Management Principles

A Contemporary Edition for Africa

Management Principles

A Contemporary Edition for Africa

Second Edition

Editors

P J Smit
G J de J Cronjé

Authors

T Brevis
M J Vrba
A de Klerk

Marketing means Business

First published 1992
Second edition 1997

© Juta & Co, Ltd
PO Box 14373, Kenwyn 7790

ISBN 0 7021 3828 2

Cover art: Isabel le Roux, Kosmos. Oil on canvas
Photograph: Koos van der Lende Photography, Pretoria
Cover design: Inspiration Sandwich, Cape Town
Book design and typesetting: Zebra Publications, Cape Town

Printed and bound in South Africa by
Creda Press, Eliot Avenue, Eppindust II, Cape Town

▨ Preface

Civilisations rise and fall on the quality of their organisations and, therefore, on the quality of their managers. This is especially true of Western and other contemporary civilisations, whose social and economic structures rest on the foundations laid by 'the organisation' and its management. During this century mankind's greatest accomplishments, ranging from tremendous increases in production and consumption to the giant leap into space, can be directly linked to increasing managerial knowledge. Proof of this is the fact that the developed countries of the world earn and enjoy 70 % of the world's income, while only 15 % of the world's population live there. It is no wonder that management is being increasingly recognised as the most critical element required for the creation of wealth, which makes peace and prosperity possible.

Yet, vast populations outside of the developed world have not achieved the level of organisation required to provide for even their most basic needs. These nations, commonly known as the Third World, have not yet been exposed to the discipline of management. They are at the crossroads. With meagre resources and largely uneducated and unskilled human resources, these nations can, despite the illusions of political freedom, only overcome perpetual poverty and socioeconomic slavery if they accept the managerial challenge. Where there are signs of rising socioeconomic standards in these countries, there is evidence of effective management. Wherever one sees glimmers of organisation in the gloom of disruption and disorganisation, one sees the presence of the business organisation and its management. The actions and decisions of managers have a profound impact on any society. The single most important thing which can help the developing world is better management of its resources.

South Africa is not an extension of Europe. It is a developing African nation desperately seeking to avoid the spiral of socioeconomic slavery and social misery. About 72 % of South Africa's whites and only 22 % of blacks have had a high school education. Only 61 % of whites and 5–10 % of blacks complete matric, as opposed to 95 % of Japan's inhabitants. Apart from this obvious need for education, there is a desperate need to break the cycle of unemployment and pauperisation. Unemployment is currently about 40 %. At the same time it is estimated that by the year 2000 South Africa will need about 100 000 new managers each year; the traditional source of managers, namely the white segment of the population, can provide only 40 000. The urgent need for management education in this country is clear.

South Africa, rich in material resources and well positioned to become the workshop for the developed world, exports its resources without adding any value to them. Skilled human resources are needed to add value to the material resources. Again one sees the need for education, especially management education. Improved and indigenous management practices will also improve South Africa's poor productivity performance — a vital aspect when it comes to competing in the expanding global marketplace.

South Africa generates 31,6 % of Africa's production. Its GDP is three times that of Egypt, which has the second largest economy in Africa. Yet Africa, which houses 12,8 % of the world's population, contributes only 1,5 % of the world's GDP. If Africa is to survive the next century, it has to managerially empower its people.

This book was written with the objective of contributing towards much-needed management education in South Africa for, as we have pointed out, management is increasingly being recognised as a most critical element required for socioeconomic development. It is a book which, like many foreign texts on general management principles, deals with the things which managers do, or should do, to improve the performance of their companies and, ultimately, to create wealth. Unlike the foreign texts, it is written by a team of South African academics who know the realities of South Africa and the educational needs of the South and southern African student. The discussion of concepts and principles is therefore richly illustrated with examples from the South African environment.

The book is organised around the traditional management process paradigm which emphasises planning, organising, leading and controlling. This framework is generally accepted as the most logical and effective way to describe the management process. Part one introduces the student to the nature and importance of management in society and gives an overview of the management process and its environment. The next four parts examine each of the four fundamental tasks of management, and part six deals with contemporary management issues. An important feature of the second edition is a heightened sensitivity to our multicultural workplace.

Helpful comments and suggestions have come from many professors, students and managers. We are keenly aware that their influence and guidance have been substantial, and wish to acknowledge our debt to those intellectual inputs.

Contents

Part 1
THE NATURE OF MANAGEMENT

Part 3
THE ORGANISING PROCESS

Part 4
THE LEADERSHIP PROCESS

Part 5
THE CONTROL PROCESS

Management Principles

Part 6
CONTEMPORARY MANAGEMENT ISSUES

18. **The Management of Diversity** 423

Introduction 423
    ■ Reasons for the increased focus on the management of diversity 425
    ■ Managing diversity 435
    ■ Summary of the general dimensions of diversity 441
    ■ Managing cultural diversity 442
    ■ Diversity training 455
    ■ Conclusion 456
    ■ References 457

19. **International Management** 459

Introduction 459
    ■ The nature of international business 460
    ■ The structure of the global economy 469
    ■ Environmental challenges of global management 473
    ■ How to compete in a global economy 480
    ■ Conclusion 486
    ■ References 487

20. **Ethics and Corporate Social Responsibility** 489

Introduction 489
    ■ Ethics 490
    ■ Corporate social responsibility 501
    ■ Conclusion 507
    ■ References 507

Index 509

Part 1

The Nature of Management

1 Introduction to Management

Key issues

- The role of the business organisation and management in satisfying people's needs
- What the management process entails and how it enables organisations to achieve their goals
- The different levels and kinds of managers in an organisation and the role that each plays in the organisation
- The skills management requires and how the skills are acquired
- The scope of management and the challenge facing it

1.1 INTRODUCTION

Existence and survival have always depended on the ability to control the environment in which one lives. To overcome obstacles and threats to their existence, people have, over the centuries, developed specific means to survive. Just as dinosaurs became specialised in size as a means of defence, humans have specialised by adapting to complexity and change. To find and secure food our ancestors invented stone axes, blades, spears, knives, hoes and tractors, and to make their lives easier, they adapted to their environment. They built shelters, used fire, made clothing and invented medicines.

Two probably unrelated developments had a revolutionary effect on human existence. About ten thousand years ago, some people noticed how barley and wheat dropped seeds annually and that these grew again during the next season. The logical step was to collect some of the seeds and plant them — the start of agriculture.

The second development was the domestication of animals. This probably developed from the hunters' close contact with wild animals and the habit of some of these animals of living near human settlements. Their young could be tamed to serve people in many ways in their pursuit of improving life. The domestication of animals and the development of agriculture caused the humans' nomadic form of existence to disappear. Populations grew, which led to the emergence of town and city life. With this came churches, markets, schools, hospitals and businesses — all new means of adapting to the environment created by the new industrial age.

To deal with the population explosion of the new industrial society of the 19th and 20th centuries and the consequent need for products and services, people were forced to invent yet another means of extending the limits of their many capacities. To satisfy the needs of an industrial society, it became necessary for groups of people to perform tasks that no individual could perform alone, and the **organisation** was invented. The organisation, particularly the business organisation — a concept only two centuries old — enormously extended our capacity to deal with the complex problems of existence.

Business organisations bring together society's resources, namely people, raw materials, money and knowledge, to produce the products and services for its many needs. All organisations, including business organisations, are created and kept together by a group of people striving towards a common purpose or goal. All organisations have plans on how they will achieve these goals and people responsible for executing the plans to achieve the goals. These people are called **managers**, and they influence the success of their organisations. The success with which an organisation achieves its objectives and satisfies the ever-increasing needs of society, depends on the competence of its managers. If managers do their jobs well, the organisation will be successful. If a country's organisations are competitive and successful, the country as a whole will prosper. Today the countries of Europe, North and South America, Japan and the new successful nations of the world such as Korea, New Zealand, Vietnam and even China are enjoying the wealth which managers create. In fact, the USA, Western Europe and Japan together earn about 70 % of the world's income, even though only 15 % of the world's population live there.[1]

According to the *Global Competitiveness Report*, by the Geneva-based World Economic Forum, the top ten most competitive countries for 1996 include the USA, Singapore, Hong Kong, Japan, Switzerland, Luxembourg, Norway, Canada, Taiwan and Malaysia. The success of these countries is due to managers who run business organisations that can compete internationally. These managers also operate in environments characterised by stable labour markets, lean governments and the application of advanced technology. New Zealand's success is attributed to privatisation, which means that managers produce products and services more productively than civil servants. Switzerland's success is attributed to advanced technology and exceptional management. Russia appears at the bottom of the list because it simply does not have managers and entrepreneurs to operate a market economy.

In contrast to the successful nations of the world, the 'wealth experiment of the century', namely socialism and communism in Eastern Europe, Africa and Cuba, claimed that the state could best satisfy the needs of people. It has led to economic, social and ecological decline, characterised by unemployment, famine and

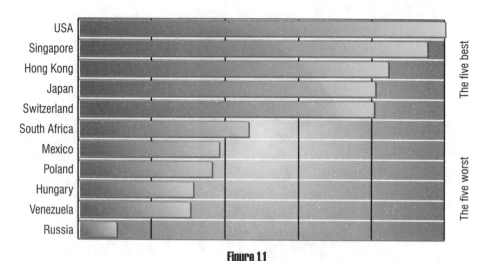

Figure 1.1
The competitiveness of countries: the five most successful and five least successful countries in the world
Source: *Time*, 10 June 1996, p 49.

despondency. Political freedom at the beginning of the nineties made these countries realise that freedom in itself does not mean bread on the table, and that their position can only improve with a market economy in which managers in private business enterprises provide for their needs.

Without managers, most organisations would not be able to achieve their goals. Managers are the people who make decisions about the qualities and quantities of products that must be produced. They also create job opportunities and provide income; promote technology; contribute to education and knowledge; provide training and health services; and ultimately bear the responsibility for a society or a country's standard of living. In the past decade, management in the USA has created about 15 million new job opportunities. In Japan this figure is about four million.[2] The more productive managers are in satisfying the country's needs, the more available scarce resources become for further needs satisfaction.

Figure 1.2 clearly shows the wealth created by a well-known South African business organisation and how it is distributed amongst its stakeholders. Some 60 % of the income went to employees in the form of remuneration and other benefits, while the providers of capital received 11 % in the form of interest and dividends, and government received 12 % in the form of taxes. It follows that a country with competent managers will have better resource utilisation and will therefore be more successful in satisfying the needs of its people. This includes political stability and social progress which go hand in hand with prosperity. This is what South Africa desperately needs and it is one of the most important reasons for studying management.

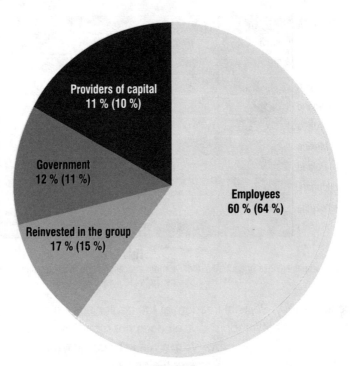

Figure 1.2
The business organisation and wealth distribution, 1995
(1994 comparatives shown in brackets)
Source: Barlow Ltd *Annual Report* 1995, p 5.

Focus

Against the background of the introductory remarks on the role of managers in society, the objective of this book is to provide a comprehensive contemporary review of management principles and their application in organisations operating in Africa. The latter refers to the pragmatic presentation of subject matter that also recognises the multicultural nature of the southern African student. A few remarks about the nature of management would be appropriate at this stage.

1.2   **ORGANISATIONS AND MANAGERS**

A century or two ago, the consumer was still part of an agricultural society and depended on himself or herself and a few individuals such as the local shopkeeper, tailor, butcher and blacksmith for products and services, unlike the modern consumer who lives in the age of the organisation, which, in this century in particular, has emerged as one of the most important social institutions. Virtually all the products and services required to satisfy the consumer's and, ultimately, society's needs are produced and provided by specialised organisations such as hypermarkets, sports clubs, universities, car manufacturers, banks, guest houses, bicycle shops, hospitals and airlines, to mention but a few. Moreover, unlike a century ago, people's lives are influenced in some way or another by the managers of these numerous business organisations. The growth in the number of organisations is, therefore, also evidence of people's ever-increasing needs and their sustained efforts to improve their standard of living.

Organisations, especially business organisations, serve society in a number of ways.

1.2.1 Business organisations serve society

Business organisations serve society by bringing together the resources to produce the products and services it needs. Table 1.1 depicts how various types of organisations bring together the human, financial, physical and information resources from the environments to produce skilled people, cars, municipal services, bicycles — even repair services.

Table 1.1
The basic resources of an organisation

Organisation	Human resources	Financial resources	Physical resources	Information resources
University of South Africa	Lecturers and administrative staff	State subsidies, contributions by private enterprises, annual fees	Buildings, libraries, lecture halls, computers	Expertise in distance teaching, research reports, annual reports
Toyota South Africa	Managers, engineers, technicians, administrative staff, workers	Shareholders, loans, profit	Assembly plants, buildings, equipment, computers	Data on the market, environmental information, statistics, skills in car manufacturing
City Council of Pretoria	Engineers, jurists, town planners, technical and administrative staff, councillors	Municipal taxes, fines, fees	Buildings, power stations, waterworks, pipelines	Statistics on urban population, annual reports, budgets, expertise in town management
Joe's Bicycle Shop	Owner manager, members of family, labourer	Owner's equity, profits	Counters, shelves, equipment	Knowledge of models, spare parts, price lists and suppliers

Source: Adapted from Griffin, RW. 1993. *Management.* Boston: Houghton Mifflin, p 5.

Organisations do not, however, achieve their objectives on their own. Someone has to deploy the basic resources that an organisation has at its disposal to help it achieve its goals. This vital element is management. Managers must activate and guide the organisation. That is, they must get things going and keep them together until the goals have been achieved. Without management an organisation is lifeless.

1.2.2 Business organisations provide careers

Business organisations provide society with job opportunities. They provide their employees with a livelihood and, depending on the management style, work satisfaction and self-fulfilment.

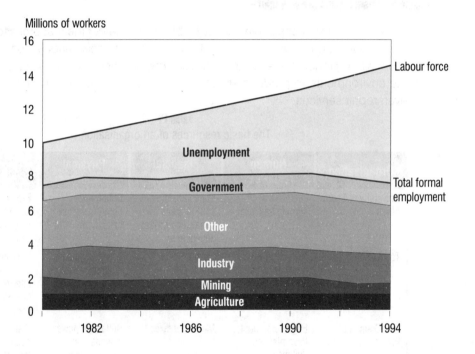

Figure 1.3
Employment in the formal sector
Source: SA Foundation, as quoted in *Finansies en Tegniek*, 8 March 1996, p 19.

Against the background of the above discussion in which the organisation, especially the business organisation, is viewed as the habitat of the manager, we can now take a closer look at management.

1.3   THE NATURE OF MANAGEMENT

It is clear from the above discussion that by coordinating the efforts of different individuals, organisations enable us to reach goals that would be impossible or very difficult for an individual to achieve. This necessitates management. **Thus management's task is to combine, allocate, coordinate and deploy resources or inputs in such a way that the organisation's goals are achieved as productively as possible.** Management goes about this by following a specific process. A process is a systematic way of doing things. All managers, regardless of their skills or the level at which they are involved, engage in certain interrelated activities to achieve their desired goals. This entails four fundamental management functions:

- planning
- organising
- leading
- controlling

It is easier to understand a process as complex as management when it is described as a series of separate parts. Descriptions of this kind are known as models or paradigms. A model is a simplification of the real world to explain complex relationships in easy-to-understand terms. This model of management evolved over many decades, even though various writers use different and frequently disparate terms to define management actions or functions. Some authors refer to planning as decision making, others regard coordination as a separate management function while others again see it as part of organising. Some writers describe the function of leading as directing. Despite these slight differences of opinion, all agree that **planning**, **organising**, **leading** and **controlling** are the central functions of management.

Figure 1.4
The four fundamental management functions constituting the management process

These fundamental functions of a manager link up in a specific sequence to form a process. Figure 1.4 depicts the process as a logical sequence of actions. It is meaningless to execute them in any other sequence, since a manager cannot decide to do something unless he or she knows what has to be done; he or she

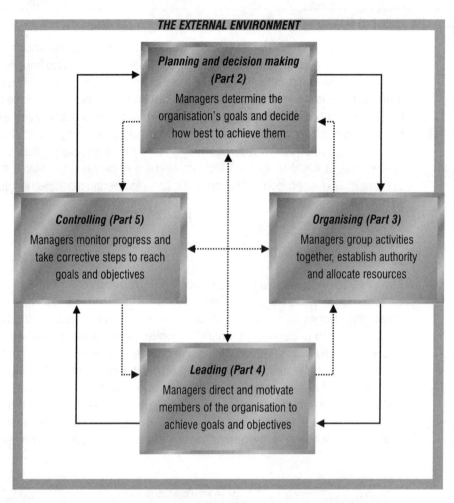

Figure 1.5
The interactive nature of the management process
Source: Adapted from Stoner, JAF & Freeman, RE. *Management*. 1995.
Englewood Cliffs, NJ: Prentice-Hall, p 13.

cannot order a job to be done before he or she has decided how it should be done. Even less can he or she control the results before the order has been given.

It is important to realise that the functions of management do not occur in a tidy, step-by-step order. Managers do not plan on Monday, organise on Tuesday, lead on Wednesday, control on Thursday and take corrective action on Friday. At any given time, a manager is likely to be engaged in several management functions simultaneously. To simplify the complex process of management, it is depicted in a model, shown in in figure 1.5. The solid lines indicate how, in theory, the functions of management are performed. The dotted lines represent the true reality of management. Figure 1.5 also serves as the framework for this book.

1.4   A DEFINITION OF MANAGEMENT

Following from the above introductory remarks about organisations and the management activities necessary for the functioning of the organisation, management can be defined as the process of planning, organising, leading and controlling the resources of the organisation to achieve stated organisational goals as efficiently as possible.

A concise description of each of the fundamental management functions will further elucidate the concept of management and the nature of the management process.

Planning is the management function that determines the organisation's mission and goals. It involves identifying ways of attaining the goals and the resources needed for the task. It entails determining the future position of the organisation, and the strategies needed to reach that position. Hence the activities of the organisation cannot be performed in a random fashion, but should follow a specific, logical, scientific method or plan.

Organising is the second step in the management process. Once the goals and plans have been determined, management has to allocate the organisation's human and physical resources to relevant departments or individuals. Duties have to be defined and procedures established to achieve the objectives. Thus organising involves developing a framework or organisational structure to indicate how people and materials should be deployed to achieve the goals. The success of an organisation lies in directing the different resources towards the achievement of a common goal. The better the resources are coordinated and organised, the more successful the organisation will be. Because organisations have different goals and resources, it stands to reason that each one should have an organisational structure that will accommodate its particular needs. Management must match the organisation's structure to its resources, goals and strategies. This process is called **organisational design**.

Leading refers to directing the human resources of the organisation and motivating them in such a way that their actions accord with previously formulated goals and plans. Managers do not act in isolation and do not only give orders — they collaborate with their superiors, equals and subordinates, with individuals and groups, to attain the goals of the organisation. Leading the organisation means making use of influence and power to motivate employees to achieve organisational goals. Leading means communicating goals through the organisation and motivating departments and individuals to perform as well as they possibly can.

Controlling means that managers should constantly make sure that the organisation is on the right course to attain its goals. The aim of control is therefore to check that performance and action conform to plans to attain the predetermined goals. Control also enables management to identify and rectify any deviations from the plans, and to take into account factors which might oblige them to revise their goals and plans.

The management process and the four functions of the process are encountered at all levels and in all departments of the organisation. We will examine this in greater detail in section 1.5.

1.5   DIFFERENT LEVELS AND KINDS OF MANAGERS IN THE ORGANISATION

Against the background of our definition of **management**, we use the term **manager** to include anyone who carries out the four fundamental functions of management. The four management functions must be performed in all organisations, but managers are responsible for different departments; they work at different levels and meet different requirements.

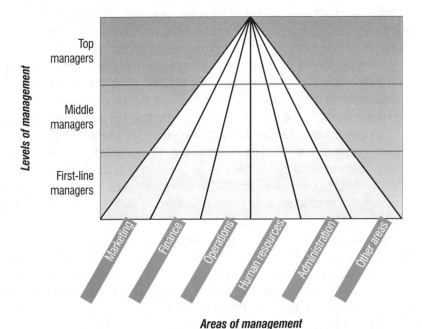

Areas of management

Figure 1.6
Classification of managers according to level and area

Managers are usually classified in two categories: according to their **level** in the organisation (the top, middle and first-line managers) and by the **area** of management for which they are responsible (the functional managers). Figure 1.6 indicates how managers within an organisation can be differentiated according to level and area.

1.5.1 Top management

Top management represents the relatively small group of managers who control the organisation and with whom the final authority and responsibility for executing the management process rest. This level of management comprises, for example, the board of directors, partners, the managing director, chief executives, as well as management committees (consisting mainly of members of top management). Top management, also known as strategic management, is usually responsible for the organisation as a whole, as well as for determining its mission, goals and overall strategies. Top management is concerned mainly with long-term planning, designing the organisation's broad organisational structure, leading the organisation (through the top executive) and controlling it. Top management also influences the corporate culture.

1.5.2 Middle management

Middle management is responsible for specific departments of the organisation and is primarily concerned with implementing the policies, plans and strategies formulated by the top management. It normally includes the functional heads, such as the marketing manager, the purchasing manager and the human resources manager. Middle management is concerned with the near future and is therefore responsible for medium-term and short-term planning, organising functional areas, leading by means of the departmental heads, and controlling the management activities of the middle managers' own departments. Middle managers also continually monitor environmental influences that may affect their own departments. The trend in recent years of corporate restructuring, delayering, downsizing and decentralisation of decision making has been responsible for large numbers of middle managers being retrenched. Electronic technology has reduced the need for middle management in some organisations. It is in the area of management information, in particular, that computers have replaced the information-gathering tasks of middle managers. Middle managers are, however, still necessary to link the upper and lower levels of the organisation and to implement the strategies developed at the top.

1.5.3 Lower/first-line management

Lower management or first-line management is responsible for even smaller segments of the organisation, namely the different subsections. In the case of, say, marketing, lower management would include product managers, promotions managers or sales managers. Lower management also includes supervisors or foremen.

The managerial functions of first-line managers are centred on the daily activities of their departments or sections, short-term planning and implementing the plans of middle management. Their primary concern is to apply rules and procedures to achieve a high level of productivity, to provide technical assistance, to motivate subordinates and to accomplish day-to-day objectives. They typically spend a large portion of their time supervising the work of subordinates. Because of this, first-line management is a vital force in the organisation. These managers hold the power to increase or decrease the productivity of most organisations. They also maintain the crucial interface between management and the body of employees in the organisation.

For the sake of clarity and convenience, we have distinguished only three levels of management. Obviously, the size of an organisation plays an important role in the number of levels encountered in practice. This is because one person can manage only a limited number of people, a consideration that will be discussed in more detail later. A one-man business, therefore, has only one level of management and the owner embodies top, middle and lower management. However, large organisations with thousands of employees have many more levels of management. We shall deal with this issue in greater detail in chapter 9 in the discussion of the organisational structure.

Although we have distinguished different levels of management, the four fundamental functions of management are still performed at each level of management, but in different combinations. Figure 1.7 illustrates how the four functions differ for the three management levels.

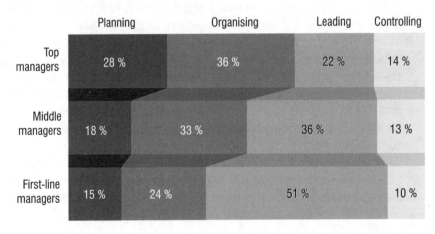

Figure 1.7
Percentage of time spent on functional activities by organisational level
Source: Daft, RL. 1995. *Management*. Orlando: The Dryden Press, p 17.

Planning and organising are primarily the responsibility of top management, while the time devoted to these activities decreases for middle and first-line managers. Leading, which includes motivation, is the highest priority for first-line managers, with the time devoted to this activity decreasing at higher levels. The time devoted to controlling is similar for all three levels, although middle and top managers spend marginally more time on this activity than their first-line colleagues.

1.6   AREAS OF MANAGEMENT

Another factor that influences the classification of managers (see figure 1.6) is the type of activity they manage. Therefore, in any organisation there may be marketing, finance, operations, human resources, purchasing and public relations managers at all three levels of management.

- The **general management** function includes an examination of the management process as a whole: the planning that management has to do, the organisation that managers have to establish to carry out their plans, the leadership that management has to assume to get things done, and the control that has to be exercised over the whole process. General management embraces the overall function through which top management develops strategies and formulates policies for the whole organisation, and also cuts through all the other functions, because functions such as planning and controlling are performed not only at top level, but also in each functional area.
- The **marketing function** entails the marketing of the products or services of the organisation. This includes the assessment of the market and the needs of consumers, as well as the development of a strategy to satisfy those needs profitably.
- The **financial function** includes the acquisition, utilisation and control of the money the organisation needs to finance its activities and to buy materials and equipment.
- The **production or operations management function** includes that group of activities concerned with the physical production of products, namely the establishment and layout of the production unit and the conversion of raw materials and semi-finished products into finished products for the market. Operations management also examines problems related to the supply of services.
- The **purchasing function** entails the acquisition of all products and materials required by the business to function profitably, namely raw materials, components, tools, equipment and, in the case of a dealer, the inventory. The purchasing manager has to be in contact with suppliers, must be aware of new products and know the prices at which goods can be bought. He or she also has to keep the inventory up to date, to ensure continuity of functioning.

■ The **human resource function** entails the appointment, development and maintenance of the human resources of the organisation. To enable the organisation to operate at a profit, the human resource manager must appoint the right people and provide them with the right training in order to make the best use of them.

■ The **public relations function** of an organisation is to create a favourable, objective image of the organisation, and to establish good relations with those directly or indirectly concerned with the business and its products or services.

These are the specialised areas of management that are identified according to the various functions of the organisation. Functional managers are mainly responsible for their own tasks or their department's specific managerial activities. Marketing management, for example, is responsible for the following:

■ **planning** the marketing department's activities — that is, marketing goals (for example, a 10 % increase in the market share for the 1998 financial year) are determined in accordance with the objectives of the organisation and plans are formulated to attain these objectives and goals;

■ **organising** marketing activities — that is, allocating tasks to people so that goals can be achieved;

■ **taking the lead** in marketing activities — that is, motivating and commanding marketing personnel to perform their duties in pursuit of the goals formulated in the marketing plans;

■ **controlling** marketing activities — that is, ensuring that marketing objectives are accomplished according to plan.

Financial managers, human resource managers, purchasing managers and the other functional managers plan, organise, lead and control in the same way. In practice, the number and importance of the specialised areas of management vary from one organisation to the next.

In the discussion above we explained the different levels as well as different areas of management in the organisation. To further clarify the essence of management, we now examine the role of managers in organisations, and the skills they require.

1.7   THE ROLE DISTRIBUTION OF MANAGERS

Regardless of the managerial level or the management area in which a manager works, the manager must play a specific role. A manager does certain things for the organisation, satisfies specific needs and accepts certain responsibilities. Mintzberg studied the activities of a group of managers and came to the conclusion that managers play about ten different roles, which, as shown in figure 1.8, can be classified into three overlapping groups, namely an interpersonal role, an information role and a decision-making role.[3]

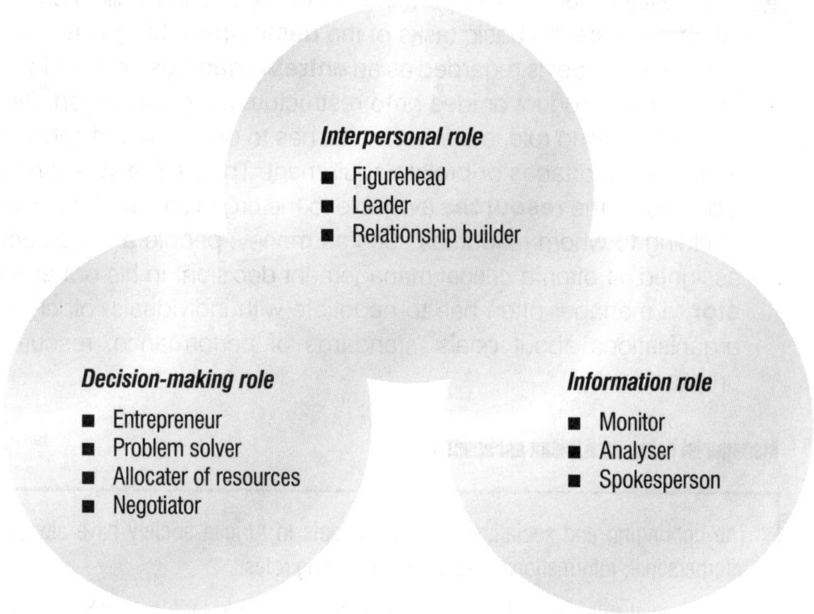

Interpersonal role

- Figurehead
- Leader
- Relationship builder

Decision-making role

- Entrepreneur
- Problem solver
- Allocator of resources
- Negotiator

Information role

- Monitor
- Analyser
- Spokesperson

Figure 1.8
The overlapping role distribution of managers

■ As far as the **interpersonal role** of a manager is concerned, three groups of activities can be distinguished. Firstly, a manager acts as a **figurehead**, for example when taking a visitor to dinner or when officiating at the opening of a new factory. Secondly, he or she plays the role of a **leader** in appointing, training, promoting, dismissing and motivating subordinates. Thirdly, managers are involved in **public relations** which aims at maintaining good relations within and outside the organisation. Within the organisation, a manager has contact with other managers and individuals, and outside it, a manager is responsible for building sound relationships with other organisations, suppliers, bankers and clients. This role often takes up half of the manager's time.

■ A manager's **information** role enables him or her to obtain information from colleagues, subordinates and department heads, as well as outside persons, and he or she can use this data for making decisions. This **information role** of the manager involves **monitoring** or gathering information on trends, and passing on relevant data to colleagues, superiors and subordinates. The manager is, therefore, a vital link in the organisation's communication process. The manager's information role also entails acting as a **spokesperson** for the department or for the whole organisation.

■ The development of interpersonal relations and the collection and analysis of information are the basic tasks of the **decision-making role** that management plays. A manager is regarded as an **entrepreneur**, using the information to introduce a new product or idea or to restructure the organisation. Secondly, in this decision-making role, a manager also has to deal with and solve problems such as strikes, shortages or broken equipment. Thirdly, managers must make decisions about the **resources** available to the organisation. Resource allocation, or deciding to whom resources such as money, people and equipment are to be assigned, is often a critical management decision. In his or her role as **negotiator,** a manager often has to negotiate with individuals, other departments or organisations about goals, standards of performance, resources and trade unions.

Managerial roles: an African perspective

The upbringing and socialisation of individuals in African society have always emphasised interpersonal, informational and decision-making roles.

Interpersonal roles are subsumed in the notion of *ubuntu* in Zulu and Xhosa, *unhu* in Shona, *botho* in Tswana, *broederbond* in Afrikaans, *bunhu* in Tsonga, *vhuthu* in Venda and *brotherhood* in English. Thus *ubuntu* is a literal translation for collective personhood and collective morality.

Therefore, a leader *(mutungamir/i* in Shona and *umukhokhel/i* in Zulu) guided by the *ubuntu* philosophy is expected to inform and communicate with his or her own group and to be their mouthpiece in external communication. Decision making is the hallmark of leadership which involves analysis of the situation at hand in consultation with others and guiding the process until a course of action is selected.

Source: Mbigi, L. 1997. *Ubuntu: The African Dream in Management.* Randburg: Knowledge Resources.

The role distribution framework is especially useful in explaining why managers cannot move systematically from planning to organising to leading and ultimately to controlling. The inconstancy of their environment requires a more flexible managerial style. The success of the above role distributions (in a nutshell, the execution of the management process) depends on whether or not management has the right skills. A few remarks about such skills are necessary at this juncture.

1.8   MANAGERIAL SKILLS AT VARIOUS MANAGERIAL LEVELS

Although management is found at all levels and in all functions of an organisation, each level and each role requires different personal skills for the performance of the management task. Figure 1.9 depicts the different skills. The skills that top management needs to perform the function of general management as productively as possible differ from those required by lower management. The following three main skills are identified as prerequisites for sound management.[4]

1. **Conceptual skills** refer to the mental ability to view the operation of the organisation and its parts holistically. Conceptual skills involve the manager's thinking and planning abilities. They also include the manager's ability to think strategically.
2. **Interpersonal skills** refer to the ability to work with people. It stands to reason that if managers spend about 60 % of their time working with people, a manager should be able to communicate, understand people's behaviour and motivate groups as well as individuals.
3. **Technical skills** refer to the ability to use the knowledge or techniques of a specific discipline to attain objectives. A knowledge of accountancy, engineering or economics is an example of the technical skills that can be used to perform a task. A manager at a lower level in particular requires a sound knowledge of the technical activities he or she must supervise. However, the time spent on technical activities decreases with progress up the managerial ladder.

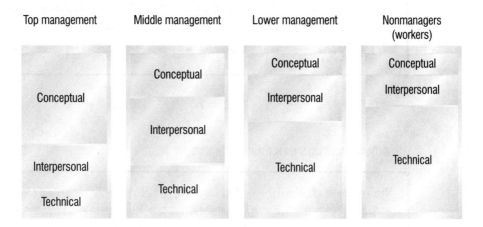

Figure 1.9
Managerial skills needed at various managerial levels

As illustrated in figure 1.9, the major difference between nonmanagers and managers is the shift in focus from technical skills to interpersonal and conceptual skills. Promotion from the nonmanager level to the lower and even middle-management level is often the result of high achievement based on technical ability. Because of this, new managers often mistakenly continue to rely on technical skills rather than on interpersonal skills which involve motivating employees and building teams. This is why management education is necessary.

Management skills and success or failure

Various studies have proved a close correlation between management skills and success. The Center for Creative Leadership in Greensboro, North Carolina, compared 21 derailed executives with 20 executives who had made it to the top of the company. The derailed executives were successful people who had been expected to go far but who had reached a plateau, were fired, or were forced to retire early. Successful and derailed managers were similar in many ways. They were bright and excelled in a technical area such as accounting or engineering. They worked hard, made sacrifices in order to achieve, and established good track records.

Those who made it to the top, however, had more diverse track records — they did not rely on a single functional skill. Moreover, they had excellent interpersonal skills. They maintained composure under stress, were able to laugh at themselves, and handled mistakes with poise and grace. They also were strong in conceptual ability and could focus on problems and solve them.

In the managers who had derailed, the single biggest flaw was a lack of sensitivity towards others. Often this characteristic was associated with other negative personal qualities, such as abrasiveness, aloofness and arrogance. These managers also failed to display conceptual skills and were unable to think strategically, that is, take a broad, long-term view.

Source: Hymowitz, C. 1988. Five reasons why managers fail. *The Wall Street Journal,* 2 May, p 16.

The difficult transition from nonmanager to manager

New managers often mistakenly continue to rely on technical skills rather than concentrating on working with others, motivating employees, and building a team. Indeed, some people fail to become managers at all because they let technical skills take precedence over human skills.

Consider Pete Martin, who has a Bachelor's degree and has worked for five years as a computer programmer for an oil company. In four short years, he has more new software programs to his credit than anyone else in the department. He is highly creative and widely respected.

However, Pete is impulsive and has little tolerance for those whose work is less creative. Pete does not offer to help co-workers and, because of this, they are reluctant to ask. Pete is also slow to cooperate with other departments in meeting their needs, because he works primarily to enhance his own software-writing ability. He spends evenings and weekends working on his programs. Pete is a hard-working technical employee, but he sees little need to worry about other people.

The difficult transition from nonmanager to manager (continued . . .)

> Pete received high merit raises, but was passed over for promotion and does not understand why. His lack of interpersonal skills, lack of consideration for co-workers, and failure to cooperate with other departments severely limit his potential as a supervisor. Pete has great technical skills, but his human skills are simply inadequate for making the transition from worker to supervisor.
>
> Source: Daft, RL. 1995. *Management*. Orlando: The Dryden Press, p 21.

1.9 ACQUIRING MANAGEMENT SKILLS

One may well ask at this point where managers acquire the skills to become successful. Figure 1.10 illustrates the various sources from which managerial expertise may be gained.

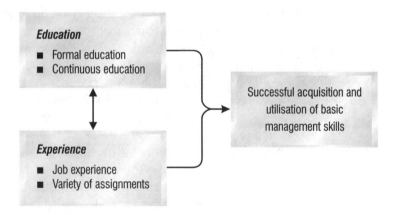

Figure 1.10
Sources of management skills
Source: Griffin, RW. 1993. *Management*. Boston: Houghton Mifflin, p 14.

1.9.1 Management education

One place to acquire management skills is in an educational setting. In South Africa this refers to management and entrepreneurship training at schools, business colleges, technikons and universities, as well as through organisations that provide in-house management education and training.

Management education in the USA and Europe

In the USA, where as much as 40 % of the population already have degrees, formal management education, including MBA programmes, is on the increase. A contemporary development in management education is the advanced MBA programme for top managers which management schools offer over weekends. The number of in-house programmes offered is also increasing.

In Europe, management education is in a growth phase. Of 45 European business schools that took part in a survey in 1989, 18 were less than five years old. In Europe, however, the emphasis is on in-house programmes rather than the MBA programme, which is said to be too long and abstract and to offer relatively poor value for money. In Eastern Europe, management education is an urgent priority to raise the subsistence level of those communities where the standard of living has been drastically curtailed by the state in the past 50 years.

Nonformal management education, often called continuous learning, refers to non-degree programmes offered by universities, organisations such as Get Ahead Foundation, IBM's Learning Centres and in-house training by business organisations themselves. The Centre for Business Management at Unisa currently presents 25 nonformal management programmes to over 3 000 students every year.

Management education is of major importance to the South African economy. The economy must grow at a rate of well above 3 % per year to reverse the spiral of population growth, economic stagnation and impoverishment. This will only be possible if there are enough skilled managers to drive the economy. It is widely recognised that a moderate real economic growth rate of 2,7 % per year will require an additional 100 000 managers each year for the remainder of this century. Since the traditional source of managers, namely white males, has been exhausted, most of the managers required will have to come from the black population. Massive management education is therefore required for the South African economy to be successful.

Various other factors also indicate the importance of management training in South Africa. These include the following:

▪ Firstly, the current crisis in education and training in the country poses an enormous challenge for management training. About 51 % of the adult population in South Africa are illiterate, compared to 1 % in Japan and 14 % in the USA. In addition, 87 % of all black teachers are underqualified and fewer than ten of every 100 black scholars who start school actually matriculate.

▪ Secondly, the shortage of managers makes specific demands on management training. Each day in South Africa, about 1400 unskilled people enter the labour market, which can offer only about 300 jobs per day — and these entries to the labour market increase the demand for managers. It is estimated that by the year

2000, South Africa will need approximately 100 000 new managers per annum. The white section of the population can supply only about 40 000. The remaining managers will have to come from other population groups.

■ A third factor that indicates the importance of management education is the dualistic nature of the economy, in which the informal sector grows by about 15 % per annum. Management education is imperative to assist the informal sector as it supplies job opportunities.

■ The fourth and principal factor that makes demands on management education is the multicultural nature of the South African population. This situation requires curricula that should be relevant to the South African environment, research that indicates the direction which management education in South Africa should take, and greater emphasis on interpersonal and intercultural skills.

■ A survey of 240 South African managers indicated that the demands that will be made on management in the next five years will be concerned with **labour relations, higher productivity, management of cultural interfaces** and the **managerial empowerment** of disadvantaged people.

■ Finally, a distinct trend emerging in developed countries is that, whereas between the late fifties and the late eighties a university graduate in the USA earned about the same as an uneducated blue-collar worker, educated people in the nineties are earning four to five times what blue-collar workers earn. The same trend is emerging in South Africa.

1.9.2 Practical experience

A second source of managerial competence is practical experience. There is no doubt that a natural aptitude for management, self-motivation and ambition play a decisive role in the development of managerial skills. Most managers have advanced to their present positions from other jobs. Through experience and by facing and meeting a variety of managerial challenges, the individual develops insights that cannot be learnt from training alone. Efficient managers, however, learn their skills from a combination of education and experience. What is needed most in South Africa in the area of management development, is the managerial empowerment of previously disadvantaged people through a system of **education, internship** and **mentorship.** Unless many more people advance in the managerial environment, the South African economy will be limited to the poor performance of the past two decades.

The acquisition of management skills through education and experience indicates that management is a science, a profession and an art. Management is a science because of the growing body of knowledge which describes how organisational performance can be scientifically achieved. The body of knowledge is acquired through scientific research and is disseminated through teaching, textbooks and articles. Management is often viewed as an art because many skills cannot be learnt from a book or in a classroom. Management requires practice and many skills, especially human skills and some conceptual skills, are learnt through experience. Becoming a successful manager, therefore, requires a blend of formal learning and practice, of science and art. Practice alone used to be enough to learn how to manage, but this is no longer the case. The study of management enables managers to see and understand aspects of organisations that others cannot.[5]

The purpose of the above discussion of management levels and skills and how these skills are acquired, is to provide a background knowledge of the nature of management. The next section explores the scope and challenges of management.

1.10   MANAGEMENT AND ORGANISATIONAL PERFORMANCE

It was explained in the introduction that the private business organisation can best satisfy the unlimited needs of society by means of the judicious application of the community's limited resources. This endeavour to achieve the highest possible satisfaction of needs with scarce resources is known as the **fundamental economic principle**. Business organisations in a free-market economy are also subject to this principle, and the managements of these organisations therefore endeavour to achieve the highest possible output (profit) with the lowest possible input. This is the reason for management's existence: to direct the organisation in its pursuit of the basic economic principle. Therefore, the task of management in a free-market economy is to manage in such a way that the organisation earns the highest possible income with the lowest possible costs, with profit as the favourable difference between the two. The ultimate responsibility of managers is, therefore, to achieve **high performance** (productivity), which is the attainment of organisational goals by reaching the highest possible output with the lowest possible input of resources. In American literature in particular, the productivity endeavours of management or the performance of management is expressed somewhat simplistically as **efficiency** and **effectiveness**.[6] **Efficiency** means doing something right, while **effectiveness** means that the right thing is done. However, the fact remains that the management of a business organisation operating in a free-market economy must adhere to the economic principle and run the organisation as productively (and therefore as profitably) as possible. Of course, this should be done with due consideration of the social responsibility of the organisation towards the community in which it operates.

Against the background of these brief remarks about the purpose of management, it is clear that management is an important contemporary social institution which, judging by the search for improved standards of living in Eastern Europe and elsewhere, continues to grow in stature. There are, however, many challenges facing management. Some of these challenges will now be discussed.

In a nutshell

Management exists for the following reasons:
- Management in a market economy is necessary to enable the enterprise to **achieve its goals at the highest possible level of productivity**. This is also a measure of management's effectiveness in carrying out its task. Ultimately productive organisations are those that are most successful at using their resources judiciously to best serve the interests of society.

- Management is necessary to **direct an organisation towards its goals**. Without the inputs of management, the organisation's resources will not be channelled in the direction of its goals. A business organisation in a market economy cannot achieve its profit objectives unless it has capable managers. It will also not continue to exist if it fails to make a profit. In a nutshell, a business organisation cannot achieve or maintain the reason for its existence without management.

- Management is necessary **to keep the organisation in equilibrium with its environment.** Managers adapt the organisation to the environment by accommodating environmental change. However, they also endeavour to maintain the equilibrium between the organisation and the environment by trying to influence the environment so that the organisation can achieve its goals more easily. They may do this, for example, by assisting with education and training in an effort to increase the standard of living of consumers in the lower socioeconomic classes.

1.11   THE SCOPE AND CHALLENGES OF MANAGEMENT

The study of management traditionally focuses on business management and, therefore, the management of business organisations. This does not mean that the management is limited to large business organisations only. In small businesses and organisations such as hospitals, universities, sports clubs, political parties and even government organisations management is essential because in each case two or more people work together to achieve a goal.

1.11.1   Large business organisations

Any successful nation needs large business organisations with the necessary resources to compete globally and smaller local businesses to act as subcontractors. In South Africa, large organisations still provide two thirds of the GDP (Gross Domestic Product). Management training is therefore imperative for large South

African business organisations because of the important role they play in competing internationally to earn much-needed foreign currency for domestic development.

1.11.2 Small business organisations

Management training for small and medium-sized business organisations (SMEs) is essential for a variety of reasons. In the economically successful countries of the world, SMEs provide as much as 85 % of the job opportunities and are therefore an important economic institution. In South Africa, SMEs need to play a greater role in the economy because their present contribution to the GDP is far less than that of similar organisations in Japan, Singapore, the USA and other countries. Various reasons why management education for small businesses in South Africa should be a priority are highlighted in a World Bank report which shows that the survival rate of new businesses in South Africa tends to be quite low. In Asia, Latin America and West Africa, the rate at which surviving firms graduate from micro-enterprises to become dynamic small and medium enterprises is, on average, 50 %. In East and southern Africa it is only about 10 %.[7] Improved management skills would increase the capability of black managers and entrepreneurs in particular and help them to deal with these constraints.

1.11.3 International management

Because of globalisation, where national boundaries become meaningless, business organisations have to be able to compete internationally. With the restructuring of the South African economy and the scrapping of protective import tariffs, South African businesses, large and small, will have to become more productive in order to survive. This challenge to business also demands more stable labour relations and therefore fewer strikes and higher productivity levels.

1.11.4 Nonprofit-seeking organisations

Although nonprofit-seeking organisations such as universities, schools, health-care facilities and government organisations may not have to be profitable to attract investors, they must still employ sound management principles if they are to survive and achieve their goals. South Africa's vast new government structure, which involves a central government, nine provincial governments and thousands of local governments, schools, clinics and service centres, will make tremendous demands on scarce resources and poses a real challenge to management.

1.11.5 Managerial and economic empowerment

Perhaps the greatest challenge to management in South Africa is to bring about the managerial and economic empowerment of previously disadvantaged people.

Under the apartheid government, job reservation and inadequate education and training were the main reasons for the poor advancement of blacks into managerial roles. Massive management training, combined with internship and mentorship programmes, is needed to empower South Africa's previously disadvantaged people and to redress the inequalities of the past.

Managerial and economic empowerment in South Africa

- Under the apartheid government, job functions were largely dictated by race. According to a survey carried out by human resources consultants FSA-Contact, nearly 90 % of senior managers are white, a change of less than 1 % over the previous three years. But this is predicted to drop to 79 % by 1999, with similar decreases in the percentage of whites filling middle management and professional jobs.

- More than 80 % of companies in South Africa now have affirmative action policies, although the level of commitment varies considerably. A study by the Graduate Business School at the University of Cape Town of 150 leading companies shows that the top 10 % in terms of black recruitment have far outstripped the rest.

- The number of nonwhite managers in those 15 'top ten' companies has more than doubled in four years, and should reach 35 % by the end of the decade. In the other companies it appears unlikely to go much beyond 10 %.

- In 1995 alone, 23 black economic empowerment deals with a value of R12,4 billion materialised. There are presently 11 black-owned companies listed on the Johannesburg Stock Exchange.

Source: *Business Times*, 1996, p 6.

1.11.6 Cultural diversity

The concern for economic and managerial empowerment reflects a new commitment to equal opportunity for everyone in South Africa. However, it also reflects of the problems and opportunities created by South Africa's cultural diversity. Diversity in the workplace is significant since 60 % of the people who enter the labour market are women, immigrants and people from other cultures. In the year 2000 only 42 % of South Africa's graduates will be white. Much information must be garnered about Afrocentric values and leadership, how they impact on business organisations and how they can be harnessed to help develop an African approach to management that will lead to improved and more productive management practices.

The above discussion on the scope and challenges of management indicates the role that management can play in improving the quality of life in South Africa and on the African continent. This book endeavours to contribute to this quest.

1.12 THE APPROACH FOLLOWED IN THIS BOOK

The foregoing discussion of various views on management and its importance, the management process, the various levels of management and the skills required to manage an organisation effectively highlights the fact that various approaches can be followed in studying management. In fact, the discussion of how management thoughts and theories developed may widen the choice of approaches which can be followed in studying management. However, the approach which most management theorists and experts follow is the management process paradigm or framework, indicated in figure 1.11.

The functions that most management experts single out as the framework for the development of a theoretical foundation in management are also the four fundamental management functions discussed earlier, namely planning, organising, leading and controlling. These functions also constitute the framework of this book. The process approach has been adopted because it provides a conceptual framework for studying management and encourages the development of a uniform management approach. Using the four fundamental management functions as the basic premise in this book, we shall discuss the concepts, principles, theories and techniques that allow the enterprise to function productively and profitably. Part 1 continues with an examination of management theories in chapter 2 and, in chapter 3, an overview of the environment in which South African managers operate.

In part 2 we examine the first fundamental management function, namely **planning**. In simple terms, planning means determining the organisation's goals and objectives and deciding how best to achieve them. Chapter 4 deals with the goals and objectives that are developed as the point of departure for the planning process. Chapter 5 examines the planning process, while chapter 6 focuses on strategic planning. Chapter 7 examines decision making, an action that is paramount in all management functions and closely related to planning. In addition, information is needed to make decisions, a phenomenon examined in chapter 8.

Once a plan has been devised, it must be executed, and people and other resources must be organised for this purpose. Part 3 discusses what happens after planning, namely the **organising process**. In chapter 9 we examine the basic elements of organisational design, while chapters 10 and 11 deal with aspects of organisation such as authority, power and organisational culture. The management of change, and how this ties in with the organisation, is discussed in chapter 11.

Part 4 deals with the **leadership process**, in which someone takes the reins in putting a plan into action. This person must assign tasks to other people to help carry out the plan. In chapter 12 we discuss the foundations of leadership and in chapter 13 we examine how subordinates are motivated by leaders. Chapter 14 deals with management communication. In chapter 15 the human dimensions of management are investigated, especially the individual, while the management of groups (teams) is examined in chapter 16.

The nature of management

- Chapter 1: Introduction to management
- Chapter 2: The evolution of management theory
- Chapter 3: Managing in a changing environment

↓

Planning

- Chapter 4: Goal formulation
- Chapter 5: Planning
- Chapter 6: Strategic planning
- Chapter 7: Managerial decision making
- Chapter 8: Information management

↓

The organising process

- Chapter 9: Organisation design
- Chapter 10: Authority, power and job design
- Chapter 11: Organisational culture and change

↓

The leadership process

- Chapter 12: Leadership
- Chapter 13: Motivation
- Chapter 14: Communication and negotiation
- Chapter 15: The human dimension of management
- Chapter 16: Groups and teams in the organisation

↓

The control process

- Chapter 17: Control

↓

Contemporary Management Issues

- Chapter 18: The management of diversity
- Chapter 19: International management
- Chapter 20: Ethics and corporate social responsibility

Figure 1.11
A conceptual framework for studying management

The fourth and final fundamental management activity, namely controlling the plan, is studied in depth in part 5. Chapter 17 examines the components of control.

Chapters 18, 19 and 20 constitute part 6, which discusses a few contemporary management issues such as the management of diversity in Africa, international management, social responsibility and business ethics.

1.13 CONCLUSION

This chapter, the first of three chapters comprising part 1, introduced the concept of management and the management process. By way of introduction, we pointed out that the business organisation in a market economy is the organisation that best succeeds in satisfying people's needs. These organisations, however, do not function of their own accord, but need professional management to achieve their objectives successfully.

Management, the process or set of activities which develops and directs an organisation's resources in such a way that it reaches its goals effectively and efficiently, is explained as a process comprising four fundamental functions. These functions are planning, organising, leading and controlling. These activities take place at various levels in the organisation and functional managers also manage these activities.

Management requires certain skills. These skills can be acquired through education and experience. Management education in South Africa should be a national priority to enable managers to meet various challenges, especially the challenge of the economic and managerial empowerment of South Africa's previously disadvantaged people.

1.14 REFERENCES

1. Sunter, C. 1987. *The World and South Africa in the '90s.* Cape Town: Tafelberg, Human & Rousseau, pp 37–38.
2. Sir Michael Edwards. *Transvaler,* 7 September 1990, p 12.
3. Mintzberg, H. 1987. The nature of managerial work, cited by Donnelly, JH, Gibson, JC & Ivancevich, JM. 1987. *Fundamentals of Management.* Plano, TX: Business Publications p 28.
4. This paragraph is based on the classical research of Robert Katz. See Katz, RL. 1974. The skills of an effective administrator. *Harvard Business Review*, October, pp 90–102.

5. Daft, RL. 1995. *Management*. New York: The Dryden Press, p 22.

6. Griffin, RW. 1993. *Management*. Boston: Houghton Mifflin, p 18.

7. The World Bank. 1993. *Characteristics and Constraints Facing Black Businesses in South Africa.* South Africa Department, The World Bank.

2 The Evolution of Management Theory

Key issues

- The study of management theory and its importance to today's management student
- The forces that shape management theory
- The main schools of thought/theories on management
- The relevance of the different schools of thought/theories for today's managers
- The systems approach to management as a contemporary management approach
- Other contemporary approaches to management

2.1 INTRODUCTION

In chapter 1 we looked at management from the perspective of a science (basic principles), a profession (one can learn and apply these principles), and an art (people approach management issues differently). There is no single best way to manage and we therefore need to look at different management theories and how the theorists behind them — at a specific time and within a certain environment — thought they had the answer to management issues. A closer look at the history of management will place these different management theories in context.

The history of management is fascinating and revealing, for it reflects society and its constantly changing needs. It explains the dominant culture of the time, and is a reflection of the political, economic, social, technological, international and ecological issues of the time.

Ancient civilisations developed and practised many of the basic principles and approaches to management discussed in this book. As early as 4000 BC, the Egyptians recognised the need for planning, organising and controlling. Before 400 BC, the Greeks recognised management as a separate art and advocated a more scientific approach to work. The Romans decentralised the management of their vast empire before the birth of Christ.

Background

> The Egyptians recognised the need for planning, organising and controlling. In the construction of the pyramid of Cheops at Giza, astronomers and architects, among others, were responsible for planning. The organisational structure was rigid, indicating definite authority lines to the 100 000 men who worked on the project. The project was controlled meticulously: the south-east corner of the 13-acre tomb is only one centimetre higher than the north-west corner.
>
> Source: Bedeian, AG. 1993. *Management.* Fort Worth: The Dryden Press, p 26.

However, **management as a science** with a unique body of knowledge and **professional management as the institution** that manages the organisation are products of this century. In the previous century, entrepreneurs were capitalists who risked their own money in organisations that they managed themselves. They were self-appointed managers who bore the risk alone and took all the profits. The conditions for success were intelligence, ingenuity, resourcefulness and an intimate knowledge of technical production. In short, experience, and not scientific management, was the prerequisite for scientific entrepreneurship. The one-man business or noncorporate entrepreneur was a typical example of how capitalism was organised. This kind of capitalism is known as **entrepreneurial capitalism**

Entrepreneurial capitalism versus managerial capitalism

> ■ In the 19th century the South African economy was characterised by entrepreneurial capitalism in which a few mining magnates such as Cecil Rhodes, Ernest Oppenheimer and Barney Barnato dominated the business world. These entrepreneurs were for the most part personally responsible for planning and decision making and bore the financial risk, while staff members merely performed the administrative tasks.
>
> ■ South Africa's industrial revolution, which was stimulated mainly by mining and the urbanisation of the population, produced entrepreneurs such as Anton Rupert, Donald Gordon, Albert Wessels, Bill Venter, Ntatho Motlana and Sol Kerzner. However, the coming of the large organisation also ushered in the age of managerial capitalism, and professional experts such as Warren Clewlow, Christo Wiese, Mzi Khumalo, Dikgang Moseneke, Allan Knott-Craig, Brand Pretorius and Eugene van As today occupy key positions in the South African business scene.

Capitalism, however, has changed drastically since the end of the 19th century. The technological innovation resulting from the Industrial Revolution, especially the invention of the steam-engine, made mass production possible. This resulted in the erection of factories where employees could come together to manufacture products previously produced on their own land — or for which there had been no need before. People had to change their agrarian lifestyle to an industrialised lifestyle. This created a need for new products, such as housing, sanitation, transport and many more.

This confluence of factors required an organisational form far larger than the individual entrepreneur to make possible the large-scale financing necessary for large-scale production. Thus the company or corporation as an organisational form, with its shareholders and suppliers of capital, was born and widened the gap between the suppliers of capital and management. **The result was suppliers of capital who did not manage, and managers who did not supply capital.**

This unique combination of circumstances in the capitalist world gave rise to a need for professional management, for it soon became clear that the management issues of the new organisational form could not be solved merely by religious dogma, military rigidity and discipline or the power of the government, as was previously the case. Managers had to invent their own solutions to management problems. Each manager had his own theories about the organisation and the management thereof — hence the different approaches to management.

Focus

> This chapter focuses on the different management theories and the dominant culture of the time in which they were formulated.

2.2 WHY STUDY MANAGEMENT THEORY?

Students often ponder the questions: Why study management theory? What can one learn from management theories developed decades ago? Do all these theories have any relevance for the contemporary organisation — especially the South African organisation with its complex business environment?

These questions are indeed relevant. We live in an era characterised by a diversity of management theories. Students are presented with quantitative, behavioural, functional and other theories or approaches in various courses. This generally leaves them with a fragmented picture of management and assumes that they will integrate these ideas for themselves. This fragmentation can partly be overcome by putting the different management theories in context — by looking at their origins, tracing their development and giving some perspective in terms of the cultural environment.

Out of the many theories about how to improve management, some parts of each theory have survived and been incorporated into contemporary theories on management. In this way, the legacy of past efforts, triumphs and failures has become our guide to future management practice.

Without a knowledge of the evolution of management, students will have only their limited experience as a basis for thought and action. History should equip management students with additional alternatives and answers to build into their decision-making models.

In short, managers should be contingency-oriented and use the appropriate classical or contemporary management concepts, tools and techniques when needed.

2.3   UNDERSTANDING THE DIFFERENT MANAGEMENT THEORIES

A **management theory** is a group of assumptions put forth to elucidate the **productivity** issue. There is no clear answer to this issue, so management experts put forward their own views on productivity.

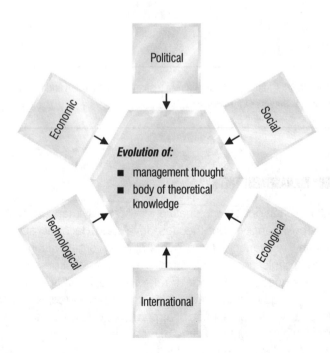

Figure 2.1
Environmental forces that shape management thought

In studying the evolution of management theory one should bear in mind that any science is shaped by environmental influences. These influences will therefore be reflected in the different theories or approaches of management experts at different times and in different situations. As shown in figure 2.1, certain environmental forces are responsible for the evolution of management theory, namely social, economic, technological, political, international and ecological forces.

As these forces change, the theoretical body of knowledge of management also changes to adjust to changing circumstances. Thus, **social** and **political** change in South Africa has led to changes in the rights of workers. The right to form trade unions, to set minimum wages, to strike and numerous other consequences of social and political changes and expectations play a decisive role in the creation of management theories on negotiation, labour relations, motivation and leadership. Likewise, **economic** factors such as the abolition of the financial rand and the fact that South Africa is now a citizen of the borderless world, the so-called global village — to mention but two major changes — influence management theory on planning, environmental scanning, organisation design, and so on. **Technological** changes also affect management practices. With present-day computer technology, up-to-date information can now be at the fingertips of every employee. **International** changes and concern for **ecological** factors have also had their impact on management theories.

2.4   THE THEORIES OF MANAGEMENT

The theories of management can be classified into two main schools of thought, namely **classical approaches** and **contemporary approaches**. At a certain point in time each of these theories was held to be the answer to the productive attainment of the goals of an organisation. However, it is important to realise that no theory dominates the field of management. Instead, the eclectic approach — the practice of borrowing management principles from different theories as dictated by circumstances — is the state of the art in management theory and practice today.

These approaches should always be seen against the dominant culture (economic, political, social, technological, ecological and international) of their time (see figure 2.2).

2.4.1 The classical approaches

The classical approaches extended from the late 19th century to the 1920s. Many of these management approaches developed simultaneously; some, on the other hand, were a direct reaction to the perceived limitations of the previous approaches. The different approaches developed in response to the needs and issues confronting managers over the years.

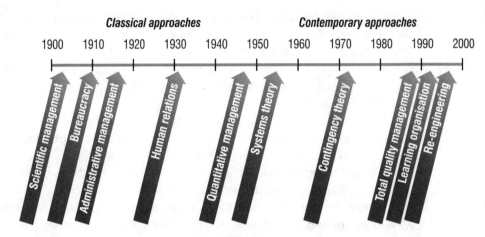

Figure 2.2
The evolution of management theory

The classical approaches to management should be seen against the background sketched above.

Background

The driving force of the Industrial Revolution was the steam-engine. This engine provided cheaper and more efficient power for ships, trains and factories, revolutionising commerce and industry. Steam power lowered production costs, lowered prices and expanded markets. A spirit of innovation led to inventions, which led to factories — and factories led to a need for organisations. The expanded market called for more employees, more machines and mass production. Workers and machines now worked under one common authority. Instead of being on their farms, workers were now shifting their efforts from the home to the factory. The need to coordinate and direct their efforts became a major issue.

The emerging factory system posed management problems different from those ever encountered before. Labour, for instance, was a major problem. The labour force consisted largely of unskilled agrarian workers and the shift from a small workshop, a farm or family-operated concern was a drastic change for these people. They were not used to the regularisation of hours, the monotony of factory work and a managerial hierarchy of authority. Training was essential but difficult as most workers were illiterate.

Discipline and motivation were also major problems. Accustomed to the craft traditions of independence and the agrarian mores of self-sufficiency, workers had to develop habits of industry, such as punctuality and regular attendance at work. Motivation, for instance, took the form of close inspection, the offering of positive inducements (the carrot) or negative sanctions (the stick).

Source: Wren, A. 1994. *The Evolution of Management Thought*, 4 ed. New York: Wiley, pp 35–55.

Scientific management school

As a supervisor at the Philadelphia Midvale Steel Company in the late 1800s, **Frederick W Taylor**, a mechanical engineer, became interested in ways of improving the productivity of workers. He studied the work of individual workers to discover exactly how they performed their tasks. Taylor believed that there was **one best way** to perform any task. He analysed each aspect of each task and measured everything measurable. Unnecessary physical movements that slowed production down were identified and eliminated, and the exact sequence of activities was determined. A standard time for the accomplishment of each task could be determined. This allowed him to describe performance objectives quantitatively, such as the number of units that a worker should produce per shift. This is known as time-and-motion study.

Taylor's scientific approach to analysing a task addressed a pressing problem of that time: how to judge whether an employee had put in a fair day's work. He believed that money motivated workers. Knowing what amounted to a fair day's work, he supported the individual piecework system as the basis for pay. If workers met a specified production standard, they were paid a standard wage rate. Workers producing more than the set standard were paid a higher rate for all the units produced, not just those exceeding the standard. His experiments to determine the best way to do a job inspired others to undertake similar studies in other industries.

Taylor's management principles and Singapore

The application of Taylor's scientific management principles has helped many of the world's underdeveloped and poor countries to become world-class competitors within one generation. Singapore is a typical example: its per capita income has increased from $800 in 1970 to $10 000 in 1990.

Source: Maital, S. 1993. A tale of two cities. *Across the Board*, vol 30, no 6, pp 50–51.

Frank and Lillian Gilbreth focused on **work simplification** as an answer to the productivity question. Being a bricklayer himself, Frank Gilbreth studied the motions of bricklayers and determined that many of the body movements of bricklayers (bending, reaching, stooping, trowelling) could be combined or eliminated.

Henry L Gantt's main concern was productivity at shop-floor level. His major contribution to scientific management is a chart showing the relationship between work planned and completed on one axis and time elapsed on the other.

Principles of efficiency were thus established during this period by using scientific methods to determine the most efficient way to do things. In short, it focused on the issue of **managing work**.

This approach has certain limitations. Firstly, workers cannot be viewed simply as parts of a smoothly running machine. Secondly, their assumptions about the motivation of employees is too simplistic. Money is not the only motivator of workers. In the third place, this approach to management creates the potential for exploitation of labour and, therefore, possible strikes by workers. Fourthly, in a broader sense, this approach can lead to ignorance of the relationship between the organisation and its external environment.

Taiwanese companies in Lesotho

Taiwanese companies believe that Lesotho is one of a few countries in the world where factories can attain the same level of productivity as in the East. The firm hand with which discipline is exercised in the C&Y denim factory in Lesotho is a typical example of Taylor's approach to management. Taiwanese supervisors constantly check their subordinates' work to ensure that they attain their goal of 100 % productivity, 100 % quality. Red and green lights indicate to workers whether the set goals have been reached for a specific time period.

The process (administrative) approach

Literature containing the reflections and observations of executives and academics began to appear in conjunction with the development of scientific management. While **scientific management** focused on increasing the productivity of the **worker**, the **process approach** to management grew out of the need to find guidelines for **managing** complex **organisations** such as factories. As output increased and operations grew in these industries, organisations had to deal with more complex problems than the productivity of workers. Planning and the organisation of people in the workplace became a focal point for consideration.

Henri Fayol, a French industrialist, is recognised as the greatest European management pioneer. His interest was in the administrative side of operations. He was concerned about the fact that different abilities were required as one moved up the organisational hierarchy. At the lower levels, an individual required greater technical skills, and at the upper levels, greater administrative skills.

Fayol's experience led him to conclude that there were five basic functions of administration: planning, organising, commanding, coordinating and controlling. **Planning** called for the formulation of objectives and an operating programme. **Organising** focused on the effective coordination of resources for attaining the set objectives. **Commanding** was the art of leading people. **Coordinating** the activities of groups to provide unity of action ensured a smoothly functioning organisation. **Controlling** involved seeing that everything was done according to the set plans.

To guide the administrative process, Fayol formulated 14 principles, listed in the box below. Fayol's approach is extremely relevant to contemporary management.

Fayol's 14 principles

■ **Division of labour:** Work should be divided to permit specialisation.

■ **Authority and responsibility:** These should be equal.

■ **Discipline:** Discipline results from good leadership at all levels of the organisation. It is necessary to develop obedience, diligence, energy and respect.

■ **Unity of command:** An employee must receive commands from one superior only.

■ **Unity of direction:** All operations with the same objective should have one manager and one plan only.

■ **Subordination of individual interest to the common good:** The interests of an individual or group should not take precedence over the interests of the organisation.

■ **Remuneration:** Rewards for work should be fair to the worker and employer.

■ **Centralisation:** The proper degree of centralisation versus decentralisation should be found.

■ **Hierarchy:** The line of authority in an organisation should run in order of rank from top management to the lowest level of the organisation.

■ **Order:** Resources should be in the right place at the right time.

■ **Equity:** Managers should be fair to their employees.

■ **Stability of staff:** A low personnel turnover rate enhances the attainment of goals.

■ **Initiative:** Subordinates should be given the freedom to conceive and carry out their plans, even though some mistakes may result.

■ **Team spirit:** This will give the organisation a sense of unity.

Source: Fayol, H. 1930. *Industrial and General Administration*. Geneva: International Management Institute.

The notion that 'managers are born, not made' is not true, seen against the principles of management that he identified, namely planning, organising, leading and controlling. According to Fayol, management is a skill — one that can be taught once its underlying principles are understood.

The First National Bank example (above) highlights the importance of planning ahead and organising the workforce to strengthen the organisation's competitive position.

A major disadvantage of the administrative approach to management is the fact that the approach postulates that formal authority should be maintained by managers. In today's turbulent business environment, organisations need to be flexible to be able to adapt to the rapidly changing needs of the customer or client. In a firm

First National Bank plans for the future

Fayol's management principles are still evident in most South African organisations. At First National Bank, planning led top management to restructure this financial institution to cope with the changing needs of its customers. The (then) managing director Barry Swart explained the situation as follows: 'During the last two years the marketplace in which we operate has changed dramatically and our business, besides growing, has also changed direction. We are in new businesses we weren't in before and it's important that our structure ensures that we can provide our customers with the holistic one-stop service they need.

'All sorts of barriers, physical, technological and regulatory, are disappearing. This has had a tremendous impact on how we do business. New opportunities are being created, both nationally and internationally. Also, competition is increasing and we have to compete against the banks of the world, both at home and abroad. To be able to exploit the new opportunities this freedom creates and to remain competitive, we must be at the forefront of change.'

Source: *First News*, 1 February 1996, p 1.

of engineers, for instance, the maintenance engineer may take instructions from the plant manager as well as from the chief engineer — contrary to Fayol's principles of division of labour and unity of command.

The bureaucratic approach

The main concern of **Max Weber**, a German sociologist, was with the more fundamental issue of how organisations are structured. Reasoning that any goal-oriented organisation comprising thousands of individuals would require the carefully controlled regulation of its activities, he developed a theory of bureaucratic management that stressed the need for a strictly defined hierarchy, governed by clearly defined regulations and authority.

Weber's ideal bureaucracy is based on **legal authority** — and not tradition or charisma. Legal authority stems from rules and other controls that govern an organisation in its pursuit of specific goals. Managers are given the authority to enforce the rules by virtue of their position. Obedience is not owed to an individual person but to a specific position in the hierarchy of the organisation. These positions would outlive the people occupying them.

Weber's approach to management has stood the test of time relatively well. In South Africa with its relatively few managers (see sec 1.8.1) and large numbers of unskilled workers, devotion to rules and other controls set by managers is still a relevant way of managing. Even organisations employing skilled workers still use the principles of Weber's approach. University administrators must handle the registration of students in a very short period of time. At the University of South Africa, for

Background

Bureaucracy developed as a reaction to the personal subjugation and cruelty of earlier administrative systems, such as monarchies and dictatorships, in which the lives of all were dependent upon the whims of a despot whose only law was his own selfish one. Weber's approach to management can best be understood against this background. He observed the world as decidedly unjust — dominated by class consciousness and nepotism. An aristocratic birth entitled one to military officership or a position of leadership in government or industry. In Weber's view, this was a waste of human resources that ran counter to his belief that the working class could also produce leaders — and not just followers.

instance, approximately 130 000 students must be registered between the middle of November and the middle of March the following year. This task cannot be accomplished using an informal, individualistic approach. Rules and procedures have therefore been developed to achieve this end.

One of the major limitations of this approach is that bureaucratic rigidity results in managers being compensated for doing what they are told to do — not for thinking. Hence rules may become ends in themselves. Limited organisational flexibility and slow decision making are also limitations which, in today's turbulent environment, can lead to the loss of golden business opportunities.

2.4.2 Human relations movement

The classical approaches to management were built on the assumption that if managers could plan, organise, lead and control (process or administrative approach) workers (scientific approach) and the organisation (bureaucratic approach), productivity would increase. These early approaches to management emphasised the technical aspect of work at the expense of its personal aspects. The Depression of the 1930s and major changes in the economic, political, social and technological environments (see 'Background') caused managers to challenge these approaches and their relevance in the business environment. Managing people became the major issue facing managers, and managers became more oriented to **human relations** and **behavioural science**.

The **human relations approach** to solving the productivity problem grew out of a famous series of studies conducted at the Western Electric Company from 1924 to 1933. These eventually became known as the **Hawthorne Studies** because many of them were performed at General Electric's Hawthorne plant near Chicago.

The Hawthorne Studies investigated the relationship between the level of lighting in the workplace and worker productivity. As lighting improved, so did productivity. Surprisingly, as lighting conditions were made worse, there was still a tendency for

Background

The 1920s were prosperous years, characterised by price stability, a doubling of industrial productivity and a 55 % rise in the real income of individuals.[1] Efficiency and mass production held costs down and increased purchasing power. The end of this decade of prosperity came on October 29, 1929, known in the United States of America as Black Tuesday. On this day the stock market crashed. Life was substantially changed by this crash and the Great Depression. Unemployment rose as businesses failed, incomes dropped, homes were lost and family savings were wiped out.[2]

In the early days of the Depression, labour and management responded positively to work sharing, by reducing the hours of work per worker per week rather than laying off workers. It also became socially acceptable for women to work outside the home. Out of economic necessity, women entered the labour force to bolster the family income.[3]

The economic temper of the times certainly shifted the social values of society. A craving for security, a turning inward of people to others who shared the same tribulations, characterised the social environment. A concern for people rather than production predominated. It is, therefore, not strange to find that management theories of this time focused on the people in the organisation.

productivity to improve. It was obvious that something besides lighting influenced the workers' productivity.

Researcher **Mayo** and his associates decided that a complex chain of circumstances had touched off the productivity increases observed. Management's concern for their wellbeing and sympathetic supervision enhanced the workers' performance. This phenomenon was subsequently labelled the **Hawthorne effect**.

The studies concluded that group pressure, rather than management demands, had the strongest influence on worker productivity. In short, employees were more motivated by social needs than economic needs. Group pressure, rather than management rules, controlled an employee's productivity. This approach to management is reflected today in the Japanese management approach of 'quality circles'. Quality circles refer to work groups that meet to discuss ways of improving quality and solving production problems.

Mayo and his colleagues pioneered the use of scientific methods in their studies of people in the work environment. Later researchers, especially psychologists, sociologists and anthropologists, used more sophisticated research methods and became known as **behavioural scientists** rather than **human relations theorists**.

Maslow and **McGregor** are two well-known behavioural scientists. Maslow suggested that humans have five levels of needs. The most basic need is the physical need for food and water; the most advanced need is the need for self-actualisation or personal fulfilment. Maslow argued that people try to satisfy their lower-order needs before attempting to satisfy their higher-order needs. Managers can facilitate this process and attain the organisational goals by removing obstacles and encouraging behaviours that satisfy both the needs of the worker and the organisation. (See chapter 12 for an in-depth discussion of Maslow's hierarchy of needs.) McGregor distinguished two alternative basic assumptions about people and their approaches to work. These two assumptions, which he called **Theory X** and **Theory Y**, take opposite views on people's commitment to work. Theory X managers assume that workers must be constantly coaxed into putting effort into their jobs. Work is distasteful to workers, who must be motivated by force, money or praise. This is consistent with the early approaches to solving the productivity problem, especially the scientific approach. Theory Y managers, on the other hand, assume that people relish work and approach their work as an opportunity to develop their talents. This approach reflects the basic assumptions of the human relations as well as the behavioural science approach to management.

In a nutshell

To solve the issue of productivity, Taylor (scientific management) focused on the **efficiency of the worker**, Fayol (administrative management) emphasised the importance of the **management functions** and Weber (bureaucratic management) stressed the **hierarchy of the organisation**

According to the human relations movement, as well as the behavioural science movement, management should focus on the **needs of the worker**.

The major contribution of the human relations approach to management is the fact that this approach viewed workers as human beings and not as machines. This aspect was emphasised by Pick 'n Pay, which held ongoing discussions between management and labour in 1995 to tackle the issue of high labour costs. Both parties agreed that natural attrition, early retirement and voluntary retrenchments should have a positive impact on the problem.

The key to the success of decreased labour cost was that instead of management dictating what would happen and to whom it would happen, employees were empowered to facilitate the process.

Both the human relations approach to management and the behavioural science perspective have their limitations. The belief that a happy worker is a productive worker is too simplistic. Economic aspects of work remain important to workers, as Taylor believed. Therefore, the human aspect of work is even more complex than originally suggested by the results of the Hawthorne studies.

2.4.3 The quantitative management theory

The quantitative school propagates that management is primarily about 'crunching the numbers'. This approach to solving the productivity problem starts when a mixed team of specialists from relevant disciplines is called in to analyse the problem and recommend a course of action to management. The team constructs a mathematical model that shows, in symbolic terms, all relevant factors bearing on the problem and how they are interrelated. By changing the variables in the model (for example, by increasing the cost of labour) and analysing the different equations of the model by means of a computer, the team can determine the effects of each change.

Background

At the beginning of World War II, Great Britian needed to solve a number of new, complex problems in warfare. With their survival at stake, the British formed the first operational research teams by pooling the expertise of mathematicians, physicists and other scientists. This enabled the British to achieve significant technological and tactical breakthroughs.

The Americans entered the war. They formed what they called operations research teams, based on the successful British model, to solve similar problems. Early computers were used to perform the calculations involved in mathematical modelling.

When the war was over, the applicability for problems in industry of operations research — with the aid of computers — became apparent.

Source: Stoner, JAF, Freeman, RE & Gilbert, DR. 1995. *Management*, 6 ed. Englewood Cliffs, NJ: Prentice-Hall, p 45.

The techniques of the quantitative management theory are a well-established part of the problem-solving armoury of large organisations. Tools and techniques used today include linear programming, PERT/CPM and regression analysis. The greatest contributions of these techniques are in planning and control activities. They can be used to develop product strategies, production scheduling, capital budgeting, cash flow management and inventory control.

This approach offered a new way of looking at management problems. However, it is seldom used by managers as the primary approach to decision making. It is used mainly as a tool or aid in decision making, since many aspects of management decisions cannot be quantified and expressed by means of mathematical symbols and formulas. The human element of management cannot be captured in a quantitative sense.

2.4.4 Contemporary approaches

The classical approaches to management provide the foundation for management and organisations as they function today. These approaches responded primarily to the pressing issues of their times, particularly the need for internal efficiency. However, they took a simplistic view of the organisation, ignoring the broader role of the organisation in its environment. This environment became increasingly turbulent after World War II and managers realised that, in order to survive, they had to take the business environment into consideration in their management decisions.

Background

> After World War II the business environment became increasingly turbulent. In the **economic** environment, competitive challenges from abroad became the rule and no longer the exception, multinational organisations became popular, trade alliances were formed. Changes in this environment continue today. South Africa is now part of the new borderless world, the so-called global village where there is an ongoing search to improve quality and productivity. The **social** environment exhibits a new concern for ethics and social responsibility, employee empowerment and managing across cultures. Major **political** changes in South Africa include the fact that this country again has access to the United Nations and supports the basic tenets of human rights. This is reflected in chapter 2 of South Africa's Constitution and has a direct implication for manager–worker relations. There is also a growing interest in employment, health and safety issues and product quality practices. Computer technology changed the face of the **technological** environment. Computer capabilities were enhanced by technology that progressed from vacuum tubes, to transistors, to miniaturised chips that could store more data and perform more applications and which eventually led to the 'information age'.
>
> To survive in this environment, management can no longer view only the organisation as its major focus. Changes in the external environment have a direct or indirect influence on the survival of organisations. This interrelatedness between organisation and external environment gave rise to the **systems approach** to management as well as many other contemporary approaches, such as the contingency approach, the learning organisation, total quality management and re-engineering.

To cope with changes in the external environment, management had to shift its focus from internal issues to focus on internal as well as external variables. The management approaches that developed as a result are the systems approach to management, the contingency approach, total quality management, the learning organisation, and re-engineering. These contemporary management approaches will be discussed in the following sections.

The systems approach

The systems approach to management developed in the 1950s. This approach compensated for the main limitations of the classical approaches, namely (1) that they ignored the relationship between the organisation and its external environment and (2) that they focused on one aspect of the organisation at the expense of other considerations. To overcome these deficiencies, management scholars based their conceptions of organisations on a general scientific approach called **systems theory**.

Background

Ludwig von Bertalanffy (1901–1971), a biologist, is credited with coining the phrase *general systems theory*. He noted certain characteristics common to all sciences, namely:

■ the study of a whole, or organism

■ the tendency of a system to strive for a steady state of equilibrium

■ an organism is affected by and affects its environment and can thus be seen as an open system.[4]

Others built on Bertalanffy's efforts. Wiener (1884–1964) adopted the word *cybernetics*. The study of cybernetics showed that all systems could be designed to control themselves through a communications loop, which fed information back to the organism, allowing it to adjust to its environment. This feedback meant that an organisation could learn and adapt to possible changes in its environment.[5]

The systems approach to management views an organisation as a group of interrelated parts with a single purpose. The action of one part influences the other parts and managers therefore cannot deal separately with individual parts. Managers should view the organisation as a whole and should anticipate the effect of their decisions on the other parts of the organisation. From a systems point of view, management should maintain a balance between the various parts of the organisation as well as between the organisation and its environment.

The open system perspective of an organisation is depicted in figure 2.3.

The approach followed in this book is based on the systems approach to management and this approach is therefore explained in depth in chapter 3.

The contingency approach

The contingency approach is based on the systems approach to management. The basic premise of the former approach is that the application of management principles depends on the particular situation that management faces at a given point in time. There is no single best way to manage. A method highly effective in one situa-

EXTERNAL ENVIRONMENT

Figure 2.3
The open system perspective of an organisation

tion may not work in another. Management has to decide whether to use the principles of the scientific, bureaucratic, administrative, behavioural or quantitative approaches — or even a combination of them. In other words, the contingency approach to management tries to direct the available techniques and principles of the various approaches to management towards a specific situation to realise the objectives of the organisation as productively as possible.

The contingency approach recognises that every organisation, even every department or unit within the same organisation, is unique. Every organisation exists in a unique environment with unique employees and unique goals. The superintendent of a hospital must realise that the environment in which medical specialists in the intensive care unit function is different from that in which nursing staff in the children's ward function. In the former case management has to adapt to specialists who function individually in an unstructured environment, each taking responsibility for his or her actions. In the case of the nursing staff, a strict hierarchy may be necessary to indicate lines of authority to senior and junior nursing staff. A different management approach is necessary in these two situations although both occur in the same hospital. The contingency approach thus calls for managers to be flexible and to adapt to the situation at hand.

Although the contingency approach emphasises a situational approach (it depends on a specific situation), it is important to stress that not all management situations are indeed unique. The characteristics of the situation are called *contingencies*, and they can be of use in helping managers identify the situation. These contingencies are:

■ the organisation's external environment (its rate of change and degree of complexity)
■ the organisation's own capabilities (its strengths and weaknesses)
■ managers and workers (their values, goals, skills and attitudes)
■ the technology used by the organisation

Management training and experience may help a manager to categorise the situation that has to be managed, based on an examination of the contingencies depicted in figure 2.4.

Figure 2.4
Major contingencies

In a sense, the contingency approach views a manager as a physician. The analogy is depicted in figure 2.5.

As in the case of the physician treating a patient, different yet potentially successful treatments may be available for the same management problem. In systems theory this is called *equifinality* (there is more than one way to reach the same goal). For instance, if the production manager needs to improve productivity in his or her department, he or she may decide on a new work method (a classical solution) or that a new motivational approach needs to be applied (a behavioural solution). Either solution may have the desired effect.

The manager and aspiring manager in South Africa — and the rest of the world — preparing for the 21st century, must learn multiple ways to compete, innovate and lead. This is precisely what the contingency approach suggests.

Total quality management

Today, a quality revolution is taking place in the business world. The term that has evolved to describe this revolution is **total quality management**, or TQM for short.

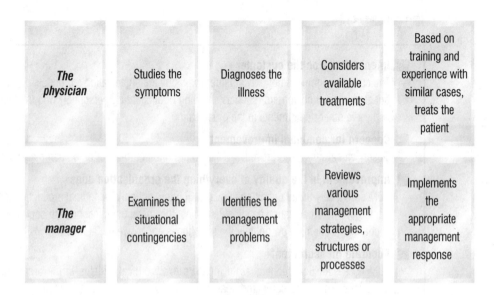

Figure 2.5
The manager as physician

It was inspired by a small group of quality experts, the most prominent of them being **W Edwards Deming**.

Deming, an American, went to Japan in 1950 and began advising many top Japanese managers on how to improve their production effectiveness. Central to his management methods was the use of statistics to analyse variability in production processes. According to Deming, a well-organised organisation was one in which statistical control reduced variability and resulted in uniform quality and predictable quantity of output.

Deming's original programme has been expanded into TQM (total quality management) — a philosophy of management that is driven by competition and customer needs and expectations. The term 'customer' in TQM is expanded beyond the traditional definition to include everyone who interacts with the organisation's product or service, either internally or externally. TQM encompasses employees and suppliers, as well as the people who buy the organisation's products or services. The objective is to create an organisation committed to continuous improvement. It is essentially about creating learning organisations and promoting an intrinsic motivation for learning instead of merely relying on extrinsic punishments and rewards. Deming believed that profound knowledge, including an understanding of a system, statistics and psychology, is required for the achievement of quality.

TQM represents a counterpoint to earlier management theorists who believed that low costs were the only way to increase productivity. The cost of rejects,

The principles of TQM

> ■ **Intense focus on the customer**
> The customer includes not only outsiders who buy the organisation's products or services, but also internal customers (such as shipping or accounting personnel) who interact with and serve other departments in the organisation.
>
> ■ **Concern for continual improvement**
> Quality can always be improved. TQM is a commitment to never being complacent.
>
> ■ **Improvement in the quality of everything the organisation does**
> TQM uses a very broad definition of quality. It refers not only to the final product or service, but to how the organisation handles deliveries, the speed of its response to complaints, its accounting systems, how politely the telephones are answered, and so on.
>
> ■ **Accurate measurement**
> TQM uses statistical techniques to measure every critical variable in the organisation's operations. These are compared against standards or bench marks to identify problems, trace them to their roots and eliminate their causes.
>
> ■ **Empowerment of employees**
> Teams are widely used in TQM programmes as empowerment vehicles for finding and solving problems.

repairing shoddy work, recalls and expensive controls to identify quality problems could lead to lower productivity.

The turbulent environment in which organisations worldwide have to operate emphasises the importance of TQM as a management approach. In this constantly changing environment, TQM can be used as a strategic weapon — as a way to build a competitive advantage. Product innovations, for example, offer little opportunity for sustained competitive advantage because they can be quickly copied by rivals. This phenomenon can be seen in the South African motor industry. Volkswagen South Africa introduced the Citi Golf Chico as a 'no-frills' car — to be quickly copied by Ford's Tracer and Mazda's Midge. Volkswagen, therefore, had to differentiate its product from the competitors by constantly improving the quality and reliability of the Chico — an advantage competitors cannot copy.

Using total quality management as a competitive advantage does not apply only to manufacturing organisations. A university, for instance, can introduce TQM in order to be more responsive to customers (students, academic staff and other groups that use its services) in an environment characterised by increased competition from universities abroad for students.

TQM should not be confused with quality control. While TQM emphasises actions to prevent mistakes, quality control consists of identifying mistakes that may already have occurred.

The learning organisation

It is rare to find a recent management text that does not either refer to or directly quote from Peter Senge's *The Fifth Discipline: The Art and Practice of the Learning Organisation.*

> 'Learning disabilities are tragic in children, but they are fatal in organisations. Because of them, few corporations live even half as long as a person — most die before they reach the age of forty.'
> (Peter Senge)

The **learning organisation** is a management approach also based on the systems approach to management. In many ways Senge's work is a direct offshoot of Deming's work on quality management, which was discussed in this section.

Organisations are really only a collection of individuals. A learning organisation therefore requires learning individuals. However, certain learning disabilities can cripple an organisation. According to Senge, the first step in curing these disabilities is to identify them. The seven learning disabilities are listed in the box on page 54.

According to Senge, five disciplines enable us to overcome these disabilities and create new futures for the organisation. These disciplines are:

■ Becoming committed to lifelong learning.
■ Challenging one's own assumptions and generalisations about the organisation and the world around it is essential to becoming a learning individual and a learning organisation.
■ Sharing a vision for the organisation.
■ Encouraging active dialogue in the organisation.
■ Promoting systems thinking.

It is vital that the five disciplines discussed in this section develop as a unit. This is why systems thinking is seen as the fifth discipline. It is the discipline that integrates the other disciplines; it keeps them from being separate gimmicks or the latest fad in organisational change.

Re-engineering

Re-engineering involves a significant reassessment of what a particular organisation is all about. It is about a fundamental reappraisal about how organisations operate. **Hammer and Champy**,[6] who invented this approach to management, urge managers to ask a very basic question about what they do: 'If I were recreating this

Senge's seven organisational learning disabilities

- **The delusion of learning from experience.** The core learning dilemma that confronts organisations is that we learn best from experience but we never directly experience the consequences of many of our most important decisions. The critical decisions made in organisations have systemwide consequences that stretch over years or decades.

- **'I hit him because he took my ball.'** We are conditioned to see life as a series of events — for every event there is one obvious cause. The primary threats to survival today come not from events — such as a shortage in fuel supply — but from gradual processes to which we are blind: environmental decay, decline in design or product quality relative to competitors' quality, and so on. Generative learning cannot be sustained in an organisation if employees' thinking is dominated by short-term events. A short-term inclination inhibits creative learning.

- **The myth of teamwork.** Often teams in business tend to spend their time fighting for turf, avoiding anything that will make them look bad personally. To keep up the image, they seek to suppress disagreement. Decisions become compromises that reflect what everyone can live with, or else reflect one person's view foisted on the group. Decisions are seldom challenged as management may view inquiring minds as threatening. This leads to 'skilled incompetence' — teams full of people who are incredibly proficient at keeping themselves from learning.

- **'I am my position.'** Workers are trained to be loyal to their jobs — sometimes to the extent that they confuse them with their own identities. When people in organisations focus only on their jobs, they have little understanding of and sense of responsibility towards the results produced when all jobs interact.

- **'The enemy is out there.'** This syndrome is a byproduct of 'I am my position' and the nonsystematic way of looking at the organisation. The 'enemy' syndrome is not limited to assigning blame within the organisation; external sources are often blamed for misfortune.

- **The illusion of taking charge.** Often 'proactiveness' is reactiveness in disguise. Fighting the 'enemy out there' is a reaction. True proactiveness comes from seeing how we contribute to our own problems.

- **The parable of the boiled frog.** If you put a frog in a pot of boiling water, it will immediately try to scramble out. However, if you put the frog in a pot of cold water and gradually turn up the heat, the frog will become groggier and groggier, until it is unable to climb out of the pot. Although there is nothing restraining it, the frog will sit there and boil. Why? Because the frog's internal apparatus for sensing threats to survival is geared to sudden changes in the environment — not slow, incremental changes. This often happens when modern organisations react only to dramatic changes in the environment, ignoring gradual processes that may be bigger threats.

organisation today, given what I know and given current technology, what would it look like?' In other words, managers should imagine that they are starting with a clean piece of paper. This could mean a quantum leap in reinventing the organisation and not merely incremental steps in doing so. It may involve abandoning what has been successful in the past as there is no such thing as a permanent winning formula.

How can a team of committed managers with individual IQs above 120 have a collective IQ of 63?

Team learning starts with dialogue. To the Greeks *dialogos* meant a free flowing of meaning through a group, allowing the group to discover insights not attainable individually. *Dialogue* differs from *discussion*, the latter usually implying a heaving back and forth of ideas in a winner-takes-all competition.

Source: Senge, PM. 1990. *The Fifth Discipline: The Art and Practice of the Learning Organisation.* New York: Doubleday, p 9.

Three labourers were working on a building site. A passerby asked what they were doing. 'Breaking stones,' the first replied. 'Earning a living,' the second answered. The third allowed a greater sense of purpose. 'Helping to build a cathedral,' he said.

Organisations may stagnate when their members, including management, focus on their immediate environments — such as their jobs and departments — rather than on the larger patterns of relationships in which they work and influence the lives of others. Re-engineering thus involves rethinking and redesigning the processes connecting organisational members with people, such as customers and suppliers, outside the organisation. Speed, quality of service and overhead costs are some of the issues that re-engineering can address.

Re-engineering considers the entire organisation, including its suppliers and customers. It is constant and relentless in its focus on integrating four key drivers — people, processes, technology and infrastructure — to create and sustain value for customers while managing costs.

Compared to TQM, re-engineering blends the best of two worlds:

■ drastic change — not merely incremental change — throughout the five to 10 core processes of an organisation, and

■ a profound respect for the smallest but most important details that make an organisation successful in the eyes of its customers.

Re-engineering : a quantum leap

Most large and established organisations cannot readily cope with the demands and challenges of business environments in the 1990s. Many of these organisations are organised along principles dating back to the 1920s. These outdated principles required that all tasks be broken down into the smallest possible subtasks and carried out by a narrow specialist (Taylor's approach to management). Managers were supposed to do the thinking (Fayol's approach) while the doing was left to the rest of the workforce. This separation of thinking from doing fitted in well with the hierarchical view of organisations (Weber's approach), in which division of labour and efficiency were the key factors in organisational design. This viewpoint worked well when the business climate was stable and the emphasis was mainly on growth.

The turbulent business environment of today calls for organisations that are more flexible and responsive, reacting to new competitive situations with the utmost speed. The window of opportunity opens and shuts very quickly. Time to market is rapidly shrinking and is becoming a crucial dimension in business.

A new approach to management is therefore essential to enable organisations to cope with these changes — an approach so revolutionary that it represents a quantum leap in management thought.

Six conditions vital for successful re-engineering programmes have been identified:
1. **Powerful external forces** for change should make change inevitable.
2. **Top management** should vigorously back the re-engineering initiative.
3. Re-engineering projects should focus on the **process improvements** that customers really care about and are willing to pay for.
4. **Thorough knowledge of the needs of customers** is therefore essential.
5. **All major departments** affected by the process(es) should be represented on the team.
6. Changes in **human resource programmes and information technology** should be closely coordinated with the re-engineering effort.[7]

Successful re-engineering is an ongoing rather than a one-off project, as well-managed re-engineering programmes encourage organisations to continually examine themselves to learn and generate new processes to meet the challenges of the 1990s.

2.5   CONCLUSION

This chapter focused on the major approaches to management during the past century. It should be clear from our discussion of the evolution of management theory that this evolution was — and still is — the result of changes in the environment. The different management approaches can therefore be studied meaningfully only if they are seen against the dominant culture of their time.

The classical approaches to management developed from the late 19th century through the early 1950s. The emphasis was on the internal functioning of the organisation. Taylor introduced the scientific management approach which looked inter alia at the 'one best way' to complete production tasks.

At about the same time the process or administrative management perspective appeared. Writers like Fayol looked at the management functions, namely planning, organising, leading and controlling, as a means of improving productivity in the organisation.

Weber attempted to establish an overall management system based on bureaucracy. His emphasis was on specialised positions, structured relationships, rules and regulations.

The human relations approach as well as the behavioural scientist approach to management focused on the worker, groups, and organisational processes as a possible solution to the productivity problem.

The quantitative management approach developed as a result of the invention of computers and enabled experts to apply mathematical techniques to management problems.

The contemporary approaches have developed since World War II. The business environment became increasingly turbulent and managers could no longer focus on internal issues only. The interaction between the external environment and the organisation became the focus of the systems theory to management. According to this theory, an organisation is an open system which is influenced by, and influences, the external environment. Any change in the system or its environments will influence the other parts of the system.

The contingency approach developed from the systems approach. According to the former, there is no 'single best way to manage'. The characteristics of the situation, called contingencies, will determine the best way to manage a specific situation.

The learning organisation approach to management is also based on the systems approach and stresses lifelong learning, scrutinising our mental models, sharing a vision for the organisation and active dialogue within the organisation.

Total quality management looks at continuous improvement and never being satisfied with quality. Re-engineering, on the other hand, propagates reinventing the organisation and not merely taking incremental steps in doing so. This could mean a quantum leap for the organisation in order to adapt to an extremely turbulent environment.

2.6   REFERENCES

1. Alloway, DN. 1966. *Economic History of the United States*. New York: Monarch Press.
2. Wren, A. 1994. *The Evolution of Management Thought,* 4 ed. New York: Wiley, p 330.
3. Ibid p 331.
4. Von Bertalanffy, L. 1951. General systems theory: A new approach to the unity of science. *Human Biology*, 23 December, p 302.
5. Weiner, N. 1948. *Cybernetics*. Cambridge, Mass: MIT.
6. Discussion based on Hammer, M & Champy, J. 1993. *Re-engineering the Corporation: A Manifesto for Business Revolution.* New York: Harper.
7. Davis, TRV. 1993. Re-engineering in action. *Planning Review* 21(4), pp 49–50.

3 Managing in a Changing Environment

Key issues

- The organisation as an open system with specific relationships with its environment
- Some concepts in systems theory and the systems approach to management
- The composition and nature of the environment in which management operates
- Ways in which management responds to the environment

3.1 INTRODUCTION

In the preceding chapters, we emphasised the importance of management in the age of the organisation, more specifically the business organisation, as an institution that creates wealth for a country. We highlighted the significance of management education and showed that management is a process comprising four fundamental management functions, namely planning, organising, leading and controlling. We also traced the evolution of the management process through various theories in the past century. However, traditional ways of thinking about management pay little attention to the environment in which managers have to operate. When most of the management theorists discussed in chapter 2 were alive, the external environment of organisations was stable and unchanging. The environment in which managers work today holds many surprises and shocks.

Who would have thought that in 1996 the rand would be worth only a quarter of its value ten years ago? How many managers realised ten years ago, in planning their communication with consumers and stakeholders, that a black newspaper, *The Sowetan*, would become the biggest in the country? How many advertisers, five years ago, could foresee that Afrikaans, a language spoken by approximately 50 million people in southern Africa and the home language of 17 % of South Africans, would virtually disappear from the main advertising medium, television? Five years ago few people would have believed that before the turn of the century South Africa would no longer have a white government.

Yet many managers still do not fully understand the implications of a changing environment, in particular affirmative action and the shift towards more Afrocentric culture and values. The surprises and shocks that the environment has in store for managers are not confined to South Africa. The American automobile and electronics industries, for example, did not foresee Japan and other Asian countries' world domination of these industries.

The so-called surprises that the environment produces are nothing more than trends that appear and disappear, only to reappear in a different form at a later stage. These trends or external environmental variables largely determine the success or failure of organisations. Economic, technological, social, political, and even ecological and international trends, pressures and influences can make it difficult for managers to achieve the goals of the organisation.

South African managers are operating in one of the most difficult business environments in the world, one where many variables have an enormous influence on their main task, namely to achieve their organisation's goals and objectives. Consider, for example, the impact of the following variables on South African managers.

- In the economic environment, variables such as the plunging rand (in the first four months of 1996 it devalued by 25 %), high interest rates and low productivity impact negatively on management. A currency that constantly devalues makes the planning of things such as imports, capital expenditure and the marketing of consumer goods difficult. The necessary high interest rates to contain inflation result in lower consumption expenditure and necessitate complex marketing strategies, especially in the case of luxury goods and property. While exporters are influenced positively by the devaluation of the rand, low productivity levels, which are the result of rolling mass actions and poor industrial relations, offset any possible gains for exporters.

- The crime wave impacts negatively on management. Each day people, including prominent executives, are murdered or have their cars hijacked and their houses burgled. Even Judge Arthur Chaskalson, president of the Constitutional Court (which abolished the death penalty), was robbed at gunpoint in August 1996. Not only does crime cause tremendous emotional stress, but security, theft, insurance, illegal imports and fraud cost the country in excess of R40 billion per annum. It is virtually impossible to bring criminals to book. The 1996 Nedcor survey on crime shows that of every 1 000 crimes committed, only half are reported, a quarter are solved, a tenth result in prosecution and less than a tenth in convictions.[1]

- The new political dispensation in South Africa is characterised by a host of variables that can be classified under what is known as 'transformation'. Managers are under tremendous pressure from politicians and politically inspired forums to adopt Afrocentric management philosophies, to managerially empower blacks by appointing more black managers and to economically empower blacks.

Some measure of success has been achieved if one considers the fact that in 1995 the number of blacks in top management positions increased by 9,5 % compared to the previous year's 2,5 %. The number of white managers decreased from 96 % to 87 % over the same period. The pressures of transformation make a manager's job extremely difficult, especially since the neglect of education under apartheid did little to produce skilled managers and workers. The solution probably lies in upgrading people's skills. According to a survey by Ernst and Young,[2] upgrading just 1 % of the black workforce's skills to the level held by whites would translate into a 2 % growth in GDP.

■ The influx of some eight million illegal immigrants from neighbouring countries has put further pressure on the deteriorating health, education, transport and municipal services. Management has to bear the cost of providing basic social services for employees. The presence of illegal immigrants also increases unemployment and crime.

■ Because of mass action and poor labour relations, South Africa cannot compete against the successful nations of the world. This is confirmed by the fact that South Africa's market share of international trade decreased from 1,35 % in 1980 to only 0,59 % in 1994. Deregulation and privatisation can improve South Africa's competitiveness.

■ Because of the changing conditions in South Africa, foreign investors are hesitant to invest in South and southern Africa. Between 1983 and 1988, sub-Saharan Africa attracted over 5 % of new foreign private investment. In the first five years of the 1990s, this figure dropped to less than 3 %. South Africa has not only lost ground to the rest of the world as an investment location, but also within Africa. The oil-producing African countries are attracting the bulk of new investment. With South Africa showing an outflow of capital, Nigeria, for example, attracted $740 million or 45 % of the annual capital flow to sub-Saharan Africa.[3]

Table 3.1
The South African management environment compared to
that in other emerging economies, 1996

Comparison	Percentage who say it is . . .		
	Better	Same	Worse
Crime and violence	3	15	79
Productivity	16	40	42
Labour relations	13	44	35
Profit potential	27	46	19
Economic policy	43	42	11
Infrastructure and raw materials	66	26	6

Source: Investor Responsibility Research Centre. *Sake-Rapport,* 28 April 1996, p 12.

The trends and forces in the management environment also impact on international investors. Table 3.1 above reflects the international business world's opinion of the South African management environment.

Focus

> An analysis of the organisation's external environment is necessary, not only to emphasise the influences of environmental variables on managerial performance, but also to further explain the functioning of management, because the management functions of planning, organising, leading and controlling are performed in continually changing conditions. A brief overview of systems theory is necessary to explain the relationship between management and the environment in which it operates.

3.2   CONCEPTS OF SYSTEMS THEORY

3.2.1   The organisation is a system of its environment

The theory of systems was first developed in physics (see page 48), but concepts of this theory are borrowed to explain the interdependence between the business organisation and its environment. A system can be defined as **a set of interrelated elements functioning as a whole**. According to this definition, there are numerous systems of some kind or another. A motor vehicle, for example, is a mechanical system consisting of hundreds of interdependent components; a flower is a botanical system of its own; a dead tree is an essential component of the ecological system; and a human being is a physiological and psychological system made up of interdependent organs, needs and expectations.

A business organisation is also a system that operates in a specific environment. The organisation and its environment depend on each other for survival. This mutual dependence is illustrated in figure 3.1 opposite.

According to figure 3.1, a business organisation obtains resources or inputs from the environment in the form of people (labour), physical resources (raw materials), capital (financial resources) and information (knowledge and know-how). The organisation then transforms these inputs from the environment into outputs in the form of products and services for the environment or, more specifically, the marketplace. Any product being manufactured or produced needs to be marketed. However, this transformation refers not only to the physical production process in the organisation, but also to the entire management process. The human resources required for the manufacturing process have to be appointed and trained, and finances have to be obtained to pay for the raw materials, labour, manufacturing equipment, marketing

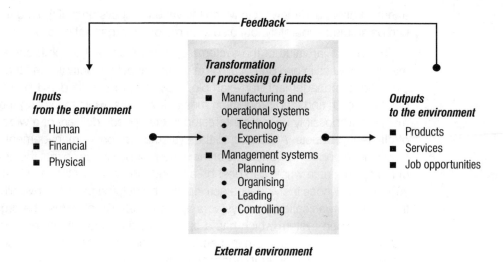

Figure 3.1
A systems perspective of an organisation

activities, and so on. Thus the transformation process — the activities involved in processing the inputs from the environment into products and services of the environment — constitutes the field of study of management. This transformation process is carried out by the organisation as a specific system of its environment.

3.2.2 The systems approach in management

When explaining systems theory and presenting the business organisation as a system, four basic concepts must be understood: **an open system (as opposed to a closed system) subsystems synergy and entropy.**[4]

1. A system is **closed** when it is self-supporting and can exist independently of a particular environment — for example, the development of a test-tube baby from conception to the foetal stage.

    A system is **open** if:

    ■ it is dependent on the environment in which it operates;
    ■ the environment is dependent on the system; and
    ■ there is a specific interaction between system and environment.

2. A **subsystem** is actually a system within a system. For example, a university's library, laboratories and administration can be regarded as subsystems, but they are also systems in their own right. Similarly, the marketing, production and finance functions in an organisation are subsystems, but can also be viewed as systems in their own right. Because the organisation is an **open system** which is dependent on its environment and consists of various **interdependent subsystems** such as marketing, finance, and so on, the systems approach in man-

agement offers a framework in which the various subsystems of the organisation can be studied separately, but also in terms of the organisation as a whole.

The particular value of the systems approach is that it emphasises the fact that the activities in one part of an organisation affect the activities in other parts. Operations management, for example, may require standardised products to obtain smooth and long production runs at low costs, while marketing management would possibly be more interested in the speedy delivery of a wide range of different products. According to the systems approach, management has to marry these opposing viewpoints of the various subsystems so that the objective of the system as a whole can best be attained, and not only those of one of the subsystems whose individual objectives may be detrimental to the overall objectives of the organisation. The systems approach also implies that the organisation is an open system which has a specific relationship with its environment. Also in this regard, management needs to be continuously attentive to changes in the environment in order to adapt timeously to such changes.

3. **Synergy** is another concept of the systems theory that can be applied to management. It means that the whole is greater than the sum of its parts, or that the individual subsystems are simultaneously applied in such a way that the result of their simultaneous application is greater than the sum of their individual efforts. In other words, if the various sections or functions in the organisation cooperate as subsystems, they become more productive than would have been the case if they had functioned individually. This also applies to the management process. The functions of management should not be seen as independent components of the management process, but rather as interdependent components that complement each other in their pursuit of synergy.

4. **Entropy**, or the process of systems disintegration, is the opposite of synergy. When a system, including an organisation, does not make the necessary adjustments to enable it to continue its existence in a particular environment, it is doomed to disintegration and failure.

The above overview of some of the concepts in systems theory that apply to management emphasises the importance of the interface between an organisation and its environment, especially the environmental influences on the organisation and its subsystems. Both entities, the organisation as well as its environment, are not self-supporting, closed systems, but depend on each other for their continued existence. Together they form a business environment or system in which they influence each other mutually. The organisation supplies the products and services that a society requires. As an employer it influences the purchasing power of the society, and its products may also affect the community's way of life. The community constitutes the market for the organisation's products. This interdependence leads to a complex relationship between a business and its environment, which becomes more complex as factors over which management has little or no control — such as technological innovation, economic trends, social changes and political developments — change the environment. These changes or environmental variables may influence management's actions within as well as outside the organisation. It is therefore necessary to examine the composition of the environment in which managers operate.

3.3   THE COMPOSITION OF THE MANAGEMENT ENVIRONMENT

The influence of the environment and change on the successful management of the organisation became apparent in the 1950s. This was partly the result of the systems approach to management, which contends that the organisation is closely intertwined with its environment, and that management should therefore adopt a policy of organisational Darwinism to ensure that the organisation does not become extinct in a rapidly changing world in which only the fittest can survive. The 1950s also ushered in a period of increasing instability in the environment that further increased the need to study environmental influences and change. The result of this interest was the creation of a framework for examining environmental change, namely the environmental concept. This concept is defined as **the sum total of the factors or variables that may influence the continued existence of the organisation** — that is, factors both inside and outside the organisation.

Background

> According to Charles Darwin's theory of evolution, species survive because they have the ability to adapt to a changing environment. Horse-drawn carts and ox-wagons disappeared in South Africa in the 1930s because other means of transport had become available. Possibly cartwrights would have survived if they had adapted themselves to develop other forms of transport, and not just horse-drawn carts.
>
> When Elvis Presley was the king of rock, the jukebox reigned supreme. However, the development of suburban residential areas and technological innovation in the reproduction of music undermined the growth of the urban milkshake parlour and the need for jukebox music became something of the past.

It is necessary to classify the numerous environmental variables that influence the organisation in order to enable one to identify certain trends for further analysis in each section or **subenvironment**. Figure 3.2 shows the composition of the management environment in the format usually encountered in the literature, on the one hand, and as a practical conceptualisation of the interaction between organisation and environment, on the other. According to the figure, the business or management environment comprises **three** different environments.

The first is the **microenvironment**, which consists of the organisation itself, and over which management has almost complete control. The variables in this environment, namely the mission, goals and objectives, as well as strategies of the organisation, various management functions and the organisation's resources, are controlled by management. Also included in the internal environment are the organisation's employees and corporate culture. When managers and employees embrace the same values and have the same goals, the organisation has a good chance of management success. Of particular interest to South African managers today is the need to advance disadvantaged people into managerial positions. Management's decisions influence the market environment through the strategies that it applies to protect, maintain and extend its share of the market. One such strategy is the marketing strategy that management applies, in which pricing, advertising or distribution are employed to increase the organisation's market share.

The second component of the environment is the **market** or **task environment** which surrounds the organisation. Here all the variables indicated in figure 3.2 are relevant to virtually every organisation in a particular *industry*, for they determine the nature and strength of competition in an industry. The key variables in this environment are consumers, whose purchasing power and behaviour in turn determine the number of entrants to the market; *competitors* who are already established in the market and wish to maintain or improve their position, and new and potential competitors; *intermediaries*, who compete with each other to handle the organisation's product or wish to handle only the products of competitors; *suppliers* who supply or do not wish to supply products, raw materials, services and even finance to the organisation; and *labour unions* which deal with the supply of labour.

All these variables create particular opportunities and threats. Management's primary task in this environment is to identify, evaluate and utilise opportunities in the market, and to develop its strategy in such a way that it can meet competition. It is for these reasons that the market environment is often termed the **task environment**. Management has no control over the components in the market environment, although its strategy may influence the relevant variables. Matters such as consumer purchasing power and consumer boycotts may also affect an organisation. At the same time, the market environment, and therefore the microenvironment, is influenced by developments in the macroenvironment. This brings us to the third component in the management environment, namely the macroenvironment.

The **macroenvironment** exists outside the organisation and the market environment. It comprises six distinct subenvironments. First, it includes a *technological environment* that is continually responsible for the pace of innovation and change; an *economic environment* that influences factors such as inflation, recessions, exchange rates and the monetary and fiscal policy of the government and the wealth of the community; the *social environment*, where people's lifestyles, habits and

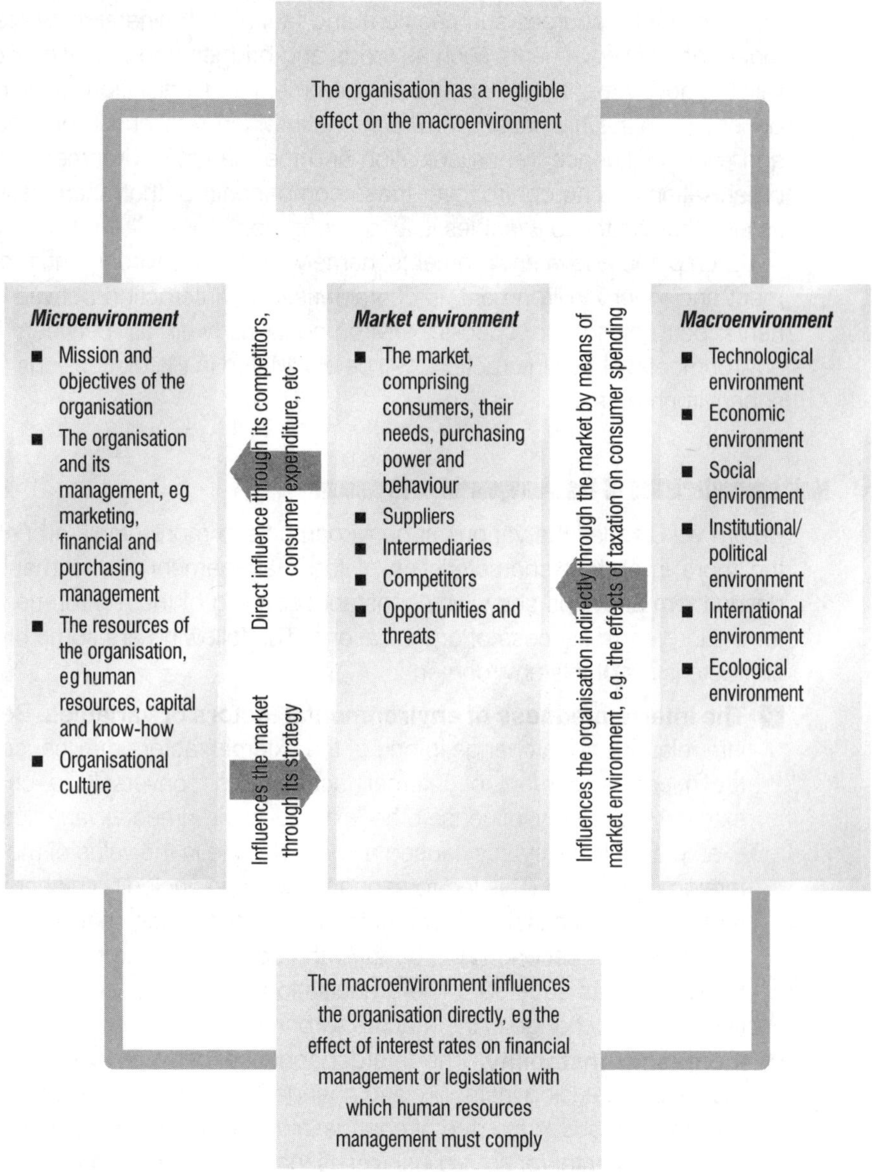

The organisation has a negligible effect on the macroenvironment

Microenvironment	Direct influence through its competitors, consumer expenditure, etc	*Market environment*	Influences the organisation indirectly through the market environment, e.g. the effects of taxation on consumer spending	*Macroenvironment*
■ Mission and objectives of the organisation ■ The organisation and its management, e g marketing, financial and purchasing management ■ The resources of the organisation, e g human resources, capital and know-how ■ Organisational culture		■ The market, comprising consumers, their needs, purchasing power and behaviour ■ Suppliers ■ Intermediaries ■ Competitors ■ Opportunities and threats		■ Technological environment ■ Economic environment ■ Social environment ■ Institutional/ political environment ■ International environment ■ Ecological environment

Influences the market through its strategy

Influences the organisation by means of market spending

The macroenvironment influences the organisation directly, eg the effect of interest rates on financial management or legislation with which human resources management must comply

Figure 3.2
The composition of the management environment
Source: Cronjé, GJ de J et al (eds). 1996. *Introduction to Business Management*.
Johannesburg: Southern, p 50.

values are shaped by the culture and, in turn, make certain demands on the organisation, particularly through consumerism; the *ecological environment,* which comprises natural resources such as flora and fauna and mineral resources as well as man-made improvements such as roads and bridges; the *institutional environment,* with the government and its political involvement and legislation as the primary components; and the *international environment,* in which local and foreign political trends and events influence the organisation and the market environment. The individual organisation has no control over these components of the macroenvironment and its influence on these variables is also negligible.

Each of the above environments, namely the microenvironment, market environment and macroenvironment, is characterised by interaction between the components peculiar to the specific environment, as well as between the different environments. These interactions will be elucidated in the discussions of the various subenvironments.

3.3.1 Main characteristics of the management environment

Before we discuss the various subenvironments in more detail, a brief overview of the more important characteristics of the management environment will help to define them and thus show why constant scanning of the environment is essential for the long-term success of organisations. The following are some of the principal characteristics of this environment:

■ **The interrelatedness of environmental factors or variables.** Because of this interrelationship, a change in one of the external factors may cause a change in the microenvironment or internal factors, and conversely, a change in one external factor may influence other external environmental variables. In 1995, for example, political events caused a sharp decline in the value of the rand against foreign currencies. This led to economic change, including higher inflation. This reduced the purchasing power of the consumer, which, in turn, led to growth in the market for second-hand cars. At the same time, the price of fuel doubled. Holiday resorts suffered, while organisations such as Sasol and exporters profited from this change in the macroenvironment.

■ **Increasing instability.** The interdependence between environmental factors results in increasing instability and change in the environment. Even if there is a general increase in the rate of change in the environment, environmental fluctuations are greater for some businesses than others. Researchers have found, for example, that the rate of change in the pharmaceutical and electronics industries is higher than in the automobile component and bakery industries.

■ **Environmental uncertainty.** This is the third characteristic of the management environment. Uncertainty about the environment is, of course, a function of the amount of information available on environmental variables as well as the confidence that management has in that information. If little information is available or the value of the information is suspect, uncertainty about the environment increases, and vice versa.

■ **The complexity of the environment.** This is the fourth characteristic of the management environment and indicates the number of external variables to which the organisation must react, as well as fluctuations in the variables themselves. A baker has far fewer environmental variables to cope with than a computer manufacturer and, therefore, functions in a less complex environment. Organisations in less complex environments have the advantage that they require less critical information for decision making. Hence not all aspects of the environment have the same importance for all organisations.

The above characteristics of the environment also stress how important it is for management to understand and have a knowledge of the environment in which the organisation operates. With this discussion in mind we shall now take a look at the various subenvironments, namely the microenvironment, the market environment and the macroenvironment.

3.4 THE INTERNAL OR MICROENVIRONMENT

The microenvironment is the internal environment of the organisation and is the main environment in which management operates. It is in this environment that management plans, organises, leads and controls the management activities of the organisation. The management process is enacted in this environment to achieve synergy between the objectives of the organisation, the resources for realising these objectives, the personal goals of employees, ownership interests, market requirements and the environment outside the organisation. Different levels and kinds of management are involved here. Most of what was discussed in chapter 1 forms part of the internal or microenvironment.

3.5 THE MARKET OR TASK ENVIRONMENT

The environment that immediately surrounds the organisation is known as the market environment. As shown in figure 3.2, it comprises the market, suppliers, intermediaries and competitors who are the source of opportunities and threats to the organisation. More specifically, this environment contains those variables that revolve around competition and pose threats or create opportunities for organisations.

3.5.1 The market

The **market** for the organisation's products or services consists of people who have needs to be satisfied and the financial means to satisfy them. The market as a variable in the market environment consists of people with particular needs and a certain behaviour in satisfying them. If a business is to achieve any success with a strategy to influence consumer purchasing behaviour in its favour in this competitive business environment, management should be informed about all aspects of consumer needs, purchasing power and purchasing behaviour. Management should also realise that these aspects are influenced directly by the variables in the macroenvironment. For example, demographic trends affect the **number of consumers**, economic factors determine the **purchasing power** of consumers, and cultural values exert particular influences on the **purchasing behaviour** of consumers. Buying power is represented mainly by the **personal disposable income** of consumers. Personal disposable income is that portion of personal income that remains after deducting direct tax, plus credit (loans from banks, shops and other institutions), which can be used to purchase consumer products and services. Figure 3.3 indicates the *per capita* disposable income of South African consumers in the nine provinces.

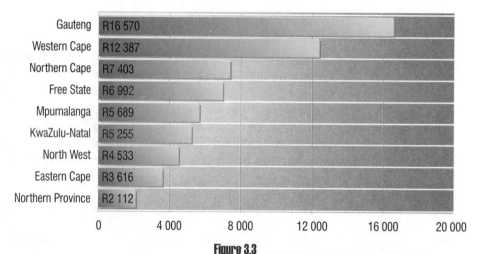

Figure 3.3
The per capita disposable income of South African consumers according to province
Source: Bureau for Market Research, 1994.

Only two of the main characteristics of the consumer market, the **number** of consumers and the **buying power** of consumers, are mentioned above. Numerous other characteristics such as language, age , gender distribution, marital status, family size, and literacy influence the consumption patterns of the consumer market.

Management should also understand that this continued interaction between market variables and variables in the macroenvironment gives rise to changes in both environments.

3.5.2 Suppliers

According to the systems approach, the organisation is regarded as a system that attracts inputs from the environment and converts them into outputs, or products and services, to be marketed in the market environment. The inputs that the organisation requires are mainly **materials**, including raw materials, equipment and energy, **capital** and **labour** which are provided by the organisation's suppliers. If one considers that in South Africa about 60 cents (60 %) in every rand is spent on purchases from suppliers, their importance as a variable in the market environment becomes clear. If an organisation is unable to draw the essential inputs of the right quality, quantity and price to reach its objectives, then it cannot hope to succeed in a competitive market environment.

Virtually all organisations, be they manufacturing, trading or contracting organisations, depend on regular supplies of materials. Organisations are also totally dependent on suppliers of capital. Banks, building societies, shareholders, mortgages and the like are such suppliers. Small organisations in particular have difficulty attracting capital. Another component of suppliers as an environmental variable on which businesses depend, is provision of **labour** by trade unions and other pressure groups, which are regarded as 'suppliers' of labour and with which organisations, particularly those in manufacturing and mining, have complex relations. Management should also realise that at present the South African workforce as a whole is different from what it was ten, or even five, years ago. Despite the large percentage of unemployed workers in South Africa and the fact that millions of workers from neighbouring countries are flooding to South Africa, the government is considering the introduction of a minimum wage. This could worsen the unemployment situation. At the same time the lifestyle and life circumstances of workers are changing. The proportion of women in the workforce is increasing; the demand for educated and skilled workers is rising, while jobs for unskilled workers are diminishing; increasingly more employees want to participate in decisions about their work lives; and in South Africa the challenge to manage cultural diversity is on the increase.

The interaction between the organisation and its network of suppliers is one of the important examples of the influence of environmental variables on the organisation.

3.5.3 Intermediaries

Besides consumers and competitors in the market environment, intermediaries also play a vital role in bridging the gap between the manufacturer and the consumer. By bridging this gap, place, time and ownership utility are created. Intermediaries are wholesalers and retailers, commercial agents and brokers. Even spazas form part of the distribution system in that they play an important role in the distribution of basic consumer goods. Financial intermediaries such as banks and insurers who are financially involved in the transfer of products and services also play a role here.

Managerial decision making on intermediaries is complicated by the following:

■ **The dynamic and ever-changing nature of intermediaries.** New trends in marketing or consumption are responsible for the development of new types of intermediaries. Examples of contemporary South African trends in this regard are extended shopping hours, the power shift from manufacturers to large retailers because of bar-coding and no-name brands, an increase in advertising by shopping centres themselves, the growing importance of black retailers in black residential areas, and the increase in the number of franchises and spazas.

■ **Decisions about intermediaries mean the formation of long-term alliances**. This may have certain implications for the marketing strategy. Thus the economic power of large retailers may have specific implications for price and advertising decisions, while product diversification is dependent on the capacity of intermediaries.

The new trends among intermediaries offer opportunities to management, but certain trends may also mean threats.

3.5.4 Competitors

A market economy is characterised by, among other things, a competitive market environment. Thus every organisation that endeavours to market a service or product in the market environment is constantly up against **competition** — and it is often competitors and not consumers who determine the actual quantity of a particular product to be marketed, including what price should be asked for it. In addition, organisations not only compete for a market share for their product, but also compete with other organisations for labour, capital and materials. Competition as a variable of the market environment can be defined as **a situation in the market environment in which different organisations with more or less the same product or service compete for the business patronage of the same consumers**. The result of this competition is that the market mechanism keeps excessive profits in check, provides an incentive for higher productivity and encourages technological innovation. Although the consumer benefits from competition, it is still a variable that management has to take into account when developing strategies to enter a market.

In its assessment of competition, management should bear in mind that the nature and intensity of competition in a particular market environment are determined by five factors:

■ the possibility of new entrants (competitors) or departures
■ the bargaining power of clients and consumers
■ the bargaining power of suppliers

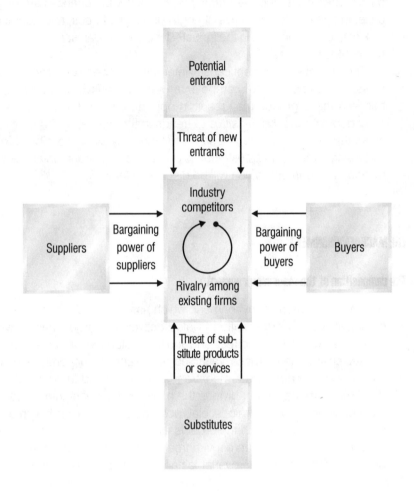

Figure 3.4
Competitive forces in an industry
Source: Pearce, JA & Robinson, RB. 1994. *Formulation and Implementation of Competitive Strategy.*
Homewood, Ill: Irwin, p 77.

■ the availability or lack of substitute products or services
■ the number of existing competitors

Figure 3.4 illustrates the five forces responsible for competition in a particular industry. This model is called 'Porter's five forces model' as it originates in the work of Michael Porter. The collective strength of these five forces determines the competitiveness in the industry and, therefore, its profitability. Competition varies from intense in industries such as tyres and retailing, to moderate in mining and cold-drinks. The weaker the five forces are, the better the chances are of good perform-ance. In spite of the collective strength of the five forces, management still has the task of finding a position in the industry where the organisation can best defend itself against these forces.

The market environment causes interaction between organisations and their sup-pliers, consumers, and competitors with alternative offerings. The interaction between these groups may result in opportunities or threats for the organisation. Management must be sensitive to trends in the market environment to enable it to make the most of opportunities and to timeously avoid possible threats. The tools that management should use for this purpose are environmental scanning and infor-mation management, which will be discussed later.

3.6   THE MACROENVIRONMENT

3.6.1   The composition of the macroenvironment

Apart from the market environment, which has a more direct effect on the futures of organisations, an organisation is also active in a larger macroenvironment con-taining variables with a direct and indirect influence on the organisation and its market environment. These variables represent the uncontrollable environmental forces, also referred to as 'megatrends'. As indicated in figure 3.2, contemporary literature on management divides the macroenvironment into six variables, namely the technological, economic, social, political, ecological and international variables or subenvironments which the organisation has to monitor and react to.

In the study of the macroenvironment, the emphasis is on the changes caused by the uncontrollable macrovariables and their implications for management.

3.6.2   The technological environment

Every new technological development or innovation creates **opportunities** and **threats** in the environment. Television was a threat to films and newspapers, but at the same time provided opportunities for instant meals, satellite communication and the advertising industry. The opportunities created by the computer for banking, manufacturing, transport and practically every industry are virtually immeasurable. Moreover, technological or scientific innovation often has unpredictable conse-quences: the contraceptive pill meant smaller families, more working women and more money to spend — hence more money to spend on holidays and luxury items that would previously have been unaffordable. The most outstanding characteristic of technological innovation is probably the fact that it constantly accelerates the rate of change.

Background

Scientists estimate the age of the earth at approximately five billion years and human beings as having existed for 250 000 years. History goes back about 5 000 years. With the exception of a few basic products, most of the products at our disposal today have been developed in the last 60 years. The latest products which are already considered to be indispensable to modern society (laser surgery, robot factories, silicon protein molecules, fibre optics and 80 % of the medicines bought in pharmacies, to mention but a few) are only ten years old! Five hundred years ago individuals spent 80 % of their day providing for their energy needs. Today this figure is in the region of 10 %. These dramatic changes in the environment are largely the result of technological innovation.

The acceleration of technology

The following ten future technologies appear to have the greatest potential for transforming society:

- Hydrogen fuel-cell vehicles will reduce pollution.
- High temperature superconductivity will carry more than 1 200 times as much current as household copper.
- Genetic engineering. Almost every week doctors find the gene responsible for a specific illness — and manipulate the gene!
- Bionics. Biomedical engineers are building limbs that resemble the real thing.
- Universal personal telephones the size of wrist watches.
- Voice-activated computers that will even allow for variations in accent!
- Nanotechnology — making small machines on a molecular scale.
- Optical electronics — ways of using light to store data, making today's computers look as primitive as the roomsize computers of the 1950s.
- Virtual reality — creating an artificial environment so convincing it cannot be distinguished from the real thing.
- New materials which are lighter and far more heat tolerant, including biological materials such as spider silk which is flexible, yet five times stronger, gram for gram, than steel.

Source: *Time*, 17 July 1995, pp 44–51.

The question that now arises is how technological innovation affects the organisation, and what its implications are for management. The fundamental implications are clear. The most basic effect of technology is probably **higher productivity**. The ability to produce more and better products threatens organisations with keener competition, compelling them to reassess factors such as organisational structure, division of labour, appointment of people, methods of production and marketing strategies. Figure 3.5 indicates the role of technology in improving productivity.

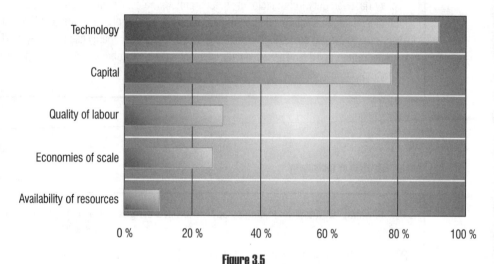

Figure 3.5
Factors that improve productivity in the world economy
Source: Hunt, VD. Mechatronics. *Finansies & Tegniek,* 26 July 1996, p 21.

Technological progress, therefore, affects the organisation as a whole, including its products, life cycle, supply of materials, production processes and even its approach to management. These influences all require management to keep abreast of technological change.

3.6.3 The economic environment

After technology, which is primarily responsible for change in the environment, there is the economy, which is, in turn, influenced by technology, politics, the ecology and the social and international environments. These cross-influences constantly cause changes in the economic growth rate, levels of employment, consumer income, the rate of inflation, the exchange rate and general state of the economy. These economic forces ultimately result in prosperity or adversity, and have specific implications for an organisation and its management. The main interfaces between the economic environment and the organisation are the economic growth rate, consumer income, inflation, monetary and fiscal policy and fluctuations in these magnitudes.

The economic prosperity of a nation is measured by the range of products and services it produces and renders. In financial terms, this standard is more or less equivalent to the gross domestic product, that is, **the total value of finished articles and services produced in a given period, usually a year, within the borders of a country**.

Background

In the thirty years after World War II, the average real growth rate of the South African GDP was about 4,7 % per annum, after which, from 1970 to the early 1990s, it declined to an average annual rate of 2,8 %. This puts South Africa's population growth of about 2,9 % per annum higher than the growth rate in the GDP — the main cause of a real decline in the standard of living in the last decade. This trend, as indicated in figure 3.6, has certain implications for management.

Source: Bureau for Market Research. 1993. *Aspects of the Marketing Environment in Developing Countries*. Research Report no 199, Unisa, p 21.

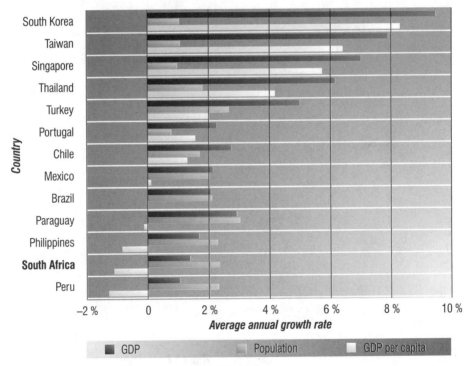

Figure 3.6
Changes in the standard of living of thirteen developing countries, 1980–1990

If a nation's economic growth rate continues to be lower than the population growth rate, there will be a constant decline in the standard of living. Organisations have to realise that declining purchasing power is accompanied by a change in buying behaviour as well as the type of products sought. With a declining income, the consumer cannot afford luxury goods and the emphasis shifts to basic products and services.

The economic environment not only influences other environments and businesses, but is itself influenced by other trends. The devastating crime wave which the country has experienced since 1996 has been responsible for a decline of 50 % in the number of tourists to South Africa, at a time when the hotel industry has spent billions of rands to provide accommodation for the expected wave of tourists to the new South Africa. Managers have to adjust their plans to cope with sudden change in the economic environment.

Another economic variable affecting an organisation and its market environment is the government's monetary policy, which affects the money supply, interest rates and the exchange rate and can cause disturbances in the environment. Fiscal policy affects the organisations as well as the consumer through tax rates and tax reforms.

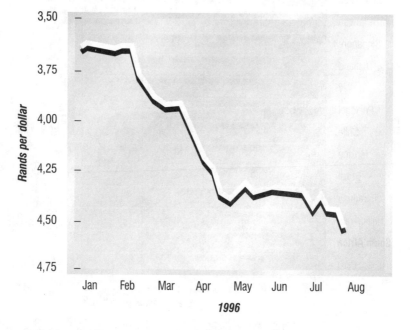

Figure 3.7
Devaluation of the rand, 1996
Source: *The Economist*, 17 August 1996, p 66.

Ultimately, a country's economic success is reflected by the value of its currency. South Africa's low productivity levels, turbulent labour situation and devastating crime wave have eroded the market's confidence in the rand, as shown in figure 3.7. The decline in the value of the rand has played havoc with importers' plans.

These economic trends, which were briefly discussed as examples of economic change, demand constant awareness on the part of management and regular consideration of the mission, goals and strategy of the organisation.

3.6.4 The sociocultural environment

The environmental variable that is probably most sensitive to cross-influences by other variables, especially technology and the economy, is sociocultural change. It is precisely because it affects management indirectly through people as consumers and as employees that its ultimate effect on the strategy of an organisation should not be underestimated.

People are products of their society: as members of a particular community, nation or population group they adopt the culture of that society — that is, they learn its language, values, faith, expectations, laws and customs. This culture — or the sum total of the way of life of a group of people — influences an individual's lifestyle. Consumption is therefore not only explained in economic terms as a function of income, but also as a function of cultural and social change. However, a culture is not static and a community's values, expectations, way of life and habits change over a period of time.

The culture of a particular country is not absolutely homogenous. There are numerous subcultures, based on nationality, religion, population group or geographical area, each of which modifies the environment and has implications for management. An organisation is at the centre of social change. It contributes to social change, on the one hand, and should always keep up with the major influences of social trends on the organisation, on the other.

The influence of crime on a single business organisation

The following are the experiences of the furniture retailer, JD Group, during 1996:

- 355 burglaries, 81 hijackings, 11 armed robberies and several security personnel killed
- the soaring incidence of crime cost the group R10,8 million in stock and cash — excluding the 81 vehicles involved in hijackings
- the group spends R20 million a year on crime prevention

Source: *Business Times*, 1 September 1996.

Appropriate standards of business conduct also vary across cultures. In Euro-centric countries, accepting bribes is considered unethical, while in many African countries this is perfectly acceptable. The shape of the market, the political influence of the culture with the political power and the attitudes of the workforce are only a few of the many ways in which culture can affect an organisation. In South Africa, new cultural values are emerging among young urban blacks, for example the extended family living under one roof is viewed with disfavour, women have become more independent and many express negative attitudes towards marriage and large families.[5] These changes in cultural values will eventually influence the marketplace and the workplace.

Aspirations of black youths in Gauteng, 1995

The hopes and aspirations of the young people were based on their ambition to be educated, successful and prosperous in a professional career or in their own business. All dreamt of living with their family in a beautiful home, either in a posh suburb or on a farm with their own car and all the trappings of wealth around them.

- The hostel dwellers tended to favour larger families (up to seven children were mentioned) and, in some instances, more than one wife. They valued the possession of livestock (cattle, sheep and chickens), television, hi-fi sets and piped water. Some dreamt of owning a spaza shop, supermarket, brewery or football club. Others wanted to become a carpenter, drive a truck, play for the National Soccer League or become a television presenter.

- The young urban women favoured smaller families (mostly one or two children were mentioned, and three or four more rarely). They were not convinced that they wanted to be married, unless to an educated and considerate husband. They dreamt of becoming professionals (such as lawyers), movie stars or owning their own business. They saw themselves travelling locally and overseas in the future, meeting a variety of people from different cultural backgrounds and making many friends. Most valued happiness, peace and rural values.

- The young urban men also mostly favoured smaller families but slightly larger than was the case with the young women. No man wanted only one child, and two or three were mostly preferred, with some saying four or five. They aspired to be successful and prosperous in their own business, to 'wake up each day with a purpose', and to experience luxury and the fun life. They were more materialistic than the young women and also more prone to risk taking, both in their desire to take part in physical activities such as scuba diving, sky diving, mountaineering and exploring caves, as well as in gambling.

Source: Bureau for Market Research. 1995. Research Report no 223, Unisa, p 41.

Another important trend in the sociocultural environment is urbanisation. Over the next 15 years, China will have to build new cities which will house more people than the millions already living in the European Community. Figure 3.8 reflects South Africa's urbanisation pattern. It is obvious that this pattern will impact on managers in the housing, transport and waste management industries, and on banks, building societies and manufacturing in general.

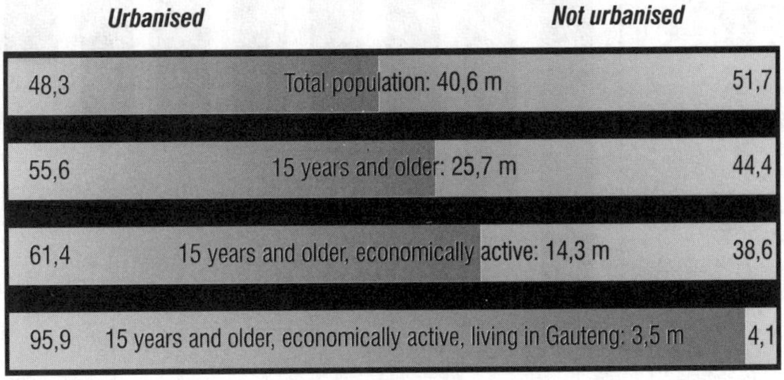

Urbanised		*Not urbanised*
48,3	Total population: 40,6 m	51,7
55,6	15 years and older: 25,7 m	44,4
61,4	15 years and older, economically active: 14,3 m	38,6
95,9	15 years and older, economically active, living in Gauteng: 3,5 m	4,1

Figure 3.8
Urbanisation in South Africa
Source: Central Statistical Services, 1994.

3.6.5 The ecological/physical environment

The ecological or physical environment contains the limited natural resources from which an organisation obtains its raw materials and is the receptacle for its waste. The latter refers to various forms of pollution. Since the 1960s, there has been a growing awareness of the need to conserve the limited resources of our natural environment; people have protested against all forms of pollution and the destruction of the environment by opencast mining and the building of roads and dams, and it has been speculated that the theories of Malthus and others on the overpopulation of the earth could become a reality. Organisations are likewise becoming increasingly aware of the physical environment. Interfaces that present opportunities as well as threats to organisations are discernible. These include a shortage of resources, the cost of energy, the cost of pollution and damage to the country's natural resources. Management must take timely steps to limit as far as possible any detrimental effects the organisation may have on the environment, in order to prevent unfavourable attitudes towards the organisation.

Of particular importance to managers in agriculture are temperatures and their influence on natural resources and food production. The earth's surface temperature could increase by 1–3 °C in the next century. This may have devastating consequences for South Africa, which is already harassed by droughts and floods.

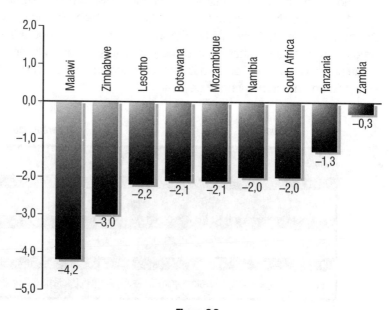

Figure 3.9
Average annual growth in food production in southern Africa
Source: International Food Policy Research Institute (IFPRI). Washington, 1996.

The declining production of food in South and southern Africa is another troublesome megatrend in the ecological environment, as shown in figure 3.9. These trends show that southern Africa is fast becoming the world's new locus of poverty. South Africa, with four million uprooted people and eight million refugees in the form of illegal immigrants, faces famine on an unprecedented scale unless it increases its food production. This variable can bring about many changes in the food industry.

3.6.6 The politicogovernmental environment

Management's decisions are continually affected by the course of a country's politics, especially political pressures exerted by the ruling government and its institutions in the business environment. As a component of the macroenvironment, the state influences the business environment and the organisation primarily as a regulating force. By promulgating and enforcing laws, it influences the environment with measures that are usually politically directed, so steering development and economic policy in a certain direction. The policy of the South African government is aimed at maintaining a market economy, private ownership and freedom of speech, but it will intervene where monopolistic or other conditions impede the functioning of the market. The government also intervenes on a large scale and influences the total environment by means of the annual budget, taxes, import control (or lack of it), promotion of exports, import tariffs to protect certain industries against excessive foreign intervention, price control in respect of certain products and services, the marketing of agricultural products, health regulations and incentives, and other measures to force development in a certain direction.

Furthermore, the government influences the organisation's market both internally and externally — internally through government expenditure, and externally through its political policy which may mean acceptance, or otherwise, of South African products on international markets. When the government acts as producer, as in the case of numerous government organisations such as Eskom, it competes with the private sector for labour, raw materials and capital. To an increasing extent it remains the task of management to study the numerous and often complex activities, legislation and measures of the government as well as political trends in order to timeously determine their influence on the profitable survival of the organisation.

3.6.7 The international environment

While each of the preceding environmental factors to a greater or lesser extent influences the business environment of each organisation, the business environment grows in complexity with more opportunities and threats if an international dimension is added to each of the environmental factors. Similarly, businesses that operate internationally find themselves in a far more complex environment because each country has unique environmental factors with its own technology, economy, culture, laws, politics, markets and competition which differ from those of other countries. International and multinational organisations in particular are affected by international trends and events.

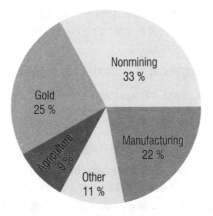

Figure 3.10
South Africa's exports, 1994
Source: Boland Bank, 1995.

South Africa's readmission to international markets should present managers with many opportunities, especially in African markets. Figure 3.10 illustrates the value of South Africa's exports for the year 1994. It is interesting to note that South Africa is one of only six food-exporting countries in the world: at R8,3 billion, food represented about 9 % of its 1994 exports. However, the scrapping of tariff protection in many industries will result in severe competition for local organisations.

Focus on global competition

Today's environment pays no respect to national boundaries. Managers must learn to cope with products, services and ideas circulating around the world. What is the environment of the new global village like?

◼ As a result of advances in transportation and communication technology in the past century, almost no part of the world is cut off from the rest and virtually every organisation is affected by the international dimension.

◼ Products and services exist in a one-world market where competitors in the global village hail from all over.

◼ Even organisations that do business in only one country may face foreign competition at home, and they often use materials or production equipment imported from abroad. The knitting industry in South Africa uses expensive German knitting machines, expensive imported yarns, local labour which is ten times as expensive as that in India or Singapore, and at the same time competes against the highly productive Asian countries, such as Taiwan.

◼ Many organisations use components manufactured in countries where labour is inexpensive, and assembled locally. Ford, for example, employs less than 50 % of its total workforce on US soil. Half of those employed in the chemicals industry in the USA work for foreign-owned companies.

◼ Successful organisations standardise and customise products to local needs.

Source: Daft, RL. 1991. *Management*. Orlando: The Dryden Press, p 69.

3.6.8 Conclusion

In a market economy the organisation exists in a dynamic environment in which technological innovation, economic fluctuations, changing ways of life, international and ecological variables as well as political trends are continually changing the environment and ultimately affecting it. Insight into trends and events in the environment, especially the ability to forecast the implications of these for managerial decision making, are now becoming a top priority for management, since past experience in the rapidly changing environment is often of little help when management has to deal with new problems. Knowledge of trends in the environment and identification of environmental dimensions that largely determine the progress of a business, are also necessary for decision making to maximise profitability. This knowledge requires scanning of the environment which enables management to timeously identify threats and challenges in the environment and, where possible, to transform them into opportunities.

In a nutshell

All organisations operate in an external and internal environment. The external environment comprises the macro- and market environments. The internal environment is also called the microenvironment. These environments can be depicted as follows:

3.7   INTERFACES BETWEEN THE ORGANISATION AND THE ENVIRONMENT

The above overview of the different dimensions of the environment in which management functions clearly shows the complexity and dynamics involved. Because an organisation is an open system, there are certain relations between it and the various dimensions of the management environment. We shall now examine how the environment influences the organisation and how the latter reacts to this.

3.7.1 Environmental change and the organisation

Change is a difficult concept to define. In simple terms it means changing the status quo — changing a state of stability to instability, moving from the predictable to the unpredictable, or from the known to the unknown. It is unmeasurable and causes uncertainty. No one factor is responsible for change and it occurs in specific areas and societies in various ways and at different rates. Furthermore, the **rate** of change often has a more profound effect on the environment than the actual **direction** of change. Change is therefore a process of continual innovation in every conceivable area of society. Consider the following inventions that changed our way of life.[6]

Background

Number of years ago	Invention
■ 100 000	Making equipment for hunting
■ 40 000	Making and using weapons
■ 15 000	Agriculture
■ 5 000	Invention of the wheel
■ 800	The timepiece and compass
■ 600	Gunpowder
■ 500	The printed book
■ 210	The steam-engine
■ 150	Electricity
■ 90	Telecommunications, aircraft and motor vehicles
■ 50	Nuclear weapons
■ 40	The computer (it has been estimated that in the early 1950s the maximum demand for computers in the USA was 100)
■ 25	Lasers
■ 20	Space travel
■ 10	80 % of the medicines now in use were invented in the last 10 years

Today people in developed countries live in a world in which communication is instantaneous, products have a short life cycle and competition is high because entry into the market is relatively easy. Contemporary change is rapid compared to historical change, even in the last 50 years. According to Toffler,[7] this rapid change has a particular implication which he terms 'future shock' for those who cannot adapt to it. This change also has specific implications for organisations. An organisation's systems, structure, strategy, style, expertise, culture and mutual values may be in equilibrium with the environment. In other words, the strategies and systems of the organisation fit into the environment in such a way that the organisation fares out-standingly and yields a good rate of return. However, change in the environment may also seriously disrupt the once harmonious relationship with the organisation. To ensure its survival, management must make adjustments in one or more of the organisation's interfaces, namely its systems, strategy, structure, and so forth. The extent of these adjustments will depend on the nature, speed and complexity of environmental change. As mentioned earlier, the environment of one organisation differs from that of another, with the result that some environments are more suitable than others. We shall now discuss a few examples of how an organisation can approach environmental change.

3.7.2 Uncertainty in the environment

An organisation's environment can be approached from two perspectives, namely the **extent of change** and the **level of complexity**.[8] The extent of change refers to the degree of stability or instability of the environment, while the complexity of the environment depends on the number of variables in the environment, resulting in either a complex or a simple environment. Interaction between these two dimen-sions, as depicted in figure 3.11, determines the level of uncertainty that the environ-ment holds for the organisation. Although figure 3.11 is a simplistic representation of environmental change, it at least explains the fact that the environments of certain organisations differ from each other.

Although no environment is without some degree of uncertainty, organisations that exist in a stable and simple environment are in a segment that experiences little uncertainty. Examples here are manufacturers of packaging materials, bakeries and cafés. Technology, legislation and inputs in this segment are fairly stable.

The combination of a simple but dynamic environment means a moderate level of uncertainty. A clothing manufacturer is an example of a business that functions in such an environment. Rex Trueform, for example, has relatively few competitors, few suppliers and limited measures or regulations that have to be complied with, but is affected by the pace at which styles, fashions and new consumer tastes emerge.

A third combination of factors entails a complex but stable environment also with a moderate level of uncertainty. Toyota South Africa exists in an environment in which it has to cope daily with numerous suppliers, regulations, trade unions and compet-itors. However, changes in design and manufacturing technology are fairly slow.

Finally, a complex and dynamic environment promotes a high level of uncer-tainty. Such an environment has many variables and the nature thereof is continually changing, owing to technological change and resultant changes in competition and market behaviour. The communication industry (cellular phones, computers, fax machines, photocopy machines and so forth) operates in an environment with a high level of uncertainty.

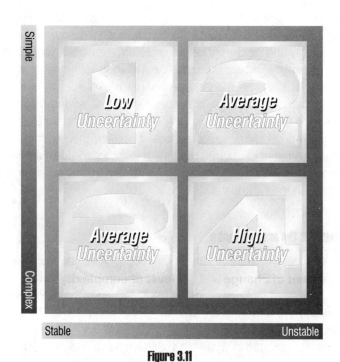

Figure 3.11
Environmental change and uncertainty
Adapted from Griffin, RW. 1993. *Management.* Boston: Houghton Mifflin, p 75

Table 3.2
Examples of crises in the South African management environment

Year	Nature of crisis	Effects
1985	Halving of rand after Rubicon speech	Importers, consumers detrimentally affected
1989	Leakage of toxic substances by Sappi's papermill in the Lowveld	Ecological pollution and bad publicity for Sappi
1990	Drought and high interest rates	Downfall of agricultural organisations
1991	Iraq-Kuwait war	Tourism industry forced to its knees world-wide
1992	President Nelson Mandela released	Mining organisations and banks threatened with nationalisation
1994	April election	A resounding victory for President Nelson Mandela brings peace and unprecedented business confidence; JSE soars to all-time highs
1996	25 % devaluation of the rand	Importers affected negatively

3.7.3 Crises in the environment

Analyses, such as the above, of the environment in which an organisation exists are no safeguard against unexpected events in the environment that can strike without warning, as depicted in table 3.2. Crises such as these influence organisations in different ways, and this is precisely why they react differently to influences from the management environment. We shall now discuss some of these reactions.

3.8 WAYS IN WHICH MANAGEMENT CAN REACT TO THE ENVIRONMENT

Insight into trends in the management environment and the ability to predict their implications for decision making are becoming management priorities. The extent to which the environment influences the management of an organisation therefore depends primarily on the type of organisation and the nature of the environment. The main response to environmental change revolves around environmental scanning (see chapter 6) and information management (see chapter 8).

3.8.1 Information management

If an organisation is to have knowledge of the environment for decision-making pur-poses, its information management system should make adequate provision for environmental scanning. The importance of **environmental scanning** — that is, the process of measuring, making projections and evaluating change in the environ-ment — finds expression mainly in the following:

■ The environment is changing constantly — hence management should make a conscious effort to explore it in an effort **to keep up with change**.

■ Environmental scanning is necessary to determine whether factors in the envi-ronment constitute a **threat** to the organisation's current objectives and strategy.

■ Scanning is also necessary to determine what factors in the environment afford **opportunities** for the more effective attainment of objectives by adjusting the present strategy.

■ Organisations that scan the environment systematically are more successful than those that do not.

The **extent** of environmental scanning, on the other hand, is determined by the following factors:

■ **The nature of the environment in which an organisation operates and the demands the environment makes on it.** The more unstable its environment is, the more vulnerable the organisation is to change — hence the more compre-hensive environmental scanning will have to be. Increasing instability is usually characterised by greater risk from the organisation's point of view.

■ **The basic relationship that an organisation has with its environment.**

■ **The source and extent of change will also influence the degree of meaningful environmental scanning.** The effect of change is seldom compartmentalised in the sense that one or two parts of the organisation are affected. Change has an interactive and dynamic effect on different facets of the organisation.

Chapter 8 deals with information management and information systems as part of the planning process.

3.8.2 Strategic responses

Once management has an adequate information base and insight into its environment, the next logical step is a strategic reaction. This may entail adapting an existing strategy or developing a new one. Management might even decide to do nothing at all. Strategic options such as mergers, takeovers or joint ventures can also be used to adapt to environmental change. Management's strategic options are discussed in more detail in chapter 6.

3.8.3 Structural change

Another type of response to environmental change is to adapt or redesign an organisation's organisational structure. Organisations in an environment with a low level of uncertainty may, for example, maintain a bureaucratic type of structure in which basic rules and a system of stereotyped actions are sufficient for successful existence. In contrast, organisations that operate in an environment with a high level of uncertainty prefer a more flexible structure with fewer levels of authority and fewer rules in order to deal with environmental change more quickly. (See part 3, chapters 9–11.)

Managers, however, are not always defenceless against environmental change. Management plays an important role in influencing the environment of an organisation through its marketing strategy, its agreements with suppliers and by providing consumers and shareholders with information. These actions require sound management which starts with proactive planning. We shall deal with this topic in the following chapter.

3.9 CONCLUSION

In this chapter we explained the nature and essence of management on the basis of the environmental concept. By way of introduction we discussed some concepts in systems theory to show that the management process endeavours to promote **synergy**. In the discussion of the systems approach we showed that the organisation is an open system that is influenced by its environment. This was followed by an in-depth discussion of the external environment to show that management does not exist in isolation, but has specific relationships or interfaces with the external environment and reacts to environmental change in particular ways. Knowledge of the environment is also a prerequisite for the successful implementation of the management process.

3.10 REFERENCES

1. *Business Times*, 25 August 1996, p 21.
2. *Business Times,* 18 August 1996, p 15.
3. *Business Times*, 16 June 1996, p 6.
4. Griffin, RW. 1993. *Management*. Boston: Houghton Mifflin, pp 57–58.
5. Bureau for Market Research. 1995. *Aspirations, values and marketing issues among black youth in Gauteng*. Research Report no 223, Unisa.
6. Makridakis, S. Management in the 21st century. *Long Range Planning*, 22(2), p 40.
7. Toffler, A. *Future Shock.*
8. Based on Griffin op cit p 74.

Part 2

. . . .

Planning

4 Goal Formulation

Key issues

- The importance of planning
- The development of organisational goals as a step in the planning process
- The planning premises
- The nature of organisational goals
- Specifications for goal setting
- Management by objectives (MBO) as a technique for goal setting

4.1 INTRODUCTION

In chapter 1 we identified **planning** as the starting point in the management process and explained it as the fundamental management function that determines what an organisation wants to attain and how it should go about this. In other words, planning involves those activities of management that determine the mission and goals of an organisation, the ways in which these are to be attained and the deployment of the necessary resources to realise them.

In chapter 3 we examined the environment in which an organisation functions. In the discussion of the external environment, we indicated how this environment, which is uncontrollable and changes constantly, creates both uncertainty for management and opportunities to be exploited.

Management formulates the goals that predetermine what the organisation proposes to accomplish in the changing environment in which it operates. To achieve its goals and to survive in a turbulent environment, the organisation needs to plan its activities carefully. Planning enables the organisation to be proactive — not reactive — in its interaction with the external environment. In this chapter we look at:

- the importance of planning
- planning as a process
- the nature of organisational goals

- specifications for goal setting
- the development of goals
- management by objectives (MBO)

Focus

> Our major focus in this chapter will be on the development of goals, which is the starting point in the planning process.

4.2   THE IMPORTANCE OF PLANNING

Some managers see **planning** as the **primary** function of management[1] — to them organising, leading and controlling are secondary. Whatever its relative importance, the other management functions cannot be executed without proper planning. Planning logically precedes the execution of the other management functions. Planning starts with setting goals for the organisation, and determines the type of organisational structure required to achieve the goals, the leadership that is necessary and the control that has to be exercised to steer the organisation as productively as possible towards its goals (figure 4.1).

Planning occurs in all organisations and at all levels. The Bafana Bafana manager who considers replacing an out-of-form soccer player in the African Cup competition is involved in planning. So, too, is the sales manager who defines sales quotas and assigns salespeople to specific areas. Top-level managers considering the closure of an unprofitable plant are involved in planning the future of the organisation. Planning is the task of all managers, although its character and scope vary according to the managers' authority and the nature of plans outlined by their superiors. Planning is important to South African organisations for the following reasons:

- Probably the most important contribution that planning makes to the managerial process is that it gives **direction** to an organisation in the form of goals, on the one hand, and in the form of plans indicating how to set about achieving those goals, on the other hand. It clarifies the goals and determines their feasibility.
- Planning promotes **cooperation** between the various departments and people in an organisation. If objectives are clearly formulated and plans developed, tasks and resources can be allocated in such a way that everyone is able to contribute to the realisation of the objectives. Scarce resources can be channelled and utilised rationally, which is a prerequisite for the productivity and ultimate profitability of the organisation.

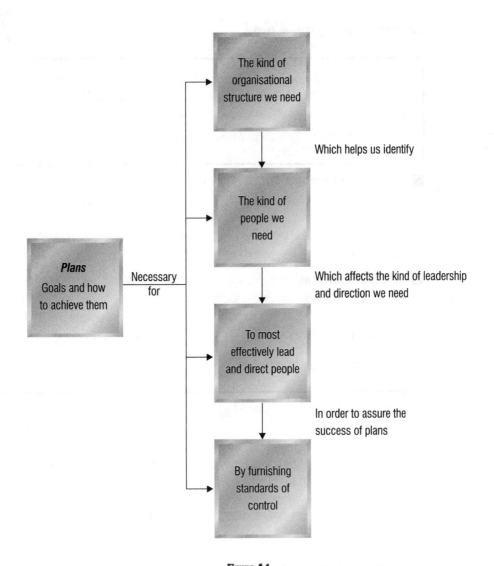

Figure 4.1

The importance of planning

Source: Adapted from Koontz, H, O'Donnell, CO & Weihrich, H. 1984. *Management,* 8 ed. New York: McGraw-Hill, p 103.

■ Planning compels managers **to look towards the future**. It eliminates crisis management by obliging management to anticipate threats in the environment and to take timeous steps to avert them. By looking back over the past and forward to the future, management can organise the present in such a way that the future is as prosperous as possible.

'Black South African executives think analytically, laying plans which aim to maximize long-term effectiveness and achieve synergy across a range of functions. Their realistic objectives are set within a framework that looks beyond the demands of the immediate situation.'

Source: AMROP, 1996. The South African executive: The challenge of diversity. *AMROP International Executive Search 3*, p 8.

■ Modern **technology** in business, especially in the development of complex products by means of complicated processes, makes heavy demands on planning. It takes about ten years to develop a supersonic aircraft or military helicopter and it is very expensive, so proper planning is critical to the success of such a project.

■ The **multicultural** composition of the South African workforce necessitates clear, well-formulated goals and plans. The 11 official languages spoken in South Africa can easily result in the misinterpretation of goals and plans and in counter-productive performance.

Goal formulation in the African culture

The goal-formulation process is well ingrained in the African cultural heritage, as evidenced by historical monuments such as the Zimbabwe Ruins and similar sites in southern Africa. The construction of these monuments was underpinned by the goal-formulation and implementation process. A goal is referred to as *chinangwa* in Shona and *inhloso* in Zulu, and a *gwara* ('direction' in Shona) must be established through the goal-formulation process. Similarly, the production of sculpture and craft products in contemporary Africa reflects high levels of goal formulation and execution.

Source: Tamangani, Z (consulting editor). 1997. Interview at the University of South Africa.

■ Probably the single most important factor — even in smaller or less complex organisations — that makes planning indispensable, is the rapid **change** in the business environment. Indeed, **strategic planning** has its origins in the instability which has characterised this environment since the 1960s. Planning encourages proactive management — that is, management that plays an active part in the creation of the future of the organisation — rather than allowing the organisation to be pulled passively along, resigning itself to change when compelled to do so.

4.3 PLANNING AS A PROCESS

As a process, planning comprises:

- an understanding of the planning premises
- the development of strategic goals and strategic plans
- the development of tactical goals and tactical plans
- the development of operational goals and operational plans[2]

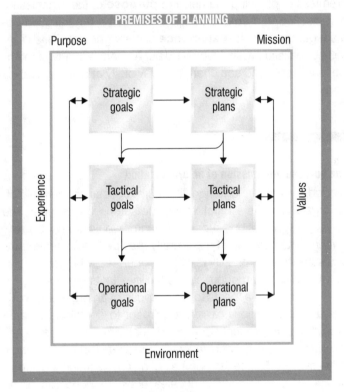

Figure 4.2
The planning process

Figure 4.2 represents the planning process schematically. Bear in mind that although planning is explained as a process in its own right, it does not take place in isolation — it is a dynamic process in which the deployment of the resources of an organisation and the influences of the business environment are constantly scrutinised.

Our focus in the rest of this chapter will be mainly on the development of goals, the starting point in the planning process. The rest of the planning process will be discussed in chapter 5. Chapter 6 is devoted to strategic planning. The turbulent environment in which South African organisations and organisations abroad operate necessitates a special focus on the issue of reconciling the organisation's resources with opportunities and threats in the external environment.

4.4 THE DEVELOPMENT OF GOALS*

Before we examine the development of goals, we need to discuss the five basic premises of planning, namely the **purpose** of the organisation, the **mission** of the organisation, the **environment** in which the organisation operates, the **values** of management and the **experience** of management. These five factors are relevant in setting realistic organisational goals. A change in any of them influences the organisation's goals and can change a previously attainable goal into an unrealistic future goal.

4.4.1 The planning premises

The purpose and mission of an organisation

A good deal of management literature focuses on the topic of what the **purpose** of an organisation is. At first, this issue seems very simple. The purpose of a profit-seeking organisation, such as Edgars, would surely be to generate profit for its owners. The purpose of a university may be to transfer knowledge, initiate research and serve the community in which it operates, whereas the purpose of a sports club may be to supply modern sports facilities to its members.

There are two aspects to the purpose of an organisation. Firstly, the organisation has a social purpose, which requires it to contribute to the welfare of society by providing safe products of a good quality at a reasonable price. Secondly, there is the purpose of the organisation, such as surviving in the long run by earning a profit for its owners. Hence the purpose of an organisation may be profit making, provision of a product, maximisation of sales, social responsibility or managerial self-interest. The purpose of an organisation may also reflect a combination of these factors.

Although it may seem obvious that the basic purpose of all organisations is survival, we should note that long-term survival may not be the most appropriate purpose for all organisations.

Management's view of what an organisation is trying to do and to become in the long term is referred to as the organisation's **mission**. This mission gives direction to its activities and is a concise organisational outline of 'who we are, what we do, and where we are heading'. Mission statements are personalised in the sense that they express an organisation's special identity, character and reason for existence.

*The terms 'goal' and 'objective' will be used interchangeably in this book.

Sun International's mission statement

> We will be recognised internationally as a successful leisure group, offering superior gambling, hotel and entertainment experiences which exceed our customers' expectations.
>
> We will create an environment in which all employees are well trained, motivated and take pride in working for the company.
>
> Innovation and fun and an obsession with service excellence and efficiency will make Sun International a formidable competitor and provide our shareholders with excellent returns.

A mission statement is a broad statement of intent, which distinguishes the company from similar organisations by focusing on those factors that make it unique and give it a competitive advantage over similar businesses. Sun Internatinal's mission statement stresses its superior entertainment facilities and service excellence as the factors that make it unique. City Lodge sets itself apart from similar suppliers of accommodation by focusing on its 'no frills' concept and tariffs which are below those of full-service hotels.

Mission formulation is based on several fundamental elements, namely:[3]

■ the belief that the product or service can provide benefits at least equal to its price
■ the belief that the product or service can satisfy a customer need currently not being met adequately for specific market segments
■ the belief that the technology to be used in production can provide a product or service that is competitive in terms of cost and quality.

The business environment

The systems approach to management views an organisation as an open system that interacts with the external environment (see chapter 3). A change in any of the environments, namely the **external or internal environment**, or their subenvironments, will have an effect on the other environments. A change in society's values, for instance, may have a direct effect on the social responsibility of an organisation. Here we can think of the growing importance of environmental conservation in South Africa and how this has affected organisations, many of which have found it necessary to reformulate their goals.

Although an organisation has no control over the external environment, it nevertheless has to assess this environment carefully in order to plan realistically, and this obviously includes revising its mission and goals in terms of the environment. Planning can prepare the organisation for possible changes in the external environment, allowing it to be proactive — not reactive — in its interaction with the external environment.

Important changes in the business environment

> The ageing South African population also has important implications for business planning. In 1980 there were approximately 1,11 million people aged 65 and older in South Africa. By the year 2020, the 65-and-older segment is expected to number more than 4,1 million. To date, business has paid scant attention to the growing number of consumers in this age bracket and their particular needs and wants. The market segment constituted by people aged 65 and older requires a wide variety of products and services, including personal financial management, housing, personal care and appearance, and recreation and entertainment.

The values of management

The values[4] of the managers in an organisation have an important influence on the formulation of goals. **Values and ethics** play a role in determining what the organisation is willing to devote to social responsibility, to the development of employees, and the like. Managerial values also influence and set the culture of the organisation. The mission statements of Sun International and City Lodge reflect divergent managerial values. Whereas the managers of Sun International see gambling as an important facility to offer to their customers, City Lodge has chosen not to pursue this type of business.

The experience of management

Experience[5] gained from previous planning cycles influences the performance of subsequent planning activities. If an organisation decides to concentrate on a specific market segment in order to sell its product but fails to sell the projected number of products, it needs to investigate how the original plan to concentrate on that specific market segment was developed — and may even decide to withdraw from that market segment.

Overcoming the shortage of managers in South Africa

> South Africa has a serious shortage of managers and managerial skills. A source of experience that should be tapped in the future is the accumulated expert knowledge and experience of people aged 65 and over. People in this age bracket will number 4,1 million in the year 2020 and they can be employed in an organisation in a part-time or full-time capacity.

Managers should use the premises discussed above as a foundation in setting goals for their organisation. These premises should constantly be scanned in order to ensure that the development of organisational goals is conducted in a realistic manner and that the goals set by management are attainable.

Now that the background against which organisational goals can be developed has been examined, the actual process of developing these goals will be discussed.

4.4.2　The nature of organisational goals

To the management of an organisation, goals are the starting point of the planning process, as illustrated in figure 4.2. The task of management can be successfully carried out only if the goals over which control is to be exercised are specified clearly. A goal is defined as a particular future state to be achieved by the organisation, or as some particular function or project of the organisation. Implicit in this definition of a goal is the fact that all organisations have multiple goals.

Goals should flow directly from the mission statement of an organisation, but they should be specific and concrete. If the mission of a hospital is 'to offer a full range of medical services to the citizens of Sasolburg', the following objectives would be appropriate:

■ to increase the number of beds by 80 within the next two years
■ to increase worker productivity by 5 % within the next three years
■ to shorten time in the emergency room before contact with the medical doctor to less than ten minutes per patient

To speak of an organisation's goals as if it had only one would be an oversimplification. Organisations and managers have multiple goals that are sometimes incompatible and may lead to conflict within the organisation. The coordination of these goals is of the utmost importance to enable the organisation to move in the desired direction.

In order to gain a better understanding of organisational goals, goals are differentiated in terms of their **organisational level**, **focus**, **degree of openness**, and **time-frame**.

Let us now discuss organisational goals in terms of these variables.

The organisational level

For the purpose of this discussion, assume that you have spoken to several managers in a hotel group that offers accommodation to holiday makers nationwide. You asked what their goals for the organisation were and received the following responses:

■ 'We want to sell affordable accommodation to all the people of South Africa.'
■ 'We want to increase our occupancy rate by 6 % within the next two years.'

■ 'We want to decrease employee turnover by 2 % during each of the next four years.'

The first goal mentioned above is fairly general and applies to the entire organisation. This type of goal is called a strategic goal.

Strategic goals are set by top management. They have to be in keeping with the mission and purpose of the organisation. The strategic goals must be clear because the tactical goals are derived from them. Tactical goals are set by and for middle managers, such as the operations manager, financial manager or marketing manager. They focus on specific functional areas. Operational goals are set by lower-level managers and are derived from tactical goals. They focus on a specific department or unit in the organisation. A restaurant manager at a Spur Steakhouse is a lower-level manager responsible for the operational goals of his or her restaurant.

The goals form a hierarchy, ranging from the broad purpose of the business to very specific individual goals. (See figure 4.3.)

The focus

In the previous section we mentioned that the different managers in the same organisation had different goals. The different goals relate to different aspects of the organisation. Some goals are financial, some focus on the development of personnel, while others again relate to the quality of the product offered by the organisation or its social responsibility.

Organisational goals usually focus on four major areas, namely finance, the environment, participants and survival. These areas are illustrated in figure 4.4.

The industry in which an organisation operates is one of the factors that will determine the focus of its organisational goals. For National Panasonic, which operates in a high-technology industry, innovation is an important organisational focus. A company in the mining sector, such as JCI Ltd, would focus more on human relations as this sector is vulnerable to labour unrest.

The degree of openness

A distinction can also be made between official and operative goals. The official goals of the organisation are those goals that society wishes the organisation to pursue. These goals are derived from the purpose and mission of the organisation, and the organisation espouses these official goals formally and publicly in annual reports and company publications.

Operative goals represent the private, unpublished goals of an organisation. The operative goals of a motorcar manufacturer might include delaying the launch of a new motorcar until after an announcement by the government of an increase in the petrol price. A university might have an operative goal of an 8 % budget increase because it recognises that its formal request of a 16 % increase is unlikely to be granted by the government.

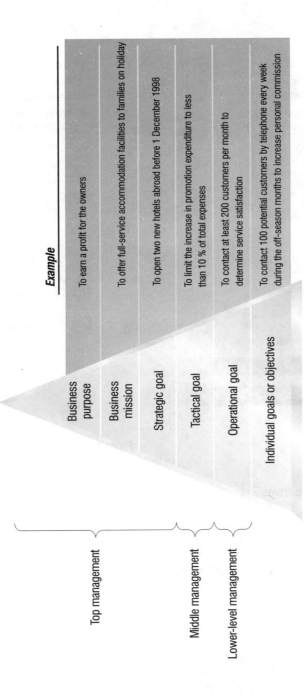

Figure 4.3
Goals according to organisational level

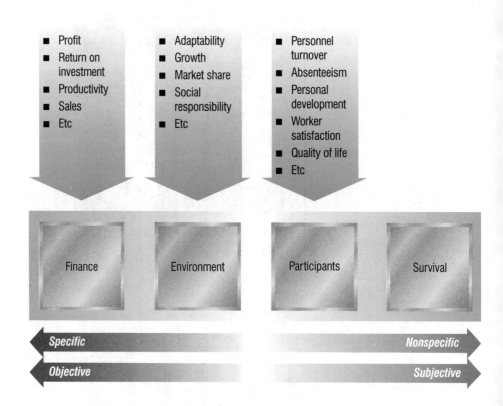

Figure 4.4
The focus of organisational goals

The time-frame

Some goals in an organisation have a short time horizon, whereas others have a long time horizon. Organisations generally distinguish three time-frames for goals, namely short-run, intermediate and long-run time-frames. The time-frame implies a degree of specificity within the goals.

Short-run goals tend to be quite specific: for example, increasing the number of units sold in the first three months of 1998 from 3 000 to 3 500, or realising a return on investment of 16 % for the current year.

Intermediate goals are slightly less specific than short-term goals. These are goals that an organisation plans to achieve within the next five years. If a company in the pharmaceutical industry is conducting research into a new medicine for the relief of migraine, it is unlikely that it will come up with a new product and promote and distribute it in less than five years.

Long-run goals are goals that will take more than five years to accomplish. For the pharmaceutical company discussed above, such a goal might be to discover a substance within the next six years that not only relieves the migraine patient's pain but also cures the patient permanently.

It can be said that the lower a department or unit is within the organisational hierarchy, the more specific and short-run its goals will be. It is also important to note that what is regarded as a short-run or long-run goal varies from one organisation to the next. The owner of a plantation may project 20 years into the future, while the owner of a small grocery store may view any goals extending beyond 18 months as long term.

4.4.3 Specifications for goal setting

For the managerial purpose of goals to be fulfilled, they need to meet certain specifications. These specifications are specificity, flexibility, measurability, attainability, congruency and acceptability.[6]

Examples of organisational goals

Example 1
- Poor
  Our goal is to maximise profits.
- Better
  We wish to increase our return on investment from the current 15 % to 18 % within the next two years, provided the prime interest rate remains below 20 %.

Example 2
- Poor
  Our goal is to increase sales.
- Better
  Our goal is to increase sales revenue from R1 500 000 in 1998 to R1 850 000 in 1999. We expect to do this by selling 1 850 units at an average price of R1 000 each.

Specificity

Good goals should possess specificity and should indicate what they are related to, the time frame for accomplishing them and the desired results. In our 'poor' goal in example 1 above it is difficult to determine what is meant by 'to maximise profits'. The 'better' goal specifies that it is related to the profit of the organisation; the specific results are indicated (from 15 % to 18 %) and the time-frame is also mentioned (within the next two years).

Flexibility

The turbulent environment in which South African organisations operate makes it necessary to allow for modification of the goals. Flexibility is often achieved at the expense of specificity. The 'better' goal in example 1 above is based on the condition that the prime interest rate will remain below 20 %. Should the prime interest rate change, the goal should be reformulated.

Measurability

Measurability means that an attempt should be made to state goals in terms that can be evaluated or quantified objectively. The statement 'to maximise profits' in the 'poor' goal in example 1 above cannot be measured. What yardstick does management use to establish whether actual profit is equal to maximum profit? An increase from 15 % to 18 %, however, is measurable.

The primary reason why goals should be measurable is to facilitate control — goals often evolve into control standards for performance appraisal.

Attainability

Goals should be realistic and attainable, but should also provide a challenge for management and personnel. People are most productive when goals are set at a motivating level — a level high enough to challenge, but not so high that it frustrates or so low that it is too easy to attain. If the salespeople in example 2 feel that it is impossible to increase sales because of the economic and political situation in South Africa, they are unlikely to be motivated to accomplish this organisational goal. However, if management assures them that the average price of their product will remain constant at R1 000 per unit from 1997 to 1999, they might regard the goal as attainable.

Congruency

Goals should be congruent with one another. Congruency means that the attainment of one goal should not preclude the attainment of another. In example 2, if the marketing department's goal is to sell 1 850 units of the product in 1999, but the production department's goal is to reduce production of the product from 1 850 to 1 500 units per year, it is likely that attainment of one of these goals will eliminate the possibility of attaining the other.

Incongruent goals may lead to friction and conflict which, if intense enough, may necessitate compromise to enable their accomplishment.

City Lodge formulates attainable goals

City Lodge owns and operates City and Town Lodges. In formulating attainable goals for 1997, top management had to consider, inter alia, the following external environmental variables:

■ the economic cycle

■ lower weekend occupancies

■ continuing high levels of crime and violence

■ the slow growth rate of international tourism

The formulation of the goals was also influenced by past results, namely an occupancy rate of 80 % in 1995.

In the light of the above, the following goal was formulated:

City Lodge would like to increase its occupancy rate from 80 % in 1995 to 81 % or higher in 1997.

Acceptability

Managers are most likely to pursue goals that are consistent with their perceptions and preferences. If managers feel that maximising profits, as in example 1, is unethical but that 'reasonable' profits are acceptable, they may ignore or even obstruct the achievement of the unacceptable goal. Acceptability implies and leads to management and employee commitment. In order to formulate acceptable goals, management should take into account the needs and values of employees.

While the other specifications of goals discussed in this section may be influenced by management, management cannot influence the acceptability of goals.

4.4.4 The process of goal setting

A question that needs to be answered at this stage is: 'Who sets these goals in an organisation?' This question is not easily answered, as different organisations use different goal-setting processes. These processes range from centralised to decentralised goal setting.

In some organisations, the board of directors set the goals. These goals encompass the entire organisation and typically result in more congruent goals, as the setting of long-term as well as short-term goals is more likely to focus on the organisation's mission. When goals are set in this way, we speak of centralised goal setting. Although centralised goal setting has important advantages, it also has significant disadvantages. One major disadvantage is that the goal-setters may know little about the specific opportunities and problems faced by lower-level managers. Lower-level managers may also resist directives coming from above if they do not understand the reasons for the goals.

Decentralised goal setting takes place when managers at each level of an organisation have the dominant influence on their unit or department's goals. Two basic approaches can be identified, namely the top-to-bottom approach and the bottom-up approach.

In the top-to-bottom approach to goal setting, the board of directors or corporate-level managers set the corporate goals and the head of each division or business unit sets the goals for his or her division or business unit. The same applies to the other organisational levels, although higher-level managers usually approve the goals of lower-level managers.

In the bottom-up approach, the lower levels set their goals, and higher-level managers set their goals to be in line with the lower-level goals. This approach is sometimes less likely to yield a coordinated effort and congruent goals, as some managers tend to fall into the trap of tunnel vision and therefore focus only on what is important for their unit.

A combination of the top-to-bottom and the bottom-up approaches is an approach to goal setting used by many organisations — this approach stresses the importance of the purpose and mission of the organisation as formulated by top management, but also takes into account the strengths and weaknesses of each division.

Whether goals are proposed from the bottom or imposed from the top, once agreement has been reached, there should be a firm commitment at all levels to provide the resources and achieve the results.

Finally, it should be noted that the decision to use centralised or decentralised goal setting affects strategy selection, the organisational structure and management of the organisation in general.

4.5   TECHNIQUES FOR GOAL SETTING

In the previous section we discussed the process of setting goals by discussing centralised versus decentralised goal setting and the advantages and disadvantages of each. We have concentrated on the establishment of goals at top, middle and lower management levels. We have not touched on the question of setting goals for the individual in an organisation.

One particular technique designed to achieve the integration of individual and organisational goals is called **management by objectives**, or **MBO**. MBO is currently a widely discussed and used planning technique and is based on the belief that the joint participation of subordinates and superiors in translating or converting broad organisational goals into more specific individual goals has an impact on

employee motivation. In other words, MBO is based on the belief that you are motivated to perform more efficiently in an organisation if you participate in selecting your
own personal goals.

The importance of objectives or goals in management can best be seen by illustrating how MBO works in practice. Figure 4.5 illustrates this process.

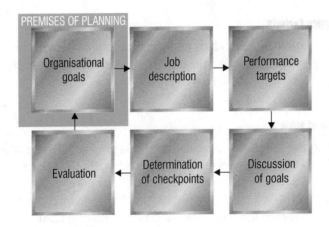

Figure 4.5
The process of MBO

4.5.1 Planning premises

For an MBO programme to be successful, the process should start at the top of the
organisation and should have the active support of the top managers. Before the
process of MBO is implemented in an organisation, top management should explain
to subordinates why it has adopted the process. The subordinates should then be
educated about MBO and their role in it. Top management should tell subordinates
what MBO will do for the organisation and should stress the fact that it has accepted
and is committed to MBO.

4.5.2 Organisational goals

Having adopted the MBO philosophy in an organisation, it is necessary for each
subordinate involved in the MBO process to have a clear understanding of the
organisation's purpose, mission, long-term goals and strategy. These should always
guide subordinates in the establishment of their own goals. Superiors should also
see to it that their subordinates are well informed about organisational and departmental goals.

4.5.3 Job description

The goal-setting process starts with a discussion between the manager and the subordinate about the content or relative importance of the subordinate's major duties — the activities that he or she is accountable for and is paid to do. Two-way communication is vital to ensure that both subordinate and superior agree on job content and responsibilities.

4.5.4 Performance targets

The subordinate formulates performance targets in predetermined areas of responsibility for a forthcoming period. Each goal should be as quantitative as possible, specific, concise and time related. It should also be in written form.

4.5.5 Discussion of goals

During this stage the subordinate meets with his or her superior on a one-on-one basis to discuss potential performance targets. The purpose of this meeting is to arrive at a set of objectives that the subordinate and the superior have developed jointly and to which both are committed. Involvement is the key element at this stage. Objectives dictated by a superior do not evoke full commitment from subordinates. By the same token, failure by a superior to participate fully and actively in this step leads subordinates to believe that management places little value on MBO.

Superiors play the critical role of counsellors in the goal-setting discussion. They should ensure, inter alia, that subordinates' goals are indeed attainable and that these goals will facilitate goals at the higher levels of the goal hierarchy (see 'The organisational level' on page 103).

The discussion between subordinate and superior should also spell out the resources that a subordinate needs in order to work effectively towards goal attainment. A subordinate should know which human resources he or she is allowed to mobilise (for example, the number of new salespeople), the financial resources available to him or her (funds), the physical resources allocated to him or her (office space, computers, vehicles, warehouses, etc) and the information resources at his or her disposal (reports, surveys, financial statements, etc).

4.5.6 Determination of checkpoints

A subordinate's progress needs to be measured periodically and checkpoints need to be established for this purpose. If the goals are established for a one-year period, it may be a good idea for subordinate and superior to meet on a quarterly basis to discuss progress to date. These periodic reviews not only monitor the subordinate's progress but also provide an opportunity to adjust objectives that have become unrealistic in the light of changing conditions or uncontrollable events, such as the unavailability of resources or a boycott by one of the organisation's suppliers of raw materials.

4.5.7 Evaluation

At the end of the predetermined performance period, the superior should meet with the subordinate to review the degree of goal attainment. The meeting should focus on goal analysis and a discussion of the results actually achieved.

From the discussion above it is clear that a great deal of planning and commitment from top management, superiors and subordinates is necessary to implement MBO successfully. It is also evident that changes in an organisation may have to be made in areas such as communication between managers and subordinates in order to facilitate the MBO process. This brings us to the question of whether it is really worth while for an organisation to adopt the MBO philosophy.

Some of the major benefits of MBO are:

■ improved employee motivation through participation in goal setting

■ increased role clarity

■ improved communication resulting from the process of goal discussion

MBO also has limitations, one of them being overburdening systems with too much paperwork and record keeping.

As can be seen from the above, MBO is not a perfect goal-setting or planning technique. However, one way to illustrate the usefulness of MBO is to consider alternatives to this planning technique.

Alternatives to MBO

■ **Management by extrapolation** (MBE)
The basic assumption of this approach is that the future takes care of itself and that things will work out all right: 'We have our act together, so why worry?' The basic game plan is to keep on doing (a) the same things (b) in the same way because (c) it works well enough and (d) has brought the organisation to where it is.

■ **Management by crisis** (MBC)
This management approach is based on the belief that the forte of any good manager is solving problems. Management devotes its time and energy to solving the most pressing problem of the day. MBC is a form of reacting to crises rather than acting; events therefore dictate management decisions.

Alternatives to MBO (continued . . .)

■ **Management by subjectives** (MBS)
This approach emerges in the absence of clear-cut directives on where an organisation is heading (its purpose and mission). Goals and plans are never clearly articulated by top management and subordinate managers are left to work out what is happening. The manager does what he or she thinks should be done.

■ **Management by hope** (MBH)
Decisions are made in the hope that they will work out and that success is just around the corner — after all, management has tried hard and long enough; things are bound to get better. Shortfalls in performance are attributed to unexpected events and the fact that the future is unpredictable. Much time is therefore allocated to hoping that things will improve; solid analysis and results-oriented action plans are absent.

The four 'planning techniques' mentioned above amount to 'muddling through'. There is an absence of effort to shape or influence the direction in which the organisation is heading and to delineate the activities in which it should engage. Although MBO has its shortcomings, as discussed earlier, it is doubtful whether managers who rely upon alternatives to MBO outperform managers who select challenging yet attainable goals and then formulate a timely, astute business plan to achieve them.

4.6 CONCLUSION

Goals or objectives are the starting point of the management process and can be defined as a particular future state of things to be achieved by an organisation, or as a particular function or project of the organisation. An understanding of the planning premises is essential in formulating the organisation's goals or objectives. The planning premises are the following: the purpose and mission of the organisation, the environment in which it operates and the values and experience of the managers. The goals give direction to the activities of the organisation and determine the strategy that will result in the attainment of these goals.

Organisations and managers have multiple goals that are sometimes incompatible and that may lead to conflict within an organisation. The coordination of goals is of vital importance to an organisation if all the goals are to move the organisation in the same direction. In order to develop congruent goals, they should be differentiated in terms of four variables, namely the organisational level, the focus, the degree of openness and the time-frame.

If the organisation is to attain its goals, the goals need to be specific, flexible, measurable, attainable, congruent and acceptable.

The procedure for setting goals may range from centralised to decentralised goal setting. Centralised goal setting takes place when the goals of an organisation are formulated by top management — these goals encompass the entire organisation. Decentralised goal setting takes place when managers at each level of an organisation have the dominant influence on their department's goals. Two basic approaches can be identified in this case, namely the top-to-bottom approach and the bottom-up approach.

A popular technique for integration of individual and organisational goals is called management by objectives (MBO). MBO is a widely discussed and used planning technique nowadays and is based on the belief that the joint participation of subordinates and superiors in translating broad organisational goals into more specific individual goals has a positive impact on employee motivation. Although MBO is not a perfect goal-setting or planning technique, it is preferred to other planning techniques in which there is a notable absence of calculated incremental effort to shape or influence the direction in which an organisation is heading.

4.7 REFERENCES

1. Surasy, A in Lussier, RN. 1997. *Management: Concepts, Application, Skill Development.* Massachusetts: South-Western, p 139.
2. Bennis, WG in Griffin, RW. 1987. *Management,* 2 ed. Boston: Houghton Mifflin, p 113.
3. Pearce, RB & Robinson, JA. 1997. *Strategic Management: Formulation, Implementation and Control*, 6 ed. Chicago: Irwin, pp 29–30.
4. Ibid p 293.
5. Ibid p 292.
6. Based on Lussier, RN. 1997. *Management: Concepts, Application, Skill Development.* Massachusetts: South-Western, pp 149–150.

5 Planning

Key issues

- The importance of planning
- Kinds of organisational plans (strategic, tactical and operational)
- Long-term, intermediate and short-term plans
- Steps in the planning process
- Barriers to effective planning
- Overcoming planning barriers
- Planning tools

5.1 INTRODUCTION

All managers engage in **planning** — some plan informally while others plan formally by documenting their plans. The following questions can therefore rightfully be asked: 'Does formal planning pay off? Is it worth while for managers to spend hours planning for the future — especially in today's constantly changing environment?'

Some critics of planning argue that planning creates too much rigidity.[1] They argue that you cannot plan in today's turbulent business environment. According to these critics 'setting oneself on a predetermined course in unknown waters is the perfect way to sail straight into an iceberg'.[2]

Others feel that planning reduces the impact of change in the environment, gives direction to the organisation, reduces overlapping and wasteful activities, establishes objectives or standards that facilitate control, and so on.[3]

Who is right — the proponents of planning or the critics? Many studies have been undertaken to test the relationship between planning and organisational performance.[4] Contrary to the arguments made by critics, the overall evidence is generally positive. Results of these studies allow us to draw, among others, the conclusion that formal planning is associated with increased growth in sales and earnings, higher profits, higher return on assets, and other positive financial results.

When we use the term **planning** in this chapter, we refer to formal planning. Formal planning encompasses defining an organisation's goals, establishing strategies for attaining these goals, and developing a comprehensive hierarchy of plans to integrate and coordinate activities. Planning is concerned with **what is to be done** as well as **how it is to be done**.

Goal formulation, the starting point in the planning process, was discussed in chapter 4. Given the clear link between organisational goals and plans (as illustrated in figure 4.2) we will now turn our attention to those issues associated with planning which have not been explained.

Focus

City Lodge's goal of increasing occupancy levels to 81 % or more in the next year indicates **where** they want to be. The issues of **what** has to be done and **how** to reach this 'destination' must still be clarified. This chapter focuses on these two issues. More specifically, we look at:

- kinds of organisational plans
- the time-frame for planning
- steps in the planning process
- barriers to effective planning
- how to overcome these barriers
- planning tools

5.2 KINDS OF ORGANISATIONAL PLANS

The formulation of organisational plans takes place in a specific context — the context being referred to as the planning premises (see figure 4.2). Hence the formulation of plans has to reflect this context. To stay within the parameters set by the planning premises, managers need to understand the different kinds of plans in an organisation. Understanding the kinds of plans that a manager has to formulate will indicate to the manager what has to be taken into consideration.

To formulate realistic plans, managers need to understand that the different kinds of plans in an organisation form a hierarchy. This hierarchy is illustrated in figure 5.1.

5.2.1 Strategic plans

Strategic plans are plans designed to meet the organisation's broad goals. These plans are formulated by top management and focus on the entire organisation. City Lodge Hotels' strategic plan to find growth opportunities by focusing on four brands,

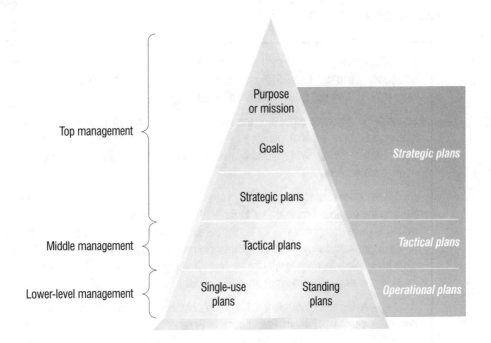

Figure 5.1
The kinds of plans

namely The Courtyard Suite Hotels, City Lodge, Town Lodge and Road Lodge is a strategic plan; it indicates **how** City Lodge Hotels intend reaching their goals, one of them being an average occupancy rate of 81 % or higher. These plans were formulated and based on certain premises about the external environment. One such premise was an expected high growth in international tourism after the 1995 Rugby World Cup. This strategic plan of City Lodge Hotels reflects the following characteristics of strategic plans:

■ Strategic plans have an extended time-frame, usually more than five years.

■ They focus on the entire organisation.

■ Strategic plans look at reconciling the organisation's resources with threats and opportunities in the external environment.

■ They focus on an organisation's competitive advantage. In City Lodge Hotels' case one of these advantages is its knowledge and experience in the business travel industry.

■ These plans also take synergy into consideration. City Lodge Hotels' four brands complement one another by offering the business traveller an option of four different types of hotels — from one star to four stars.

Planning at City Lodge Hotels

In 1996 the group produced another impressive financial performance, maintained high room occupancies, and laid the foundation for further solid growth of its four brands — The Courtyard Suite Hotels, City Lodge, Town Lodge and Road Lodge.

Strong demand for accommodation was experienced from corporate travellers, but the expected high growth of international tourists after the 1995 Rugby World Cup did not materialise. The second half of the year was affected by rises in interest rates and the signs of a general slow-down in the economy.

Average room occupancy levels at City Lodge, Town Lodge and Road Lodge increased from 81 % in the previous financial year to 82 %. With the inclusion of the five Courtyard hotels, overall average occupancy was 81 %, compared with 80 % in the previous year. The maintenance of high occupancy levels and an improvement in operating margins were major contributors to excellent financial results for the year. Group turnover grew by 71 %, pretax profit grew by 31 % and attributable earnings after exceptional items were up by 47 %.

Ongoing refurbishment took place at the group's hotels. Construction began on two new lodges during the year: a 142-room Town Lodge in Grayston Drive, Sandton, and a 92-room Road Lodge at the N1 City complex in the Cape Peninsula. Prospects for both lodges are excellent as they meet the growing need for affordable accommodation in two of the country's major growth areas.

Through the ongoing expansion of its four distinct brands, covering the one- to four-star selected services hotel market, the group is ideally positioned to take advantage of any future growth in the economy and to benefit from an increase in local and foreign business and leisure travel.

Occupancies in the forthcoming year are likely to remain at high levels despite the concern about saturation in the upper end of the accommodation offered in certain regional markets.

Source: McGregor Information Services. City Lodge Hotels Ltd, Chairman's statement, 23 January 1997.

In order to survive in the turbulent environment in which the modern organisation operates strategic planning is essential. Because of its importance to the modern manager, the whole of chapter 6 will focus on strategic planning. This chapter (section 6.3.5 on page 155) also looks at the different strategies available.

Strategies do not attempt to outline exactly how an organisation is to accomplish its goals. Tactical and operational plans are more specific and should guide the actions of managers at the middle and lower levels of management.

5.2.2 Tactical plans

Whereas strategic plans focus on the entire organisation and its interaction with the external environment, tactical planning deals primarily with people and action and has a more specific and concrete focus. The focus could be on the functional areas in an organisation, ie the marketing, finance, operations, human resources, and other functions. A tactical goal of the operations manager at City Lodge Hotels could be to refurbish the breakfast rooms at all City Lodges within the next two years. The **tactical plan** to attain this goal should take more specific issues into consideration than the strategic plans, such as:

- strategic goals, plans and tactical goals (see figure 4.2)
- resource allocation and time issues
- human resource commitments

A realistic tactical plan for the operations department at City Lodge could — in the light of the above — be to appoint interior designers on a contract basis for the next twelve months. This plan should enable the operations department to realise this goal within one year and cause a minimum of inconvenience to current employees and clients.

Other specialist areas in the City Lodge Hotel group should also formulate tactical plans to attain the tactical goals of City Lodge Hotels. Other tactical plans should focus on marketing, finance, purchasing, and so on. Of importance in formulating these tactical plans for the different functional areas is the issue of **synergy**. All of these plans should be congruent, ie they should contribute to the attainment of the organisation's overall goals. This could mean that some of the tactical plans will have to be reformulated to accommodate the plans from other functional areas.

> You have probably heard the phrase 'winning the battle but losing the war'. Tactical plans are to battles what strategy is to war.

5.2.3 Operational plans

Operational plans are developed by middle-level and lower-level managers. These plans focus on carrying out tactical plans to achieve operational goals. Operational plans are narrowly focused and have relatively short time horizons (monthly, weekly and day to day). For instance, the breakfast-room manager at the Waterfront City Lodge may formulate a plan outlining the steps to be followed in removing all movable equipment from the breakfast room in order to have it refurbished.

There are two basic forms of operational plans, namely **single-use plans** and **standing plans**. Single-use plans are used for nonrecurring activities, such as the refurbishment of the South African Airways' information desks at airports. Plans that remain roughly the same for long periods of time are called standing plans. Specific types of single-use and standing plans are illustrated in figure 5.2.

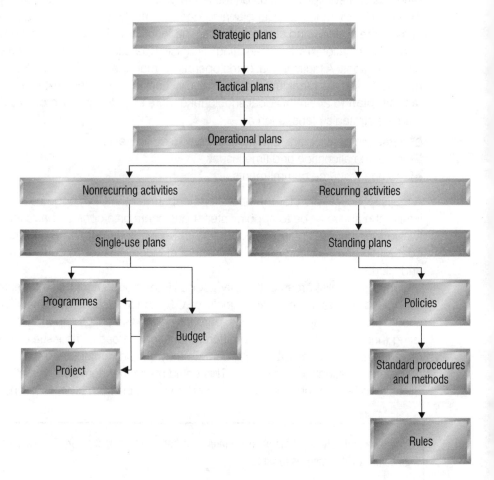

Figure 5.2
Types of operational plans
Source: Adapted from Stoner, JAF & Freeman, RE. 1992. *Management,* 5 ed. London: Prentice-Hall, p 227.

A **programme** is a single-use plan for a large set of activities. The Reconstruction and Development Programme (RDP) is a programme to uplift the previously disadvantaged people of South Africa. This should be done within a fixed time period. However, not all programmes are as complex as this one; to change an organisation's culture can also be seen as a programme.

A programme can consist of different **projects**. A project often shares some of the characteristics of the overall programme of which it is part. A project in the RDP could be to supply electricity to the Diepkloof squatter camp.

A **budget** is a numerical plan for allocating resources to specific activities. Before starting on the Diepkloof project, plans had to be submitted to indicate the number of workers required to complete the project, the raw material needed to construct the electricity lines, and so on. A budget is frequently thought of in financial terms only. However, budgets are also used to plan the allocation and utilisation of human, physical and information resources.

Programmes, projects and budgets are all single-use plans. Policies, standard procedures and methods and rules, on the other hand, are standing plans.

Policies are general statements that guide decision making in an organisation. Policies limit an area in which decisions are to be made and ensure that the decisions are consistent with the organisation's goals. One of the policies that could guide the managers of the project to supply electricity to Diepkloof could be that local labour will always be given preference.

Standard procedures and methods refer to the series of related steps or tasks expressed in chronological order to achieve a specific purpose. Before purchasing raw material for the Diepkloof project, managers had to obtain three written quotes, which had to be sent to the regulatory body which referred the quotes to a higher body for final approval.

A **rule** is a statement that either prescribes or prohibits action by specifying what an individual may or may not do in a specific situation. Workers on the above project were prohibited from smoking near petrol stations.

For managers to formulate realistic operational plans, they need clear guidance from strategic and tactical plans. Only if the different kinds of plans are understood, will lower-level managers be able to derive their sections' plans from plans at a higher level.

5.3   THE TIME-FRAME FOR PLANNING

Why do managers responsible for town planning plan ten years ahead whereas the managers at a clothing boutique have no plans that extend beyond a year or two? These differences have nothing to do with the quality of management. The reason for the different time-frames has to do with the future impact of the decisions that these managers currently make. The decision to plan a new town entails an investment of millions of rands that will take decades to recoup. The clothing boutique turns over its entire inventory every season and may have only a one-year renewable lease.

Top management usually makes plans that commit resources for long time periods. Supervisors, on the other hand, rarely make plans that commit the organisation well into the future. This shows us that plans made at different management levels cover different time-frames. This is illustrated in figure 5.3.

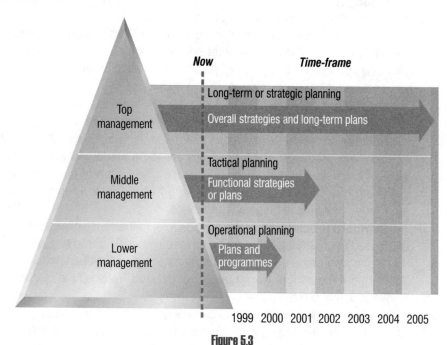

Figure 5.3
The levels and time-frames of plans
Source: Adapted from Cronjé, GJ de J, Neuland, EW & Van Reenen, MJ. 1987. *Introduction to Business Management.* Cape Town: Southern, p 29.

5.3.1 Long-term plans

Strategic planning is long-term planning which gives direction to an organisation, with its mission as the ultimate aim to achieve. The time span for long-term planning varies from one organisation to the next. Long-term planning for an organisation in the forestry industry could span up to 40 years or more; for a clothing boutique for teenagers, the time span of the long-term plans could be 12 months.

The following characteristics of a long-term plan are apparent:

- It is carried out by **top management** — the board of directors, the partners, the managing directors or the chief executives, including management committees comprising mainly members of top management.
- It has a **time-frame** of five years or more, depending on the type of industry.
- It is focused on the organisation **as a whole**.
- It is **future-oriented** and constantly on the look-out for changes in the environment.
- It requires **constant adaptation** to the environment in order to survive in the long run.

In a nutshell

Characteristics of different kinds of plans

Plan characteristic	Strategic planning	Tactical planning	Operational planning
Alternative name	Long-term planning	Medium-term planning	Short-term planning
Responsibility	Top management	Middle management	Lower management
Time-frame	3–10 years or more	1–5 years	Less than 1 year
Detail	■ Organisation as a whole ■ Purpose, mission, goals, strategies ■ External environment	Functional goals	■ Day-to-day activities ■ Policies, procedures and rules ■ Programmes, budgets, projects
Information	■ Broad, general guidelines ■ Vague, qualitative	■ More detailed than strategic plans ■ More specific	■ Fine detail ■ Specific, quantitative

■ It does not concern itself with **details** but with broad, general guidelines to keep the organisation on course.

■ A long-term plan helps management to constantly **develop the resources and skills of the organisation to face the opportunities and threats in the business environment** in order to steer the organisation as profitably as possible towards attaining its mission and surviving in the long run.

These characteristics distinguish long-term plans from tactical and operational plans in which the emphasis is more on medium-term, short-term and comprehensive plans for particular functional areas. Long-term plans — namely the development of a mission and long-term objectives in a business, and the choice of one or more long-term strategies to fulfil them — require tactical and operational plans to put the overall or grand strategy into effect.

5.3.2 Intermediate plans

Intermediate plans refer to the medium-term planning carried out by middle management for the various functional departments to realise tactical goals, which are derived from the strategic goals. This includes planning for the marketing, financial, production, personnel, administration and general management and other functions. Intermediate plans are components of long-term goals and plans. Since long-term goals and plans are exposed to many uncertainties and changes in the business environment, intermediate plans, especially in very unstable environments, form the nucleus of the planning activities of some organisations.

5.3.3 Short-term plans

Short-term (or operational) plans are concerned with periods of no longer than a year. They are developed by lower management to achieve the operational goals. Short-term plans are concerned with the day-to-day activities of an organisation and the allocation of resources to particular individuals in accordance with particular projects, budgets, and so on, to fulfil certain aims.

5.4 STEPS IN THE PLANNING PROCESS

Now that we have discussed the different kinds of plans as well as their time-frames, we should be able to understand the different steps in the planning process. Figure 4.2 has already indicated the clear link between goal formulation and planning. In this section we look deeper into planning and discuss each step in the planning process.

Planning is carried out in identifiable steps. Essentially the same steps are followed in planning, irrespective of the complexity of the situation — be it for developing a new motor car or staging a tennis tournament for schoolchildren. As minor plans are usually simple to execute, the following eight practical steps are of general application.[5]

Step 1: Being aware of opportunities

Being aware of an opportunity or problem is the first step in planning. A realistic diagnosis of the opportunity or problem situation is required. This requires a clear understanding and knowledge of the organisation's capabilities, possible future opportunities and a vision of what can be gained by utilising the opportunity.

Step 2: Establishing goals

The second step is to establish goals (see chapter 4). Organisational goals should give direction to all major plans. They should be reflected in departmental goals and in goals of subordinate departments.

Step 3: Drawing up premises

The third step is planning assumptions or premises — in other words setting up the expected environment in which plans are to take place (see figure 4.2). As discussed in chapter 3, the external environment (the macro- and market environments) in which South African organisations operate is constantly changing. So, too, is the internal environment. Forecasting is therefore important with regard to premises. Management should ask itself questions such as: 'What kinds of markets will there be? What about technological developments? What wage rates will be acceptable to our employees? What will the political and social situation be like in the future South Africa?'

It would be surprising if the individual members of an organisation's management team agreed about the organisation's future. One manager might expect an increase in the inflation rate for the next five years, whereas a colleague might expect a sharp decline in inflation for the same period. The use of different sets of premises can be extremely costly to an organisation. Consistent premises should therefore be agreed upon by top management to ensure that subordinate managers plan upon the same premises.

Step 4: Developing various courses of action

It seldom happens that there is a plan for which there are no alternatives. The fourth step in the planning process is, therefore, to search for and examine various courses of action.

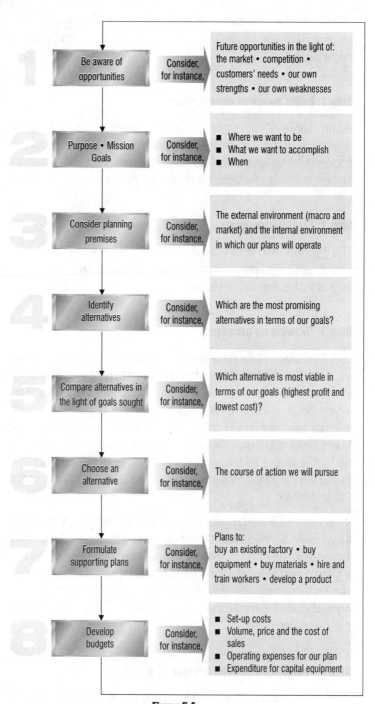

Figure 5.4
Steps in the planning process
Adapted from Koontz, H, O'Donnell, CO & Weihrich, H. 1984. *Management,* 8 ed. New York: McGraw-Hill,
p 114.

> Volkswagen South Africa had to search for alternative solutions to increase sales of its 'old-shape' Volkswagen Golf. One of the alternatives was to withdraw the car from the market and replace it with a 'new-shape' Golf. Another alternative was to modify the 'old' Golf and sell it as the Citi Golf.

Step 5: Evaluating various courses of action

The fifth step in the planning process is to evaluate the options by weighing up the various factors in the light of the premises and goals. One option may appear to be extremely profitable but may require the replacement of current machinery with expensive new machines; another option may seem less profitable but may not require the replacement of the machines currently in use; yet another may suit the enterprise's mission and goals better.

The number of options in most situations is legion and the numerous variabilities and limitations may be complex. This makes the evaluation of options a difficult task. A number of newer techniques have come into use for the evaluation of possible options. Among the most widely used of these techniques are risk analysis, decision trees and the preference theory.

Step 6: Selecting a course of action

The real point of decision — the sixth step — is now reached. The manager selects the course of action that he or she wishes to follow or may even decide to follow several courses rather than a single one.

Step 7: Formulating derivative plans

Planning is seldom complete when a decision is made. If a university decides to get involved in computer-based training, this decision is the signal for the development of a host of derivative plans dealing with the acquisition and positioning of computers, the training of personnel, financing of the project and so forth. These derivative plans — the seventh step — are required to support the basic plan.

Step 8: Budgeting

The eighth and final step in the planning process is the conversion of the plans to budgets. Through budgeting, managers ensure that they have the resources available to carry out the plans to reach the organisation's goals.

5.5   BARRIERS TO EFFECTIVE PLANNING

At this stage of our discussion of planning as the fundamental function of management, it is interesting to note that not all managers are keen planners. Why is this so?

5.5.1   Lack of environmental knowledge

The dynamic and complex environment in which managers work requires careful consideration during planning. One of the biggest mistakes that a manager can make is to assume that conditions in the environment will remain constant. The fact that an organisation is successful today does not mean that it will still be a success in the future. A bank which is successful in the 1980s will not be a success in the 1990s if it does not adapt to changes in the environment; the personal contact between bank manager and client has to some extent given way to instant banking because of major technological changes affecting this industry.

Unless a manager has insight into the technology affecting the organisation, competition, changes in customer profiles, new legislation and many other things, he or she is on very shaky ground. In order to survive in the long term, management has to reconcile its scarce resources with opportunities and threats in the external environment. One could say that the answer to survival lies in the external environment. However, forecasting uncontrollable external events is extremely difficult and certainly complicates the planning process.

5.5.2   Lack of organisational knowledge

In order to plan effectively, managers need a clear understanding of which resources their organisation can utilise in order to attain the purpose, mission and goals of the organisation. They need to understand the strategy that the organisation is following. They also need to understand the goals of their own and those of other subunits (departments, divisions or sections). The easy way out for managers would be to adhere to tried and trusted plans for fear of conflict with other departments. Concentrating on proven plans and neglecting future plans is, however, certain to lead to their downfall.

5.5.3   Reluctance to establish goals

The reluctance of some managers to establish goals for their subunits is another barrier to effective planning. A lack of confidence in their own ability and that of their subordinates is usually the reason for this reluctance. Fear of failure may be another reason why managers are reluctant to formulate goals; by not setting goals for their subunits, managers cannot be accused of not attaining their goals.

5.5.4   Resistance to change

One of the principal barriers to the planning process is resistance to change. Almost by definition planning involves changing one or more aspects of an organisation's current solutions to enable it to adapt to the ever-changing external environment.

Background

> *Future Shock*, Alvin Toffler's popular book, emphasised that change has become part of life. Toffler tells us that if we divide the last 50 000 years into 800 lifetimes of 62 years each, we will find that the human race spent 650 of those lifetimes in caves. Electric motors have been around for only two lifetimes. Most of the technology that we take for granted has existed for a single lifetime or less.

Organisational changes can be made in one or more elements of the organisation: the organisational structure, span of control, salary structure, replacement of typewriters by computer terminals, work hours, to mention but a few.

In planning for change, management almost inevitably encounters resistance. This resistance may be so severe that a manager may decide not to implement his or her plans for the sake of not 'rocking the boat'.

> The chains of habit are too weak to be felt until they are too strong to be broken.
> (Samuel Johnson)

5.5.5   Time and expense

Planning is time consuming and expensive. Managers sometimes become so involved in their day-to-day activities that they neglect their management task of planning. Setting up a planning system and gathering information to make it work require time and effort from many people. This high cost of planning — especially when it is introduced into an organisation for the first time — is often expected to be justified with tangible results. Since this is difficult to do, planning is often reduced to a superficial process.

Although the barriers to planning might seem insurmountable, there are guidelines that managers can use to **overcome** planning barriers.

■ Effective planning should start at the top of an organisation. Top management's sincere involvement in planning sets the stage for subsequent planning at middle and lower management levels and stresses the importance of planning to everyone in the organisation.

■ Management should realise the limitations of planning. Although it may sound paradoxical, good planning does not necessarily ensure success — adjustments and exceptions are to be expected as a plan unfolds.

■ The role that line and functional managers play in the planning process cannot be overemphasised. Since they are the individuals who have to execute the plans, their involvement in planning is obvious. People are more committed to plans they have helped to shape. Employees at all levels of an organisational hierarchy should be involved in planning of some sort.

■ Communication plays a vital role in planning. Planning initiated at the top should be communicated to others in the organisation. Managers and all other employees involved in the planning process should have a clear understanding of the grand strategy of the organisation (for example, horizontal diversification), the functional strategies (for example, the marketing and production strategies) and how they are interrelated.

■ Plans should constantly be revised and updated. New information, the completion of short-term plans, an unexpected strike by factory workers or the discovery of a hazardous substance in a pharmaceutical product being developed are examples of events that make planning a dynamic process.

■ Contingency planning may be very useful in a turbulent environment. Contingency planning is the development of alternative courses of action to be taken if an intended plan is unexpectedly disrupted or rendered inappropriate. City Lodge Hotels had to rely on contingency planning when their assumption that there would be an increase in international tourism after the 1995 Rugby World Cup proved to be incorrect.

5.6   PLANNING TOOLS

To overcome any resistance they have to planning, managers can use planning tools. These tools enable managers to plan scientifically and not simply look into a crystal ball. These tools include forecasting, budgeting and scheduling tools.

5.6.1   Forecasting

An important prerequisite for planning is to have some idea of what is likely to happen in the future as far as an organisation is concerned. A forecast is thus a projection of conditions expected to prevail in the future by making use of both past and present information.

Forecasting starts with the identification of factors that might provide opportunities or pose threats to an organisation in the future. Areas of forecasting that are of

Poor forecasting

> The abolishment of pain in surgery is chimera. It is absurd to go seeking it today. Knife and pain are two words in surgery that must forever be associated in the consciousness of the patient.
> (Dr Alfred Velpeay, 1839)
>
> The population of the earth decreases every day, and if this continues, in another ten centuries the earth will be nothing but a desert.
> (Montesquieu, 1743)
>
> That (the atom bomb) is the biggest fool thing we have ever done ... The bomb will never go off, and I speak as an expert in explosives.
> (Admiral Will D Lehy to President Truman, 1945)
>
> My figures coincided in fixing 1959 as the year when the world must go to smash.
> (Henry Adams, 1903)
>
> What, sir, would make a ship sail against the wind and currents by lighting a bonfire under the decks? I pray you excuse me. I have no time to listen to such nonsense.
> (Napoleon to Robert Fulton, inventor of the steam-engine)
>
> The demonstration that no possible combination of known substances, known form of machinery and known form of force can be united in a practical machine by which man shall fly long distances through the air, seems to the writer as clear as it is possible for the demonstration of any physical fact to be.
> (Simon Newcomb, astronomer, 1903)

the utmost importance to most organisations are sales and revenue forecasting and technological forecasting. **Sales forecasting**, as the term implies, is concerned with predicting future sales. Monetary sources, derived mainly from sales, are necessary to finance both current and future operations. Knowledge of future sales is thus vital to an organisation.

The term 'sales forecasting' is appropriate not only to organisations that sell something. All kinds of organisations depend on financial resources, which necessitate forecasting. A university must forecast future student numbers when planning to expand its library facilities; a hospital needs to forecast its income from patients. In these cases, **revenue forecasting** would seem to be a more appropriate term than the more conventional term 'sales forecasting'.

Technological forecasting focuses on the prediction of which future technologies are likely to emerge and when they are likely to be economically feasible. Managers must be able to anticipate new technological developments in their industry. This gives the organisation an advantage over its competitors. Recent technological innovations include cellular phones, the Internet, and much besides.

Although sales and revenue forecasting and technological forecasting are vital, other types of forecasting are also important to many organisations. **Resource fore-**

casting projects future needs for human, financial, physical and information resources. **Economic forecasting** focuses on factors such as the inflation rate, interest rates and the potential level of unemployment in a country. Some organisations undertake **market forecasting** and the forecasting of possible new legislation that might affect them. In fact, virtually any component in an organisation's external environment is an appropriate area for forecasting.

5.6.2 Budgeting

A budget is a plan that deals with the future allocation and utilisation of various resources with regard to different organisational activities over a given period. Budgets are typically thought of in financial terms, but also in terms of the allocation and utilisation of raw material, labour, office space, machine hours, computer time, and so on. A budget can be seen as a tool that managers use to translate future plans into quantitative terms.

Although budgeting is an important part of planning, it also serves as a control mechanism for evaluating organisational activities. A budget exercises control in two ways:

- It sets limits on the amount of resources that can be used by a department or unit.
- It establishes standards of performance against which future events will be compared.

Generally, budgets serve the following purposes:

- They help managers to coordinate resources and projects.
- They help to define the standards needed in all control systems.
- They provide clear guidelines on an organisation's resources and how they are expected to be utilised.
- They facilitate performance evaluations of managers and units.

Characteristics of budgets

- They are most frequently stated in monetary terms.
- They cover a specific period (usually one year).
- They contain an element of management commitment.
- They are reviewed and approved by an authority higher that the one that prepared them.
- Once approved, they can be changed only under previously specified conditions.
- They are periodically compared with actual performance, and variances are analysed and explained.

Although budgeting is an important aspect of planning and a useful control device, it has its limitations. One of the major limitations of budgets is overemphasising it at the expense of other considerations. Often one finds that managers focus almost exclusively on meeting their budgets while neglecting other elements that cannot be measured in quantifiable terms. The development of a supervisor's management skills, for example, is a goal that a certain organisation should pursue but, since it is usually not included in the financial budget, it receives little attention.

5.6.3 Scheduling

The Gantt chart is a graphic planning and control method in which a project is broken down into separate tasks. Estimates are then made of how much time each task requires as well as the total time needed to complete the entire project. The starting and end dates of the tasks are indicated on the chart.

When planning a conference, the essential activities of the project must be determined. This is depicted on the vertical axis in figure 5.5. It is clear from the chart that some of the activities require the completion of other activities before they can begin (for example, the mailing labels must be completed before the announcement can be mailed).

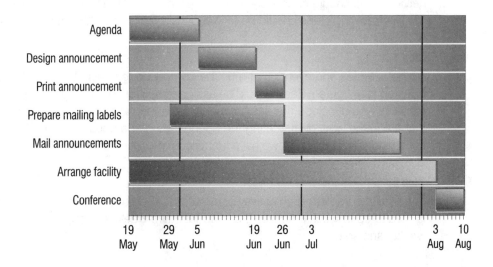

Figure 5.5
Gantt chart
Source: Bateman, TS & Zeithaml, CP. 1990. *Management Function and Strategy*. Homewood, Ill: Irwin, p 152.

Once the basic activities have been determined, a target completion date must be set. This is depicted on the horizontal axis. The next step is to determine the duration of each activity. If the conference is scheduled for 3 August, the announcements must be mailed at least a month in advance. Therefore 3 July is the latest mailing date for the announcements.

Once the activities as well as the activity duration, completion time and latest starting time have been determined, the Gantt chart can be drawn.

Managers can monitor the progress of the project by comparing actual progress with planned progress.

5.6.4 PERT

PERT, an acronym for Programme Evaluation and Review Technique, is a planning tool that uses a network to plan projects involving numerous activities and their interrelationships.

The key components of PERT are activities, events, time, the critical path and possibly cost (see figure). These components will be explained in the following example. Building a house would be an event; completion of the house would require multiple activities. Time can be measured in a variety of ways (seconds, minutes, hours, days, months, and so on) to determine the critical path. A knowledge of a critical path is essential, because it determines the length of time it will take to complete the house by identifying how long each activity will take. The critical path is the longest or most time-consuming sequence of events and activities in a PERT network. This should enable one to work out the time it will take to build the house.

The following steps should be followed in developing a PERT network:

Step 1

All the activities and events that must be completed to realise the objective should be listed (see figure). Each should be assigned a letter. In building a house, relevant activities would include the design, municipal approval of the plans, felling of trees that are in the way, demarcating the boundaries of the house, digging the foundations, and so on. In figure we have identified nine such activities.

Step 2

The time to complete each activity or event should be determined. In figure 5.5, time is measured in weeks. Activity 2 should take two weeks to complete; activity 3 six weeks; and so on.

Step 3

Arrange tasks in the sequence in which they should be completed. In figure , for instance, E must be completed before H can begin. Note that activity D is independent of the other activities. The numbered circles signify the completion of an event. In figure , 1 represents the start of the project and 9 the completion date.

Step 4

The critical path should be determined. To do this, one totals the time it takes for each path from start (1) to end (9). Path 2 – 6 – 8 – 9 takes 2 + 7 + 4 + 1 weeks, thus 14 weeks. Path 1– 3 – 6 – 8 – 9 takes 16 weeks. Path 1 – 4 – 7 – 8 – 9 takes 18 weeks. Path 1 – 5 – 9 takes 10 weeks. The critical path is 1 – 4 – 7 – 8 – 9. The project should therefore take 18 weeks to complete.

PERT allows managers to monitor a project's progress, identify possible bottle-necks and shift resources as necessary to keep the project on schedule.

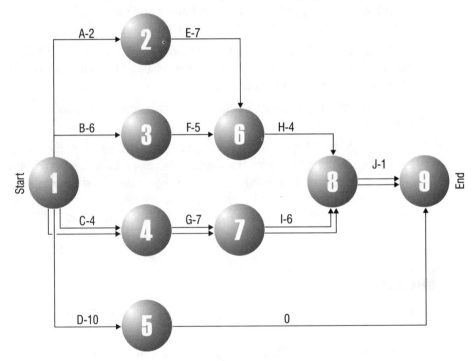

Circles=Events
Arrows and letter=Activities
Numbers=Time in days
Double arrows=The critical path, or how long it should take to complete the project

Figure 5.6
A PERT network
Source: Lussier, RN. 1997. *Management: Concepts, Applications, Skill Development.* Massachusetts: South-Western, p 188.

5.7   SUMMARY

Chapter 5 focused on planning — the first management function. Once goals have been developed for an organisation, managers need to plan in order to attain them.

Different kinds of organisational plans can be identified, namely strategic, tactical and operational plans. These plans form a hierarchy — from broad strategic plans at the top to detailed operational plans at the bottom of the hierarchy. Strategic plans focus on the entire organisation, are formulated by top management and have an extended time-frame of five years or more. Tactical plans are more specific and concrete than strategic plans. These plans are formulated by middle management and focus on areas such as marketing, finance, purchasing, human resources and so on. The time horizon of tactical plans is usually from one to five years. Operational plans are narrowly focused and have relatively short time horizons. They are usually formulated by middle-level and lower-level managers.

There are two basic forms of operational plans, namely single-use plans and standing plans. Single-use plans are formulated for nonrecurring activities and standing plans for recurring activities.

The planning process has been looked at by discussing each step in this process.

Although planning is the fundamental management function, managers are sometimes reluctant to plan. The reasons for this reluctance could be managers' lack of environmental knowledge, a lack of organisational knowledge, resistance to change and other reasons. To overcome resistance to change, managers can use planning tools such as budgets, forecasts, the Gantt chart and PERT.

5.8   REFERENCES

1. Mintzberg, H. 1994. *The Rise and Fall of Strategic Planning*. New York: Free Press.

2. Mintzberg, H. 1987. The strategy concept II: Another look at why organisations need strategies. *California Management Review*, Fall, p 26.

3. Robbins, SP. 1997. *Managing Today*. Upper Saddle River, New Jersey: Prentice-Hall, p 132.

4. Ibid p 133.

5. Griffin, RW. 1993. *Management*. 4 ed. Boston: Houghton Mifflin, p 159.

6 Strategic Planning

Key issues

- The concept of strategic planning
- The strategic plan\gning process
- The levels of strategy
- Each component of the strategic planning process
- Behavioural considerations affecting strategic choice\g

6.1 INTRODUCTION

The first half of the twentieth century, especially the period before World War II, was characterised by a steady business environment in which inflation was virtually unknown, interest rates remained steady, urbanisation was not seen as a viable alternative to farming and the business environment was an unexplored field. During this era there was no shortage of natural resources and the rate of technological development was much slower than it is today. There were few unforeseen changes in the business environment and little effort was required to keep up with the pace of change.

However, this situation has changed drastically since the end of World War II. Today's business environment is more turbulent than ever. South African organisations are particularly hard pressed because of South Africa's recent entry into the global economy. South African organisations now have to compete in a borderless world against established competitors such as the United States of America and Singapore.

This borderless world is characterised by the following:

- Highly educated, technically oriented 'knowledge workers' are replacing manufacturing employees as the worker elite.
- The downsizing of major organisations is a reality worldwide and South African organisations seem to be following suite.
- Businesses will focus more on providing services than on making products.

■ Work will become less predictable and less routine and will require constant learning and complex thinking.

■ Employees will have more independence than workers had in the past; they will be expected to know more about the overall business, to take greater responsibility and risks, and to be accountable for business results.

South Africa: on the starting line

The United States of America has become the leader in world competitiveness, a position previously held by Japan. The USA's success is based on:

■ its large and resilient domestic economy

■ the introduction of new technology

■ a very flexible attitude towards work structures

■ financial strength

■ internationalisation

The USA is followed by Singapore (second), Hong Kong (third) and Japan (fourth). India (38th), South Africa (44th) and Russia (46th) are still on the starting line.

Source: *The World Competitiveness Yearbook.* 1996, pp 18–20.

Focus

For the above and countless other reasons, managers have turned to strategic planning as a means of surviving in a hostile environment. In the rest of this chapter we focus on this sophisticated planning process which should prepare the organisation for possible turbulence in its environment. To explain the strategic planning process, we will constantly refer to figure 6.1.

6.2   STRATEGIC PLANNING: WHAT IT ENCOMPASSES

Strategic planning can be defined as the **process** of reconciling the organisation's resources (**internal environment**) with threats and opportunities in the **external environment** (see chapter 3).

The following characteristics of strategic planning will elucidate this definition:

■ Strategic planning is an ongoing activity (process).

- It requires well-developed conceptual skills and is performed mainly by top management.

- It focuses on the organisation as a whole.

- It is future oriented.

- It is concerned with the organisation's vision, mission, objectives and strategies.

- Strategic planning aims at integrating all management functions.

- It focuses on opportunities (or threats) that may be exploited (or dealt with) through the application of the organisation's resources.

Figure 6.1 depicts the strategic planning process.

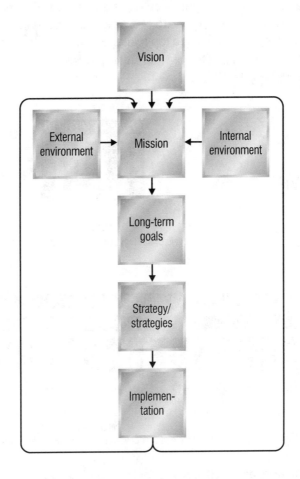

Figure 6.1
The strategic planning process

The discussion in this chapter will be based on the above figure. However, before we discuss this figure, it is important to understand the difference between strategic planning, tactical planning and operational planning, as depicted in figure 5.1. It is crucial to grasp the following points before we discuss the strategic planning process:

■ Strategic planning is performed by **top management** with input from managers at the other levels.

■ Tactical and operational planning are performed by **middle** and **lower management**.

A major implication of the above is that one group of managers (top management) formulates the strategic plans, whereas other groups of managers (middle and lower management) have to put these plans into action. Top management therefore has to make sure that the plans are clear and understandable. The principles discussed in this chapter should guide top management in this regard.

It is also important to note that strategic planning takes place at corporate as well as at business level.

Figure 6.2
The levels of strategy: single-business organisations

Figure 6.3
The levels of strategy: multiple-business organisations

The **corporate strategy** (also called the 'grand' strategy) is the course charted for an organisation as a whole and specifies what set of businesses the organisation should be in. Cullinan Holdings (figure 6.3) decided at corporate level to focus on three businesses: electrical, property and industrial ceramics. The set of decisions about which new businesses to enter, which businesses to buy and possibly which businesses to sell, represents Cullinan's corporate strategy. In short, the corporate strategy focuses on the organisation's scope of activities and resource deployment.

Business strategy determines how best to compete in a particular industry or market. It is concerned with the strategies for each unit or business within a corporation. Cullinan Holdings has a business strategy for each of its businesses: electrical, property and industrial ceramics. The business strategies for these businesses may differ in order to gain a specific advantage in the industries in which they operate. Although each business has its own strategy, the formulation of the strategies does not take place in isolation. The objective of the business strategies is to achieve synergism, that is, to cooperate with a view to the cumulative or overall effect, rather than concentrating on the optimal strategy for each individual business.

6.3   THE STRATEGIC PLANNING PROCESS

Although each of the components of the strategic planning process is explained separately in the sections that follow, one should always remember that these components are interdependent. For instance, when formulating the mission statement, top management needs information on the internal and external environments. A realistic mission statement should take into account the capabilities (internal environment) of the organisation, as well as threats and opportunities in the external environment.

6.3.1   The vision

For top management to lead the organisation to success in the future it needs a 'strong vision'.[1]

Having a vision implies that managers need to think about ways to carry their organisation into the future. South African managers face the challenge of surviving in a global environment in which new technologies and political alignments are important realities. In the tertiary education industry, for example, the manner of disseminating knowledge is changing. At many universities, students now obtain an MBA degree without ever seeing the campus or a lecturer. Computer technology makes this possible.

The world is being reshaped not only by technological innovation but also by changing political boundaries and alliances. A few years ago it was unheard of for South African institutions to form alliances with communist countries, such as Cuba. Today many Cuban doctors are being recruited to work in South Africa.

Background

'People in the political arena are particularly good at developing visions and they often excel at articulating them. Such people are inspirational because, when there is dissatisfaction with the existing *status quo*, they recognise it, are able to present an acceptable alternative, and rally others around them to make it happen. For example, Mahatma Gandhi had a vision of an independent India where Muslims and Hindus would live together in peace. Martin Luther King had a vision of harmony between blacks and whites. John F Kennedy, when he was president, had a very specific vision of wanting a man on the moon by the end of the sixties. Then there were the darker visions of Adolf Hitler's thousand-year Reich' (Kets de Vries, MFR. 1994. The leadership mystique. *Academy of Management Executives*, 8(3), p 14).

President Nelson Mandela's vision of a democratic South Africa — a 'rainbow nation' — earned him, amongst others things, the coveted Nobel Peace Prize.

A clear vision is important to an organisation for the following reasons.[2]

■ **A vision promotes change.** A vision serves as a road map for organisations as they move through accelerated change. It is a vehicle for driving change.

■ **A vision provides the basis for a strategic plan.**

■ **A vision enhances a wide range of performance measures.** It has been found that companies with a clear vision statement outperform those companies that do not possess a vision. This should be considered by shareholders when selecting companies in which they can invest.

■ **A vision helps to keep decision making in context.** Visions provide focus and direction. Organisations with a clear vision help employees to focus their attention on what is most important to the organisation, discouraging them from exploiting short-term opportunities they may otherwise seize.

In South Africa, as well as in other countries, organisations tend to become managerially leaner and flatter; decision making becomes more decentralised. A clear vision can affect the perspectives or premises that people use to make decisions in the absence of direct supervision.

■ **A vision motivates individuals and facilitates the recruitment of talent.** A vision should enable employees to see how their effort contributes to the organisation's success. The vision should also indicate the attributes valued by the organisation, for example innovation, knowledge, and so on.

■ **A clear vision has positive consequences.** When top management effectively communicates the vision, there is a significantly higher level of job satisfaction, commitment, loyalty, pride, esprit de corps, clarity about the organisation's values, productivity and encouragement.

Many organisations articulate their vision through a vision statement. NovoNordisk, the Danish pharmaceutical company, emphasises the company's 'desire to improve human life by preventing and treating human diseases'.

Vision statements may be longer and written in conversational prose. Some are crisply outlined in point form; some are vague and abstract on some topics while clear and precise on others. There is no template for the style of a vision statement.

Creating a vision: looking backwards and forwards

> The black South African executive group has a strong strategic emphasis. Their focus is not so much on short-term hurdles but on longer-term objectives. They are fairly traditional leaders who prefer tried and trusted practices. Their hesitancy to experiment may blind them to real opportunities which offer a competitive edge.
>
> They believe that specialist knowledge is an important resource, so they prepare themselves thoroughly, consulting relevant sources of information. This can slow the decision-making process, taking up time which could be better spent. Greater efficiency needs to be developed.
>
> Source: AMROP International. 1996. *The South African Executive: The Challenge of Diversity.* Johannesburg: AMROP, p 18.

6.3.2 The mission statement

With the vision clearly articulated, managers should now consider the next step in the strategic planning process, namely the formulation of the mission statement.

The mission statement was briefly discussed in section 4.4.1. In this section the mission statement of an organisation was defined as the **fundamental, unique purpose** that sets the organisation apart from other organisations of its type and identifies the scope of its operations in (i) **product**, (ii) **market** and (iii) **technological** terms.

A mission statement, therefore, provides answers to the following questions:

- ■ **What** is (are) our business(es) (in other words, our **product**)?
- ■ **Who** is our client (our **market**)?
- ■ **How** will we provide this product or service (**technology**)?

The answers to these three questions should clearly set the organisation apart from similar organisations. A mission statement should ensure unanimity of purpose within the organisation, and serve as the basis for resource allocation. The mission statement also sets the parameters within which all decisions should be made.

Eli Lilly, the pharmaceutical giant, stated its unique purpose as follows: 'Eli Lilly and Company is a global research-based pharmaceutical, medical instruments, diagnostic products, and animal health products company. The company markets its products in 110 countries around the world.'

The core components of Eli Lilly's mission statement

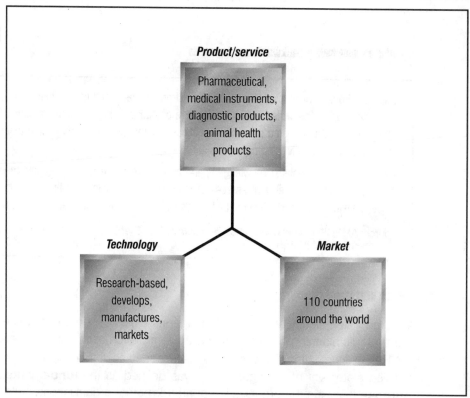

The Eli Lilly mission statement cited above clearly indicates how this company sets itself apart from similar companies such as Lennons. For instance, Eli Lilly not only produces and markets its products but also does the research and development of its products. Lennons, on the other hand, is a generic pharmaceutical house that does not get involved in research on new pharmaceutical products. It produces products based on the recipes of research-based pharmaceutical companies such as Eli Lilly.

Organisations should also address the following components in their mission statement — or should state them in an addendum to the mission statement, often referred to as the philosophy of the organisation:

■ the organisation's intention to secure its survival through sustained growth and profitability

- the organisation's culture (its beliefs and values)
- the organisation's public image
- the self-concept of the organisation (its capabilities — that is, where its strength lies)
- the organisation's social responsibility towards its internal stakeholders (eg employees and shareholders) and outside stakeholders (eg the government and general public)

The importance attached to re-engineering and total quality management (TQM) in contemporary management emphasises two additional components that should be addressed by the mission statement, namely:

- the customer, and
- quality.

When formulating a mission statement, management should be very sensitive to the claims of stakeholders, both inside the organisation and outside. Inside stakeholders such as employees would like to see their economic, social and psychological needs being addressed in the mission statement. The general public, an outside stakeholder, may want its concern for the conservation of the environment to be addressed in the mission statement.

Figure 6.4 depicts the internal and external stakeholders that should be considered when formulating a mission statement.

Figure 6.4
The organisation's mission: stakeholders
Source: Pearce, JA & Robinson, RB. 1994. *Formulation, Implementation, and Control of Competitive Strategy.* Homewood, Ill: Irwin, p 49.

Mission formulation was discussed in this section. We looked at what a mission statement is, what components it should have, and at stakeholders and their claims. However, both the internal and external environments should be scanned to indicate to top management whether the mission statement is realistic.

In the next section we will consider the internal environment.

6.3.3 The internal environment

The internal analysis of an organisation (organisation profile) would identify the strategically important strengths and weaknesses on which the organisation should base its strategy. The analysis should indicate to top management what its capabilities are.

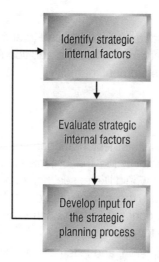

Figure 6.5
Steps in the development of an organisation profile

Figure 6.5 illustrates internal analysis as a three-step process. By following these steps, management is able to identify those factors that give the organisation a competitive advantage, those that meet the basic business requirements and those that make it vulnerable.

Step 1: Identify strategic internal factors

In step 1, managers identify and examine key aspects of the organisation's basic capabilities, limitations and characteristics — those internal capabilities that are most critical to success in a particular industry or competitive area. Factors strategic to organisations in the building industry, for example, would be quite different from those of organisations in the catering industry.

Strategic factors can also vary between organisations in the same industry. For example, the strategies of Edgars Stores and a very exclusive ladies' boutique would be based on different internal strengths: Edgars on its strength in mass marketing, extensive advertising and specialised managerial skills; the exclusive ladies' boutique on high quality, image and customer loyalty.

You may be wondering at this stage how managers decide which factors are truly strategic. To help managers with this challenging task, the following approaches have been identified.

■ **The evaluation of functional segments.** The functional approach concentrates on in-depth studies of the functional areas of an organisation. To Cullinan Holdings (figure 6.2) this would mean a thorough analysis of its marketing, financial, production, human resources, research and development, and external relations functions. In table 6.1, the focus is on general management as one of the key internal factors in an organisation, and the factors listed have been identified as potential strengths or weaknesses. This table serves as an illustration of how one of the functional segments of the organisation has been assessed in terms of those factors critical to its success.

According to table 6.1, the major strengths of the organisation involved are its clear and realistic mission statement, its leadership, its top management's vision and capabilities and its reaction to external changes. Weaknesses in the general management function are the organisational structure and communication systems.

■ **The evaluation of the mission and objectives.** An organisation's purpose or the reason for its existence is found in its mission statement. Components of the mission statement refer to the organisation's **product**, its **market**, its **technology** or ways in which it serves its market, and its basic philosophy on management, employees and society in general. These components should be regarded as the factors critical to the success of the organisation.

■ **The analysis of historical trends.** In the search for strengths and weaknesses inside an organisation, management can learn a lot by asking questions about the organisation's past performance: What did the organisation do particularly well in the past?

■ **The value chain.** Another method of identifying key success factors in the internal environment is the so-called 'value chain method'. The whole process through which a product goes until it reaches the consumer is divided into value-added stages. Each stage is scrutinised and analysed to improve productivity, quality, and so on.

■ **The product–market evolution.** The requirements for success in an organisation's product–market relationship change over time. Management can therefore apply the framework of a product life cycle to identify strengths and weaknesses in the internal environment as an ongoing exercise. Based on this concept, key success factors during the introductory phase of the product's life cycle would revolve around the marketing capabilities to create awareness of the product, while key factors in the decline phase would encompass cost advantages, good supplier relations and financial control.

Table 6.1
Steps in the development of an organisation profile

Key internal factor	Potential strengths and weaknesses			
	++	+	–	– –
1 Clear and realistic mission statement	■			
2 Organisation's record — achieving objectives		■		
3 Organisational structure			■	
4 Communication systems			■	
5 Leadership	■			
6 Effectiveness and utilisation of control systems		■		
7 Organisational culture		■		
8 Decision making		■		
9 Top management's vision and capabilities	■			
10 Reaction to external changes	■			

Step 2: Evaluate strategic internal factors

Now that the strategic internal factors have been identified, the next issue that arises is: What are the potential strengths and weaknesses of an organisation? A factor is considered a strength if it is a competency or competitive advantage of an organisation. For example, Rolls Royce's image and quality are two distinct competencies for that organisation and these competencies should be exploited to the full. A weakness, on the other hand, is something that an organisation does poorly. For any organisation operating in a turbulent environment, a lack of management vision can be considered to be a major weakness, as this lack of vision hampers the organisation in its attempt to keep pace with the changing business environment.

How do managers evaluate key internal factors and activities as strengths or weaknesses? Four basic perspectives on the evaluation of strategic internal factors can help managers in this task. These perspectives focus on:

■ a comparison with the organisation's performance in the past
■ a comparison with competitors
■ a comparison with key success factors in the organisation's industry
■ bench marking

Many managers start their planning efforts by comparing their current results with **previous results of the organisation**. These are the capabilities and problems with which they are most familiar. A major problem of this very popular approach, however, is that managers might develop tunnel vision: 'This has worked well in the past so why rock the boat?'

Comparing the organisation's capabilities with those of major **competitors** is a second approach that managers might use to evaluate the organisation. The full-service facilities that it provides for travellers are a major strength of the Holiday Inn Group, whereas this is a relatively unimportant factor for the City Lodge Hotel Group, which focuses on the basic needs of its clients. This is an example of organisations in the same industry having different marketing skills, managerial vision, financial resources, accommodation facilities, locations and so forth. Before deciding on a feasible strategy to follow, each organisation would have to know whether it really has a competitive advantage in those areas critical to its success.

The key determinants of success in an **industry** can also be used to identify the internal strengths and weaknesses of an organisation. For instance, when entry into an industry is difficult, organisations already in it have a measure of protection from competition. In this regard one can think of the difficulties in starting a communication network such as Vodacom as compared with opening a video shop. In starting a communication network, the organisation has some protection from competition owing to the legal restrictions pertaining to starting such a business. In the case of the video shop, there is far less protection from competition because of the relative ease of entering this industry.

A substitute product from inside or outside an industry can also introduce tough competition. Companies in the contact lens industry are now threatened by Lasik, laser treatment for poor eyesight, which takes approximately 20 minutes per eye to perform. This could make contact lenses obsolete.

The situation is complicated by two further forces that shape competition in an industry, namely the power of suppliers and that of customers. Powerful suppliers can squeeze profitability if the organisation cannot pass on added costs to the customer. Customers, likewise, can force down prices, demand better service, higher quality, and so on.

Bench marking is another approach that can be used to identify an organisation's strengths and weaknesses. Bench marking is the search for the best practices among competitors and noncompetitors which lead to their superior performance. A car manufacturer, for instance, can list all the features customers perceive as important and then set about finding the products which are the best in these areas. The spray paint used on aeroplanes could set the standard for paintwork whereas the design of the Lamborghini could set the bench mark for superior aerodynamic design. Bench marking can focus on employee, supplier or technological performance, cost performance, financial performance, customer service performance, and other areas.

Although the identification and evaluation of key internal factors have been discussed as two separate steps, it should be stressed that, in practice, they are not differentiated.

Step 3: Develop input for the strategic planning process

The results of the second step could be applied to determine those internal factors that:

- provide an organisation with an edge over its competitors — factors around which to build the organisation's strategy
- are important capabilities for the organisation to have but are typical of every competitor
- are currently weaknesses in the organisation — managers should avoid strategies that rely on those key vulnerabilities

The results obtained in this final step in the internal analysis process serve as inputs into the strategic planning process. In the next section we discuss environmental analysis as another input into the strategic planning process.

6.3.4 The external environment

Chapter 3 deals in great detail with the organisation and the environment in which it operates. Only a brief overview of this very important component of the strategic planning process is given in this section. Since organisations do not operate in a vacuum, they should constantly be aware of key variables in their external environment. These variables may be in the macroenvironment or the market environment.

The macroenvironment includes forces that originate beyond any single organisation's immediate environment. This uncontrollable, remote environment is composed of the economic, political, technological, societal, ecological and international environments. In assessing the economic environment, managers should analyse factors such as the stage of the economic cycle, inflation and interest rates, and unemployment levels. An assessment of the political environment should address environmental protection laws, tax laws, special incentives, and other issues. The societal environment includes factors such as attitudes towards quality of life, women in the workforce, the population growth, and the career expectations of the population.

The market environment includes those factors that both directly affect and are affected by an organisation. These factors include competitors, customers, suppliers, potential entrants and substitute products.

The macroenvironment and market environment are subject to constant change, thus presenting opportunities that can be exploited or threats that can be converted into opportunities. An organisation's survival depends to a large degree on the ability of management to anticipate changes in the environment and to prepare in advance for these changes. It is therefore necessary to predict the type of environment that the organisation will face in the future. In this regard the steps illustrated in figure 6.6 should be taken.

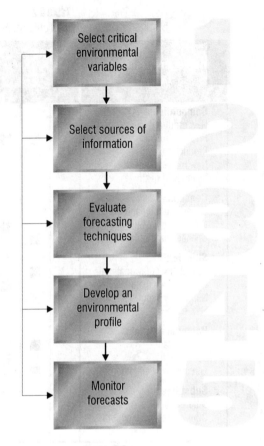

Figure 6.6
Steps in environmental forecasting

The selection of **critical environmental variables** is usually a responsibility of top management. Time and money constraints obviously preclude the forecasting of all possible variables. The most important variables that should be forecast are those that force sharp growth or decline in the marketplace. For instance, the birth rate of the population is significant for manufacturers of educational toys for children. The birth rate of the population, in turn, is greatly affected by variables such as the educational level of parents and the lifestyles of the population.

Many organisations find that environmental forecasting is beyond their capabilities. They therefore obtain basic forecasts from sources such as government agencies and professional research firms. Important South African **sources of information** for forecasting include the Bureau for Market Research at the University of South Africa, the Department of Statistics, the Bureau for Financial Analysis at the University of Pretoria and the Institute for Futures Research at the University of Stellenbosch.

Table 6.2

Market environmental profile for Boats (Pty) Ltd

Market environmental factors	Strong ++	+	Weak −	−	Significance for Boats (Pty) Ltd
Competitive:					
New product				■	− −
Pricing structure			■		0
Product life cycle	■				+
New marketing strategies				■	− −
Intensity of rivalry				■	− −
Consumer:					
Changes in demand				■	− −
Changes in wealth			■		0
Changes in population		■			0
Supplier:					
Availability of raw materials		■			0
Prices of raw materials			■		0
Number of suppliers		■			0
New materials				■	−
Potential entrant:					
Cost of plant		■			+
Ease of entry			■		−
Threat of new entrants		■			0
Substitute:					
Different boat models				■	− −
Other recreational opportunities				■	− −

Significance designations:
+ = positive impact
0 = neutral impact
− = negative impact
The more pluses there are, the more positive the impact will be and the more minuses, the more negative the impact will be.

Publications such as the *Financial Mail, Finance Week,* the *South African Journal of Business Leadership* and *Business Day* also provide useful information. It is important to note that the ultimate responsibility for the evaluation and interpretation of the information supplied by these institutions and publications lies with the organisation and not the forecasters.

If an organisation is capable of gathering primary data, a number of quantitative and qualitative **forecasting techniques** can be applied. The choice of technique depends on considerations such as the nature of the forecast decision, the usefulness and accuracy of available information, the accuracy required, the time available, and the cost and importance of the forecast. Popular approaches to forecasting are described in chapter 5.

The next step in forecasting environmental variables is the **development of an environmental profile**. An environmental profile is a summary of the key environmental factors. Each factor is listed and evaluated for its potential impact on the organisation.

Table 6.2 illustrates a market environmental profile for the company Boats (Pty) Ltd.

The final step in environmental forecasting is to **monitor** the critical aspects of management forecasts. These aspects include those referred to in steps 1 to 4 in figure 6.6.

Once an organisation is thoroughly aware of its own strengths and weaknesses and of the opportunities and threats in the external environment, it is in a position to identify and evaluate realistic strategies that are in line with the organisation's mission and objectives.

6.3.5 Strategic analysis and choice

So far our discussion of strategic planning has focused on where the organisation would like to be in the future. We have not yet asked the question of **how** it will get there. Our discussion in this section should address this question.

Strategic analysis and choice entail the simultaneous selection of long-term objectives and the grand strategy of a business organisation.

When formulating a strategy, strategic planners study their opportunities in order to determine which are most likely to result in the achievement of various long-term objectives. They try to forecast whether an available grand strategy can take advantage of preferred opportunities so that the specific objectives can be met. Since we have already discussed long-term objectives in detail in chapter 4, we focus in the next section on the different strategies available to strategic planners.

6.4 CORPORATE STRATEGIES

Corporate strategies define what business or businesses an organisation is in or should be in, how each business should be conducted and which new business the organisation should get into. Corporate strategies are also called 'grand strategies'. Grand strategies should be developed for both single-business and multiple-business organisations (figure 6.2). Single-business organisations limit their operations to one major industry. A case in point is City Lodge Hotels in South Africa, which is involved in the lodging industry only. Multiple-business organisations operate in more than one industry. Cullinan Holdings is an example of a company involved in the electrical, property and ceramics industries.

A multibusiness organisation such as Cullinan Holdings develops a business strategy for each business. Single-business organisations address the same issues as multiple-business organisations, but their scope is more limited. To these organisations, corporate and business strategies are essentially the same.

City Lodge Hotels, for instance, has to look at the different strategies to find out which strategy, or combination of strategies will enable it to attain a goal of 82 % room occupancy. It should consider three categories of grand strategies, namely growth, decline or coporate combination strategies. The choice of strategies is depicted in figure 6.7.

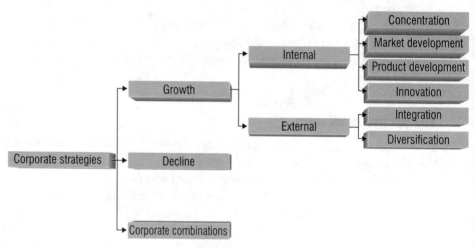

Figure 6.7
Corporate strategies

6.4.1 Growth strategies

Internal growth strategies

Should City Lodge Hotels or any other organisation decide to choose an **internal growth** strategy, it has the following options.

A **concentration growth strategy** implies 'sticking to the knitting'. It involves concentrating on improving what one is already doing. Resources are directed towards the continued and profitable development of a single product, in a single market, using a single technology. What these (product, market, technology) are, will be found in the mission statement, as they are the core components of a mission statement.

A concentration growth strategy can be accomplished by attracting new consumers, increasing the consumption rate of existing users or 'stealing' from the competition.

Known skills and capabilities are a major advantage of this low-risk strategy. However, organisations choosing this strategy are susceptible to new competitors and innovations. Should City Lodge Hotels choose this strategy, it will have to compete with 30 new hotels in the Cape Town region only, which have added 6 000 new beds to the Peninsula's stock.[3]

Market development is very closely related to a concentration strategy. This strategy also builds on existing strengths and skills. Market development is a strategy according to which an organisation sells its present products in new markets by opening additional new outlets or attracting other market segments. Protea Hotels' decision to manage a hotel in Ghana is an example of market development. Another example of this strategy would be a university designing nondegree courses for students who wish to obtain a professional qualification but who have not passed matric.

Product development implies substantial modification of existing products or additions to present products to increase their market penetration within existing customer groups. The Southern Sun Group has introduced its own brand of economy hotel — the Holiday Inn Express — thus attracting customers who might previously have used City Lodge Hotels' economy accommodation for executives.

While the first three internal growth strategies discussed here are relatively low in risk, **innovation** is a very risky strategy. Organisations choosing this strategy continuously search for original or novel ideas. The rationale for this strategy is to create a new product life cycle, thereby making existing products obsolete.

External growth strategies

The internal growth strategies discussed in the previous section are primarily concerned with improving competitive strategies for existing businesses. Higher-risk **external growth strategies,** comprising **integration** and **diversification,** should also be considered.

Backward vertical integration is the strategy followed by an organisation seeking increased control of its supply sources. The organisation can create its own source of supply or can purchase an existing supplier. This strategy is very attractive if there is uncertainty about the availability, cost or reliability of the deliveries of suppliers. It does, however, require a large capital investment. An example of this strategy would be Sappi (paper producer) acquiring a plantation to secure raw material supplies (see figure 6.8).

When the strategy involves the acquisition of a business nearer to the ultimate consumer, it is called **forward vertical integration**. An example would be a paper producer purchasing a bookstore. Forward vertical integration is an attractive alternative if an organisation is receiving unsatisfactory service from the distributor of its products. However, this strategy adds to the level of capital investment involved in a business.

Horizontal integration is a long-term growth strategy by which one or more similar organisations are taken over for reasons such as scale-of-operations benefits

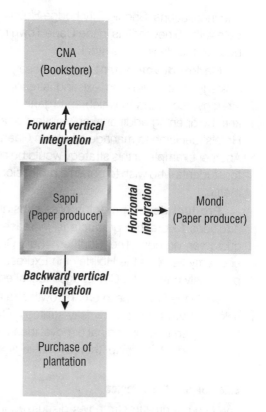

Figure 6.8
Integrative growth strategies

or a larger market share. Such acquisitions provide access to new markets, on the one hand, and get rid of competition, on the other. The integration of two paper producers, two restaurant chains or two world boxing associations, for example, would be classified as horizontal integration.

Diversification growth strategies may be appropriate to organisations that cannot achieve their growth objectives in their current industry with their current products and markets. Reasons for an organisation to diversify include the following:

- The markets of current businesses are approaching the saturation or decline phase of the product life cycle.
- Risk can be distributed more evenly.
- Current businesses are generating excess cash that can be invested more profitably elsewhere.
- Synergy is possible when diversifying into new businesses.

Concentric diversification involves the addition of a business related to an organisation in terms of technology, markets or products. In this type of grand strategy, the new business selected must possess a high degree of compatibility with the current businesses. The key to successful concentric diversification is to take advantage of at least one of the organisation's major strengths. Vodacom's introduction of fax lines on cellular phones illustrates concentric diversification based on expertise in communication networks.

Horizontal diversification involves seeking growth by appealing to current markets with new products that are technologically unrelated to present products. A meaningful strategic fit should be provided by some aspect of the new product, for example, through the use of the present channels of distribution or target customer demands. Vodacom, for example, can opt for a horizontal diversification strategy by diversifying into the publication of a magazine focusing on communication issues.

Conglomerate diversification involves seeking growth by acquiring a business because it represents the most promising investment opportunity available. Neither the new markets nor the new products have to be technologically related to the products currently being offered by an organisation. This strategy can be chosen to offset deficiencies such as seasonality, a lack of cash or a lack of opportunities in the marketplace. However, this strategy is not without its pitfalls, the primary one being the lack of managerial experience in the new business.

6.4.2 Decline strategies

One often reads about relatively successful organisations selling off some of their major assets or even selling a division of the organisation, resulting in the elimination of many jobs. The question may rightfully be asked why an organisation would make such a drastic decision.

The situation described above could be justified in situations where an organisation needs to regroup its activities to improve efficiency after a period of fast growth, where long-run growth and profit opportunities are unavailable, where other opportunities are more attractive or where there is a period of economic uncertainty.

An organisation can find itself with declining profits for many reasons but still be worth saving. Poor management, inadequate financial control, price and product competition, high cost structure and a change in the pattern of demand are possible reasons that can lead to a decline in profits.[4] In such circumstances **turnaround** is an appropriate strategy, as it is a strategy that focuses on eliminating inefficiencies in an organisation. Top management usually looks at cost and asset reduction to reverse declining sales and profits. Closing unprofitable factories or reducing the number of employees are ways of achieving this.

Divestiture is closely related to retrenchment. The primary difference between these two strategies is often a matter of the degree or scale of the decline. The more permanent the decline is, the more likely it is that the strategy adopted will be one of divestiture. A divestiture strategy involves the sale of a business or a major component thereof to achieve a permanent change in the scope of operations.

Reasons for divestiture vary. Divestiture may arise when top management recognises that one of its businesses does not have the expected strategic fit with its other businesses. A second reason for choosing a divestiture strategy may be the financial needs of an organisation; the cash flow or financial stability of an organisation can be greatly improved if businesses or components of businesses with a high market value can be sacrificed.

Harvesting is an appropriate strategy when an organisation seeks to maximise cash flow in the short run, regardless of the long-term effect. Harvesting is generally pursued in organisations that are unlikely to be sold for a profit but are capable of yielding cash during the harvesting. Management can decrease investments, cut maintenance, and reduce advertising and research, in order to cut costs and improve cash flow.

In selecting **liquidation**, the owners and strategic managers of an organisation admit failure and recognise that this least attractive of all strategies is the best way of minimising the loss to the stakeholders of the organisation. Liquidation can therefore be seen as the most extreme form of the decline strategies in that the entire organisation ceases to exist. Planned liquidation may be a worthwhile strategy for an organisation, because the organisation can liquidate its assets for more cash than the market value of its shares.

Although the different strategies discussed above are treated as separate strategies, organisations can implement multiple grand strategies simultaneously.

6.4.3 Corporate combinations

Recently, four corporate strategies have gained popularity in South Africa and many countries abroad, especially for multinational organisations. The first of these strategies is called a **joint venture**. When two or more companies lack a necessary component for success in a particular environment, they can join resources to form a separate company. Equity positions are usually taken by the participants. The manufacture of the popular 4x4 Musso is the result of a joint venture between a Korean motor manufacturer and Mercedes Benz.

A lesser form of participation, which may or may not involve equity participation, involves **strategic alliances**. In many instances strategic alliances are synonymous with licensing agreements. Service and franchise-based organisations — including Avis, Holiday Inn and McDonalds — have formed strategic alliances as a way of entering new markets.

While only some resources of each of the companies are used in a joint venture and strategic alliance, a **merger** involves the total pooling of resources by two or more organisations. Compared to an **acquisition**, a merger is usually far more collaborative, voluntary and is entered into mutually. Acquisition occurs when the organisation being taken over agrees to sell a controlling interest to the dominant company — willingly or unwillingly. The reason for choosing acquisition as a strategy would include economies of scale, gaining access to customer bases and maintaining control over price in the industry.

Strategies of a major South African organisation

> 'With South Africa's readmittance into the international fold, there has been great interest shown in the South African economy by foreign investors. The extensive cost reduction programmes that the Group has undertaken over the last three years will stand it in good stead as it prepares for intensified competition from international entrants. It is no longer enough to be the lowest-cost producer in South Africa but rather the challenge is to be world-class competitive, and companies in the Group are now bench marking themselves, where possible, against leading multinational food companies. To this end a number of international linkages and strategic alliances have been forged, both through formal licence agreements and also through informal arrangements. In addition, one of the prime areas of focus for the group is to drive down costs and improve product quality.'
>
> Source: CG Smith Foods Ltd. 1995. Chairman's statement. *Annual Report*, p 3.

6.5   THE SELECTION OF CORPORATE STRATEGIES

Now that you have studied the various corporate strategies available to an organisation, you might ask how an organisation selects a particular strategy or strategies that could result in the attainment of its mission and objectives. In order to address this strategy selection process, we shall discuss the four steps illustrated in figure 6.9.

The foundation for selecting strategies is a thorough identification and understanding of an organisation's **current strategy or strategies**. External factors (such as the organisation's posture towards external threats) and internal factors (such as the organisation's mission and corporate and business objectives) should be well understood. Behavioural considerations affecting the choice of strategies in an organisation should also be well understood. This is discussed in section 6.7.

Organisations competing in an industry, offering products with similar demand characteristics, have a one-item business portfolio. Karos Hotels, for instance, needs focus only on the lodging industry when formulating a strategy. What is the case, however, with companies such as Cullinan Holdings, which is involved in the electrical, property and ceramics industries? Knowing how to manage diversified businesses or units calls for a knowledge of **portfolio management**. The portfolio approach is a useful aid to multibusiness organisations in which each business is managed as a separate business or profit centre. The portfolio approach provides a

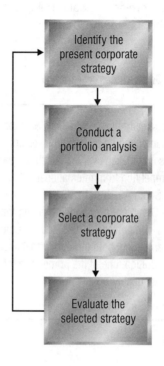

Figure 6.9
The grand strategy selection process

visual way of identifying and evaluating alternative strategies for the allocation of corporate resources. Although many different approaches to portfolio management can be identified, we shall focus only on the Boston Consulting Group Growth/Share Matrix, a widely used approach in this regard.

In the Boston Consulting Group Growth/Share Matrix (or the BCG Growth/Share Matrix), each of an organisation's strategic business units (SBUs) is plotted according to its market growth rate (percentage growth in sales) and relative competitive position (market share). In figure 6.10, the horizontal axis represents the market share of each SBU relative to the industry leader. For example, 0,2 means that the SBU has one fifth of the market share of the industry leader. The vertical axis represents the annual market growth rate for each SBU's particular industry. SBUs are plotted on the matrix once their market growth rates and relative market shares have been computed. Figure 6.10 represents the BCG matrix for a company with multiple SBUs, such as Cullinan Holdings. Each circle represents a business unit. The size of the circle represents the proportion of corporate reserves generated by that SBU.

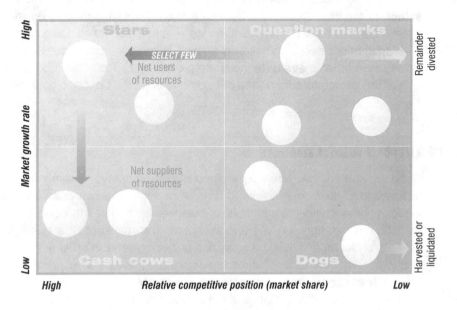

Figure 6.10
The Boston Consulting Group growth/share matrix

On the BCG matrix, businesses are classified as stars, cash cows, question marks and dogs.

Stars are businesses in rapidly growing markets with large market shares. These businesses should be quite profitable. They require substantial investment to maintain their dominant position in a growing market. This requirement is often in excess of what can be generated internally.

If an SBU has a low market growth but a high market share, it often generates a large amount of cash that can be used to support other SBUs, especially question marks. These cash-generating businesses are called **cash cows** because they can be 'milked' for resources to support other businesses. Cash cows are the foundation of the corporate portfolio.

Question marks are high-growth, low-share SBUs that normally require a lot of cash to maintain. Management must decide whether they want to invest additional cash to convert these SBUs into stars or phase them out.

The BCG matrix calls SBUs with a low market share and market growth the **dogs** in an organisation's portfolio. A dog is usually a candidate for divestiture or liquidation. Such an SBU is in a saturated, mature market with intense competition and low profit margins.

If a portfolio analysis is conducted, management should be in the position to **select** a corporate strategy for the corporation. A strategy for dog businesses, for instance, would be to cut on maintenance — a strategy called harvesting.

Management needs to ask and answer several searching questions about its strategies in order to **evaluate** the strategies selected. The most important question is: 'Will the strategies achieve the mission and objectives of our organisation?'

6.6 THE SELECTION OF BUSINESS STRATEGIES

Once the strategy has been determined at corporate level, the managers of each business unit develop their own business strategy. The corporate level strategist views the organisation as a portfolio of business units to be managed in such a way that the organisation survives and prospers. The manager of a business unit or single-product organisation has only one unit to manage. In order to be competitive and to survive, the manager of the business unit develops a business unit strategy, often called a **competitive** or **performance strategy**.

The manager of a business should understand the five forces that determine industry competitiveness (see Porter's model, chapter 3). This should guide the manager in choosing a business strategy.

According to Porter, a business can gain a competitive edge over its rivals in the market by adopting one of the following strategies:

■ overall low-cost leadership
■ differentiation
■ business focus

Business units that adopt an **overall low-cost leadership** strategy attempt to maximise sales by minimising costs per unit and hence prices. Several things can be done to minimise costs. Firstly, as workers gain more experience in producing a particular product, productivity increases and unit costs decrease. This is called a learning curve or experience curve. Secondly, an organisation can expand the size of its operations. As the size of operations increases, the costs per unit decrease because the fixed costs (plant, equipment and others) are shared by a larger number of products. This is referred to as economies of scale. An example of this is the reduction in the price of pocket calculators over the years as a result of economies of scale.

Differentiation is the second generic strategy that distinguishes an organisation's products or services from those of its competitors. The rationale for differentiation is that the organisation can charge higher prices (and make more profit per unit) for a product that customers perceive to be different from similar products offered by rivals. Differentiation may be in terms of quality, the production process, design, reputation or any number of other attributes.

Virgin Atlantic Airways differentiates its service

> Six weeks after Virgin Atlantic Airways' South African debut, the airline achieved a 90 % load factor on its upper class, which is probably a record for any airline embarking on a new route.
>
> The airline differentiates its service by offering, among other things, complimentary chauffeur services to the airline's upper-class passengers in South Africa. Land Rover Discovery vehicles are used for this purpose.
>
> Source: *Business Report*, 20 November 1996, p 6.

The third strategy is to **focus** on a specific product line or a segment of the market that gives an organisation a competitive edge. City Lodge Hotels' focus is on accommodation for the business community.

A business can adopt more than one of the above strategies simultaneously in striving to gain a competitive advantage over other similar businesses.

6.7 BEHAVIOURAL CONSIDERATIONS AFFECTING STRATEGIC CHOICE

The choice of a strategy or strategies at corporate and business levels requires a clear decision that allows an organisation to attain its goals. If an examination of the different strategies identifies a clearly superior strategy, the decision is relatively simple. However, such clarity is the exception, which makes most decisions in this regard judgmental. Several factors influence the decision to implement a specific strategy. We discuss some of the more important factors below.

'A strategy, once initiated, is very difficult to change because organisational momentum keeps it going.' This finding is confirmed by Mintzberg's research, which suggests that **past strategy** strongly influences current strategic choice. The older and more successful a strategy is, the harder it is to replace. Mintzberg also found that, even when a strategy begins to fail because of changes in the business environment, strategists often increase their commitment to that strategy. It seems that, in order to change unsuccessful past strategies, an organisation may have to replace key strategists to lessen the influence of the past strategies on future strategic choices.

Some organisations are extremely dependent on one or more **external factors** such as suppliers, customers or competition. These organisations may have to choose a strategy that they would normally not choose in order to maintain their relationship with specific external factors. A gymnasium offering aerobics and weight-lifting facilities, for example, may have to expand to offer swimming facilities and a miniature running track as well because of the threat posed by health clubs offering a broader range of facilities.

Top management's **attitude to risk** — and more specifically the chief executive officer's attitude — strongly influences strategy selection. Where attitudes favour risk, the range of strategic choices expands; where management is risk-averse, strategic choices are limited, as risky alternatives are eliminated before strategic choices are made. Risk-averse managers also have stronger ties with their past strategy compared to risk-prone managers, who have fewer ties with the past strategy of their organisation.

The **personality** of a manager also affects the choice of a strategy. Kets de Vries[5] argues that the 'inner theatre' of a manager — in other words, the manager's personality — has a direct influence on the choice of a strategy, the corporate culture and even the structure of the organisation.

Pressures from an organisation's **mission**, **objectives** and **culture** heavily influence strategic choice. The mission statement and all objectives have to be analysed to determine whether a specific strategy fits in with the direction and entire set of objectives that management chooses. Furthermore, if a strategy is compatible with the norms and values (culture) shared by management and employees, the likelihood of success is very high.

Virgin Atlantic Airways' culture

> Virgin Atlantic Airlines' Richard Branson joined the United Kingdom's billionaires club with a fortune estimated at $1,64 billion — four times that of Queen Elizabeth.
>
> His aura lingers long after he founded Virgin Atlantic Airways. Branson's values are imprinted on the organisation's managers and employees and systems. His appreciation for the unconventional can even be seen in the creative paintwork on his aeroplanes.
>
> Source: *Business Day*, 14 October 1996, p 1.

The success of an organisation's strategies is also dependent on proper **timing**. A seemingly good strategy may be disastrous if undertaken at the wrong time. A home-building organisation that decides to concentrate on the first-time home owner for the following two years may be detrimentally affected by a sharp increase in interest rates and continuing unrest. The same strategy may be very successful if the organisation decides to hold off entering this market until interest rates and unrest have settled down.

6.8   CONCLUSION

In a stable business environment an organisation is seldom surprised or disturbed by unforeseen changes in the environment. This, however, is hardly the situation that businesses have faced since World War II. Changes in the business environment are almost the only 'stable' aspect of the environment that businesses face today. As a result of the constant changes in the environment, management processes have become more sophisticated. Perhaps one of the most significant improvements in management processes came in the 1970s with increasing emphasis being placed on the assessment of the external and internal environment and on environmental forecasting in order to reconcile organisational resources with threats and opportunities in the environment. This approach is known as strategic planning.

Strategic planning addresses issues such as the formulation of the vision and mission, the assessment of the external and internal environment, the formulation of long-term goals and the choice of a strategy.

To develop an understanding of strategic planning it is important to take note of the different levels of strategy, namely corporate strategy and business strategy. Corporate strategy is the course charted for the total organisation which specifies the businesses the organisation intends to be in. Business strategy determines how best to compete in a particular industry or market.

In order to clarify strategic planning, we discussed this concept as a process, starting with the formulation of an organisation's vision and mission, then assessing the organisational capabilities and threats and opportunities from the external environment and, finally, formulating long-term goals for the organisation. Once these steps have been completed, management is in a position to choose a realistic strategy that can lead to the attainment of the organisation's mission and goals.

We discussed various grand strategies that organisations can implement at corporate level, and the strategy selection process — also at business level.

In the examination of the different strategies, it was evident that a superior strategy seldom comes to the fore, which makes most decisions in this regard judgmental. We therefore also discussed behavioural considerations affecting strategic choice.

6.9   REFERENCES

1. Lipton, M. 1996. Demystifying the development of an organisational vision. *Sloan Management Review*, Summer, pp 83–92.

2. Ibid pp 84–85.

3. *Business Day,* 12 July 1995.

4. Channon, D (ed). 1996. *Strategic Management. The Blackwell Encyclopaedia of Management*, vol II, pp 282–286.

5. Kets de Vries, MFR. 1994. The leadership mystique. *Academy of Management Executives*, vol 8, no 3, pp 73–92.

7 Managerial Decision Making

Key issues

- Types of managerial decisions
- Conditions under which managers make decisions
- The rational model of decision making
- Techniques for improving group decision making
- Quantitative tools for decision making

7.1 INTRODUCTION

Decision making is a central aspect of the planning function. In developing goals, or in planning the future of the organisation, managers at all levels of the organisation are confronted with decisions. In a decentralised organisation (see 'Centralised and decentralised authority' on page 243) most members of the organisation participate in decision making. In contrast, in a centralised organisation, the most important decisions are made by one person. In South Africa, empowerment has become a very important management issue. Empowerment, which means the sharing of power with subordinates, implies that more employees will be involved in decision making in future. Regardless of its goals, an organisation's long-term survival depends on its managers' decision-making skills.

A decision is a choice between two or more options. Mercedes Benz SA is currently facing major decisions. With sales not rising as they should, the company has to decide whether to expand its operations into Africa. Mercedes Benz SA has to consider all viable options before making a final decision. This, indeed, is a daunting task, as the decision should take into account the mission of the organisation, possible changes in the external and internal environment, and many other factors.

Because all planning involves decision making, we will explore the decision-making process as we continue our discussion of the planning function.

Background

> The course of history has been shaped by decisions made over the centuries. Some of these decisions have been good, while others have had horrendous results.
> ■ Christopher Columbus decided to leave Spain on three ships in August 1492. This decision made Columbus the first explorer to travel from Europe to the Americas, which set in motion an avalanche of change.
> ■ The decisions that led to World War II had catastrophic results for countries around the globe.
> ■ The decision to free Nelson Mandela in February 1992 was the first step on the way to a new democratic South Africa.

Focus

> A decision implies that managers are faced with a problem or opportunity. Various courses of action are proposed and analysed, and a choice is made that is likely to move the organisation in the direction of its mission and goals. In making a choice, a manager comes to a conclusion and selects a particular course of action that he or she feels might enhance the success of the organisation. Fortunately, certain principles can be applied to help managers when they are faced with a major decision. We discuss these principles in this chapter, and distinguish between programmed and nonprogrammed decisions. Next, the conditions under which managers make decisions are specified, followed by a discussion of the rational model of decision making. The concept of group decision making and techniques for improving group decision making will also be examined. Finally, we look at quantitative tools for decision making.

7.2 TYPES OF MANAGERIAL DECISIONS

Although managers in large organisations, government offices, hospitals and schools may be separated by background, lifestyle and distance, they must all make decisions involving several options and outcomes. These decisions, however, vary in terms of their content and relative uniqueness. Vodacom's decision to enter into a joint venture with Lesotho Telecommunication Corporation, for example, necessitated extensive investigation of options, as this decision will have far-reaching financial and strategic implications for both organisations. However, if a manager has to decide whether to promote an employee or not, less intensive analysis will be required, since the employee must meet certain criteria to qualify for promotion.

In general, the decisions made by managers are either **programmed decisions** or **nonprogrammed decisions**. Rather than being distinct categories, these types of decisions represent a continuum, with highly programmed decisions at one end and highly unprogrammed decisions at the other.

7.2.1 Programmed decisions

Decisions are programmed to the extent that they are repetitive and routine. In some decisions there are definite methods for obtaining a solution, so that the decisions do not have to be investigated anew each time they occur. The managers of most organisations face large numbers of programmed decisions in their daily operations. Such decisions should be made without spending unnecessary time and effort on them. Examples of programmed decisions include the processing of payroll vouchers in an organisation, the processing of graduation candidates at a university, and processing the admission of athletes to a sports club.

Managers can usually handle programmed decisions by means of rules, standard operating procedures and the development of specific policies (see chapter 5). These enable the decision maker to eliminate the process of identifying and evaluating options and making a new choice each time a decision is required. While programmed decisions do, to some extent, limit the flexibility of managers, they free the decision maker to devote attention to other, more important decisions.

7.2.2 Nonprogrammed decisions

Decisions are nonprogrammed to the extent that they are novel and ill structured. Nonprogrammed decisions have never occurred before, they are complex and elusive and there is no established method for dealing with them. Managers at all levels of an organisation make nonprogrammed decisions. The decision made by the Southern Sun Group to introduce the Holiday Inn Express — its own brand of economy hotel — was a nonprogrammed decision made by top management. Nonprogrammed decisions made by lower management include firing an employee or changing the work-flow procedures in a department. The most difficult managerial situations involve nonprogrammed decisions and require the use of creative problem solving. Techniques to encourage creative problem solving are discussed in sections 7.6 and 7.7.

7.3   DECISION-MAKING CONDITIONS

By identifying the type of decision, as well as the conditions under which it will be made, managers should be in the position to make better decisions. The Southern Sun Group's decision to compete in the economy hotel market was made under the condition of risk. The group had conducted thorough research on the spending pattern of economy hotel users and knew what the probabilities were of attaining an occupancy rate of 80 % at different room rates. What they *were* certain about, was that a long-term loan would cost them 21 % interest and a building loan only 19 %.

From the above discussion it should be clear that management decisions are made under different conditions. These conditions are **certainty**, **risk** and **uncertainty**, and they are depicted in figure 7.1.

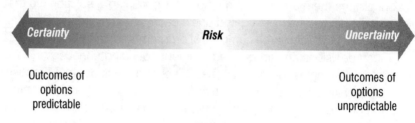

Figure 7.1
Decision-making conditions

7.3.1 Certainty

A decision is made under conditions of certainty when the available options and the benefits or costs associated with each are known. In such situations, there is perfect knowledge about available options and their consequences. No element of change intervenes between the option and its outcome. Under conditions of certainty, managers are faced simply with identifying the consequences of available options and selecting the outcome with the greatest benefit.[1]

As one would expect, managers rarely make decisions under conditions of certainty, because the future is rarely known with perfect reliability. The purchase of a government treasury bill is made under at least near certainty. Barring the fall of the government, R1 000 invested in a treasury bill for one year at 10 % will yield R100 in interest. Knowing that income taxes are due on 15 April, a financial manager can also make decisions under conditions of near certainty.

7.3.2 Risk

A decision is made under conditions of risk when the available options, the potential benefits or costs associated with them, and the probability of their occurrence are known. Decisions under conditions of risk are perhaps most common. Options are already known, but their outcomes are uncertain.[2]

Probability falls into two categories. **Objective probability** is based on historical evidence. It refers to the likelihood that a particular state of things will occur, based on hard facts and figures. Managers cannot be sure that certain events will occur but, by examining past records, they can determine the likely outcome of an event.

The probability of obtaining either heads or tails on the toss of a fair coin is 50 %: the coin is equally likely to land face up or face down. Thus, there is a condition of risk.

In many cases, historical evidence is not available, so a manager must rely on a personal estimate and belief, or **subjective probability**, of the situation outcome. A motorcar manufacturer is thinking about increasing the price of his vehicles. He is trying to determine the effect of a 10 % price increase on the average number of vehicles sold per annum. He might estimate that there is a 30 % chance of sales dropping by 5 %, a 10 % chance of sales dropping by 10 % and a 50 % chance of sales staying the same. Not knowing for certain what will happen to vehicle sales, the manufacturer must decide whether to increase prices at the risk of losing sales.

7.3.3 Uncertainty

A decision is made under conditions of uncertainty when the available options, the probability of their occurrence, and their potential benefits or costs are unknown.

Eskom's decision to investigate a new solar-driven car was made by top management who had to rely solely on 'gut feeling'. They had no trends to analyse in the South African market, no indication of possible success and little experience in the solar industry. Decisions made under conditions of uncertainty are unquestionably the most difficult. In such situations, a manager has no knowledge on which to base an estimate of the likelihood of various outcomes. No historical data are available from which to infer probabilities, or the circumstances are so novel and complex that it is impossible to make comparative judgments. Although managerial intelligence and competence are widely available, the ability to deal with uncertainty is rare. Perhaps the most common occasions for decisions under conditions of uncertainty are those involving the introduction of new technology or new markets, where management has to rely on its 'gut feelings'.[3]

The decision to exclude Francois Pienaar from the Springbok rugby team was made under conditions of uncertainty. Springbok coach André Markgraaff did not know what the reaction of the other Springbok players would be, or what the reaction of the rugby supporters would be. The likely outcome of his new approach to rugby was also unknown.

Table 7.1 gives a summary of decision-making conditions and level of certainty.

Table 7.1
Decision-making conditions and level of certainty

Certainty	Risk	Uncertainty
All alternatives known	Likelihood of alternatives known	Likelihood of alternatives unknown
Each alternative leads to certain outcome	Outcome associated with each alternative known	Outcome associated with each alternative unknown
Decision is a sure thing	Decision is a 'gamble'	Decision requires 'guts'
Complete certainty	**Some uncertainty**	**Complete lack of certainty**
Source: Bedeian, AG. 1993. *Management*, 3 ed. Orlando: Dryden Press, p 203.		

7.4 DECISION-MAKING MODELS

After looking at the type of decision and the conditions under which the decision has to be made, managers also need to look at the two primary decision-making models: the rational model and the bounded-rationality model. In the case of the **rational model** (see section 7.4.1), the decision maker should select the best possible solution. This is known as optimising. In the case of the **bounded-rationality model**, the decision maker uses satisficing — selecting the first option that meets the minimal criteria.

Managers need to know which model to use, and when. They should optimise when they are making nonprogrammed, high-risk decisions in conditions of uncertainty. The steps explained in section 7.4.1 should help in this regard. When managers are making programmed, low-risk or certain decisions, they should select the first option that meets the minimal criteria, in other words, they should satisfice.

7.4.1 The decision-making model

Why did City Lodge Hotels decide to expand into the luxury accommodation business with its Courtyard Suites Hotels while Southern Sun decided on the complete opposite by introducing economy class hotels? Did they follow different decision-making principles?

In most decision situations, managers go through a number of stages that help them think through the problem and develop alternative solutions. Figure 7.2 summarises each step in the normal progression that leads to an optimal decision. Note that these steps are more applicable to nonprogrammed decisions than to programmed decisions. Problems that occur infrequently with a great deal of uncertainty require the manager to utilise the entire process. In contrast, problems that occur frequently with a great deal of certainty are often handled by rules, standard operating procedures and specific policies, making it unnecessary to develop and evaluate alternatives each time these situations arise.

In a nutshell

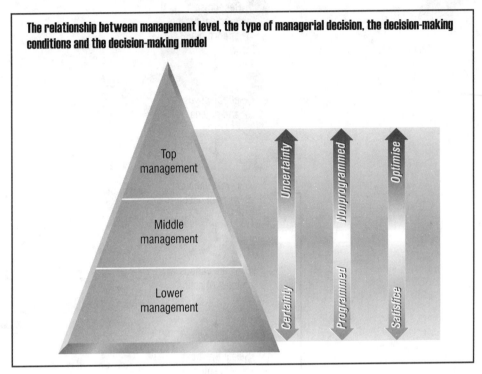

The relationship between management level, the type of managerial decision, the decision-making conditions and the decision-making model

Recognise a problem or opportunity

The first step in decision making is recognising that there is a problem or an opportunity. Recognising problems or opportunities is not as easy as one would expect. For example, a conscientious worker who suddenly starts arriving late at work should not be defined as an 'absenteeism situation'. Being late is a symptom of the problem, not the cause. The cause could be illness, personal problems, a lack of motivation, or something else entirely. Management should recognise and look at the cause. If the situation is incorrectly identified or defined, any decisions made will be directed towards solving the wrong problem.

Set objectives and criteria

Generally, in programmed decisions, steps 2 to 5 need not be followed as criteria have been set for these decisions. The criteria can be found in policies and such like. However, in the case of nonprogrammed decisions, no objectives or criteria have been set. The manager will be responsible for this task. He or she can make an individual decision or involve a group in decision making (see sections 7.5 and 7.6).

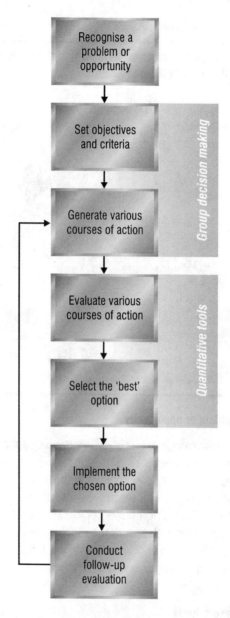

Figure 7.2
The decision-making process/model

The objective should state what the decision should accomplish (see Sappi example above). If the marketing manager resigns, a new manager should be appointed. The objective would be to hire a marketing manager before 31

December. The required criteria would include a marketing degree and at least five years' experience in a specific industry.

To realise Sappi's objective of becoming the number one producer of wood-free coated papers, management was confronted with different options. Top management decided to
- acquire a 75 % share in SD Warren, the world's largest producer of wood-free coated papers
- modernise and upgrade facilities in southern Africa, the United Kingdom and Germany.

Source: Sappi Annual Report, 1995, p 2.

Generate alternative courses of action

Once a problem or an opportunity has been recognised and objectives and criteria have been set, the next step is to identify various courses of action to deal with the situation. Bear in mind that it is impossible to identify all available options. However, a systematic effort should be made to identify as many courses of action as possible.

Innovation and creativity play a major part in generating various courses of action. Using groups to generate solutions could enhance this process (see sections 7.5 and 7.6). The availability of information (chapter 8) and technology should also be considered.

The number of available options identified is limited by certain constraints, mainly time and money. Rarely do managers have enough time or money to identify, let alone evaluate, an unlimited number of options. Indeed, there may be times when doing something immediately may be more important than taking a different action at a later date. Managers should often balance time and expense against identifying additional options. During this stage managers need to decide whether they want to consider all options and optimise their decision (rational model) or search only until a 'satisficing' option (bounded rationality) has been reached.

Evaluate various courses of action

Once various courses of action have been identified, the next step is to evaluate the options. Each option should be evaluated in terms of its strengths and weaknesses, advantages and disadvantages, benefits and costs. Because each option is likely to have both positive and negative features, most evaluations involve balancing anticipated consequences. The evaluation of options may be intuitive or may use a more scientific approach. Some of these approaches are discussed in section 7.7.

Selecting the 'best' option

In the previous two steps, options were identified and evaluated. The next step is to select the 'best' option. This step calls for the careful evaluation of each option by a manager against the objectives and criteria set during the second stage, with a view to ranking the options in order of priority. In practice, selecting an option is often subjective. The manager's experience, values, internal politics and so on influence this choice (see section 6.6).

Implement the chosen option

Once an option has been selected, appropriate actions should be taken to ensure that it is properly implemented. A decision is only an abstraction and needs to be 'put into action'. It is possible for a 'good' decision to be damaged by poor implementation, while a 'poor' decision may be helped by good implementation. Therefore, implementation may be just as important as the actual activity of selecting an option.

Decisions should be explained in such a way that all the relevant parties understand them. Those concerned should understand not only the logic behind a decision, but also what they are supposed to do. A suitable organisational structure, good leadership, a strong organisational culture and fair reward system will enhance the implementation of decisions.

Conduct follow-up evaluation

Once a decision has been set in motion, evaluation is necessary to provide feedback on its outcome. Adjustments are invariably needed to ensure that actual results compare favourably with planned results — as determined in step 2 of the decision-making process.

The process of evaluation closes the feedback loop shown in figure 7.2. The soundness of a decision may be evaluated against planned results. If necessary, modifications can be made and further options identified and evaluated. This should be seen as an opportunity for acquiring new knowledge to improve future decisions.

Decision-making characteristics of black South African executives

- Black executives are conservative risk-takers who rely on past experiences and work within existing parameters.
- They give attention to detail, and the quality of the final decision, while valuable in itself, does slow down their decision making.
- They favour professional, well-considered decisions over the quick and opportunistic.

AMROP. 1996. *The South African Executive: The Challenge of Diversity*. Rosebank: AMROP International, pp 5–19.

7.5   GROUP DECISION MAKING

Stages 2 and 3 of the decision-making process, namely the setting of objectives and criteria and the generation of optional courses of action, rely heavily on creativity and innovation. Group decision making can enhance this process, especially in the case of nonprogrammed decisions where there is usually a great deal of uncertainty about the outcome. The complexity of many of these decision-making situations requires specialised knowledge in a number of fields. Southern Sun's decision to become involved in the economy class hotel business was such a complex decision that the

Group decision making among the Zimbabwean Shona people

Group decision making is an integral framework for resolving and deciding matters at the *family unit* and *community level* among the indigenous people of Zimbabwe. The process entails a collective, transparent and consultative approach undertaken through a *dare/indaba* (forum/setting). The *dare/indaba* is a goal-oriented gathering of all relevant people at a specific place and time to consider the pertinent issue(s). (Matters for consideration include, at community level — communal resource allocation, intercommunity disagreements; and family unit level — marriage, death, family assets, etc.)

The decision-making process is underpinned by the notion of idea sharing and consultation embodied in idioms like *zano marairanwa* (ideas/decisions need to be shared) and *zano ndega akasiya jira mumasese* (lone decider makes costly decisions). The *dare/indaba* process follows a clear protocol whereby designated persons (mostly junior or a designated person) set the motion by publicly informing the gathering of the purpose of the meeting by way of addressing the elders (through informing next up in seniority who in turn does the same until the message gets to the most senior and the response follows the same communication route). Similarly questions and answers by members of the audience to and from the elders follow the same 'formal' protocol largely through probing and detailed elaboration of key issues and exploration or delineation of symptoms and causes of the issue/problem(s).

The final decision on what has to be done, depending upon the issue at hand, is supposed to be explicated through the participative question and answer process, otherwise alternative solutions — bar the selection — is a collective effort. However, tradition renders the ultimate decision making to the elders who have to reconcile the selected decision(s) with generally accepted traditional values, beliefs and norms, in particular upholding the principle *hunhu-ubantu* (oneness and moral standards).

In essence, the decision-making process embodies a collective, participative and transparent process, guided by the experience and wisdom of elders.

Source: Tamangani, Z. 1997. Interview on 12 February.

strategic planning department had to share its vision of the group with many other experts. The financial manager had to forecast, among other things, the possible return on investment; the marketing manager had to explain the possible reaction of clients to this new product; and the operations manager had to give input on the layout of the hotels.

Whether groups make better decisions than individuals working alone has been the topic of extensive discussion. Groups are subject to social processes when making decisions. These processes include social conformity, the level of communication skills, dominance by a specific group member, and so on. While groups make better decisions than the average group member, their decisions consistently fall short of the quality of decisions made by the best individual member.[4] However, group decision making has certain advantages and disadvantages. The advantages of group decision making are as follows:[5]

- A variety of skills and specialised knowledge can be used to define and solve a problem or recognise an opportunity.
- Multiple and conflicting views can be taken into account.
- Beliefs and values can be transmitted and aligned.
- More organisation members will be committed to decisions, since they have participated in the decision-making process.

Group decision making, on the other hand, also has some potential disadvantages:[6]

- It may be more time consuming.
- It may lead to feeble compromises.
- It may, conversely, lead to more risky decisions.
- It may inhibit creativity.

Group decision making in South Africa

Ubuntu places great importance on working for the common good, as captured by the expression: 'Umuntu, Nqumintu, Ngalantu', literally translated: A person is a person through other human beings; I am, because you are, because we are.

Source: Khoza, R. 1993. The need for an Afrocentric approach to management, in Christie, P, Lessem, R & Mbigi, L. 1993. *African Management*. Randburg: Knowledge Resources.

White South African leaders, on the other hand, strive for individual success, often at the price of harmonious interpersonal relationships.
The above calls for sensitivity from both parties to accommodate the different viewpoints and work out acceptable solutions to problems.

Source: AMROP. 1996. *The South African Executive: The Challenge of Diversity*. Rosebank: AMROP International, p 18.

In what follows, we examine techniques for improving group decision making.

7.6 TECHNIQUES FOR IMPROVING GROUP DECISION MAKING

To overcome the disadvantages and to capitalise on the advantages of group decision making, various techniques have been suggested to make group decision making more creative. In this section, a small selection of the many techniques available will be presented. These techniques are **brainstorming**, the **nominal group technique**, the **Delphi technique**, and **group decision support systems** These techniques are illustrated in figure 7.3.

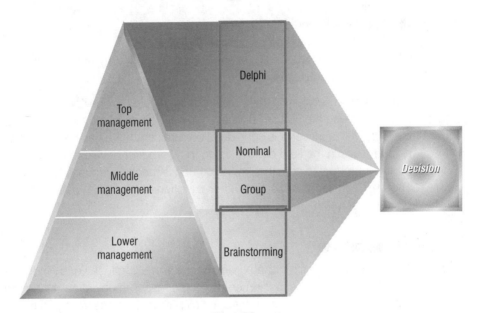

Figure 7.3
Group decision-making techniques
(This figure indicates where the different techniques are mainly used. However, the techniques can be used at any management level.)

7.6.1 Brainstorming

One of the problems of decision-making groups is that over time group norms develop and group members tend to conform to dominant group opinions. As a result, the creativity of a decision-making group declines after having peaked early in the forming of the group (see chapter 16).

Brainstorming is a technique used to stimulate creative or imaginative solutions to organisational problems. Group participants informally generate as many ideas as possible without evaluation by others. This prohibition should lower the barriers to contributions from members who are particularly shy, have divergent ideas or have low status within the group. During idea generation, group members are encouraged to build on, but not criticise, ideas produced by others. This cross-fertilisation is assumed to produce a synergistic effect. The object is to generate as many ideas as possible in the belief that the greater the number of ideas, the greater the likelihood of one outstanding idea emerging.

The following four rules govern brainstorming sessions:[7]

■ Criticism is prohibited. The judgment of the creative or imaginative solutions to organisational problems should be withheld until all the solutions have been generated.

■ Imaginative solutions are welcome. The wilder and more 'far out' the solution, the better.

■ Quantity is important. The greater the number of solutions, the greater the likelihood that there will be an outstanding one.

■ The combination of various solutions and the improvement of suggested solutions are encouraged.

Brainstorming sessions usually last from 30 minutes to one hour. A one-hour session is likely to generate 50 to 150 ideas. Typically, most of the ideas will be impractical, but a few will merit serious consideration. Brainstorming has been used with encouraging results in the field of advertising, new product development, and so on.[8]

It is important to note that brainstorming is merely a process for generating ideas. The next two techniques go further by offering methods of actually arriving at a preferred solution.

7.6.2 Nominal group technique

This technique is a structured group decision-making technique. The nominal group technique restricts discussion or interpersonal communication during the decision-making process. Group members are all physically present, as in a traditional committee meeting, but members operate independently.

A problem is usually presented with the following steps taking place:

■ Seven to ten members meet as a group. Before any discussion takes place, each member independently writes down his or her ideas on the problem.

■ The group leader systematically gathers information from all participants. Each member presents one idea to the group. No discussion takes place until all the ideas have been recorded.

■ The ideas are clarified through a guided discussion.

■ The group leader then instructs participants to vote on their preferred solutions.

■ Each member silently and independently ranks the ideas.

■ The process may conclude with an acceptable solution.

The nominal group technique is appropriate for situations in which groups may be affected by a dominant person, conformity or 'group think' because it minimises these effects.

7.6.3 Delphi technique

Decisions often have to be made by experts in different geographical areas. In this case neither brainstorming nor the nominal group technique can be used, as both techniques require the presence of participants. The Delphi technique is a decision-making technique that does not require the physical presence of the participants. Iscor Ltd, which exports 47 % of its iron and steel products, could use the technique for technological forecasting by involving its managers in Pretoria, Vanderbijl Park and Newcastle to project the next computer breakthrough and its effect on the industry.

Background

> **Origin of the Delphi technique**
> This technique gets its name from Delphi, a place that was famous before the time of Christ as the seat of the most important temple of the Greek god Apollo. Kings and other powerful rulers from all over the ancient world came to Delphi to consult with Apollo through his priestesses, whom they believed could foretell the future.

The Delphi technique involves using a series of confidential questionnaires to refine a solution. In this technique the group's members never meet face to face.

The following steps characterise the Delphi technique. Firstly, the problem is identified and members are asked to provide potential solutions through a series of carefully designed questionnaires. Secondly, each member anonymously and independently completes the first questionnaire. Thereafter, the results of the first questionnaire are compiled at a central location, transcribed and reproduced. Each member then receives a copy of the results. After viewing the results, members are again asked for their solutions. The results typically trigger new solutions or cause changes in the original position. The last two steps are repeated as often as necessary until consensus is reached.

Brainstorming, the nominal group technique and the Delphi technique should not be seen as competing choices, but as complementary techniques.

7.6.4 Group decision support systems

Group decision support system (GDSS) is a generic term used to refer to various kinds of computer-supported group decision-making systems. Most of the GDSSs can be used to support face-to-face groups as well as groups that communicate through electronic media.

The process of brainstorming can be supported by sophisticated computers, called **electronic brainstorming**. In an electronic brainstorming session, the participants have at their disposal networked work stations. Instead of contributing their ideas in a round-robin fashion, they simply type in their suggestions. These ideas are disseminated to the other group members without an identifying mark. Thus anonymity is preserved and the group members can react more freely than in a conventional brainstorming session.

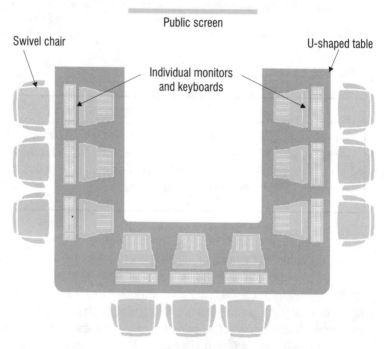

Figure 7.4
Typical GDSS configuration for a face-to-face meeting

Figure 7.4 depicts another example of a group decision support system, namely the **electronic meeting**. This technique blends the nominal group technique with sophisticated computer technology. Group members sit around a horseshoe-shaped table, empty except for a series of computer terminals. Issues are presented to participants and they type their responses onto a computer screen. Individual comments, as well as aggregate votes, are displayed on a projection screen in the room. Electronic meetings can be as much as 55 % faster than traditional face-to-face meetings.

In a **real-time Delphi**, a computer conference is substituted for the mail questionnaires of the conventional Delphi. This allows participants to respond immediately to the comments anonymously entered by the other members of the group. In this way the time required to complete the Delphi is much reduced.[9]

In deciding which of the techniques to use for improving group decision making, management should consider issues such as time and/or money costs, the potential for interpersonal conflict, commitment to the solution, and many more. In general it can be said that top management commonly uses the Delphi technique for a specific decision. Brainstorming and the nominal group techniques are frequently used at middle and lower management level where work groups are involved.

7.7   QUANTITATIVE TOOLS FOR DECISION MAKING

Another way for managers to improve their planning and decision-making skills, is by using various quantitative tools. Many of these techniques have their origin in the quantitative management school (see chapter 2) and propagate the use of mathematical relations in solving management problems.

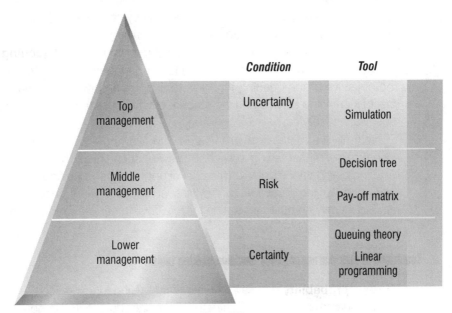

Figure 7.5
Conditions of decision making and decision-making tools

Our objective in this section is to make you aware of these techniques — not to make you a mathematician. For the same reason, we will use the dominant structure used in this part of the book as a basis for our discussion (see section 7.3). The conditions of decision making, namely certainty, risk and uncertainty, will guide our discussion. Figure 7.5 will serve as the point of reference for our discussion in this section.

7.7.1 Conditions of certainty: decision-making tools

Linear programming

Of all the quantitative tools identified, linear programming is perhaps the most frequently and extensively used. It is a quantitative tool for optimally allocating scarce resources among competing uses to maximise benefits or minimise losses. The resources in question may be human, financial, physical or informational.

The so-called 'travelling salesman' problem is a classic linear programming application. The problem is to determine the shortest or least costly route for a salesperson to travel to visit a set list of cities. The salesperson must visit each city only once, never retrace any steps, and return to the starting city. Linear programming is capable of determining which route is the shortest or least costly to follow.

Queuing theory

South African Airways introduced self-check-in systems for its passengers travelling with hand luggage only to avoid unnecessary waiting in check-in lines. The decision-making tool management used to reach this decision is called **queuing theory**.

The queuing theory is a quantitative tool for analysing the costs of waiting lines. The objective of the queuing theory is to achieve an optimal balance between the cost of increasing service and the amount of time individuals, machines or materials must wait for service.[10]

Not only are there costs associated with allowing a waiting line, but also costs associated with increasing service to prevent such lines. The problem is to determine the best balance between the cost of upgrading service and the amount of time users of a service must wait in line. In such situations, the queuing theory can be used to identify an optimal solution for maximising service while minimising costs.

7.7.2 Conditions of risk and uncertainty: decision-making tools

The term **probability** refers to the estimated likelihood, expressed as a percentage, that an outcome will occur. Southern Sun, in introducing its economy hotels, could have determined — objectively or subjectively — what the probabilities were of an 80 % occupancy rate under conditions of high inflation versus conditions of low inflation. Management could then compare this outcome to an alternative course of action. This alternative could be to rather invest in the renovation of its current hotels. A mathematically calculated answer should indicate the value (in rands) of each alternative to management.

There are two complementary approaches to using probability analysis, namely **pay-off matrices** and **decision trees**. Both are among the most helpful quantitative tools available to a manager.

The pay-off matrix is a technique for indicating possible payoffs, or returns, from pursuing different courses of action. Each option is pursued under different states of nature, or circumstances beyond the control of the decision maker.[11]

Table 7.2

Pay-off matrix showing alternative pay-offs

Alternatives	States of nature (level of inflation)	
	Low	**High**
Economy hotel	R12 m	R5 m
Refurbishment	R6 m	R3 m

Table 7.2 shows the possible pay-offs to the Southern Sun Group from pursuing each alternative under the two levels of inflation. As indicated in the pay-off matrix, if the Southern Sun Group becomes involved in economy hotels under a low level of inflation, anticipated revenues will be R12 m. If the Southern Sun Group becomes involved in refurbishment under a high level of inflation, anticipated revenues will be R3m. The anticipated revenues can now be used in a decision tree.

A decision tree is a graphic illustration of the various solutions available to solve a problem. It is designed to estimate the outcome of a series of decisions. As the sequence of the major decision is drawn, the resulting diagram resembles a tree with branches.[12]

The expected value of becoming involved in the economy hotel business is R7,8 million (according to figure 7.6). This is higher than the R4,2 million expected value of refurbishing existing hotels. Management would therefore opt for the first alternative, namely becoming involved in the economy hotel business.

Simulation is a quantitative tool for imitating a set of real conditions so that the likely outcomes of various courses of action can be compared. These methods involve constructing and testing a model of a real-world phenomenon. South African Airways use simulators to train and retrain pilots. These simulators are particularly useful for solving complex problems such as the failure of one of a Boeing 747's engines on take-off. It is too costly and dangerous to expose each South African Airways pilot to these conditions. Pilots are exposed to real-life situations but on a manageable scale.

In business, simulation can be used with mathematical models to predict the possible outcomes of investment and pricing decisions, proposed inventory control systems, assembly-line scheduling routines, various design specifications and various competitive strategies. Organisations are making increasing use of computers to run business simulations. This allows managers to save time and money and brings more information to those who use it, allowing them to make better decisions.

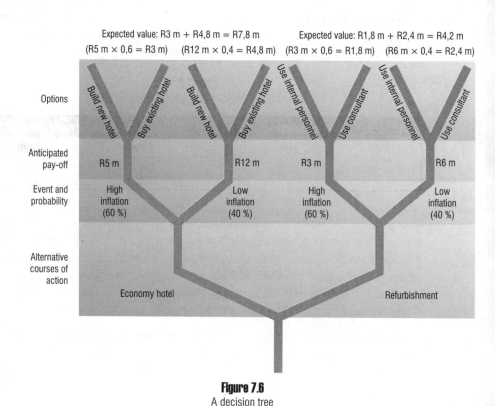

Figure 7.6
A decision tree

7.8   CONCLUSION

In its narrowest sense, decision making can be defined as the process of choosing between various courses of action. Decision making can be classified by its relative uniqueness. Programmed decisions are those decisions that are made by habit or policy and involve simple, common, frequently occurring problems. Nonprogrammed decisions deal with unusual or novel decisions and require creative thinking. This chapter is mainly concerned with nonprogrammed decision making.

Managers usually make decisions under conditions of certainty, risk or uncertainty. Under conditions of certainty, all available options and the benefits and costs associated with each are known. A decision is made under conditions of risk when the available options, the probability of their occurrence and the potential benefits or costs associated with it are known. Decisions under conditions of risk are perhaps most common. A decision is made under conditions of uncertainty when the available options, the probability of their occurrence, or their potential benefits or costs are unknown. Decision making can be seen as a process, starting with the recognition of a problem or opportunity. The other steps in this process are the setting of objectives and criteria, the generation of various courses of action, the evaluation of these courses of action, the selection of the best option, the implementation of the chosen option and follow-up evaluation.

To overcome the disadvantages and to capitalise on the advantages of group decision making, various ways of making group decision making more creative have been suggested. Techniques discussed in this chapter are brainstorming, the nominal group technique, the Delphi technique and group decision support systems.

Lastly, quantitative tools for decision making were discussed, namely linear programming, queuing theory, pay-off matrix, decision trees and simulations.

7.9 REFERENCES

1. Bedeian, AG. 1993. *Management*, 3 ed. Orlando: Dryden, p 202.
2. Ibid p 203.
3. Ibid p 205.
4. Brown, R. 1988. *Group Processes: Dynamics Within and Between Groups.* Oxford, UK: Blackwell.
5. Noorderhaven, N. 1995. *Strategic Decision Making*. New York: Addison-Wesley, p 107.
6. Ibid pp 107–108.
7. Bedeian op cit p 220.
8. Ibid.
9. Noorderhaven op cit p 208.
10. Bedeian op cit p 224.
11. DuBrin, AJ. 1994. *Essentials of Management*, 3 ed. Ohio: South-Western, p 142.
12. Ibid p 149.

8 Information Management

Key issues

■ The link between decision making and information systems
■ Definition of an information system
■ The basic components of an information system
■ Classification of information systems
■ Steps in developing an information system

8.1 INTRODUCTION

In the introductory discussion of general management, we learnt that the managerial functions of planning, organising, leading and controlling are supported by supplementary activities such as decision making and communication. In the discussion in the previous chapters one thing is clear: managers are constantly feced with situations that require them to make decisions. In decision making, management relies on a steady stream of information on what is happening in and beyond an organisation. Only with accurate and timely information can managers monitor progress towards their goals and turn plans into reality. If managers cannot stay on track — anticipating potential problems, developing the skills to recognise when corrections are necessary, and making appropriate corrections or adjustments as they progress — their work may be fruitless and costly.

In the late 1940s, Herbert A Simon popularised the notion that management was primarily a decision making process. He later received the Nobel prize in economics for his work on managerial decision making. He argued that all managerial activities involve conscious or unconscious selection of particular actions. In many cases, the selection process consists simply of an established reflex action or habit. In other cases, the selection is the product of a complex chain of activities. He suggested that for any decision there are numerous possible solutions, any of which may be selected. By the decision-making process, the possible options are narrowed down to the one that is selected.

Background

> The modern computer has many origins. Early manual computing devices and the use of machinery to perform arithmetic operations were important advancements. The earliest data-processing devices included the use of fingers, stones and sticks for counting, and knots on a string, scratches on a rock, or notches in a stick as record-keeping devices. The Babylonians wrote on clay tablets with a sharp stick, while the ancient Egyptians developed written records on papyrus using a sharp-pointed reed as a pen and organic dyes for ink. The earliest form of a manual calculating device was the *abacus*. Pebbles or rods laid out on a lined or grooved board were early forms of the abacus and were used for thousands of years in many civilisations. The abacus originated in China and it is still in use as a calculator.
>
> The introduction of machinery to perform arithmetic operations is frequently attributed to Blaise Pascal of France and Gottfried von Leibnitz of Germany who developed the *adding machine* and the *calculating machine*, respectively, in the 17th century. The calculators of Pascal and Von Leibnitz — and other early mechanical data-processing devices — were not reliable machines. The contributions of many persons were necessary over the following centuries before practical, working data-processing machines were developed.
>
> Source: O'Brien, JA. 1991. *Introduction to Information Systems in Business Management*, 6 ed. Homewood, Ill: Irwin, p 26.

Essential to the process of narrowing down options is **information** — which is provided by an organisation's **information system**. The quality of the decision is related to the quality of the information, whereas the quality of the information depends on the accuracy with which data are gathered, coded, processed, stored and presented. These are the main elements of an information system. Managers at all levels are finding that computer-based information systems provide the information necessary for effective decision making.

Focus

> The purpose of this chapter is to introduce and provide an overview of information management. As a manager, you need to understand the uses of information systems in today's business environment. We discuss the fundamental concepts of information systems, examine ways in which information systems can support managerial activities and classify information systems. Lastly, we also discuss the development of an information system.

8.2   THE LINK BETWEEN DECISION MAKING AND INFORMATION

In chapter 3, the external and internal environments in which the organisation operates were discussed. An information system transforms data from an organisation's
external and internal environments into information that can be used by managers in
the decision-making process (see figure 8.1).

The Southern Sun Group did intensive research into executives' spending patterns with regard to accommodation before deciding to introduce its economy class
hotels. The decision was guided by information on trends in the external environment, such as rises in interest rates and new entrants into the accommodation
industry. Information on the capabilities of the Southern Sun Group (internal environment) confirmed that the decision capitalised on the organisation's strengths.

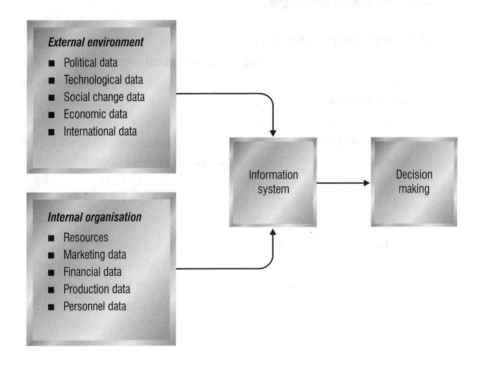

Figure 8.1
The relationship between an organisation's information system and decision making
Source: Adapted from Bedeian, AG. 1993. *Management.* Orlando: Dryden, p 598.

The environment in which management must operate today is becoming more
complex than ever before. This has an impact on managerial decision making, discussed in chapter 7. Decision making today is more complicated than it was in the
past. Firstly, the number of available options is much larger today than ever before,

owing to improved technology and communication systems. Secondly, the cost of making errors may be excessive, owing to the complexity and magnitude of operations, automation, and the domino effect of an error in other parts of the organisation. By the same token, the benefits may be numerous, if correct decisions are being made.[1]

Because of these trends and changes, it is extremely unwise to rely on a trial-and-error approach to decision making. Managers need to become more sophisticated — they must learn how to manage the information in their fields.

In what follows, we focus on information systems that support managerial decision making in organisations.

8.3   WHAT IS AN INFORMATION SYSTEM?

8.3.1   A definition of an information system

We tend to use the terms **data** and **information** interchangeably, although there is a definite distinction between the two concepts. Data are **raw, unanalysed numbers and facts** about events from which information is drawn. The operating income of Engen Limited for 1993 was R578 million and for 1994 R547 million.[2] Information is **processed data** that are relevant to a manager. In the case of Engen Limited, the given data can be processed into information. The financial manager can calculate a drop in operating income of 5,4 %. He may also conclude that the changes in the regulatory framework and restructuring changes in the company were the major causes of the decline.[3]

Management information is information that is timely, accurate and relevant to a particular situation. Management information enables management to establish what should be done in a specific situation. The drop in operating income of Engen Limited can be seen as management information, since it implies immediate action: management should ascertain how operating income can be increased in the next financial year.

A **system**, as defined in chapter 1, is a number of interdependent components or entities that form a whole. These components are linked and interact in such a way that they achieve a goal.

An **information system** can now be defined as the people, procedures and other resources used to collect, transform and disseminate information into an organisation. Stated differently, an information system is a system that accepts data resources as input and processes them into information products as output.

8.3.2 The basic components of an information system

An information system utilises hardware, software and human resources to perform the basic activities of input, processing, output, feedback, control and storage. This is illustrated in figure 8.2.

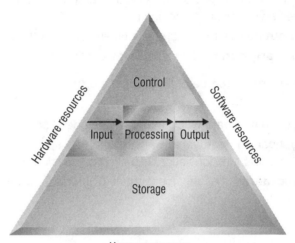

Figure 8.2
An information system model
Source: Adapted from O'Brien, JA. 1990. *Management Information Systems: A Managerial End User Perspective*. Homewood: Ill: Irwin, p 19.

Information systems receive data as **input**. The Edgars Group receives data on the sales in its 545 stores in southern Africa. The information system needs to **process** this data by organising and analysing it in a meaningful way to provide information as **output** to managers. Managers in the Edgars Group would like to know the sales realised by each of the 545 stores, the previous month's sales versus current sales, the average income of customers, and so on. The information, and not the data, should enable management to make decisions. This information must then be stored. **Storage** refers to the activity whereby data and information are retained for subsequent use. Edgars could use magnetic tapes, computer disks or other means of storage for this purpose. Finally, an information system provides **feedback** on its activities in order to determine whether the system meets established performance standards.

Information systems include certain resources that contribute to their information-processing activities. **Hardware resources** is a broad term to denote the physical components of a computer system. The four main categories of computer system components are the following:[4]

■ **input devices**, such as keyboards, optical scanning devices and magnetic ink character readers which allow one to communicate with one's computer

■ a **central processing unit** (CPU), which consists of electronic components that interpret and execute the computer program's instructions. The CPU can be seen as the 'brain' of the computer

■ **output devices**, for example, printers, audio devices and display screens

■ **auxiliary storage**, for example, magnetic disks and tapes, and optical disks.

Software resources are the programs or detailed instructions that operate computers. These include:[5]

■ **system software** which manages the operations of a computer

■ **application software** which performs specific data-processing or text-processing functions such as a word-processing package or a payroll program

■ **procedures** that are the operating instructions for users of an information system.

The various types of CPU chips

In the personal computer (PC) world people often categorise computers by the model of CPU chips they contain, saying things like 'I have a 386' or 'My computer is a 486'. The CPU chips currently used in PCs include the 8088 at the low end, 80286, 80386, 80486 and, at the high end, the Pentium — the generation after the 486 — and the P6. People usually omit the first two digits when referring to 80286, 80386 and 80486 chips. If someone tells you they have a 486 computer, they mean an IBM-type computer with a 80486 chip. (You can tell it's an IBM computer or clone because they're the only computers that use 80486 chips.) In the Macintosh world, people distinguish between models that contain the new Power PC chips and those that contain one of the 68000 series chips by Motorola.

Source: Biow, L. 1996. *How to Use Your Computer*. Emeryville, Cal: Z D Press, p 24.

Human resources refer to resources required for the operation of an information system and include specialists and end users. **Specialists** are people who develop and operate information systems, such as systems analysts, programmers and computer operators, while **end users** are people who use the information produced by a system. Managers are end users.

8.4 CLASSIFICATION OF INFORMATION SYSTEMS

Information systems perform operational and managerial support roles in organisations. Figure 8.3 provides a conceptual classification of information systems into two categories: *operations* and *management* information systems.

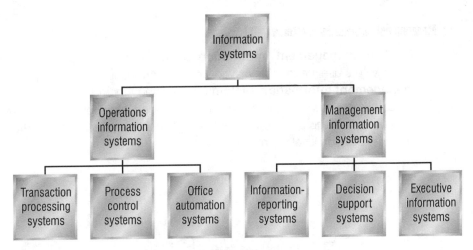

Figure 8.3
The classification of information systems
Source: Adapted from O'Brien, JA. 1991. *Introduction to Information Systems in Business Management,* 6 ed. Homewood, Ill: Irwin, p 46.

8.4.1 Operations information systems

The purpose of operations information systems is to support business operations. These systems process data generated by and used in business operations. The major categories of these systems and the roles they play are as follows:

■ **Transaction processing systems (TPS)** record and process data resulting from business transactions, such as sales, purchases and inventory changes. They produce a variety of documents and reports for internal and external use. They also update the data bases used by an organisation for further processing by its management information system.

■ Operations information systems can make routine decisions that **control physical processes**. Edgars Stores may implement an automatic inventory reorder system. Reordering then becomes a programmed decision. Decision rules outline the actions to be taken when the information system is confronted with a certain set of events. Information systems in which decisions adjusting a physical production process are automatically made by computers are called **process control systems (PCS)**

■ Office automation systems (OAS) transform traditional manual office methods and paper communications media. These systems support office communication and productivity. Instead of using typewriters to produce customers' monthly accounts, Edgars Stores can use word-processing systems. Other examples of office automation applications are electronic mail, desktop publishing and teleconferencing.

8.4.2 Management information systems (MIS)

The term **management information systems** has several popular meanings. Many writers use the term as a synonym for information systems. In this text we use **management information systems** to describe a broad class of information systems, the goal of which is to provide information on and support for decision making by managers. Figure 8.4 illustrates the relationship between management information systems and levels of management.

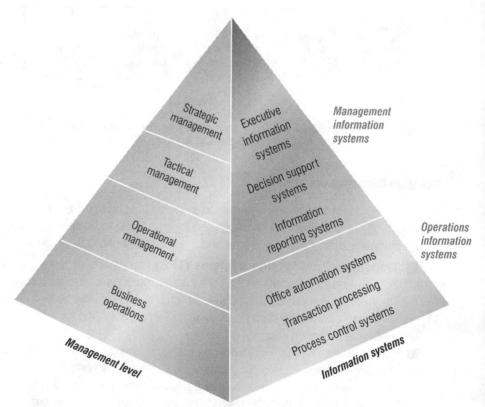

Figure 8.4
The relationship between management information systems and levels of management
Source: O'Brien, JA. 1991. *Introduction to Information Systems in Business Management,* 6 ed. Homewood, Ill: Irwin, p 49.

Management information systems support the decision-making needs at the operational, tactical and strategic levels of management.

At the **operational level**, structured decisions mainly occur, and management information systems process transactions as they occur in order to update internal records and provide reports and documents. Edgars Stores captures the details of each sale at the cash registers. Customers are provided with a receipt of the transaction. At the end of the day, summary records are produced and orders are electronically transmitted to suppliers to replenish inventories of certain goods.

At the **tactical level**, decisions are semistructured, and middle managers receive results from the operational level. At this level information is needed on important matters such as problems with suppliers, abrupt sales declines, or increased consumer demand for a particular product line. In addition, middle managers also access data from external sources to support their own planning and control activities.

At the **strategic level**, decisions are unstructured. Top management needs information from internal and external sources which is used to gauge the organisation's strengths and weaknesses, as well as market opportunities and threats. Information on the financial performance of the organisation is derived from internal sources and is needed by top management to make sound financial decisions. Management needs information on quarterly sales and profits, on other relevant indicators of financial performance (such as share value), on quality levels, on customer satisfaction and on the performance of competitors. Information from external sources is more difficult to obtain and computerise than is internal information. Top management needs information on interest rates, possible changes in tax laws, the latest technological breakthroughs, substitute products, and other variables (see chapter 2).

Providing information and support for managerial decision making at all levels of management is a complex task. Several major types of information systems are needed to support a variety of managerial end-user responsibilities. These types of management information systems are indicated in figure 8.3 and are information-reporting systems, decision support systems and executive information systems.

Information-reporting systems (IRS)

Information-reporting systems provide managerial end users with the information reports they need for making decisions. These systems access data bases on internal operations containing information previously processed by transaction-processing systems. Data on the external environment are obtained from external sources. A sales manager of Edgars Stores could receive instantaneous visual displays at his or her work station on the sales of a particular product or product line, or weekly sales analysis reports evaluating sales by product, product line or branch.

Decision support systems (DSS)

Decision support systems are a natural progression from transaction-processing systems and information-reporting systems. They are computer-based information systems that provide interactive information support to managers during the decision-making process. Decision support systems use (1) analytical models, (2) specialised data bases, (3) the decision maker's own insights and judgment, and (4) an interactive, computer-based modelling process to support the making of semistructured and unstructured decisions by the individual manager. Electronic spreadsheets and other decision support software allow a managerial end user to receive interactive responses to ad hoc requests for information posed as a series of 'what-if' questions. When using a DSS, managers are exploring possible options and receiving tentative information based on different sets of assumptions.

When Edgars Stores wanted to introduce the new Oshkosh range for kids, a DSS could be used to assist managers in making pricing, sales effort, promotion, advertising and budgeting decisions for the new product line. A DSS produces sales forecasts and profitability estimates using internal and external data on customers, competitors, retailers, and other economic and demographic information.

Executive information systems (EIS)

Executive information systems are management information systems tailored to the strategic information needs of top management. The goal of computer-based executive information systems is to provide top management with immediate and easy access to information on the organisation's critical success factors — that is, the factors critical in accomplishing the organisation's strategic objectives. Executives of Edgars Stores would consider the group's promotion efforts and product line mix as factors critical to its success and survival.

8.4.3 Other classifications of information systems

Several major categories of information systems provide more unique or broad classifications than those just mentioned. That is because these information systems can support business operations as well as managers at the operational, tactical or strategic levels of an organisation. Examples are expert systems and business function information systems.[6]

Expert systems (ES)

When an organisation has a complex decision to make or problem to solve, it often turns to experts for advice. These experts have specific knowledge and experience in the problem area. They are aware of the alternatives, the chances of success, and the costs the organisation may incur. Organisations engage experts for advice on matters such as equipment purchases, mergers and acquisitions, and advertising strategy. The more unstructured the situation, the more specialised and expensive the advice is. Expert systems are an attempt to mimic human experts.

Typically, an expert system is a decision making and/or problem-solving package of computer hardware and software that can reach a level of performance comparable to — or even exceeding that of — a human expert in some specialised and narrow area. It is a branch of applied artificial intelligence (AI). The logic behind expert systems is simple. Expertise is transferred from the human to the computer. This knowledge is then stored in the computer and users call on the computer for specific advice as needed. The computer can make inferences and arrive at a specific conclusion. Then, like a human consultant, it advises nonexperts and explains the logic behind the advice.[7]

The application of expert systems in business

> American Express uses an expert system to assist its credit authorisation staff in sorting through data from up to 13 data bases. Because American Express must review cardholder credit history and authorise the purchase each time a cardholder makes a large purchase, response time is crucial. With an expert system, the credit review and authorisation take only seconds. These systems permit an expert's knowledge to be available in many locations at once.
>
> Source: Bedeian, AG. 1993. *Management.* Orlando: Dryden, p 602.

Expert systems are used today in thousands of organisations and they support many tasks. Their capabilities can provide organisations with improved productivity levels and increased competitive advantages.

Business function information systems

Information systems directly support the business functions of accounting, finance, human resource management, administration, purchasing, marketing and opera-

In a nutshell

> Information systems can be classified as either *operations or management information systems.* Examples of operations information systems are transaction-processing systems, process control systems and office automation systems. Examples of management information systems are information-reporting systems, decision support systems and executive information systems. However, some information systems cannot be classified as either operations or management information systems, because they may support operations, management or strategic applications. Examples of these are expert systems and business function information systems.

tions management. Such business function information systems are needed by all business functions. For example, marketing managers need information on sales performance and trends provided by marketing information systems. Financial managers need information on financing costs and investment returns provided by financial information systems.

8.5 DEVELOPING AN INFORMATION SYSTEM

Most managers are not information system specialists. However, they are information system users in line and staff departments, such as accounting, operations, marketing, purchasing, and so forth. Their performance will, in part, depend on the quality of the information systems support available. It is therefore imperative for end users to manage the development efforts of information systems specialists to ensure that the system meets their information requirements.

An information system is usually conceived, designed and implemented through a systematic development process in which end users (managers) and technical staff design systems based on an analysis of the specific information requirements of an organisation or departments in an organisation. In this way, a systems development life cycle emerges, as illustrated in figure 8.5. All the activities involved in the development cycle are closely related and interdependent, with the result that several development activities can, in practice, occur at the same time.

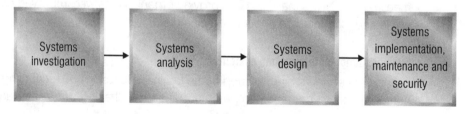

Figure 8.5
The information systems development life cycle

8.5.1 Systems investigation

The first step in the information systems development life cycle is to determine the nature and scope of the need for information. If the need is incorrectly or incompletely defined, the entire process could address the wrong issues.

Management at Tavistock Collieries Limited may need information on its annual coal sales to different buyers to establish its contribution to the JCI Group earnings. Management has to define this need clearly so that the systems specialist knows which systems to utilise to generate the information.

Since the developing process may be costly, systems investigation frequently requires a preliminary study, known as a **feasibility study**, to be conducted. The purpose of the feasibility study is to evaluate different systems, to analyse the costs and benefits of each option and to propose the most feasible system for development. A feasibility study therefore determines the information needs of prospective users and the objectives, resource requirements, cost benefits and feasibility of proposed projects. The findings of a feasibility study are usually formalised in a written report and submitted to management for approval before development begins.

8.5.2 Systems analysis

Systems analysis involves many of the activities used when a feasibility study is conducted, but is a more in-depth study of end user information requirements. Systems analysis, firstly, involves a study of the information requirements of an organisation and its end users. Managers at Tavistock Collieries Limited should state clearly that they need information on the millions of tons of coal sold to Eskom, export sales and inland sales. They should also state that they need to compare Tavistock's contribution to the JCI Group earnings for the last five years.

The second step in systems analysis is to understand the current system that is to be improved or replaced, and to determine the importance, complexity and scope of the problem at hand. Much of this phase involves gathering information on what is being done in this regard, why it is being done, how it is being done, who is doing it and what major problems have developed.

The third step is to determine the system requirements for a new or improved information system. This requires an end user's specific information requirements and the information processing capabilities required for each system activity to meet these information needs. Management at Tavistock could specify to the systems specialist that they want the information in bar chart form and they want only top management to access the information on their own personal computers.

8.5.3 Systems design

Whereas systems analysis describes **what** a system should do to meet the information requirements of end users, systems design specifies **how** a system will accomplish this objective. The systems specialist plays the major role because the area being focused on is seldom one in which management plays an active part. Systems design involves logical and physical design activities.[8] **Logical design activities** involve the development of a logical model of the proposed system. A logical data flow diagram is used to depict the system, its procedures and flow of information graphically. **Physical design activities** entail the process of developing specifications for a proposed physical system. This process includes the design of report layouts, screens and input documents, forms and physical file structures. The design specifies what types of hardware, software and human resources are needed.

Once the proposed system has been designed, it is implemented.

How Nedbank uses information technology to gain competitive advantage

Nedbank is the only bank currently offering secure full-service banking via the Internet, called Netbank. Netbank gives 24-hour access to accounts for non-cash transactions via a personal computer and modem. The facility can be used by any Nedbank account holder registered with an Internet service provider. Netbank offers the following facilities: balance enquiries; transfers between linked accounts; payment of third-party accounts; cheque book orders; PIN changes; statements; foreign exchange rates; and other menu-driven transactions.

Using the Internet for banking facilities gives Nedbank a competitive advantage. It offers Nedbank account holders advantages such as:

■ Convenience: bank from home or office, night or day.

■ Ease of use: the system displays clear instructions.

■ Affordability: a minimal subscription fee of R22,80 per month to access Netbank.

■ Security: access only when PIN is entered, no need to carry cash around or send cheques by post.

■ Independence: print your own mini- or full statement via your personal computer and printer.

■ Time-saving: no need to queue, complete transaction forms, travel or find parking.

8.5.4 Systems implementation, maintenance and security

The **systems implementation** phase involves acquiring hardware and software, developing software, testing programs and procedures using both artificial and live data, developing documentation and carrying out a variety of other installation activities. Systems implementation also involves the training of end users and operating personnel.

Systems maintenance involves monitoring, evaluating and modifying or enhancing a system once it is up and running. It includes a post audit, which establishes whether a system satisfies the system specifications and how efficiently the system investigation activities were conducted.

Systems security is an issue that must be addressed in the design and implementation stages. At Tavistock, only top management should have access to data pertaining to coal sales to Eskom, export sales and inland sales. This is confidential information which Tavistock's competition (for example Australia, Indonesia and China) could use to outperform Tavistock.

As users of information systems, managers have a major role to play during the systems investigation, systems analysis and — to a lesser extent — systems design phases. Lack of end user involvement in systems development almost certainly guarantees the failure of an information system because it will not satisfy the requirements of the organisation.

8.6   CONCLUSION

Computer-based information systems play a vital role in the operations, management and strategic success of organisations. Information systems transform data obtained from an organisation's external and internal environments into information that can be used in decision making.

An information system uses the resources of hardware, software and people to perform input, processing, output, storage and control activities that transform data resources into information products. Data are first collected for processing (input), then manipulated or converted into information (processing), stored for future use (storage), or communicated to the ultimate user (output) according to the correct processing procedures (control).

Conceptually, information systems can be classified as either operations or management information systems. **Operations information systems** process data generated by and used in business operations. The major categories of such systems are transaction-processing systems, process control systems and office automation systems.

Management information systems describe a broad class of information systems, the goal of which is to provide information and support decision making by managers. Types of management information systems needed to support a variety of managerial end user responsibilities include information-reporting systems, decision support systems and executive information systems.

Several major categories of information systems provide more unique or broad classifications than operations information systems and management information systems. Examples are expert systems and business function information systems.

An information system is usually conceived, designed and implemented through a systematic development process comprising the following steps: systems investigation, systems analysis, systems design, systems implementation, maintenance and security.

8.7   REFERENCES

1. Turban, E. 1993. *Decision Support and Expert Systems,* 3 ed. New York: Macmillan, p 8.
2. The Johannesburg Stock Exchange. June/August 1995, p 151.
3. Ibid.
4. Bedeian, AG. 1993. *Management*, 3 ed. Orlando: Dryden, pp 602–606.
5. O'Brien, JA. 1991. *Introduction to Information Systems in Business Management,* 6 ed. Homewood, Ill: Irwin, p 20.
6. Ibid p 51.
7. Turban op cit pp 16–18.
8. Schultheis, R & Sumner, M. 1995. *Management Information Systems: The Manager's View.* Homewood, Ill: Irwin, p 623.

Part 3

. . . .

The Organising Process

Part 3

The following chapter

9 Organisation Design

Key issues

■ 'Organising' in the management sense of the word
■ How organising fits in with the other functions in the management process
■ Designing the structure of an organisation
■ The uses and limitations of the various kinds of structures

9.1 INTRODUCTION

In part II the planning process was discussed in great detail. However, plans need to be put into action or, in other words, implemented.

For plans to be implemented, someone must **perform** the necessary tasks to attain the organisation's objectives. Management must determine an effective way of combining and coordinating tasks and people. It must set objectives and support them with strategies, procedures, people and other resources. Leading and controlling, it will be shown, are also crucial in ensuring that people perform tasks effectively. However, organising is the function most visibly and directly concerned with the systematic coordination of the many tasks of the organisation and, consequently, the formal relationships between the people who perform them.

Organising is the process of creating a structure for the organisation that will enable its people to work together effectively toward its objectives.

Organisation refers to the result of the organising process.

The process of organising consists of assigning to the relevant departments and jobs the work necessary to achieve the objectives, and then providing the necessary coordination to ensure that these departments and jobs fit together. In a small enterprise or a small department this task is not very difficult — it is usually a matter of deciding what tasks need to be done, and allocating them to various subordinates. In large enterprises, however, the process of organising may become quite complex. It involves dividing the work of the organisation, allocating it logically to divisions, departments and sections, delegating authority, and establishing coordination, communication and information systems to ensure that everyone is working together to achieve the objectives of the organisation.

The task of dividing up the work, allocating responsibility, establishing chains of command, and so on, is referred to as the **design of the organisation structure**. An **organisation structure** may be defined as **the basic framework of formal relationships among responsibilities, tasks and people in the organisation**. A typical way of illustrating an organisation structure is by means of an organisation chart. This is a graphic representation of how an organisation is put together. It shows, among other things, authority and communication relationships between jobs and units. A simplified organisation structure for a property developer is depicted in figure 9.1.

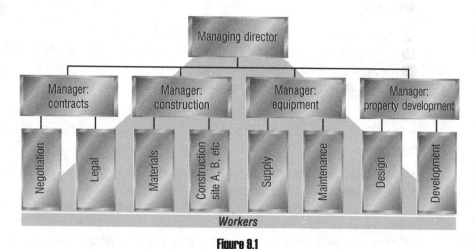

Figure 9.1
A simplified organisation structure for a property development company

Each divisional manager, such as the manager of contracts in the figure above, is responsible for several departments, which in turn may be headed by a manager with his or her subordinates. Under the construction manager, for example, there could be several managers in charge of different construction sites.

Focus

In this chapter the focus is on issues pertaining to the design of an organisation structure, such as the one depicted in figure 9.1. More specifically, we focus on:
■ the reasons for organising
■ the design of an organisation
■ the basic principles of organising
■ factors influencing organisation design

9.2   REASONS FOR ORGANISING

Organising is an indispensable function in the management process. Plans devised and strategies formulated will never become reality if human and other resources are not properly deployed and the relevant activities suitably coordinated. Leadership is not possible if lines of authority and responsibility are not clear. Likewise, control is out of the question if people do not know what tasks they are responsible for.

More specifically, organising is necessary for the following reasons:

- Organising leads to an organisation structure that indicates clearly who is responsible for what tasks. It therefore clarifies subordinates' **responsibilities**.
- **Accountability** implies that the responsible employees will be expected to account for outcomes, positive or negative, for that portion of the work directly under their control. Accountability links results directly to the actions of an individual or a group.

Background

> Accountability has its roots in the classical management theories (see chapter 2), in the division of labour into parts, and in explicit job specifications. Consistent with Taylor's scientific management, and with the norms of fairness, employees in organisations are deemed accountable for that portion of the work under their direct control.

- Clear **channels of communication** are established. This ensures that communication is effective and all information required by employees to perform their jobs effectively reaches them through the correct channels.
- Organising helps managers to **deploy resources** meaningfully.
- The principle of **synergy** enhances the effectiveness and quality of the work performed.
- The total **workload is divided into activities** to be performed by an individual or a group of individuals.
- Organising means systematically **grouping** a variety of tasks, procedures and resources. This is possible because the organising process also entails in-depth analysis of the work to be done, so each person is aware of his or her duties.
- The related tasks and activities of employees are **grouped** together meaningfully in specialised sections or departments so that experts in various fields can deal with certain tasks.
- The organisation structure is responsible for creating a mechanism to **coordinate** the entire organisation.

All the above-mentioned reasons for organising direct the organisation towards attaining its goals. The different alternatives in organisation design will now be discussed.

9.3   THE DESIGN OF AN ORGANISATION

Organisation design is the decision-making process in which managers construct an organisation structure appropriate to the strategies and plans of the organisation, as well as the environment in which the strategies and plans must be carried out.

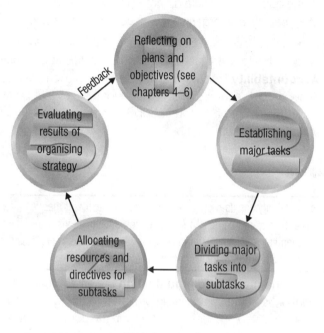

Figure 9.2
Five main steps of the organising process
Source: Certo, SC. 1994. *Modern Management*. Boston: Allyn & Bacon, p 215.

The five main steps in the organising process, depicted in figure 9.2, are (1) reflecting on objectives and plans, (2) establishing major tasks, (3) dividing major tasks into subtasks, (4) allocating resources and directives for subtasks, and (5) evaluating the results of the implemented organising strategy. As the figure implies, managers should continually repeat these steps. Through repetition they obtain feedback that will help them improve the existing organisation structure.

The example of the property development company illustrates how the organising process or the process of designing an organisation structure might work.

As depicted in figure 9.2, management would initiate the organising process by reflecting on the development of the organisational objectives and plans. Because planning involves determining how the organisation will attain its objectives, and organising involves determining how the organisation's resources will be used to activate plans, management must start to organise by understanding planning. The objectives and plans of the property development company may, for example, include the following:

■ A plan to increase its share of the lower-income housing market, thereby exploiting the opportunities created by the RDP in the new South African environment. This could entail the creation of a separate department to implement this plan, or it could mean a reorganisation of the company's present contracts and construction departments.

■ A plan to focus more on the market for luxury homes, in line with the present trend in South Africa to construct security villages adjacent to golf courses. In this case the company needs a department dealing with town planning, the provision of township services, the design of the township and the marketing thereof.

■ A plan to tender for the construction of large office buildings in the upmarket areas of South Africa's major cities. This could mean a restructuring of the construction division to facilitate building office blocks in different regions.

The possibilities are endless, but management cannot even start to design an organisation structure without reflecting on the mission, objectives and plans (strategies) of the organisation.

The second and third steps of the organising process focus on tasks to be performed within the management system. The manager of the property company must designate major tasks or jobs to be performed within the company. Such tasks may include the negotiation of construction contracts or the task of constructing houses or office buildings. The tasks must then be split up into subtasks. For example, constructing houses might include the procurement of building materials besides the physical construction of the houses.

The fourth step in the organising process is to determine who will be in charge of construction, who will procure building materials and who will execute the building of the houses. The details of the relationship between the individuals involved must be spelt out.

In the fifth step, the manager evaluates the results of a particular organising strategy, and gathers feedback on how well the implemented organising strategy is working. This feedback may furnish information that could be used to improve the existing organisation structure.

There is, however, a vast body of knowledge which underlies the steps in designing an organisation, and a knowledge of the fundamentals of organisation design — or the basic principles of organising — is important.

9.4   THE BASIC PRINCIPLES OF ORGANISING

Much has been written about the principles underlying the design of an organisation. However, most of the principles can be grouped into the following four categories:

1. principles involving the **division of work** or how to divide the total workload into tasks that can logically and effectively be performed by individuals or groups
2. principles which have to do with the **organisation structure** — this refers to reporting lines in the organisation
3. principles which have to do with combining tasks in a logical manner — the grouping of employees and tasks is generally referred to as **departmentalisation**
4. principles concerning **coordination** — this involves setting up mechanisms for integrating the activities of individuals and departments into a coherent whole.

These principles will be discussed in the sections that follow.

9.4.1   The division of work

The basic principle underlying organising is that of **specialisation**; a task is broken up into smaller units in order to take advantage of specialised knowledge or skills to improve productivity. The best example of specialisation or division of work is still the **assembly line**, usually attributed to the inventive mind of Henry Ford. This pioneering concept opened the way to mass production, which had a profound effect on Western societies in the early decades of this century. The division of a task into smaller units, however, means that the various units have to be coordinated, which makes organising indispensable.

> The principle of specialisation or division of labour is generally ascribed to Adam Smith. In his famous work *An Enquiry into the Wealth of Nations*, he describes how specialisation is applied in a pin factory to increase productivity. One man unrolls the wire, another straightens it, a third cuts it, a fourth sharpens the tip, and so on. In that way, says Smith, ten men can produce 48 000 pins a day, while one man on his own can make only 20 a day!
>
> Source: Smith, A. 1960. *The Wealth of Nations*. New York: JM Dent, p 5.

The way in which the principle of work specialisation evolves in an organisation can be illustrated by means of a hypothetical case study, such as the one in figure 9.3.

Suppose a young carpenter decides to set up his own small construction company. First, he tenders on a few alterations and, with the help of one or two labourers,

Phase 1
The single entrepreneur

Building, negotiation, bookkeeping,
design (owner-manager)

Phase 2
The small business

| Building, negotiation, design (owner-manager) | Bookkeeper (part-time) |

Phase 3
The growing business

Phase 4
The large organisation

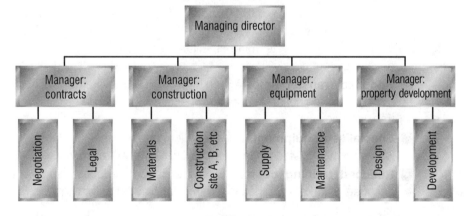

Figure 9.3
The evolution of specialisation

does the building work and carpentry himself. He also negotiates contracts, buys the materials and does his own bookkeeping. Because of the quality of his work, the business soon grows too big for him to do all these things himself. He then obtains the services of a part-time bookkeeper who relieves him of some of the workload. At this stage, as phase 2 in the figure shows, he is beginning to specialise. As the business grows, he builds homes and schools and is compelled, in phase 3, to get somebody to help him with the negotiation of contracts. At the same time he also hires someone to help him manage the different construction sites, and the part-time bookkeeper is appointed full time so that the owner can devote more of his time to the general management of his business. Eventually, he arrives at phase 4, at which point his business is becoming a large organisation. At this stage he has to consider an organisational structure (see section 9.4.3) which will enable him to attain his goals.

The growth of the business, as depicted in figure 9.3, is characterised by two developments in particular:

1. the total task load of the organisation increases
2. there is constant pressure to split up the total task into smaller units

Put differently, the growing organisation is continually compelled towards specialisation or the division of work. Besides this evolutionary pressure towards specialisation, there are other reasons that justify specialisation.

The following are examples:

■ **Individual ability.** If an individual concentrates on one task, he or she acquires a certain degree of skill in that area, and can perform that task as a specialist quicker and better than anybody else, with obvious advantages for the business. South Africa currently has thousands of unskilled workers. Unskilled workers employed by, say, a knitting factory manufacturing all the knitwear for Edgars and Woolworths, could benefit a great deal from specialisation. By specialising in one task, like the steaming of knitted items, an employee not only personally develops a certain skill, but also becomes an asset to the organisation.
■ **Reduced transfer time.** A worker who does several jobs loses time when switching from one job to another. Specialisation eliminates such nonproductive transfer time.
■ **Specialised equipment.** Specialisation leads to the development of specialised equipment, which increases the productivity of each worker.
■ **Reduced training costs.** Division of labour reduces the cost of training, because a worker is trained in a particular part of the total task.

Increased productivity is the main purpose of specialisation. Although specialisation has traditionally been applicable mostly at operational level, it is increasingly becoming applicable at managerial levels too.

However, excessive specialisation may have a negative effect on productivity. It is argued that the extreme division of labour focuses on efficiency and economic benefit to the detriment of the human variable. Work that is extremely specialised tends to be boring and production rates may therefore go down. Clearly, it is necessary to strike a balance between specialisation and motivation.

Specialisation in the African society

> Skill specialisation begins at an early age in the African society, continues through life and is passed on to future generations. This is achieved through approaches which combine mentoring, coaching, hands-on training and apprenticeship programmes. Special skills developed through these processes include those of traditional healers, hunters, traditional musicians, blacksmiths, builders, beer-brewers, farmers, and so on. The specialists take great pride in their trades, which are much valued within their communities.
>
> The strong preference for specialisation runs directly counter to the new management approach of multiskilling employees. South African managers need to be very sensitive to the preferences of their employees and not follow international trends slavishly.
>
> Source: Tamangani, Z (consulting editor). 1997. Personal interview, Unisa.

9.4.2 The organisation structure

In any organising effort, managers must choose an appropriate organisation structure. **Structure** refers to designated relationships between resources of the management system. Its purpose is to facilitate the use of each resource, individually and collectively, as the management system attempts to attain its objectives. Organisation structure is represented primarily by means of a graphic illustration called an **organisation chart**. Traditionally, an organisation chart is constructed in pyramid form, with individuals close to the top of the pyramid having more authority and responsibility than individuals lower down. The relative positioning of individuals within boxes on the chart indicates broad working relationships, and lines between boxes designate formal lines of communication between individuals.

Figure 9.1 is an example of an organisation chart. The triangular area shaded grey is not part of the organisation chart but serves to illustrate its pyramid shape. The positions nearest to the property development company's managing director have more authority and responsibility while the positions further away have less authority and responsibility. The positioning of boxes indicates broad working relationships. For example, the positioning of the construction manager over the materials and site managers indicates that he has authority over them and is responsible for their performance. The lines between the materials and site managers and the managing director indicate that formal communication between them must go through the construction manager.

Two basic types of structure exist within management systems: formal and informal structures. **Formal structure** is defined as the relationships between organisational resources as outlined by management. It is represented primarily by the organisation chart, as in figure 9.1.

Informal structure is defined as the pattern of relationships that develops because of the informal activities of organisation members. It evolves naturally and tends to be moulded by individual norms, values or social relationships. In essence, informal structure is a system or network of interpersonal relationships that exists within, but which is usually not identical to an organisation's formal structure. Although it is omitted from the formal structure, it affects decisions within it. For example, during a busy period or a crisis, one employee may turn to another for help rather than go through a manager. Informal structures or relationships help organisation members to satisfy their social needs and get things done.

The design of an organisation is also influenced by **underlying forces**. And that is the reason for the continuous change and evolution of an organisation's structure. Figure 9.4 illustrates this evolution. These forces refer to the following:

1. **The way managers perceive the organisations and organisational problems.** Naturally, background, training, knowledge, experience and values influence the manager's perception of how the formal structure should exist or be changed. Suppose two young engineers start an engineering organisation. The organisation grows rapidly and soon they are forced to employ more people. Because they have been in charge of all the activities in the organisation and have been trained as engineers and know all the current projects, they will probably still want all the new employees to report to them directly.
2. **The task itself may influence the structure.** Forces in the task include the degree of technology involved in the task and the complexity thereof. As task activities change, a force is created to change the existing organisation. The organisation structure of a road construction company like LTA will be different to the organisation structure of a partnership of medical doctors. In LTA, the organisation structure will reflect the fact that different projects are running at the same time. The medical doctors' tasks are complex and cannot be delegated. This will greatly influence organisation structure.
3. **Forces in the environment.** These include the customers and suppliers of the organisation, and existing political and social structures which may change and impact on the organisation's structure. Forces in the environment of South African organisations include the political and social changes in the country. Black people are becoming more affluent. Coca Cola SA previously targeted whites as its target market, but the strategy has changed in order to increase market share in the black population sector. This strategy forced the organisation

to empower black managers and supervisors, which had an influence on the structure of the organisation, as participative management became more important.

4. **The needs and skills of subordinates.** These also impact on the organisation structure. Unskilled labourers, like the labourers working in the gardens of the City Council of Pretoria, need a lot of supervision and this will influence the structure of the organisation in that there will be more levels of management.

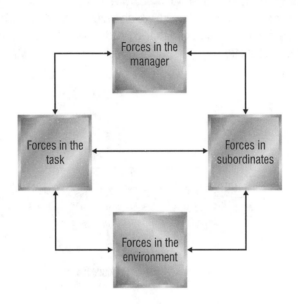

Figure 9.4
Forces influencing the evolution of organisation structure
Source: Certo, SC. 1994. *Modern Management: Diversity, Quality, Ethics and the Global Environment*, 6 ed. Boston: Allyn & Bacon, p 223.

9.4.3 Departmentalisation

The next principle underlying organising is the formation of departments. This is a result of specialisation, on the one hand, and promotes specialisation, on the other, as necessitated by the logical grouping of activities that belong together. The reasons for departmentalisation are inherent in the advantages of specialisation and the pressure in a growing business to split up the total task of management into smaller units. As soon as a business has reached a given size, say, phase 4 in figure 9.3, it becomes impossible for the owner-manager to supervise all his employees, so that he finds it necessary to create new managerial positions according to departments which are based upon a logical grouping in manageable sizes of the activities belonging together.

The various departments created constitute the organisation structure of the business as they appear on the organisation chart. By considering factors such as the size of an organisation, the kind of business and the nature of its activities, various organisation structures can be developed through departmentalisation.

Let us discuss some of the basic forms of organisation.

1. **The functional organisation structure**, as shown in figure 9.5, is the most basic structure, in which the activities belonging to each management function are grouped together. One set of activities, for example, comprises advertising, market research and sales, which belong together under the marketing function, while those concerned with the production of goods are grouped under the production function.

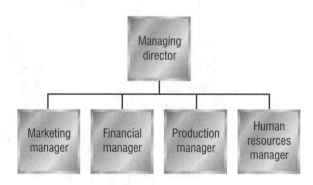

Figure 9.5
A functional organisation structure

2. **Product departmentalisation** is illustrated in figure 9.6. Departments are designed in such a way that all activities concerned with the manufacturing of a specific product or group of products are grouped together in product sections. This means that all the specialists associated with particular products are grouped together in product sections. The rationale for this structure is that the marketing, financing and personnel needs involved in the production of, say, diesel engines will differ considerably from those in the manufacture of cigarettes. The organisation structure of the Barlow Group is illustrated below. Note that this organisation is departmentalised according to products.

   This is a logical structure for large organisations providing a wide range of products or services. The advantages of this structure are that the specialised knowledge of employees is used to maximum effect, decisions can be made quickly within a section, and the performance of each group can easily be measured separately. The disadvantages are that the managers in one particular section concentrate their attention almost exclusively on their particular products and tend to lose sight of those of the rest of the organisation. In addition, the administrative costs increase, because each section has to have its own functional specialists, such as market researchers and financial experts.

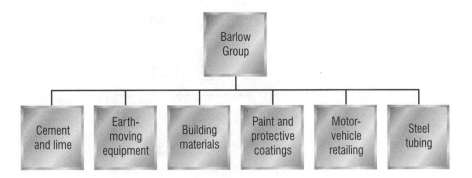

Figure 9.6
Departmentalisation according to product

3. **Location departmentalisation** is illustrated in figure 9.7. This is a logical structure for a business manufacturing and selling its goods in different geographical regions — for example SA Breweries, which operates and markets its range of products all over the country. This structure gives autonomy to area managers, which is necessary to facilitate decision making and adjustment to local business environments. This structure is also suitable for a multinational business because each country in which the multinational operates, will be culturally unique and will have to be approached differently.

Figure 9.7
Departmentalisation according to location

4. **Customer departmentalisation** is appropriate when a firm concentrates on a particular segment of the market or group of consumers, or, in the case of industrial products, where the firm sells its products to only a limited group of users.

Figure 9.8 illustrates this structure. The structure has the same advantages and disadvantages as departmentalisation according to product and location.

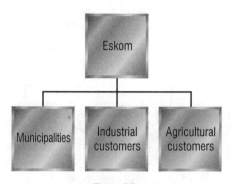

Figure 9.8
Departmentalisation according to customer

Unlike a functional structure in which activities are grouped according to knowledge, skills, experience or training, a structure based on product, location or customers in some respects resembles a small privately owned business. It is more or less autonomous in action, and is accountable for its profits or losses. However, unlike an independent small business, it is still subject to the objectives and strategies of the whole organisation.

City Lodge Hotels departmentalised

> The management structure of City Lodge Hotels Limited is departmentalised according to function, namely financial director, operations director, marketing manager and purchasing manager. The financial function is departmentalised according to function in the lower levels. The operations and marketing functions are departmentalised according to product (City Lodge, Town Lodge, Courtyard and Road Lodge). The property development manager fulfils a staff function. Figure 9.9 illustrates this structure.

9.4.4 Authority relations

In the previous sections we discussed the process of task distribution. We said that it includes subdividing the total task of the organisation into smaller specialised units and allocating these units to certain departments and persons. But this is not the end of the task of organising. The allocation of tasks to sections and members of staff also entails the allocation of **responsibility** and **authority** to each post in an organisation structure. This entails the creation of organisational relations — that is, stipu-

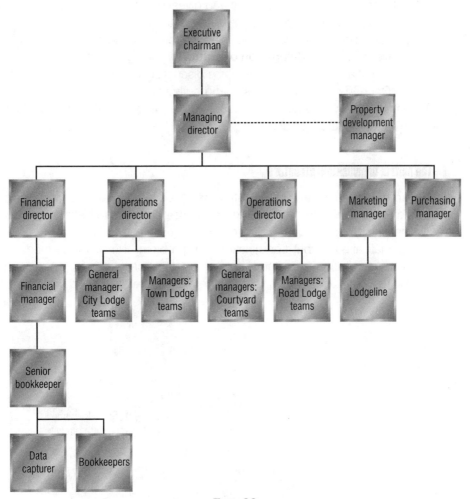

Figure 9.9
City Lodge Hotels Limited

lating the persons from whom a subordinate receives instructions, to whom he reports or to whom and for what he is accountable.

Responsibility is a particular **obligation** or commitment on the part of a manager (especially middle or lower) or, to a more limited degree, a subordinate, to carry out a task in accordance with the instructions received. This also means that a subordinate should be able to account for what he or she has done.

Authority, on the other hand, is the right to **command or to give orders**. It also includes the right to take action to compel the performance of duties and to punish default or negligence. In the formal organisation structure, several examples of which have already been discussed, the owners of an organisation possess the final authority. They appoint directors and give them authority, and the directors appoint managers, who in turn, assign limited authority to subordinates, and in this way authority flows down along the line. This formal authority passed downwards from above is known as **delegation of authority**. Delegation may be viewed as the main source of authority. This point will be discussed in greater detail in chapter 10.

Once the allocation of tasks and authority has been completed, management has to design an organisation structure that will enable the various jobs to be done in a coordinated fashion.

9.4.5 The matrix organisation structure

No organisation structure, whether designed according to function, product, location or customer, will necessarily meet the organisational needs of a particular organisation. If departments are formed according to function, there is sophisticated specialisation — but coordination is a problem. If they are formed according to product, location or customer, certain products or regions may be successful while the rest of the organisation may not reap the benefits of good organising.

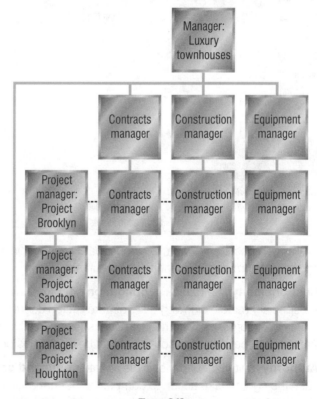

Figure 9.10
The matrix organisation structure

To overcome these problems, which occur mainly in large organisations and in those handling specific projects, the **matrix organisation structure** has been created to incorporate the advantages of various organisation structures into one. As indicated in figure 9.10, this means that the horizontal (staff) and vertical (line) authority lines occur in the same structure so that project managers (horizontal) and functional managers (vertical) both have authority.[1]

This organisation structure is particularly suited to ad hoc and complex projects requiring specialised skills. For example, the property developer in figure 9.10 created a matrix structure for the development of luxury townhouses, and disbanded the team on completion of the contract. In other businesses, the matrix structure may be permanent, for example, a car manufacturer that continually develops certain models as projects. The major advantage of the matrix structure is that specialist project managers can help manage complex projects while the advantages of functional specialisation are retained. The disadvantage of this structure is division of authority — both project leader and departmental head can exercise authority over the same subordinates. The unit of command is affected, and there is a serious risk of soured relations between the project and functional executives. Also, it places subordinates who have to satisfy two bosses in a difficult position.

9.4.6 Network departmentalisation

Network structures describe the interrelationships between different organisations. This is a method of organising that temporarily ties together the resources required to achieve specific tasks.[2] In a network structure, the business will typically maintain small central headquarters, while contracting other organisations to perform specific tasks, such as marketing, manufacturing or public relations. An illustration of a hypothetical network structure is shown in figure 9.11. The following three types of network organisations can be distinguished:[3]

1. **Internal networks.** These networks arise to capture entrepreneurial benefits. In this case the organisation owns most or all of the assets associated with the particular business. Managers are encouraged to operate their units according to demands and prices in the marketplace. These managers are expected to constantly seek innovations to improve performance. If these organisational arrangements are carried to the extreme, the parent organisation will play the role of broker, as shown in figure 9.12. The corporate headquarters become a holding company that maintains an interest in a wide variety of specialised businesses.

    An example of this is Denel, which has 19 divisions and subdivisions, managed as different business groups. Each of the divisions is encouraged to sell its services internally as well as on the open market. Figure 9.12 shows Denel Insurance Company (Pty) Ltd, an insurance broker; OTB, which offers in-flight performance measurement; the Business Development Group, which offers

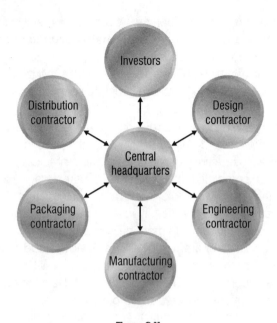

Figure 9.11
Network departmentalisation
Source: Bedeian, AG. 1993. *Management*, 3 ed. Orlando: Dryden Press, p 251.

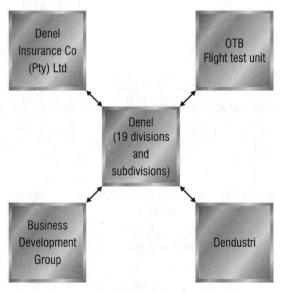

Figure 9.12
Internal network

management and business consultancy services; and Dendustri, which sells excess manufacturing capabilities to external industry.

2. **Stable networks.** These networks employ partial outsourcing and inject flexibility into the system. In a stable network, assets are owned by several organisations but dedicated to a particular business. BMW is organised as a stable network. Any part of a BMW is a candidate for outsourcing and 55 to 75 % of total production costs at BMW come from outsourced parts. Figure 9.13 shows how a set of vendors is organised around a core firm to form a stable network.

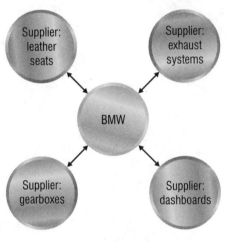

Figure 9.13
Stable network

3. **Dynamic networks.** The capabilities of the network structure are extended to the limit by the **dynamic network**. Businesses such as fashion houses and toy manufacturers allow organisations to outsource extensively. The Baygen Power Group of SA makes use of independent designers, manufacturers, marketers and investors. This concept is illustrated in figure 9.14.

In conclusion, there are certain aspects of departmentalisation that one should always bear in mind. Firstly, the units into which an enterprise is subdivided in the process of departmentalisation are given different names. One speaks of departments, sections, divisions, units, and so on. The underlying philosophy is that these designations refer to a number of tasks grouped together according to certain principles. Secondly, virtually all large enterprises are subdivided into departments on the basis of many different criteria. At top level, departmentalisation may occur according to, say, product, as shown in figure 9.15. The second level of departmentalisation in this figure is according to function. Note that the most senior manager responsible for housing loans has three functional departments, namely

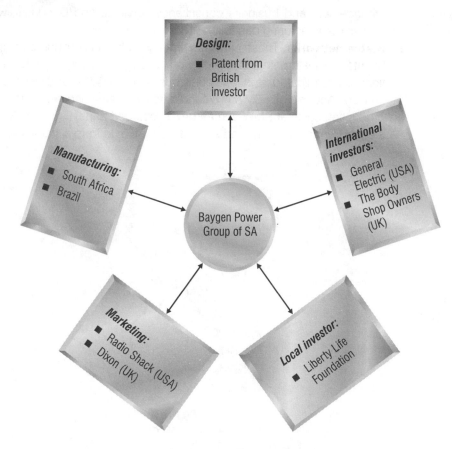

Figure 9.14
Dynamic network

marketing, administration and human resources. The next level of departmentalisation is according to geographic location (with northern and southern divisions that report to the marketing department); according to process (with a bookkeeping section and a typing section that report to the administrative manager); and according to customer (with management-related and other personnel activities). Thus there may be various bases for departmentalisation within departments at each level.

9.4.7 Chain of command

On completion of the process of departmentalisation, the organisation is divided into different departments or sections, which makes effective coordination vital. **Coordination** is the process in which the activities of individuals and work groups are integrated in order to achieve the overall objectives of the organisation. Effective coordination is achieved by systematically arranging positions and jobs — a man-

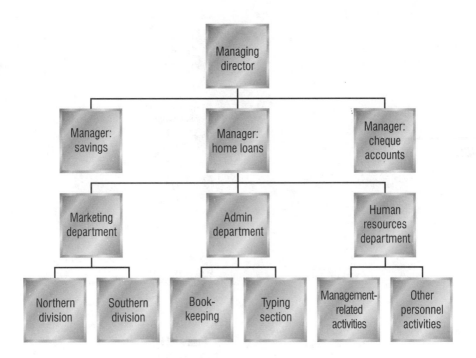

Figure 9.15
Departmentalisation according to multiple bases

agement hierarchy develops out of this process of arranging. This is called the **chain of command**.[4] The chain of command develops each time an individual becomes the subordinate of another individual. In other words, the 'chain of command' defines the reporting lines of individuals and groups.

Since ancient times, it has been recognised that this is a good way to structure unified working systems. The resulting pyramidal form — also called a bureaucracy — is often challenged and criticised, and it is said that the hierarchy kills initiative and crushes creativity. The reason why this hierarchical organisation of work is often found in business, however, is because it enables an organisation to employ large numbers of people and yet preserve accountability for the work people do.[5]

The functions of the **chain of command** are as follows:

- Degrees of authority and individual discretion are indicated, as are reporting lines.
- Information and guidelines are directed upwards and downwards in the organisation.
- The chain of command provides a basis for remuneration and status.
- The different links of the chain of command define routes for promotion or career movements from lower to higher levels.

Figure 9.16
Chain of command

The **disadvantage** of the chain of command is inherent in its pyramidal structure. Pyramids concentrate authority and result in a lack of security, which inhibits interaction and communication.

9.4.8 Unity of command

The principle of unity of command implies that each subordinate must have only one manager to whom he or she reports. This principle also applies to managers. It is vital, therefore, that there should be no confusion about who makes the decisions and who implements them. Such confusion will have a negative effect on productivity and employee morale.

The principle of **unity of command** clarifies areas of responsibility and who is responsible to whom. Unity of command also shows clearly who is responsible for each organisational activity.

9.4.9 Span of control

The chain of command and the principle of unity of command explain authority in the vertical structure of the organisation; **span of control** explains the horizontal structure.

Span of control refers to the number of subordinates working under a particular manager. It determines the complexity of a manager's task. It is easier for a manager to manage three people than nine people. Questions on the subject of span of control concentrate on how many people a manager can manage effectively.

This concept determines the **form** or **configuration** of the enterprise.

The following two reasons indicate the importance of choosing the correct span of control:

1. Span of control influences the work relationships in a specific section or department. If the span of control is too wide managers are overworked and subordinates not adequately led and controlled. Managers will have to make allowances for mistakes. Employees may have to wait a long time for feedback from managers and may become frustrated. Conversely, a span of control that is too narrow leads to inefficient management since managers are underutilised.

2. Span of control influences the speed of decision making. A **narrow** span of control leads to a **tall** structure with many levels between the lowest and the highest levels of management. This leads to a long chain of command and slow decision making, which is a great disadvantage in a dynamic and quick-changing environment. A **wide** span of control results in a **flat** structure with few management levels. Figures 9.17 and 9.18 illustrate tall and flat structures in organisations.

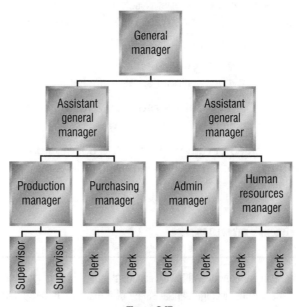

Figure 9.17
Span of control: a tall structure

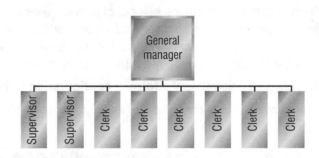

Figure 9.18
Span of control: a flat structure

9.4.10 Downsizing and delayering

Downsizing refers to a managerial activity which results in the reduction of the size of an organisation's workforce. It may be achieved by reducing the number of employees in one or more departments, leaving the organisational unit intact, or by eliminating a departmental unit by, for example, outsourcing the cafeteria to a private vendor. The general purpose of downsizing is to promote greater organisational efficiency.

Delayering is the removal of a level of management from an existing organisation structure. The advent of computers has reduced the need for multiple layers of management in organisations, which inevitably impede the flow of communication. Delayering promotes a more rapid flow of communication in the organisation.

One can have downsizing without delayering by reducing the number of people working in one or more departments, but it would be difficult to remove an organisational level (delayering) without some reduction in staff.

Rainbow Chicken **downsized** in July 1996 by cutting down on the number of employees in an effort to contain runaway costs.

Amalgamated Beverage Industries (a bottling franchise of Coca Cola) started a **delayering** process in 1996 by removing several management levels. This resulted in a flatter organisation structure.

Flatter structure saves on salaries

> Wider spans of control and fewer management levels bring about savings of millions of rands in salaries. If the average annual salary of a manager is R150 000, the cost in management salaries for the tall structure in figure 9.17 is six times R150 000, that is R900 000 per year.

Managers can implement downsizing successfully in their organisations by empowering employees. This means that employees at lower levels have more authority than previously. This not only eliminates costs in the form of salaries, but motivates employees and leads to higher productivity.

As can be imagined, delayering has certain disadvantages. Employees find themselves in a cul de sac: there are fewer chances of promotion because there are fewer management levels on the way to the top. The solution to this problem would be to create more lateral employment opportunities that are not based on promotion and salary increases, but promote the personal growth of employees. Not only will the norms for judging a successful career have to be changed (lateral moves will become more acceptable), but employees will in all probability have to carry a larger workload.

9.4.11 Coordination

Organising means dividing up the total task of the organisation into smaller units to take advantage of specialisation and achieve the aims of the organisation as productively as possible. This subdivision of the work into smaller jobs immediately raises the problem of cooperation, however. The divided tasks and the objectives of the various departments must be coordinated or integrated to achieve the primary objective of the organisation.

Without coordination, individuals and departments lose sight of the organisation's primary objective and of their own particular part in that effort. Coordination is the synthesis of the separate parts to form a unity, and it is the binding factor in the managerial process. It requires the integration of objectives and tasks at all levels and of all departments and functions to enable the organisation to work as a whole. Timing is also crucial, since the various tasks have to be scheduled to dovetail with one another.

Thus coordination is an endeavour by management to develop congruence, or harmony of aims, in the task of organising. It begins with the setting of objectives, for the objectives which the organisation is striving to attain constitute the principal means by which coordination is achieved. Other means or mechanisms to promote coordination are the organisation chart, the budget, committees, the broad policy and procedures in accordance with which tasks are carried out, and the information system of the organisation. Coordination will be discussed in detail in chapter 10.

9.5   FACTORS INFLUENCING ORGANISATION DESIGN

Organising can be carried out effectively only if the organisation structure has been developed in such a way that it optimises the execution of the strategies and plans. In other words, the plans can be successfully implemented only if the organisation structure makes this possible. Planning, leading and controlling are facilitated if management has an effective and dynamic organisation structure. This raises the question: Which organisation structure is the best? It is difficult to answer this question other than by saying that an organisation with a structure best suited to its particular activities will achieve greater success than one whose structure is not as well adapted to its strategy and requirements.

Organising is carried out amid many factors, each of which may provide a certain input in designing the organisation structure. Some experts believe that the environment within which an organisation operates is the decisive factor. Others emphasise the connection between strategy and structure. Obviously the size and complexity of the organisation, the competence of the employees, and the nature of the product and the market all play an important part. Moreover, the organisation climate or corporate culture should not be ignored in designing the structure and in forming departments and distributing tasks. Above all, according to modern management theory, whatever structure is designed, it should be adaptable to changes in the business environment. Let us briefly explore the above factors to round off our study of organising.

9.5.1 The environment in which an enterprise operates

The environment within which management operates may be taken as a basis for designing an organisation structure, because it is the starting point for the development of strategy, on the one hand, and because the organisation structure is the mechanism that should keep the business in touch with its environment, on the other. As we have already said, an organisation has to adapt itself to its environment to be able to survive. The following points may serve as a guide:

1. A **stable environment** is one that does not change much or is not subject to unexpected change. Product changes are the exception rather than the rule and, when a change does occur, it is possible to make plans to cope with it in good time. Demand for the product is regular, with only a few slight fluctuations. Technological changes are small or infrequent. A foundry manufacturing manhole covers and a workshop making violins are good examples here.

   Albany Bakeries is a large industrial bakery. It delivers bread to cafés and supermarkets such as Shoprite Checkers and Pick 'n Pay. Albany Bakeries operate in a stable environment because there is a steady demand for bread. The product hardly ever changes.

   In a stable environment the functional structure is suitable, because there is little innovation and no great need for coordination and cooperation between departments. Businesses with few competitors are under less pressure to develop products to satisfy consumers' needs. A manufacturer of nuts and bolts will have a functional structure with few specialists. Decision making takes place mainly at the top level.

2. A **turbulent environment** is one in which changes are the norm rather than the exception: competitors unexpectedly bring out new products, and technological innovations cause revolutionary changes in the manufacturing process or the product itself. The pharmaceutical industry is an example of such an environment, which necessitates many specialists for market research, product development and production, and close coordination and communication between them. In such an organisation, departmentalisation according to product is particularly suitable, since this speeds up decision making. Looking at it from a different angle, it may be said that businesses in stable environments are less differentiated in structure than those in turbulent environments. Moreover, more decisions are made in the individual departments than by top management.

3. In a **technologically dominated environment** — that is, when some particular technology forms the basis of an organisation's product — the design of the organisation will be influenced by the level of technological sophistication. Technologically complex firms tend to have more managers and more levels of management, since specialised technicians work in small groups with a narrow span. Technology — and especially technological innovation — requires an adaptable organisation structure, based on some form of departmentalisation.

9.5.2 The relationship between strategy and structure

The close relationship between the strategy of an organisation and the organisation structure or the infrastructure to implement the strategy was highlighted by Chandler's empirical findings that changes in the strategy of a business give rise to changes in its organisation structure — hence the well-known managerial maxim that **structure follows strategy**. The truth of this hypothesis is self-evident, because the strategy is the realisation of the mission and objectives, the strengths and weaknesses of the organisation, and management's perception of the environment, while the structure is the instrument to carry out the strategy and plans. The strategy provides a direct input in the design of the organisation structure and the structure cannot be separated from the strategy.

9.5.3 The size of the business

It is equally obvious that the structure also depends on the number of employees and managers to be coordinated. An increase in the size of the business creates a need for greater specialisation, more departments and more levels of managers. There is always a danger in large organisations of bureaucratic management resulting from detailed procedures, strict job demarcation, and a lack of emphasis on initiative and regeneration.

9.5.4 Staff employed by the business

There is also a close relationship between the organisation structure and the competence and role of its staff. In the managerial framework, especially in top management, the strategy influences the preferences of top management about how things should be done. Most managers have a personal preference for a particular organisation structure; they have their own views regarding authority and the degree of formality they favour in their relationship with subordinates. The trend today is to move away from strictly formal bureaucratic structures to more informal structures.

9.5.5 The organisation climate and culture

The organisation climate plays an important part in the organisation design. This so-called culture can be defined as the beliefs and values shared by people in an organisation. It is the 'personality' of the organisation. Unless management analyses the organisation's culture correctly, it will not know why people do, or do not do, certain things in the organisation. Corporate culture consists of the basic assumptions that are reflected not only in the organisation's behavioural patterns, but also in elements such as the organisation's architecture, office decor, dress regulations and the way things are done.

The type of structure that will lead to the successful implementation of tasks will depend on the current culture of the organisation. The structure of an organisation with a formal culture will differ from one with a more informal culture. The concept of culture will be discussed in detail in chapter 11.

These are some of the considerations that may influence the design of the organisation structure. They are, however, no more than guidelines for organising. Since organisations often already exist, the organising process is not always used for a new structure. Nevertheless, the organisation structure has to be revised from time to time when existing strategies or plans are changed.

9.6 SUMMARY

In this chapter we explained the second element of the management process — organising. Organising has been identified as the process of creating a structure for the organisation that will enable its people to work effectively towards its objectives.

Organisation design is the decision-making process according to which managers construct an organisation structure appropriate to the strategies and plans of the organisation. Certain basic principles, such as division of work, departmentalisation and coordination underlie the structure of an organisation. Some of these basic principles are dealt with in greater detail in chapter 10.

9.7 REFERENCES

1. Certo, SC. 1994. *Modern Management: Diversity, Quality, Ethics, and the Global Environment*, 6 ed. Boston: Allyn & Bacon, p 223.
2. Stoner, JAF & Freeman, R. 1992. *Management.* Englewood Cliffs NJ: Prentice-Hall, p 275.
3. Bedeian, AG. 1993. *Management,* 3 ed. Orlando: Dryden, p 252.
4. Stoner, JAF, Freeman, RE & Gilbert, DA. 1995. *Management*, 6 ed. Englewood Cliffs, NJ: Prentice-Hall, p 318.
5. Ibid p 275.

10 Authority, Power and Job Design

Key issues

- Authority as it ties into management
- Distinguishing between various types of power
- Analysis of delegating, and understanding the link between authority, centralisation and decentralisation
- Explaining the importance of coordination
- Highlighting aspects of job design

10.1 INTRODUCTION

It has been stated previously that the organisation structure provides a formal framework within which its members function. The organisation structure also provides a stable and logical framework of relationships within which managers and employees can work towards organisational goals. People need to interact with each other through the framework set by the organisation structure. However, rules are necessary for interaction within this structure. Managers set and apply these rules by virtue of **authority** and **power**.[1]

Managers can clearly not do everything that has to be done to achieve the organisational objectives themselves. Hence they have to decide how to delegate authority, or the responsibility to carry out a task, to the lower ranks.

Focus

> This chapter deals with managerial decisions about distributing authority in the organisation structure. More specifically, this chapter will focus on:
> - the nature of authority
> - centralisation and decentralisation of authority
> - delegation of authority
> - coordination

10.2   AUTHORITY

10.2.1 Introduction

The previous chapter discussed the division of the total task of an organisation into a number of subtasks and the allocation of tasks to individuals or departments. It was also indicated that groups of workers should be assigned to a specific manager so that units or departments can be properly managed. The allocation of tasks to individuals or departments is, however, not an indication that the organisational task has been accomplished. Certain organisational relationships must still be established to clarify to employees which person will assign their tasks to them and to whom they must report. This entails allocating **responsibility and authority**.

Responsibility is a particular **obligation** or commitment on the part of a manager to achieve organisational objectives. When strategic, tactical and operational objectives are set (see chapter 4), the managers responsible for achieving them should be clearly identified. Suppose a property developer places a manager in charge of all the building equipment. Three subordinates report to the equipment manager. The equipment manager is responsible for ensuring that the equipment is always in good working order and available to the contract managers without delay. He will have the authority to deploy resources, in other words, to make use of the skills of his subordinates, in order to achieve his objectives.

Authority is the right to **command or to give orders**. It includes the right to take action to compel the performance of duties and to punish default or negligence. In the formal organisational structure, several examples of which were discussed in chapter 9, the owners of an organisation possess the final authority. They appoint directors and give them authority, and the directors appoint managers, who in turn give a certain authority to subordinates — and in this way authority flows down along the line. This formal authority passed downwards from above is known as **delegation of authority**. Delegation can be viewed as the main source of authority.

Authority resides in positions, rather than in people — managers acquire authority by means of their hierarchical position in the organisation, rather than their personal characteristics. When a manager steps down from his or her position, that authority is relinquished.

Accountability (see section 9.2) is the evaluation of how well individuals meet their responsibility. In the example above, even though the equipment manager would have the authority to delegate some of the work to his subordinates, he would still be accountable for the way they maintain the equipment.

Managers are responsible for goal attainment in their departments. They should delegate responsibility and authority to perform tasks. But the manager will be accountable for everything that happens in that department.

Authority resides in positions, not in people

> When Mr FW de Klerk stepped down as President, he lost the authority that he previously had. This authority was transferred (delegated) to Mr Nelson Mandela, the new President.

10.2.2 Types of authority

Line and staff authority

Line authority is the responsibility to make decisions and issue orders down the chain of command (see section 9.4.7).

Line managers are those managers in the organisation who are directly responsible for attaining the organisation's objectives. **Line functions** are those activities essential for realising the organisation's objectives through the delegation of authority, allocation of work and supervision of employees. Line authority originates at top management, with the directors, and is delegated through the various hierarchical levels to the level at which the basic activities of the organisation are carried out.

Staff authority is the responsibility to advise and assist other personnel. **Staff managers** are those individuals who render services and advise line managers. **Staff functions** are those activities that directly influence the line functions by means of advice, recommendations, research and technical know-how. **Staff authority** is based primarily on expert power (see section 10.3). Partners in a law firm or a firm of architects may appoint staff members to run the business side of a firm. The presence of the staff specialists frees lawyers or architects to practise law or architecture — their line function.

Figure 10.1 depicts a typical mix of line and staff authority in an organisation. In this figure the legal adviser is in a staff position, whereas the other managers are line managers.

Certain people in staff positions function only as specialists in an **advisory capacity**. This means that line managers may choose whether or not to ask the advice of a specialist. A typical example is an economist at a bank. He advises the line managers on the prevailing economic variables such as interest rates, inflation and Reserve Bank policy.

A staff position may also involve the authority of **compulsory advice**. In the above example (see figure 10.1), the manager will be obliged to consult the staff manager (legal adviser) on matters relating to the staff position, in other words, legal matters. However, he may choose not to follow the advice.

Concurring authority is another kind of authority linked to a staff position. Here a line and a staff manager must agree on a certain plan of action. Thus the staff

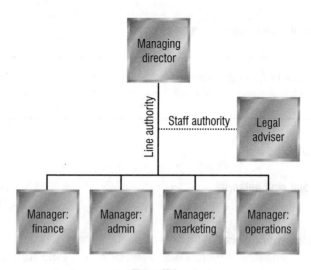

Figure 10.1
Line and staff authority and positions

Background

> The concept of advisory personnel is certainly not a contemporary development. In the past, kings, parliamentary governments and dictators appointed individuals as advisers; for example, Joseph analysed Pharaoh's dreams and advised him on how to handle his wheat crop in the future.

manager's authority is extended while that of the line manager is limited to certain areas. Hence, for example, both the line manager and the legal adviser must agree on a plan of action. If they cannot reach agreement, the decision will have to be referred to a higher authority.

Conflict may arise between people in line and staff positions because of **demographic factors** such as differences in age, ambition and level of education. As a rule, people in staff positions are younger and at a higher educational level than those in line positions. Conflict sometimes arises, because line managers regard staff managers as a **threat to their authority**. Thus staff managers are not consulted, and complain that they are underutilised. As soon as line managers are obliged to rely too heavily on the advice of staff managers, they feel that they are too **dependent** on their **expertise** and this may make them feel inferior. Differences in **perception** may also cause conflict, especially if line managers feel that staff managers are infringing on their lines of authority, have a too idealistic perspective or are usurping the honour of the line managers. However, the staff manager's perception may be that the other party unnecessarily opposes all new ideas.

10.2.3 Centralised and decentralised authority

General

The major difference between centralised and decentralised authority is who makes the important decisions in an organisation. In **centralised authority** important decisions are made by top managers. In **decentralised authority** important decisions are made by middle and lower management.

Decentralisation has become very popular in South African organisations as a method of empowering employees. By decentralising power and authority, a more democratic organisation is created where managers at the lower levels can decide on issues such as the allocation of resources in their departments, differentiated salaries for employees, and so on.

In deciding whether to centralise or decentralise authority, the following should be considered:

1. **The external environment.** The more complex the environment and the greater the uncertainty, the greater the tendency is to decentralise.

Decentralisation in a technology-based firm

> Omega Holdings, a South African firm engaged in marketing a range of consumer electronic entertainment products, was the 1996 winner of the EmPower Award, sponsored by the SABC and *Professional Management Review*. This award was given for Omega's efforts in empowering its employees.
>
> The firm suffered a loss in 1995 in the very competitive electronic marketplace, but was restructured in 1996. As a result of this restructuring, the firm reported an operating profit for 1996.
>
> A major focus on the restructuring was to flatten the management structure to provide for more decision making further down in the organisation.
>
> Source: Omega Holdings — Empowering its employees. Empowering the community it serves. *Professional Management Review*, December 1996, pp 38–39.

2. **The history of the organisation.** Organisations tend to do whatever they have done in the past. Hence there will be a tendency to follow the history of the organisation when it comes to centralisation and decentralisation.
3. **The nature of the decision.** The more risky the decision and the higher the costs involved, the more pressure there will be to centralise decision making. If Iscor Mining has to decide whether to buy new mining equipment for R4 million, it will be a centralised decision because of the high cost of the equipment. Lower management may be authorised to buy machinery and equipment up to the amount of R10 000.

4. **The strategy of the organisation.** The strategy of the organisation determines the type of markets, technological development and competition to which the organisation is subject. Alfred Chandler found that large organisations which obtained new products through a strategy of research and development advocated product diversification and therefore utilised decentralised structures. Organisations that did business in more predictable industries became increasingly centralised.

5. **Skills of lower-level managers.** If lower management is not in a position to make sound decisions, decision making in the organisation will probably be centralised. If lower-level managers are well qualified, top management can make the most of their skills by decentralising. The property developer mentioned in chapter 9, who builds houses for the low-cost housing market, will make use of centralised decision making because most of the employees are unskilled workers who do not have the ability to make important decisions.

6. **The size and growth rate of the organisation.** It is impossible to manage a very large organisation without decentralising. The larger and more complex an organisation is, the greater the need for decentralisation will be. In an organisation that is growing rapidly, management will have to bear the burden of an increasing workload, and therefore be obliged to shift some of the decision-making authority to lower levels, and thus to decentralise. As the business of a property developer becomes bigger, he will employ site managers who will have decision-making authority on matters pertaining to their specific sites. The business will have grown so much that the property developer is unable, because of the workload, to make all the decisions.

Pick 'n Pay decentralises decision making

> The management of Pick 'n Pay makes use of decentralised decision making because every shop or branch manager has certain decision-making power. This means that a branch manager can take decisions regarding staff and stock levels, for example, without referring to top management.
>
> Top management is thus able to concentrate on strategic issues, while decisions concerning staff at the branches are made quickly and effectively. Managers at the branches can display these management and decision-making skills to top management.

Advantages of decentralisation

The workload of top management is reduced, enabling it to devote more attention to strategies. Decision making improves because decisions are closer to the core of action and time is not wasted by first referring the matter to a higher authority. There is improved training, morale and initiative at the lower levels of management. These managers feel that they participate in managing the organisation and are prepared for greater responsibilities. They experience a great deal of job satisfaction. Decentralisation of decision making is more flexible and faster. This is necessary in a rapidly changing environment. Decentralised authority also fosters a competitive climate in the organisation. Managers are motivated to participate in this competition because their performance is constantly compared with that of their colleagues.

Disadvantages of decentralisation

The primary objective of organising, namely integrating subunits, will be defeated without a certain degree of centralisation. Too much decentralisation will result in subunits or departments moving away from the centres of decision making. This is why a high degree of decentralisation can lead to loss of control. There is the danger of duplicating tasks. For example, there could be human resource sections in the decentralised subunits that keep personnel records, while these records are also being kept up to date at head office. Decentralisation of authority requires more expensive and more intensive management training to enable managers to execute delegated tasks. It also demands sophisticated planning and reporting methods. Even if there is delegation, top managers are and will always be accountable for attaining the goals and objectives of the organisation and they must continually receive feedback on the situation.

Table 10.1
Advantages and disadvantages of decentralisation

Advantages	Disadvantages
■ Reduced workload for top management	■ Defeats integration of subunits
■ Improved decision making	■ Potential loss of control
■ Improved training, morale and initiative	■ Danger of duplication
■ More flexible and faster decision making	■ More expensive and intensive training required
■ Fosters a competitive climate	■ Demands sophisticated planning and reporting methods

The shift towards decentralisation in South African organisations and organisations abroad does not come without challenges. More individual authority at middle and lower management levels requires thorough management training. Managers need to be aware of the impact that their decisions could have on the survival of the organisation. A prerequisite for this knowledge in the current turbulent business environment is continuous management training.

Decentralisation in a large SA firm

Metropolitan Life Ltd of Cape Town has recently decentralised by restructuring its internal investment group from being a corporate office service department to a separate investment business unit. This new investment business can be more effective now since it has its own marketing function. Philip Morrall, the new general manager of the business, says the restructuring is already paying dividends in that the division is currently negotiating a deal in excess of R100 million with its first client.

Source: Hasenfuss, M. 1997. Metlife shows changes soon pay dividends. *Business Report*, 27 May, p 19.

Decentralisation demands management training

The Vodacom Academy was established for the purpose of training junior and middle managers.

SA firm's efforts in training of employees

The PX Division of Transnet Ltd is engaged in container and small parcel delivery. PX is undergoing a restructuring to become more market focused through intensive training and development of its employees. PX is a winner of the 1996 EmPower Award, sponsored by the SABC and *Professional Management Review*, for its development and training of personnel.

Great emphasis has been placed on internal development and training to ensure that black employees are equipped with skills needed for advancement. The company spent R12 million in 1996 on training, representing 3,5 % of the company's labour cost. PX put in place a very rigorous training and development programme (skills training and general education) of lower level managers and employees.

PX is already seeing a huge paradigm shift — a cultural turnaround in the attitudes of management. PX's progress is noted in that management has moved from 9 % black to 13 % in 1996; the target for 1997 is 19 % and 70 % by the year 2000.

Source: PX — change or perish. *Professional Management Review*, December 1996, pp 18–21.

10.3 POWER

Power is the **ability to influence the behaviour of others** within an organisation. Both managers and leaders possess power as a result of being in a position of authority over others. However, some people also possess a personal charisma which gives them power over others. A person with both **positional authority** and **personal power** is more likely to accomplish organisational objectives successfully than an individual with less personal power.

Individuals differ in their desire to seek and acquire power. Some individuals strive to acquire and exercise power, whereas others shun it. **Power** can be **used for personal gain** or it can be used **to benefit others**. The power of a manager is elusive, is difficult to measure, and is often dependent on subordinates. This means that followers can determine the nature and degree of power exercised by managers and/or leaders.

It is a clear advantage for a manager to possess power for, used correctly, it can substantially enhance the manager's effectiveness in achieving organisational results. It is helpful at this point to review the various sources of power. Research by French and Raven,[2] which is generally accepted in literature on management, identifies the following kinds of power:

1. **Legitimate power.** This refers to the authority that the organisation grants to a particular position. Thus a manager has the right to compel subordinates to perform their duties and to dismiss them if they do not. Legitimate power is therefore the same as authority. However, the fact that a manager does have legitimate power does not necessarily make him a good leader.

2. **The power of reward.** This is the power to give or withhold rewards. Such rewards may include raises in salary, bonuses, recognition or interesting assignments. The greater the number of rewards conferred by a manager and the more important these rewards are to his or her subordinates, the greater the reward power will be.

3. **Coercive power.** This is the power to enforce compliance through fear, either psychological or physical. Criminals and gangsters often exercise this power through physical violence. Physical violence is not accepted in contemporary organisations, but psychological or emotional fear of dismissal, or social exclusion from a group, is a kind of power that managers can use to bring pressure to bear on subordinates.

4. **Referent power.** This refers to personal power and is a somewhat abstract concept. In this situation, subordinates follow their leader simply because they like him, respect him or identify with him. In other words, the leader's personal characteristics make him important. Such a leader is said to have charisma.

5. **Expert power.** This is power based on knowledge and expertise and a leader who possesses it has special power over those who need this knowledge or

information. The more important the information and the fewer the people who possess it, the greater the power of the person who commands it.

Managers and subordinates can possess and use power. Managers, for instance, sometimes depend on their subordinates for information; a subordinate may have social influence over others whose cooperation is needed; or a subordinate may have specialised knowledge or a unique ability to perform a task that others cannot do. Managers should, therefore, realise that subordinates also have power, and they should use their own power judiciously and only to the extent necessary to realise their objectives. An effective manager uses power in a way that maintains a healthy balance between his or her own power and that of subordinates.

10.4 DELEGATION

10.4.1 Introduction

The job of a manager is to get the work done through the efforts of others. It is not desirable, nor possible in many instances, for the manager to perform all the work for which he or she is held responsible. Part of the manager's job must be done by others, and this is accomplished through the delegation process. **Delegation** is the process through which a manager **assigns** a portion of his or her total **workload to others**. In this process, authority is also passed on to an employee, who in fact then has the authority to deploy the necessary resources in order to complete the task.

The main reason why managers delegate is to **get more work done**. Another important reason is that a subordinate, and not the manager, often has the **specialised knowledge** required for a particular job. Thirdly, delegation is useful in **training** personnel. By participating in decision making and problem solving, employees also improve their managerial skills.

Even though managers delegate authority, they remain accountable for the completion of the job. They are accountable both for their own actions and those of their subordinates. Managers may hold subordinates responsible for a job, but are still accountable to their own superiors for the work. Therefore a manager must accept the responsibility, and the blame, for a subordinate's failure to accomplish any assigned duties.

However, according to the parity principle, neither the manager nor the subordinate should be held responsible for things beyond their control or influence. The **parity principle** stipulates that **authority and responsibility** should be **coequal**.[3] This means that when a manager assigns a task to be performed — responsibility — he or she must also give the subordinate the full authority to perform the task. For example, if an employee is asked to drive across town and pick up a load of timber (responsibility), then he should also be given the right (authority) to check out a vehicle from the garage to accomplish the task. This principle is often violated. Employees almost always feel they have been assigned more responsibility than authority to act.

10.4.2 Principles to improve delegation

The delegation process is essential to every manager for this is how he or she gets others to share in the performance of work of the organisation. A common failing of the less effective managers is that they try to be responsible for everything. In so doing, they are overloaded, and not very efficient. Consequently, the subordinate staff suffer because of the manager's failure to delegate. The delegation process may be viewed as a developmental process for it provides subordinate staff members with an increasing amount of work to be performed. It also teaches subordinates the practice of good management. Below are some principles which can be used as guidelines to help one be more effective at delegation.

1. **Set standards and objectives.** Employees should participate in the process of formulating objectives and should also agree with the criteria laid down for measuring performance. This participation will foster successful delegation.
2. **Ensure clarity of authority and responsibility.** Subordinates must understand the tasks and authority assigned to them, recognise their responsibility and be held accountable for results.
3. **Involve subordinates.** Managers should motivate subordinates by including them in the decision-making process, informing them properly at all times and improving their skills. Motivated employees will accept well-designated tasks and perform them properly.
4. **Request the completion of tasks.** By providing the necessary direction and assistance, managers can see to it that employees complete the tasks assigned to them.
5. **Provide performance training.** The effectiveness of delegation depends on workers' ability to perform tasks. Managers should continually evaluate the responsibilities delegated, and provide training to help workers overcome shortcomings.
6. **Apply adequate control measures.** Timely and accurate reports should be issued to workers on a regular basis. This will enable them to compare their performance with predetermined standards and to overcome their shortcomings.

10.4.3 The advantages of delegation

The process of management relies on the concept of **delegation**. When a firm moves from a one-person to a two-person organisation, there is no choice from that point onward — delegation is a requirement. So it is important for aspiring managers to understand the concept and to know the advantages of delegation. It has been determined that delegation has several important advantages when applied properly.[4] Firstly, managers who train their staff to accept more responsibility are in a good position to accept more authority and responsibility from higher levels of management. Secondly, delegation encourages employees to exercise judgment and accept accountability. This improves self-confidence and willingness to take initiative and is a great training method. Better decisions are often taken by involving employees who are 'closer to the action' and know more about the practical execution of tasks. Lastly, quicker decision making takes place. If subordinates have the necessary authority, they do not have to refer to top management before taking certain decisions.

10.4.4 Barriers to delegation

When one is given something to do and one knows how to do it well, there is a natural tendency to do that task rather than give it to someone else. One of the first things managers need to learn is to delegate those things that they know best. By delegating the things that one knows best, one can move on to other things which will represent further personal growth. Also, it is easy to supervise staff members doing things of which one has detailed knowledge. There are a number of different personal and psychological barriers which impede the delegation process for managers. A further review of these barriers may be helpful to you as a manager.

A manager may fear that his or her own performance evaluation will suffer if subordinates fail to do a job properly. The manager may also feel that the subordinate will not do the job as well as he or she can do it. This may be because of a lack of confidence in the subordinates and the perception that they are not up to doing the job. Managers are often too inflexible or disorganised to delegate, or sometimes feel that it takes too long to explain to subordinates how to do the job and that they may as well do it themselves. They may also be reluctant to delegate because they fear their subordinates will do the job better than they can.

Subordinates, on the other hand, sometimes fear that they will fail and thus expose themselves to disciplinary action. They may try to avoid work responsibilities and risk, and feel that there are no additional rewards for completing a task. Sometimes there is confusion about who is actually responsible for the job.

Managers often inherit organisations that are designed by others. It is possible that the current design of the organisation itself may be an impediment to delegation. If there are problems in delegation, managers should review all the elements of the organising function to determine the root cause of such organisational stumbling blocks. The following are examples of organisational stumbling blocks:

1. Delegation is not effective if authority and responsibility are not clearly defined. If a manager does not know what tasks to delegate and what is expected of him, he will not be able to delegate decision making to his subordinates. This situation requires a clarification of duties from above or from the manager's boss.

2. When a manager does not make subordinates accountable for task performance, there is a likelihood that their responsibilities will be passed on to others,
   creating additional staff and burdensome communications.
3. In the absence of, or with poorly developed job descriptions, individuals may not
   have a good understanding of what is expected of them.

10.4.5 Removing barriers to delegation

Most of the stumbling blocks and barriers to communication can be minimised by a
greater awareness on the part of the manager that such obstacles exist. Other stumbling blocks and barriers may be reduced or eliminated by continually training and
motivating subordinates to accept more responsibility. However, these problems
cannot be resolved overnight. In addition to training, the manager can use some
ideas to assist in removing barriers to delegation.

Firstly, managers should realise that there is **more than one way** to deal with a
situation and they should, therefore, not compel subordinates to apply their
methods. After appropriate training, managers should give subordinates maximum
freedom in performing their delegated tasks. When mistakes are made, they should
be assisted in finding solutions to problems. Improved **communication** between
subordinates and managers removes obstacles to delegation. Close communication will reveal the strengths and weaknesses of employees and this enables managers to know which tasks can be appropriately delegated with the knowledge that
the job will be done properly. **Training** helps subordinates to better understand their
responsibilities, authority and accountability. Subordinates will soon realise the
extent of their contribution in achieving the objectives and goals of the organisation.
Managers should have the **ability** to **analyse** the organisation's goals and task
requirements and to determine to what extent the employees have the capability to
perform the task they wish to delegate. They should be able to **trust their
employees** and have faith in their ability to complete the task successfully. When
employees cannot perform the job effectively, the job of the manager is to teach
them how to do the task.

10.4.6 The delegation process

We have discussed how essential the delegation process is to the manager. Similarly,
the process is also essential to the growth and wellbeing of subordinates. Delegation
does not take place automatically — it is something a manager must initiate. Conditions are constantly changing in today's organisations, so it is important for a manager to review these changing requirements with his subordinate staff. Of course, in
the case of new staff members, a greater amount of time is required to ensure that
they understand their jobs and what is expected of them. The following are some
recommended steps according to which the delegation process can be carried out:[5]

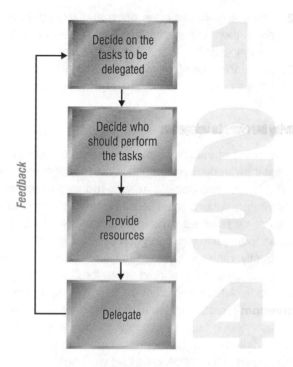

Figure 10.2
The delegation process

1. **Decide on the tasks to be delegated.** Tasks of a repetitive nature or minor chores can easily be delegated. It is important, however, to delegate more challenging tasks in order to develop employees and create self-confidence. Try delegating those tasks you best know how to do.

2. **Decide who should perform the tasks.** In this instance, the time, competency and experience of the subordinate should be taken into account. You may also want to rotate certain tasks among employees in order to create a more flexible workforce.

3. **Provide sufficient resources for carrying out the delegated task.** These resources include staff, time or financial resources without which the subordinate cannot perform the task. This is the nature of authority. All too often the manager delegates the work to be done, but fails to give the individual the necessary resources to perform the task.

4. **Delegate the assignment.** The delegating manager should provide all the relevant information on the task to be performed, including expected results. He or she will not normally prescribe the methods to be used in performing the task, unless they are not known to the subordinate. Open channels of communication

should exist between the manager and the subordinate regarding the delegated tasks.

5. **Be prepared to step in, if necessary.** Problems could be experienced with the execution of a task if resources are insufficient, or if the subordinate experiences difficulties, or lacks performance skills. Managers should be prepared to assist in cases where it may be necessary, and the subordinate should be made aware of this.

6. **Establish a feedback system.** This is vital because the outcome of the delegation process is important information that serves as input for the next delegation process.

10.5   COORDINATION

10.5.1 Introduction

Once an organisation has been divided into specialised functions or departments, and the corresponding objectives have been formulated, management should see to it that the different departments will be able to work together. Thus departments should be informed about the activities and objectives of other departments so that they can all work together in harmony.

Coordination is the synthesis of the separate parts to form a unity, and is the binding factor in the managerial process. It means the integration of objections and tasks at all levels and of all departments and functions to enable the organisation to work as whole.

Lack of coordination often leads to frustration and waste (especially of time). Hence employees who are able to work together are a real asset to an organisation. The cooperation needed in an organisation may be compared to teamwork in different sports, where at practice sessions, the coach encourages members of the team to make a joint effort. Although each player may have a specific function in the team, he or she still has to coordinate each action with those of the other players, and with the team as a whole. All activities should be coordinated to achieve a common purpose — in this case, winning the match.

Figure 10.3 shows the kind of coordination required in an organisation. The arrows indicate departments or managers at different levels that have to be coordinated.

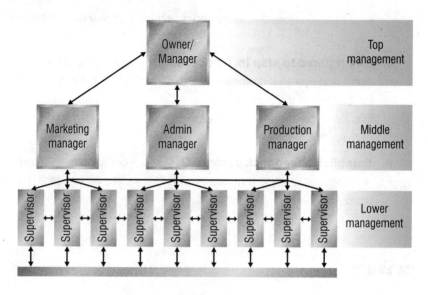

Figure 10.3
Relationships in an organisation that need to be coordinated

10.5.2 Interdependence

In general, the degree of coordination between tasks depends on their interdependence. Departments depend on each other for information and resources, for example, sales and production are interdependent because sales provide production with information about how much to produce to satisfy customer needs. The greater the interdependence between departments, the greater the coordination required.

Thompson[6] has identified three major forms of interdependence: pooled interdependence, sequential interdependence and reciprocal interdependence.

Pooled interdependence

In groups that exhibit **pooled interdependence**, the units operate with little interaction; the outputs of the units are pooled at organisational level. Failure of any unit could threaten the entire organisation and thus other departments.

The Menlyn branch of Edgars Stores may not interact all that much with the Eastgate branch of Edgars Stores, but they both contribute to the profits of the organisation as a whole. The branches are interdependent to the extent that the final success or failure of a branch affects Edgars Stores and so also the other branches.

Sequential interdependence

In **sequential interdependence**, the output of the one unit becomes the input for the next unit. The second unit is directly dependent upon the first unit to finish its work before it can begin its assigned task. Take the example of a bakery. The unit that bakes the cakes must finish its work before the unit responsible for the icing and decorating of cakes can start its activities. Sequential interdependence is typically found in a production-line setup.

Reciprocal interdependence

This form of interdependence refers to a situation in which the outputs of one work unit become the inputs for the second work unit, and vice versa. In a hospital, the units such as intensive care, paediatrics, and so on, provide inputs to surgery. After surgery, patients are sent back to the respective units.

10.5.3 Types of coordination

There are four basic types of coordination: informal coordination, programmed coordination, liaison coordination and group coordination.

1. **Informal coordination.** This occurs voluntarily. This includes spontaneous gestures that keep an organisation's social processes going, but are not directly part of task performance. Informal coordination is helpful in all instances of interdependence.

2. **Programmed coordination.** This becomes more important as organisations grow larger. This involves establishing routines. Repetitive problems are often specified in standing plans, policies, procedures and rules. Programmed coordination is particularly useful in cases of pooled or sequential interdependence.

3. **Liaison coordination.** This type of coordination is often found in large organisations where coordination problems between units are common. Separate liaison positions are established for resolving disputes. The individual in a liaison position coordinates two or more interdependent units by acting as a common point of contact.[7] Two engineering groups working on component systems for a large project might interact through a liaison officer who is familiar with both units. He or she can serve to integrate the activities of both groups and also disseminate relevant information.

4. **Group coordination.** This occurs when work group representatives meet formally. Committees are the best-known means for this purpose. Group coordination is especially useful in situations of sequential and reciprocal interdependence.

10.6　JOB DESIGN

10.6.1　Introduction

Job design is a result of efforts of employees 'to be heard'. The current generation of employees has brought more abilities, higher expectations and a desire for self-responsibility to the workplace.[8] Workplace reform and employee empowerment have followed. **Job design is concerned with designing the content of jobs to enhance feelings of achievement and other intrinsic outcomes.**

Over the years, three different approaches to job design have emerged: the mechanistic, motivational and biological approaches to job design.[9]

1. **Mechanistic job design.** This was inspired by FW Taylor, who attempted to make jobs simple and efficient by dividing jobs into different tasks and assigning one or more tasks to a person or a group of people. This approach is typically followed with factory workers on an assembly line. This practice is generally referred to as specialisation.

2. **Motivational job design.** This originated from the ideas of Hackman and others who identified five core job dimensions: skills variety, task identity, task significance, autonomy and feedback. The closer a job comes to having all five of these dimensions, the more likely it is that the employee will be highly motivated and satisfied. The term **empowerment** is used to describe the efforts of management to redesign jobs accordingly. **Job enlargement** and **job enrichment** are two empowering ways to redesign jobs.

3. **Biological job design** is a biological approach called **ergonomics**, which is a systematic approach to making the workplace safer. Attention is focused on factors such as designing pleasant and safe offices and comfortable work stations.

Let us now examine specialisation, job enlargement and job enrichment as vehicles of job design.

10.6.2　Specialisation

Job specialisation refers to the narrowing down of activities to simple, repetitive routines. This term should not be confused with **person specialisation** which refers to individuals with specialised training, such as doctors, lawyers and engineers.

Job specialisation, also referred to as division of work, originated with the work of Adam Smith when he described the work in a pin factory.

Job specialisation or division of labour was discussed in chapter 9.

Background

The famous opening words of Adam Smith's book *Wealth of Nations* describe a basic form of specialisation in a pin factory and the subsequent increased productivity. Smith puts it as follows: 'One man draws the wire, another straightens it, a third cuts it, a fourth points it, a fifth grids it at the top for receiving the head. Ten persons, therefore could make among them upwards of forty-eight thousand pins in a day ... But if they had all wrought separately and independently, and without any of them having been educated to this peculiar business, they certainly could not each of them have made twenty. This would have meant that 200 pins at most would have been made instead of 48 000.'

Source: Campbell, RH, Skinner, AS & Todd, WB (eds). 1976. *Adam Smith— An Inquiry into the Nature and Causes of the Wealth of Nations*, p 15.

Background

In the 19th century, writers such as Karl Marx and Friedrich Engels regarded division of labour or specialisation as a kind of trap for individuals: 'Division of labour offers us the first example of how ... man's own deed becomes an alien power opposed to him which enslaves him instead of being controlled by him. For as soon as the distribution of labour comes into being, each man has a particular, exclusive activity ... from which he cannot escape. He is a hunter, a fisherman, a shepherd ... and must remain so if he does not want to lose his means of livelihood.'[10] Although this statement is somewhat strong, there is a hint of truth in it.

10.6.3 Job enlargement

Job enlargement stems from the thinking of industrial engineers. They wanted to increase a job's scope in order to break the monotony of a limited routine. A job is enlarged when an employee carries out a wider range of activities of approximately the same level of skill, such as a secretary who is designated as a second manager. The expanded job will be more interesting because it is more varied.

10.6.4 Job enrichment

Job enrichment is implemented by adding depth to the job. It is based on Herzberg's two-factor theory of motivation[11] which is described in detail in chapter 13. Herzberg argued that job rotation (moving employees from one job to another) and job enlargement do not enhance employee motivation. A worker should be provided with actual control over the task. **Job enrichment** entails increasing both the **number of tasks** a worker does and the **control** the worker has over the job.

10.7   CONCLUSION

In this chapter the necessary rules by which people interact in the organisation and within the organisation structure were discussed. These rules are applied by virtue of authority and power. Authority is granted to an employee by the organisation to enable him to give orders and develop resources. A true leader has power over people to influence them to behave in a certain way. Different types of power exist: legitimate power, the power of reward, coercive power, referent power and expert power.

Delegation is a process by which authority is passed on to an employee. Centralisation and decentralisation refer to the degree to which delegation is carried out. Coordination of activities and relationships is necessary to direct the organisation towards goal achievement. There are four basic types of coordination: informal, programmed, liaison and group coordination.

Job design became important when employees insisted on being heard and appreciated. Aspects of job design, such as specialisation, job enlargement and job enrichment, were discussed.

In chapter 11 the forces for change and the relationship between culture and change will be discussed.

10.8   REFERENCES

1. Stoner, JAF, Freeman, RE & Gilbert, DA. 1995. *Management*, 6 ed. Englewood Cliffs, NJ: Prentice-Hall, p 244.
2. French, JRP & Raven, B. The bases of social power, in Cartwright, D (ed). 1959. *Studies in Social Power*. Michigan: University of Michigan, pp 156–164.
3. Bedeian, AG. 1993. *Management*, 3 ed. Orlando: Dryden Press, p 275.
4. Stoner et al op cit p 355–356.
5. Ibid p 358.
6. Thompson, JD, in Rushing, WA & Zald, MN. 1976. *Organizations and Beyond*. Lexington, Mass: DC Heath, p 41.
7. Griffin, RW. 1987. *Management*, 2 ed. Boston: Houghton Mifflin, p 313.
8. Bedeian op cit p 292.
9. Stoner et al op cit p 363.
10. Karl Marx & Friedrich Engels, in Stoner, JAF & Wankel, C. *Management*, pp 233–234; and Griffin op cit p 276.
11. Herzberg, F. *Work and the Nature of Man*. 1968. London: Crosby Lockwood Staples.

11 Organisational Culture and Change

Key issues

- Planned versus reactive change
- The forces of change
- Types of change
- The change process
- Resistance to change and how to overcome this
- Methods to introduce change
- The relationship between culture and change

11.1 INTRODUCTION

The international and national business environments are continually exposed to change. Not only technological changes, but also economic, political and other changes have an influence on organisations worldwide. Organisations in South Africa are not excluded from the consequences of change. This country has experienced drastic economic and political changes since 1994, including a change of government, affirmative action and a changing education system.

Focus

This chapter describes how to manage change successfully. The forces of change are explored and a change process is described. The role that corporate culture plays in bringing about change is highlighted. More specifically, we will focus on:

- the nature of change
- forces of change
- the change process
- resistance to change
- culture and change

In order to stay competitive, businesses have to continually adapt to change. Far-sighted managers see change as a challenge, as an opportunity to take advantage of changing conditions and of becoming more competitive.

11.2   PLANNED VERSUS REACTIVE CHANGE

Organisational change can be defined as a process in which an organisation takes on new ideas to become different. The necessity for change may be brought about by factors in the external environment of the business, or within the business itself.

All organisations undergo minor adjustments in reacting to change. The forms for credit applications are adjusted in order to supply more information to the creditor's clerk. The human resources department may initiate certain training programmes. These changes are called routine changes and are distinguished from planned change in magnitude and scope. **Routine changes** are minor changes and do not affect the organisation as a whole. These changes are also called **reactive** because they are a response to problems as they develop. Such a response is sometimes done in haste and poorly planned and executed.

In the apartheid era no decent liberal foreign (the British were particularly important for histor- ical reasons) family would be seen with a bottle of South African wine on the table. Well, not with a South African label anyway. But with the first democratic general election in 1994, all this changed. Suddenly South African wine was very much in demand.

New cultivars, such as pinotage, became the vogue, encouraged by the lavish praise of British wine connoisseurs.

Cooperatives that had the foresight, during the difficult times, to get ready for change, had a considerable edge.

Simonsvlei Cooperative Wine Cellars in Paarl, Swartland Cooperative Winery and Vredendal Cooperative Wine Cellar, with its intriguing Khoi San brandname, Gôiya Kgeisje, are among the cellars that made their mark abroad at an early stage.

Simonsvlei is an outstanding example of a wine cellar that has not only increased its export volumes but also the actual value of these exports. In 1992, for instance, the cellar exported a total of 575 000 litres of red wine and 940 000 litres of white wine to the value of R1,13m and R1,26m respectively.

The corresponding figures for 1996 were 1,7m litres of red wine and 3,15m litres of white wine, with income of R12,5m and R21,4m respectively (see table 11.1).

Planned change involves the entire organisation or a major part of it, to adapt to significant changes in the organisation's goals or direction, in reaction to expected change in the external environment, and so on. Planned change is designed and implemented in an orderly and timely fashion **in anticipation of future events**.

South African managers with foresight planned affirmative action long before political changes came about. The affirmative action programmes could be executed properly without undue pressure. This was **planned change**. Other South African managers did not foresee the need for affirmative action and were forced into quick, superficial change because of political pressure. Such **reactive change** is often poorly planned and executed, as explained above.

Next we will discuss the forces of change that exist within and outside the organisation.

Table 11.1
Wine export planning to the year 2010 (litres)

Cultivars	1996	2000	2005	2010
Red				
Cabernet Sauvignon	250 000	750 000	1 000 000	1 250 000
Pinotage	250 000	500 000	750 000	1 000 000
Shiraz	200 000	300 000	400 000	500 000
Merlot	100 000	400 000	500 000	600 000
Cinsaut	900 000	1 000 000	1 500 000	1 750 000
Subtotal	**1 700 000**	**2 950 000**	**4 150 000**	**5 100 000**
White				
Chenin Blanc	3 000 000	3 000 000	3 000 000	3 000 000
Sauvignon Blanc	50 000	50 000	200 000	400 000
Semillon	–	50 000	200 000	400 000
Chardonnay	100 000	500 000	800 000	1 100 000
Subtotal	**3 150 000**	**3 600 000**	**4 200 000**	**4 900 000**
GRAND TOTAL	**4 850 000**	**6 550 000**	**8 350 000**	**10 000 000**

Source: *F & T Weekly,* 17 January 1997.

11.3   FORCES OF CHANGE

Forces of change exist both within the organisation and in its external environment. Consequently, change results from both internal and external forces.[1] This concept is illustrated in figure 11.1.

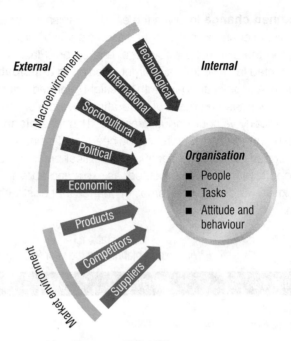

Figure 11.1
External and internal forces of organisational change

11.3.1 Internal forces

A variety of forces inside the organisation may cause change. Internal forces arise from the challenge of creating an organisation structure capable of facilitating the attainment of organisational goals. Change in the organisation's goals or objectives is likely to result in organisational change.

Some internal forces may actually be indirect reflections of external forces. As sociocultural values shift, workers' attitudes toward their work may also change.[2] In the new South Africa, a lot of attention is paid to issues of humanity and equality between genders. This resulted in paternity leave (maternity leave for fathers). The new Mine Health and Safety Act caused management at JCF Ltd to introduce new structures to promote greater cooperation between management and workers. New communication channels, among other things, had to be established; supervisor competency training had to be implemented.

11.3.2 External forces

External forces for change derive from the organisation's macroenvironment and market environment. In the **international element** of the macroenvironment, a foreign competitor may introduce a new product or increase or decrease prices. In the **political element**, new laws and regulations, such as new labour laws, affect the organisation. The knowledge explosion since World War II has brought **new technology** to organisations. Modern computers have made high-speed data-processing possible. Automation has not only affected production techniques, but also the social conditions of work.

External forces of change: the international element

> Under a government plan that began in 1988, Australia is on course to reduce protection against imported cars to 15 % by the year 2000. This could open up a major export market for South Africa.
>
> Some South African manufacturers have already adapted to the external forces of change by beginning to export to Australia.
>
> Motorists in both countries drive on the left, and SA plants have plenty of capacity to meet the extra load. BMW SA is already the sole supplier of certain 3-series models to Australia.
>
> Source: *Financial Mail*, 7 February 1997.

The **market environment** often has an even greater influence on the organisation. Competitors, suppliers and customers may force the organisation to change. Alistair McArthur of the Mr Price stores recognised that 'wearing jeans and a pullover during weekends makes you one of the people'. He targeted Mr Price's weekend leisurewear at 14- to 25-year-olds.[3] Casual clothing is becoming increasingly popular in South Africa, a country in which even the President dresses casually.

11.4 TYPES OF CHANGE

Organisations may undertake change in the following four areas: strategy, structure, technology and people. When a change is made in one of the above areas, that change will generally also bring about change in another area. For example, a change in technology may require hiring new people who understand the new technology and/or training existing personnel. The four major types of change are discussed below:

1. **Change in strategy.** Most firms have strategic plans outlining the future course of the business, taking into consideration the internal and external environments. South African firms are making major changes in their strategic plans as businesses move from producing and serving local markets to entering the world marketplace. Illovo Sugar is moving into Mozambique and Kenya in order to expand its sugar-producing capacity.

2. **Change in structure.** This change involves change in the basic components of the organisation, decentralisation, increasing authority and span of control. For example, Telkom is undergoing a change in its organisation structure as it incorporates its two new equity partners, SBC Communications from the USA and Malaysia Telecom.

3. **Change in technology.** Technological changes may involve altering equipment, engineering processes, research techniques and/or production processes. T&N Industries made major changes to their automobile radiator production upon acquiring a new alloy discovered by a British inventor.

4. **Change in people.** This change involves changes in the performance, skills, attitudes, perceptions, behaviours and expectations of people. A change in organisation culture is also regarded as change in people. Major changes are currently underway in South Africa in the empowerment of previously disadvantaged individuals.

11.5   CHANGE AS A PROCESS

Change is a process which has four distinct steps, namely denial, resistance, exploration and commitment.[4]

1. **Denial.** During periods of change, employees often ignore the facts or pretend that the change will not affect them personally. When people first heard that Cape Town was going to put in a bid for the 2004 Olympics, some people were against the idea and did not even wish to discuss it.
2. **Resistance.** Once employees actually realise that change is taking place and they have digested the facts, they often resist change. It is quite natural for human beings to resist change and this often influences the effectiveness of change in organisations. Some Capetonians launched campaigns resisting the Olympic bid.
3. **Exploration.** Once change has been implemented, employees are exposed to new information and training. This leads to better understanding. Once the Olympic bid was made and advertising campaigns launched in Cape Town, people started realising that it had certain advantages, such as an increase in trade and tourism.
4. **Commitment.** Exploration leads to some level of commitment from employees: it may be low at first and increase as the process continues, or it may start off and continue to be low or high. It may also start high and decrease during the process. Many Cape Town residents are now committed to an Olympic bid for Cape Town in the future.

11.6   RESISTANCE TO CHANGE

Most organisational change efforts run into some form of employee resistance. Change triggers emotional reaction because of the uncertainty involved. In planning for change, management should always take resistance to change into account. This can be done by understanding the reasons why people resist change. These reasons are depicted in figure 11.2.

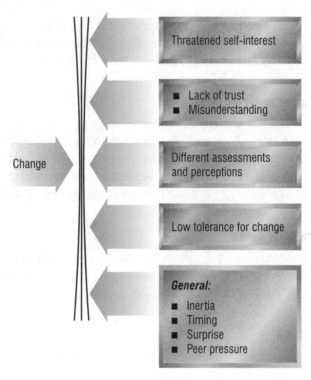

Figure 11.2
Reasons for resistance to change

11.6.1   Threatened self-interest

People care less about the organisation's best interest than their own best interest. They will resist change if they think it will cause them to lose something of value.

What could people fear to lose? At worst, their jobs, as in the case of a plant or unit closing down. A sample listing of personal goals which, when threatened, will provoke resistance, is as follows:[5]

■ **power** over organisational resources
■ **money** in the form of current or future income
■ **prestige** and respect from people responsible for hiring, promoting and firing

- **convenience** as far as personal effort is concerned
- **security**, personal power, prestige or income
- **professional competence**, including respect from peers for knowledge and technical proficiency
- **client service** — effectiveness in client service

11.6.2 Lack of trust and misunderstanding

Even when management proposes change that will benefit everyone, people will still resist if they do not fully understand the purpose. Such a situation is most likely to occur when there is a lack of trust between the parties involved. Distrust and suspicion often result in rumours and distorted information.

11.6.3 Different assessments and perceptions

Evaluations of the costs and benefits of a proposed change depend on what individuals think change will mean for themselves and their organisation. Differing assessments of the benefits of proposed change occur when information on the change is not properly disseminated. Employees are often exposed to different, often less, information than management and may not understand the full consequences of change.

11.6.4 Low tolerance for change[6]

People resist change because they fear they will not be able to develop the new skills necessary to perform well. Although individuals often understand the necessity for change, they are emotionally unable to make the change.

11.6.5 General reasons

There are also several general reasons why people resist change, regardless of the actual content of the change:[7]

- **Inertia.** People do not want to change the status quo. The old way of doing things was comfortable and easy.
- **Timing.** Change is resisted because of poor timing.
- **Surprise.** People do not react favourably to surprises. If the change is sudden, unexpected or extreme, resistance may almost be a reflex reaction.
- **Peer pressure.** Work groups sometimes resist new ideas because of anti-management attitudes.

Note that resistance to change should always be regarded as an important signal for further inquiry. Employees' assessment may be more accurate than that of management; they may know that a change will not work. In this case, resistance to change is good for the organisation.

11.7   OVERCOMING RESISTANCE TO CHANGE

Resisting change is a human response and management should take steps to counter it. Reducing resistance may cut down on the time needed for change to be accepted. A number of methods useful in decreasing resistance to change are examined below.

11.7.1 Education and communication

People should be educated about upcoming changes before they occur. The **nature** as well as the **logic** behind the change should be communicated to employees. This can be done by means of one-on-one discussions, presentations to groups or reports and memos.

Communication improves labour relations

Seardel, the biggest clothing and textile manufacturer in South Africa, employing more than 25 000 people, is driving an initiative to transform labour relations in the industry.

Thorny issues dividing the parties persist, but at least they **are talking more openly with each other.**

An industry summit between employers and union leadership resulted in agreement on several issues such as:

- the establishment of a productivity forum
- a permanent invitation for workers' leaders to meet employers quarterly.

Source: Seardel. A corporate report. *Financial Mail*, 21 March 1997, p 28.

11.7.2 Participation and involvement

Participation is generally considered the most effective technique for overcoming resistance to change. Participation gives employees a chance to express their fears about proposed changes. It is also important in bringing together those affected to help implement the change.

11.7.3 Facilitation and support

Facilitation involves providing the necessary resources employees need to carry out the change and properly perform their jobs. This often includes decentralising authority. **Support** is more psychological in the sense that it involves listening to problems and being understanding.

11.7.4 Negotiation and rewards

It is often best to negotiate a proposed change with the parties involved and to reach an agreement. Negotiated agreements involve giving something to the other party to reduce resistance.

11.7.5 Coercion and manipulation

In using explicit and/or implicit **coercion**, the manager engages in threatening behaviour. He threatens employees with job loss, reduced promotion opportunities or loss of privileges. This type of behaviour often creates bad feelings or hostility.

Some managers use more subtle, covert tactics to implement change. One form of **manipulation** is **cooptation**, which involves giving a resisting individual a desirable role in the change effort.

11.8 CULTURE AND CHANGE

11.8.1 Introduction

The changes that many organisations are forced to make in an ever-changing business environment are often so fundamental that they involve transforming an organisation's very essence — its corporate culture.

Every organisation has a particular culture, which is almost like a personality. It comprises an omnipresent set of assumptions which is often difficult to fathom and which directs activities within the organisation. In a nutshell, **corporate culture may be defined as the beliefs and values shared by people in an organisation.**[8]

Just as an individual's personality determines his behaviour, shared values and beliefs form the foundation of a particular culture that influences the actions and activities in that organisation.

11.9 DEFINITION OF THE CONCEPT OF CULTURE

Organisations are made up of people and not simply of buildings, production facilities, products, markets, strategic analyses and technological innovations. Every organisation has its own unique personality, which is known as its corporate culture. This means that the impressive buildings that one observes when driving past the Armscor complex are not necessarily the only reflection of the personality of the organisation. The heart and soul of an organisation are its people. Each of these individuals has his or her own value system and code of conduct. Furthermore, there are certain fixed patterns of behaviour, and leaders also have their own value systems in the organisation. A combination of all these factors gives an organisation its particular personality and corporate culture. The concept is difficult to define. One should first study a number of perspectives of the meaning of culture before attempting to define the concept.

Background

Corporate culture attracted the attention of leaders as much as 2 000 years ago.[9] Pericles, the greatest manager and father of Athens's golden years, coined the concept. The concept of culture first came to light in Pericles' oration at the funeral of Athenian soldiers, when he referred to the concept of culture and the role of culture in the creation of an ideal community. Pericles' age-old description of the ideal culture for Athens finds a response in contemporary statements about shared beliefs and values. More recent statements about the concept of corporate culture range from formal academic definitions that emphasise the shared values and beliefs of the people in an organisation to definitions that claim that the corporate culture of an organisation is that 'something' that makes it more successful than others.

Culture in an organisation, also termed corporate culture, **can be defined as the beliefs and values shared by people in an organisation**. It is akin to the personality of the organisation. It therefore refers to a set of basic assumptions that work so well that they are regarded as valid assumptions within the enterprise. These assumptions are upheld as the correct way to do things or understand problems in the particular enterprise. The term 'basic assumptions' refers to the following:[10]

- **Beliefs** or convictions about the world and how it works. These beliefs are based on and reinforced by personal experience. A person's beliefs can be influenced by the individuals with whom he associates.
- **Values** are the community's assumptions about what ideals are worth pursuing, for example, striving for success or avoiding debt. Values are also based on personal experience and the influence of the members of the community with whom an individual associates.

11.9.1 Elements that determine a corporate culture

An organisation's culture is determined by numerous elements, such as symbols, rituals, ideologies, language, tales, assumptions, relationships and humour.

Symbols

The symbols of organisational culture include the following:

1. the architecture of the buildings
2. the arrangement of offices

3. the name of the organisation and the use of departmental title
4. the way outsiders are dealt with

Dorbyl moved out of its massive Dorbyl Park headquarters in Bedfordview and into offices for a staff of 17 in Parktown at the end of March 1997. The move was seen as symbolic of the end of the old company. A **profit-driven culture** was introduced and those parts of its business which did not achieve appropriate returns have been sold.

Source: *Financial Mail*, 7 February 1997, p 70.

The following is said of Toyota:

'The climate in the company is conducive to easy interaction between people. At the same time, exceptionally high performance demands are made. In other words, Toyota is a company espousing a winning and a team culture,' says the 36-year-old top executive.

In his simple, functional office, with a glass of water in hand, he talks fluently and enthusiastically about vehicle manufacture, his life, the country and the challenges awaiting it. He is obviously very much at ease at Toyota.

'The fact that the chief executive of the company is Bert Wessels (son of the founder) still makes for a family atmosphere,' he says. 'It creates an easy environment in which people are challenged to use their own initiative and achieve their potential.'

Source: *F&T Weekly*, 8 November 1996, p 55.

Engen filling stations throughout the country are recognised by their characteristic red and blue colour scheme. The head office of Volkskas Bank in Pretoria, an impressive skyscraper, reflects its image as a modern progressive bank.

Organisation culture is often reflected and created by the **building** and **offices** of the organisation. The physical environment of the organisation reflects employees' pride in their work, the importance of ostentation and tradition for them, and the relative status of members of the organisation. In many organisations such as Volkskas and Nedbank, top management always occupies the top floors in the building.

Likewise, the **physical arrangement of offices** also has certain cultural implications. The arrangement of chairs and tables at meetings makes an explicit statement about the relationships between employees, managers, customers, and so forth.

Additional characteristics manifested by culture are the name of the organisation, departmental titles, and slogans used within the organisation. A specific slogan introduced together with a new strategy may be extremely forceful.

Commercial banks tend to make great use of symbols when it comes to offices and buildings. Certain banks, such as Volkskas, build impressive skyscrapers in which their offices are situated. People's positions in the organisational hierarchy are often reflected in the level of their offices in the building. Thus top management frequently occupies the top floors of a building.

Commercial banks also use specific colour combinations in their interior decorating. Examples are Volkskas Bank's grey and red and Standard Bank's blue and grey. Each of these organisations endeavours to reflect something about its culture through these symbols.

The way in which **outsiders** are handled in their dealings with the organisation symbolises organisational values and the relationship of the organisation with the environment. A reception area with a friendly receptionist who greets all visitors with a charming smile and gives them her undivided attention conveys a totally different image to the setup in which visitors have difficulty attracting the receptionist's attention on arrival. Another manifestation of this relationship is in the way prospective employees are greeted and taken into service in an organisation. Socialisation of new employees is another aspect that indicates organisational culture.

Rituals

Rituals refer to practices and reactions that occur repeatedly and have a certain significance within the organisation. These rituals set certain boundaries and relationships between employees, managers, customers, unions, and so forth. Such rituals include farewell parties, the allocation of parking bays and the size of offices. In short, they are indicative of values upheld in an organisation. At Unisa, for example, only senior members of staff have privileges such as undercover parking. In addition, seniority also determines how many chairs an employee has in the office, the size of the desk and whether or not the office has a carpet.

Ideologies

The beliefs, moral principles and values underlying decision making within an enterprise may be explicit and set the pace, or be barely visible at all in the organisation. It has been found that many of the most successful organisations make clear and strong expressions of corporate values. Ironically enough, the strong guidelines and ideologies that foster motivation and commitment are often not even set down in writing.

The most significant values and beliefs within an organisation are those of top management. These values filter through in memos, guidelines and personal and other behaviour. Values within an organisation are supported and reinforced by various rules and procedures in respect of recognition, remuneration, punitive measures and socialisation, as well as tales and hero figures in the organisation.

Sometimes the value systems of various managers in an organisation differ radically and are totally conflicting. An endeavour should be made to resolve such problems and to tighten up the organisation's ideologies. This may be achieved by open discussion of the value systems of different managers, their differences and the implications thereof.

Language

Language and language usage are important manifestations of corporate culture. One of the components here is that certain language groups have certain values and customs. Thus one might find in a predominantly English organisation that there are different value systems compared to, say, a predominantly Afrikaans or Xhosa organisation.

Moreover, the continual use of certain words and phrases tells its own story about the prevailing corporate culture within an enterprise. In certain enterprises strong, aggressive words and phrases such as 'destroy all competitors' and 'price wars' clearly depict the type of culture that prevails. Consider the language and the way in which Shoprite Checkers, Pick 'n Pay and the Hyperama advertise their products.

Tales

Often certain stories circulate in an organisation depicting certain unique qualities and characteristics considered unique to the organisation. Tales about the organisation can be subdivided into three general themes:[11]

1. **Equality.** The basic value of equality among members of an organisation is demonstrated in these stories. In this way, stories may be told about a certain superior/manager who behaves inhumanely. Other stories may revolve around the characteristics and action necessary to achieve success in the organisation.
2. **Security.** These stories revolve around the action of an organisation when an employee, for instance, makes a mistake.
3. **Control.** This theme concerns the way in which certain people deal with particular internal and external problems. This demonstrates the sources and degree of control applied.

Assumptions

Different groups in an organisation may have different assumptions about how certain tasks should be performed. These differences may result in misunderstandings and conflict. Some enterprises may even have the experience that people with different professional training belong to different groups with divergent assumptions. Even employees who belong to different unions can manifest different assumptions. It is a well-known fact that engineers and accountants often have disagreements. It is vital that an organisation recognises the various groups.

Relationships

This refers to relationships that may arise as manifestations of a particular corporate culture. The reference here is to specific types of relationships:

- relationships between managers and subordinates
- relationships between managers
- relationships between different departments
- relationships between people in the same department
- relationships between employees of the organisation and outsiders

Communication between various groups in the organisation in which different relationships prevail is vital.

Humour

Humour can convey certain messages about corporate culture. Jokes about cultural outsiders indicate a definite boundary between 'we' and 'they'. In this way, employees identify with the organisation. Such humour may subtly focus attention on divergent or corresponding assumptions.

11.10 CONCLUSION

In this chapter change and culture were discussed. Forces of change exist both within organisations and in the external environment. Change may be described as the following process: denial, resistance, exploration and commitment.

Change triggers emotional reaction because of the uncertainty involved and most organisational change efforts run into some form of employee resistance. Resistance to change can be overcome by education and communication, participation and involvement, facilitation and support, negotiation and rewards, and coercion and manipulation.

Organisational culture has a major influence on change because change often entails transforming basic values and beliefs. Organisational culture can be defined as the beliefs and values shared by people in an organisation. Culture is determined by numerous elements which were discussed in this chapter.

11.11 REFERENCES

1. Bedeian, AG. 1994. *Management*, 3 ed. Orlando: Dryden Press, p 312.
2. Griffin, RW. 1987. *Management*, 2 ed. Boston: Houghton Mifflin, p 358.
3. Truswell, H. 1995. Die meneer van Mr Price. *Finansies & Tegniek*, 11 August, p 43.

4. Lussier, RN. 1997. *Management: Concepts, Applications, Skill Development*. Ohio: South-Western College Publishing.

5. Patti, RJ. 1974. Organisational resistance and change: The view from below. *Social Service Review*, vol 48, pp 367–383.

6. Ivancevich, JM, Donnelly, JH & Gibson, JL. 1989. *Management: Principles and Functions*, 4 ed. Homewood, Illinois: Irwin, p 576.

7. Stanislao, J & Stanislao, BC, in Bateman, TS & Zeithaml, CP. 1990. *Management: Function and Strategy*. Homewood, Illinois, p 714.

8. De Klerk, A. 1989. *'n Ondersoek na Aspekte van Korporatiewe Kultuur by Eskom*. Unpublished MCom dissertation. Pretoria: University of South Africa, pp 1–5.

9. Clemens, JK. 1986. A lesson from 431 BC. *Fortune*, vol 114, pp 161–162.

10. Sathe, V. 1985. *Culture and Related Corporate Realities: Text, Cases and Readings on Organisational Entry, Establishment and Change*. Homewood, Ill: Irwin, pp 11–12.

11. Wilkins, in Ulrich, WL. 1984. HRM and culture: History, ritual and myth. *Human Resource Management*, vol 23, no 2, pp 117–128.

Part 4

. . . .

The Leadership Process

12 Leadership

Key issues

- The importance of leadership as a fundamental management function
- The nature and components of leadership
- Leadership versus management
- Different leadership models
- Contemporary perspectives on leadership
- The interfaces between leadership and organisational politics

12.1 INTRODUCTION

If organisations consisted of machines that could execute management's orders promptly, predictably and with mechanical precision, only the planning and organisational tasks of management would be necessary for its objectives to be attained. But organisations are made up of machines **and** people. It is people who give life to the organisation — hence they are one of its most important resources. People are probably also the most complex resource in the organisation, because they are unpredictable and different. Each individual in an organisation has a different combination of interests, capabilities, habits, skills and objectives and is differently motivated. In fact, the latest research on motivation shows that a significant percentage of people dislike work because of **genetic factors**, while others have a predisposition for work.[1] Thus each person has a personal agenda that does not necessarily put the interests of the business organisation first. An organisation's human resources are therefore extremely complex.

Directing this complex resource of the organisation — guiding the behaviour of or leading the employees of an organisation — requires a complicated management activity, namely leadership. Because of the complexity of the human resource and its management, this section examines specific topics necessary for a better understanding of leadership. Chapter 12, the introductory chapter in this section, provides a basic framework for leadership. Chapter 13 discusses the motivation of people by leaders as part of the leadership process. One can better understand the focal point of this chapter, namely the nature of leadership and certain perspectives of leadership models, against this background. Chapter 14 deals with communication, and chapters 15 and 16 with the human dimension and groups in management.

The nature and components of leadership will now be examined.

12.2 THE NATURE AND COMPONENTS OF LEADERSHIP

12.2.1 Introduction

Leadership is one of the most controversial and researched subjects in management. Leadership, or the process of leading, is one of the four fundamental management functions according to which this book is structured. If an organisation is to attain its objectives, someone must set certain activities in motion and keep them going. In the preceding sections, the first two of the four main management functions were discussed, namely planning and organising. These two functions set the wheels of the management process in motion, but the process is by no means complete, because the plans formulated to achieve the objectives must become reality. Thus the management activities that are **set in motion** must also be **kept in motion** for the objectives to be attained. It is here that the third fundamental function of management comes into play, namely the initiative that management takes to set the organisation's activities in motion. In leading, management also gives **direction** to the organisation's activities so that all its resources are deployed as effectively as possible to realise its objectives. Once management has provided the necessary leadership to set the management process in motion, it must periodically monitor the situation to see that the activities and resources are applied properly to enable the organisation to continue functioning **productively**. Thus **control** is exercised; this is the fourth fundamental management function, and is discussed in chapter 17.

12.2.2 The nature of leadership

Leadership is the process of directing the behaviour of others towards the accomplishment of certain objectives. It involves taking the lead to bridge the gap between formulating plans and reaching objectives, in other words translating plans into reality. Leadership is a somewhat elusive concept and is difficult to define precisely. It involves elements such as influencing people, giving orders, motivating people, either as individuals or in groups, managing conflict and communicating with subordinates. Although, from a management perspective, there are various facets of leadership, it is fundamentally the task of management to direct the activities and performance of people so that the objectives of the organisation can be attained.

Top South African business leaders of the 20th century

A study by the University of Cape Town's Graduate School of Business surveyed the opinions of 100 top executives from a sample of the 500 largest companies. They were asked to name three people they regarded as the country's greatest entrepreneurs of this century.

Casino and hotel supremo Sol Kerzner and tobacco magnate Anton Rupert have been voted by their peers as South Africa's top entrepreneurs of the 20th century.

Mr Kerzner and Mr Rupert were joint first, Liberty Life's Donny Gordon was third, followed by Raymond Ackerman of Pick 'n Pay, Anglo's Sir Ernest Oppenheimer and Christo Wiese of Pepkor. Close behind came Anglo's Harry Oppenheimer, Altech's Bill Venter, Tony Factor, Barlow Rand's Punch Barlow, estate agency boss Aida Geffen and Toyota's Albert Wessels.

Sixty-two entrepreneurs were mentioned, most coming from the business and industrial sectors. Some sportsmen, including Ali Bacher and Gary Player, were mentioned, as were President Nelson Mandela and FW de Klerk. The study showed that the traits most often associated with entrepreneurship were strong leadership abilities, persistence, resourcefulness, risk taking and self-confidence.

Source: *Business Times*, 11 February 1996, p 6.

Leadership is, therefore, the activity that infuses energy into the organisation to activate its members and resources to get things moving and keep them in motion.

Leadership, more specifically, entails activities such as transmitting information to subordinates; formulating the organisation's mission, objectives and plans and explaining these to subordinates; giving orders and instructions to subordinates; deliberating with subordinates; supervising the work of subordinates; taking steps to improve the performance of subordinates; disciplining subordinates; and dealing with conflicts.[2] Included in this is the fact that a leader also motivates his or her people, has a knowledge of how people behave as individuals and in groups, and communicates well — in the interests of higher productivity and performance. In short, taking the reins of leadership is a duty that is performed by someone who is in charge of the activities of others. In its simplest form, leadership is the relationship and interaction between superior and subordinate. Leadership is the influence of a leader on his or her followers and, conversely, the influence of a subordinate on a leader. The latter refers more specifically to information and reactions fed back to leaders, which enable them to adjust their style of leadership and plans.

Against this overview of the nature of leadership, leadership can now be defined from a management perspective as **influencing and directing the behaviour of individuals and groups in such a way that they work willingly to pursue the objectives and goals of the organisation**. This task involves knowledge of the behaviour of individuals (chapter 15) and groups (chapter 16), motivation (chapter 13) and communication (chapter 14).

Leadership differs across international boundaries

> **Americans** emphasise coordination, cooperation with people, understanding and delegation as the most important leadership qualities. This is possibly a reflection of their democratic way of life.
>
> The **British** set great store by general fortitude, integrity, discretion and willpower.
>
> **Europeans** stress the quality of leadership or supremacy, natural authority, discipline and inspiration and see themselves as a reflection of the European aristocratic tradition (Napoleon, Bismarck and De Gaulle).
>
> The **German** management elite manifests authoritarian tendencies to retain the leadership function (*Führung*) for themselves, and tend to delegate authority only for routine functions (*Leitung*).
>
> Source: Dr AE Rupert. Leierskap vir die toekoms. Lecture as honorary professor at the University of Pretoria, 3 September 1965.

12.2.3 The components of leadership

Against the preceding overview of the nature of leadership, it is clear that it is a complex management function and that the definition formulated above is merely an attempt to give direction to the numerous perspectives on the concept. If one wishes to formalise the complex process of leadership from the preceding discussion and definition, certain components emerge, namely **authority, power, influence, delegation, responsibility and accountability**.

Authority is the right of a leader to give orders and demand action from subordinates. **Power**, however, refers to the ability of a leader to influence the behaviour of others without necessarily using this authority. **Influence** is the ability to apply authority and power in such a way that followers take action. Military leaders influence soldiers in such a way that they kill people, and in the context of the organisation, followers are often influenced to make personal sacrifices for the sake of the organisation. At times the task of a leader might also involve passing his or her authority on to a subordinate to do something on his or her behalf. This is known as **delegation** and entails subdividing a task and passing a smaller part of it on to a subordinate together with the necessary authority to execute it. The final component of leadership is accepting **responsibility** and **accountability**. Leaders have the responsibility of performing a task according to orders, and have a duty to account for their actions. Figure 12.1 depicts the five components of leadership.

For the sake of good leadership and the effective management of the organisation the delicate balance of the different leadership components should be maintained. Therefore, excessive authority may mean an autocratic leadership style, which could undermine the motivation of subordinates. Similarly, a subordinate can accept responsibility for a task and account for himself or herself only if management delegates enough of the right sort of authority to him or her. Knowledge of the interaction and maintenance of the balance of the components of leadership is important to an understanding of the concept of leadership. To further explain the concept of leadership, it is necessary at this stage to discuss the above components in more detail.

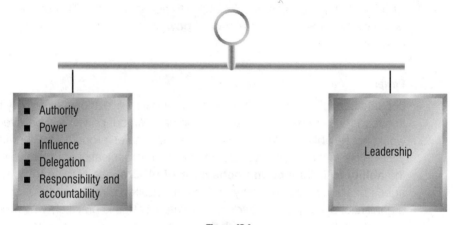

Figure 12.1
The balance of the components of leadership

Authority

On occasion, every leader, regardless of the level of management at which he or she operates, is also a manager who has to ensure that his or her subordinates work together to attain the objectives of the organisation. Without authority a manager cannot manage — cannot set the management process in motion and keep it going. Authority, therefore, entails having the right to perform certain actions according to specific guidelines, the right to say who must do what, the right to expect people to do their duty and to punish failure or negligence.[3] It involves the right to insist on action by subordinates and the right to act against them. Authority ultimately resides in the owners or shareholders, who delegate it to the directors, who, in turn, pass it on to the top managers, who again delegate it to middle management, and so on, right down to the lower levels of management.

Delegation is in a certain sense the source of authority, and management delegates authority to subordinates so that they, in turn, can perform certain actions and enforce action on the part of others. In this way, certain bank managers may have the authority to enter the bank safe, others may have the authority to sign cheques on behalf of the organisation and others again may have the authority to negotiate on behalf of the organisation and the power to enter into contracts. The organisation delegates this authority to them, and this refers particularly to **formal authority**

The most obvious example of formal authority is the defence force, in which the bearers of particular authority wear badges signifying their rank. Thus a major has authority over a lieutenant, who, in turn, is of higher rank than a sergeant, and so on down the line. Managers in a civilian organisation do not wear visible signs of their recognised authority, but authority is assigned to a specific position or rank in the organisation in the same way. The right to expect others to act, however, is allocated to a particular manager not only by the organisation, but also by members of a group who feel that this person has the ability to act as a leader. This concept of informal authority overlaps with the concept of **power** and merits more comprehensive discussion.

Power

Leaders can influence their followers and apply their authority effectively because a true leader has power of one kind or another. Without power, it is believed, a leader would not be able to influence his or her subordinates properly to voluntarily perform their duties in the productive attainment of the organisation's objectives. Power, or the **ability to influence the behaviour of others**, has nothing to do with a manager's position in the hierarchy and is not acquired through a title or an entry in an organisational diagram. A leader has to earn it. This is precisely why a person who has both authority and power, that is, a manager with power, is far more effective than a manager who only has authority.

Research by French and Raven,[4] which is generally accepted in literature on management, identifies the following kinds of power.

Legitimate power

This refers to the authority that the organisation grants to a particular position. Thus a manager has the right to compel subordinates to perform their duties and to dismiss them if they do not. Legitimate power is, therefore, the same as authority. However, the fact that a manager does have legitimate power does not necessarily make him or her a good leader.

The power of reward

This is the power to give or withhold rewards. Such rewards may include raises in salary, bonuses, recognition or interesting assignments. The greater the number of rewards conferred by a manager and the more important these rewards are to subordinates, the greater his or her reward power.

Coercive power

This is the power to enforce compliance through fear, either psychological or physical. Criminal gangsters often exercise this power through physical violence. There is certainly no question of physical violence in a contemporary organisation, but psychological or emotional fear of dismissal or social exclusion from a group is a kind of power that managers can use to bring pressure to bear on their subordinates.

Referent power

This refers to personal power and is a somewhat abstract concept. In this situation, subordinates follow their leader simply because they like, respect or identify with him or her. In others words, the leader's personal characteristics make him or her attractive. Such a leader is said to have charisma.

Expert power

This is power based on knowledge and expertise and a leader who possesses it, has special power over those who need this knowledge or information. The more important the information, and the fewer the number of the people who possess it, the greater the power of the person who commands it.

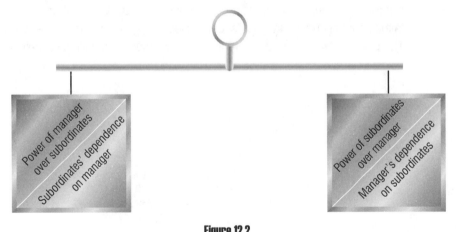

Figure 12.2
Balancing the power of management and of subordinates

A manager who possesses all five kinds of power is a strong leader. However, not only managers or leaders have power — subordinates also possess it. Managers, for instance, sometimes depend on their subordinates for information; a subordinate may have social influence over others whose cooperation is needed; or a subordinate may have the ability to perform a specific task. Managers should therefore realise that subordinates also have power, and they should use their own power judiciously and only to the extent necessary to realise their objectives. Effective managers use their leadership or power in a way that maintains a healthy balance between their own power and that of their subordinates. Figure 12.2 illustrates this balance.

In addition to authority and power, which were discussed above as two of the foundations of leadership, let us now examine some of the characteristics of leadership.

The preceding discussion of the nature and most important components of leadership indicates the significance of leadership in the management process.

12.2.4 The importance of leadership

The performance of any organisation, small or large, is directly related to the quality of its leadership. In fact, the business world has many examples in which the success or downfall of a particular organisation can be attributed to a specific leader. Dr Anton Rupert, for example, built the Rembrandt group into an international business empire. Likewise, Raymond Ackerman of Pick 'n Pay established what was to become the biggest retail operation in South Africa. The success of these business organisations is not necessarily due to these individuals' competence as managers but rather to their ability as leaders. Similarly, in numerous other fields, for instance in the political and military fields, certain leaders give direction to people's existence. The point we wish to make here is that good managers will lead their organisations

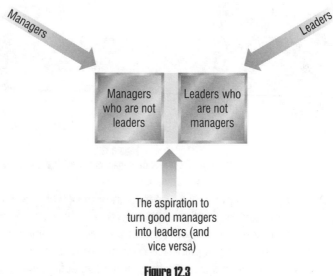

Figure 12.3
The integration of leadership and management

Leaders and successful organisations

There are many ways for an investor to value a share. Most involve assumptions made from historical financial data. Important as these may be, especially over the short term, the past does not necessarily reflect the future — as seventies investors in oil stocks found out in the eighties.

One way of getting some logical indication of how a company will cope with the uncertainties of the future is to assess the personality and mental agility of the chief executive. He sets managerial attitudes, the corporate climate and the financial goals. In fact, there are some investors who believe all else pales beside the quality of the man at the top. They quote examples of the impact a CE can have on a company — Lee Iacocca at Chrysler, for instance. Another example can be seen in the behaviour of the share price of Rembrandt. The company tells the public so little in its financial statements that an investment in it amounts to an act of faith in chairman Anton Rupert.

- Simply put, when investors buy a share, they are in reality buying a man. Others minimise a CE's importance. One Johannesburg stockbroker suggests that the CE probably accounts for only about 15 % of the share price of a company; but he admits that investors need to see someone firmly in charge. When Gencor had three men in control, the share was given a low rating. The perception changed when Derek Keys took charge.

- Bill Venter, Altron founder and executive chairman, has an image almost inseparable from that of his companies — which are very highly rated. He puts it this way: 'The fact that a company attracts attention — and favourable attention — will depend upon the person in charge and his track record. A record of having produced results draws the attention of the press and the analysts. If a competent CE leaves a company, there is a gap; and if he goes to a badly managed company, that company will receive attention.'

- Liberty Life chairman and founder Donald Gordon is emphatic that the CE's role in linking the company with the community outside is vital, and the public relations departments cannot do the job alone: 'The CE is the face of the company and the banner bearer.' And Gordon should know — his company is the most highly rated in the insurance sector.

- Meyer Khan, previous MD of South African Breweries, suggests that the entrepreneur tends to be more high-profile than the professional manager who has worked his way up. 'People love winners and they build charisma around them.']

Source: Kenney, P. 1989. Shares in the man. *The Executive*, April, pp 11–15.

to greater heights of achievement, productivity and profitability if they are good leaders as well. It is here that good leadership is so important from a management perspective. Good managers are not necessarily good leaders. To increase the performance of the organisation, it is obviously desirable that all managers should also be good leaders, which is why organisations seek, and train, people who are good managers and leaders. Turning managers into leaders so that they can become better managers is the underlying principle behind the study of leadership. There is already a considerable body of knowledge on leadership, and this knowledge can be productively applied to increase managerial effectiveness. Figure 12.3 illustrates this aspiration.

12.3   LEADER VERSUS MANAGER

Leading is not the same as managing. Leadership and management are related, but they are not the same. A person can be a manager, a leader, both, or neither. Management is much broader in scope than leadership and deals with all the functions of management, including leading. Some basic distinctions between management and leadership are summarised in table 12.1.

Table 12.1
The distinction between management and leadership

Activity	Management	Leadership
■ Creating an agenda	■ Planning: Establishing goals and objectives and formulating strategies and plans to reach the goals	■ Establishing direction: Develop a mission and strategies for change
■ Developing a human network to achieve the agenda	■ Organising and staffing: Develop a structure for the assignment of tasks and resources	■ Aligning people: Motivate people and teams to follow a vision
■ Outcomes	■ Produce the results expected by stakeholders	■ Produce change and often dramatic results

Source: Griffin, RW. 1993. *Management*. Boston: Houghton Mifflin.

Managers focus on **nonbehavioural** aspects of management such as the systematic selection of goals and objectives, the development of strategies to achieve these goals, the design of the organisation and the control of the activities required to attain the goals. In contrast, leaders focus on the **behavioural** aspects of management; the leaders focus on energising people to change what needs to be changed and to steer the organisation in a certain direction. Organisations need both management and leadership to be effective.

Johan Kotter on leadership and management

> **Leadership** involves bringing about change, envisioning a new future for the organisation and impassioning people to commit and dedicate themselves to the new directions.
>
> **Management**, on the other hand, is more directed to maintaining the *status quo*, albeit very effectively, and availing the sustained effort needed to maintain new directions. It has a flavour of bureaucracy, system and procedure.
>
> Source: *People Dynamics*, August 1997, p 27.

Because the **influence** that leaders have on subordinates has such a profound effect on the performance of the organisation, numerous efforts have been made to establish exactly what it is that enables leaders to influence their subordinates. We now examine the foundations of leadership that have emerged from years of studying and searching for good leadership qualities.

In a nutshell

> ■ Leadership is the ability to influence others to cooperate willingly.
> ■ Management includes leadership in addition to other functions of management, such as planning, organising and controlling.

12.4   LEADERSHIP MODELS AND THE FOUNDATIONS OF LEADERSHIP

12.4.1 Introduction

The preceding discussion on the importance of good leadership in effective management shows clearly why this subject has been so widely researched. It has to be determined exactly what it is that makes a person a good leader. And some people are still convinced that good leaders are born and not made — an opinion with which many researchers disagree. In analysing the concepts of leadership, and searching for the traits that make good leaders, various leadership models have been researched, developed and tested in an effort to pinpoint the most important modes of behaviour that good leaders manifest. The research centred on the assumption that identifying the leadership qualities that make certain people outstanding leaders would be to the advantage of both organisations and society, because organisations and nations would become more sophisticated in their selection of leaders. Only true leaders would then be appointed, which would mean that the organisation and the community would function more effectively.

Spurred on by the assumption that certain personality traits and models of behaviour are decisive for the success of a leader, research into leadership and leadership models has investigated leadership characteristics and behaviour, as well as all sorts of approaches to, and theories of leadership, including a few contemporary perspectives. An overview of the research that gave rise to specific leadership models, theories and perspectives will now help to throw more light on the issue of leadership and management.

12.4.2 Leadership characteristics

The first organised efforts by psychologists and other researchers to learn more about leadership involved the analysis and identification of the personal qualities of leaders. The underlying idea was that strong leaders have certain basic traits that distinguish them from nonleaders, and if these traits could be isolated and identified, then potential leaders could be recognised. In their search for identifiable leadership traits, the researchers followed two basic approaches.[5] First, they tried to compare the characteristics of those who had come forward as leaders with those who were not leaders and, secondly, they compared the characteristics of effective leaders with those regarded as ineffective leaders.

Most of the studies fell into the first category and researchers held that leadership traits include qualities such as intelligence, assertiveness, above-average height, a good vocabulary, attractiveness, self-assurance, an extrovert personality, and similar characteristics.[6] Literally thousands of studies were conducted to identify important leadership traits. However, the researchers were disappointed time and again with the results because there were so many exceptions. For each set of 'leadership' traits identified, they found millions of people who were not leaders but who had those attributes. Napoleon, for example, was short of stature and Abraham Lincoln was an introvert, yet both were outstanding leaders. Another possibility that emerged from the research was that individuals become more self-assured and communicate better after they have achieved leadership positions. In other words, traits that come to the fore after a while are the **result** of the leadership position rather than the **cause** of it. The second category of research, namely a comparison of the traits of successful and unsuccessful leaders, failed to contribute anything startling. The studies did, however, show that effective leadership is not the result of a specific set of traits but rather how well a leader's traits correspond with the qualities required for a specific position.

Research into leadership traits can be regarded as unsuccessful. The lack of any progress in constructing a leadership model, however, did serve as an incentive to researchers to study other variables concerned with leadership.

Divergent characteristics of leaders in the same organisation 1948–1992

In an interview with Helen Suzman on her political career spanning 36 years under five prime ministers, the following leadership traits of these leaders emerged:

■ DF Malan was a dour person who seldom smiled.

■ HF Verwoerd was the most unpredictable of them all. He was the only man that Mrs Suzman had ever been afraid of.

■ John Vorster was a charming person who communicated well.

■ PW Botha was arrogant and always wanted to have his own way.

■ FW de Klerk was unconventional, courteous and communicated well with people.

Source: *Sarie*, 19 February 1992, p 31.

Leadership studies

■ The latest studies on leadership show that women are less likely to emerge as leaders than men, but are just as effective as men when they do.

■ Certainly one of the most famous female leaders of all time is Margaret Thatcher, former Prime Minister of Britain.

■ Subordinates regard women in managerial positions as being just as competent as men.

Source: Stoner, JA & Freeman, RE. 1992. *Management*. Englewood Cliffs, NJ: Prentice-Hall, p 474.

12.4.3 The behavioural approach to leadership

In the research into the behaviour of leaders, the new hypothesis was that the behaviour or actions of successful leaders differed from those of unsuccessful leaders. Thus, instead of trying to establish what a successful leader was, the researchers tried to determine what successful leaders do — how they delegate, communicate, motivate their subordinates, and so on. The opinion was that behaviour, unlike **traits**, can be acquired. Thus managers who are trained in the 'right' behaviour variables become more effective leaders. This research also showed, however, that leadership behaviour that seems to be appropriate in one situation is not necessarily valid in another. The successful manager of a hypermarket will not necessarily be effective in electronics manufacturing. The research into leadership behaviour did bring to light the realisation that by participating in a group a person can manifest and establish certain leadership behaviour. To function effectively, a group needs **someone** to perform two important functions, namely **job-related functions** that concern problem solving, and **social functions** that are necessary to maintain the group. Against the background of the preceding assumptions, both the University of Michigan and Ohio State University conducted studies in this field, and both came up with the finding that leaders manifest certain **leadership behaviour**.

The Michigan studies, under the guidance of Likert, identified two basic forms of leadership behaviour, namely:[7]

1. **Task-oriented leader behaviour**, in which the leader is concerned primarily with careful supervision and control to ensure that subordinates do their work satisfactorily. This leadership style implies pressure on subordinates to perform. For task-oriented leaders, subordinates are merely instruments to get the work done.
2. **Employee-oriented leader behaviour**, in which the leader applies less control and more motivation and participative management to get the job done. This leadership style focuses on people and their needs and progress.

The leadership style of Derek Keys

'I don't think of myself as a manager,' he said. 'I have never managed anything. I have acted as an intelligent audience watching some very remarkable managers, trying to be helpful and constructive. I try to be a loving, critical audience. The only way to develop an excellent manager is to give that kind of setting.

'Why love? Contrary to external appearance, a chief executive is a sensitive flower. If he thinks you are not with him he can't communicate. He has to feel you don't represent a threat. He should be presented with a picture of himself as he could be. People need help in seeing the next stage in their own development.

'Why critical? If you are not critical, you are not doing your job. You have to raise the other point of view, generate an alternative scenario that could actually be better. I stress that one is an audience because you are a passive spectator. You can't interfere with a manager in full career.

'Finally, you have to provide the applause. That's why I see my role in Gencor as being a loving, critical audience to superior people so that they can become the stars they really are.'

Source: Derek Keys, former chairman of Gencor and Minister of Finance, *Business Times*, 21 October 1990, p 3.

So, whereas the first leadership style stresses the actual job, the second concerns the development of motivated groups. Likert showed a preference for the second approach,[8] probably because the Michigan research found that production performance was higher among employee-oriented leaders than task-oriented leaders. In the first group, job satisfaction was high and labour turnover and absenteeism low, while exactly the opposite was true under task-oriented leaders.

One conclusion drawn from the Michigan research which identified the two divergent leadership styles is that leadership does not have only one dimension, and that both dimensions (task-oriented leadership and employee-oriented leadership) may be necessary for success.

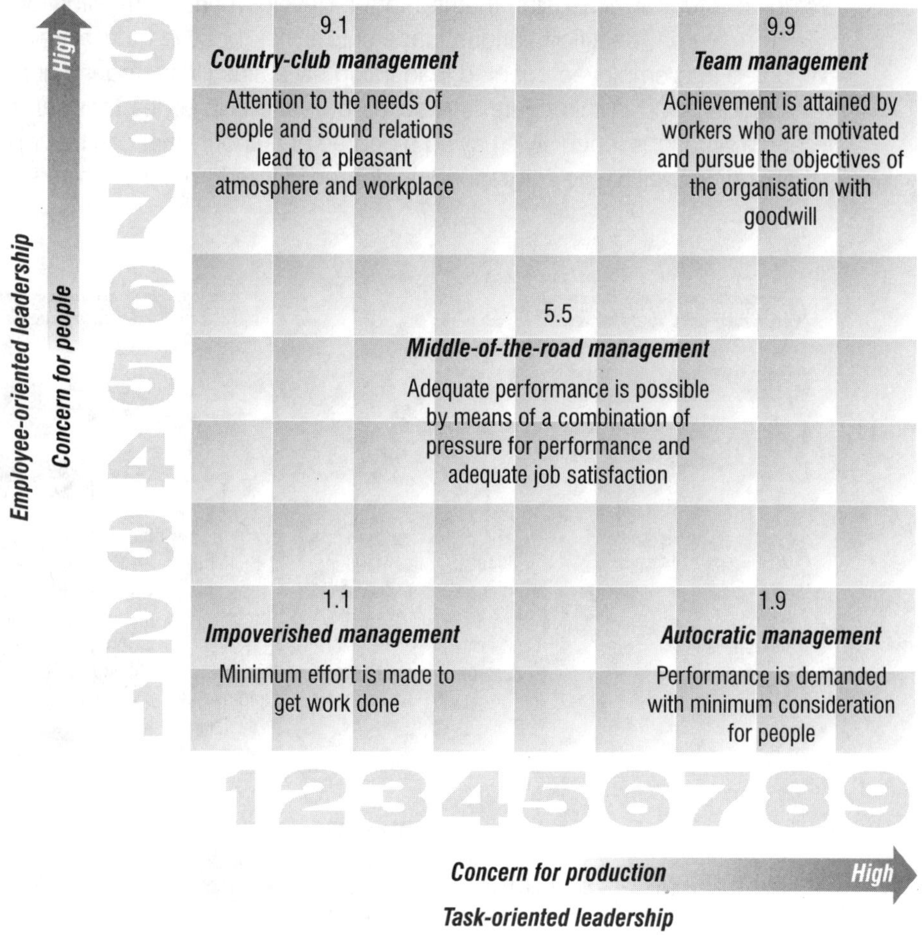

Figure 12.4
The leadership grid
Source: Blake, RR & McCanse, AA. 1991. *Leadership Dilemmas: Grid Solutions*. Scientific Methods, p 29.

On the basis of these two leadership behaviour models or leadership styles, the **leadership grid**[9] was developed as an instrument to identify a suitable leadership style so that managers can be trained and directed towards the 'ideal' leadership style. Figure 12.4 shows how the leadership grid works. The task-oriented leadership style is situated on the horizontal axis, and the employee-oriented leadership style on the vertical exis, the ideal style being at the top right where production is optimised by means of democratic management and therefore a well-motivated team of workers.

To complement the Michigan research, which studied the behaviour of leaders in an effort to develop the ideal leadership model, Tannenbaum and Schmidt[10] studied a further dimension that led to the development of the situational models. Their research identified various leadership styles between the extremes of task-oriented and employee-oriented leadership styles, as illustrated in figure 12.5. The model depicted in this figure is a series of leadership styles that can be used in certain situations, each style having a degree of authority that can be applied by the manager as well as the corresponding degree of freedom within which subordinates can act.

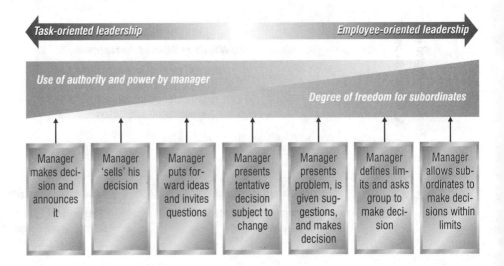

Figure 12.5
A continuum of leadership behaviour
Source: Tannenbaum, R & Schmidt, WH. 1973. How to choose a leadership pattern. *Harvard Business Review*. Harvard College.

A movement from left to right in the model also indicates a change from autocratic to democratic leadership, depending on the particular situation, which demands a certain style of leadership. Consequently, a group that works well together reacts better to more freedom than to strict supervision. However, if a group is too large or is geographically dispersed, a participative or democratic style of management is difficult to apply.

12.4.4 The contingency or situational approaches to leadership

To complement the trait and behaviour approaches to leadership and to tie in with Tannenbaum and Schmidt's multidimensional view on leadership, which gave rise to the contingency or situational approach to leadership, researchers started identifying factors in each **situation** that influence the effectiveness of leadership. The reason for this approach and the shift in emphasis was that the trait and behaviour approaches indicated that no single trait or style is equally effective in all situations, and that good leadership is the result of additional variables. Hence leaders' success can be attributed partly to certain traits and behaviour patterns that they manifest, but is determined primarily by how good their traits and behaviour are in satisfying **the needs of their subordinates and the situation**. Leaders' success is often determined by their ability to sum up a situation and adapt their style of leadership accordingly. This is the contingency or situational approach to leadership. Instead of searching for the best style of leadership, managers should rather learn to establish interfaces with regard to themselves, the situation and the needs of their subordinates.

Various models were developed against the background of this explanation of the situational approach to leadership, the most prominent being Fiedler's contingency model, Hersey and Blanchard's life-cycle model of leadership and the Vroom-Yetton-Jago model. These models will now be examined briefly to show the direction in which research into leadership was moving.

Fiedler's contingency theory of leadership[11]

Fiedler's contingency or situational theory of leadership is based on the assumption that for lack of a single best style, successful leadership depends on the fit with regard to the leader, the subordinate and the situation. In short, a leader's effectiveness is determined by how well his or her style fits the situation. According to Fiedler, a manager can maintain this fit by :

- understanding his or her style of leadership (task-oriented or employee-oriented style)
- analysing the situation to determine whether or not the style will be effective (an autocratic style may be needed)
- matching the style and the situation by changing the latter so that it is compatible with the style, because a leader cannot change his or her style to tie in with the situation. An example here would be to select an autocratic leader to fill a position that requires a task-oriented leader, or adapting a position to give an autocratic leader more formal authority over his or her subordinates.

Hersey and Blanchard's model[12]

A well-known situational leadership model is that of Hersey and Blanchard, which presupposes that the most effective management style for a particular situation is determined by the **maturity of the subordinates**. The maturity of the subordinate in this regard is defined as that person's need for achievement, willingness to accept responsibility and task-related ability and experience. The degree or level of maturity is illustrated in different quadrants in figure 12.6.

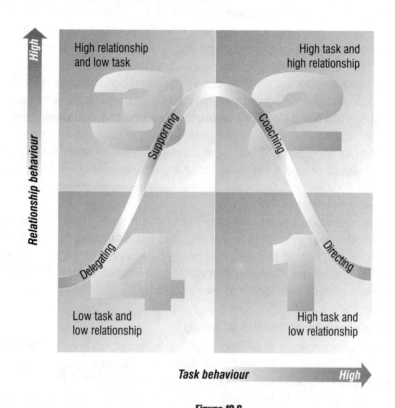

Figure 12.6
The life-cycle model of leadership
Source: Adapted from Hersey, P & Blanchard, K. 1988. *Management of Organisation Behaviour: Utilising Human Resources*. Englewood Cliffs, NJ: Prentice-Hall, p 171.

When subordinates are too immature for a task and lack the necessary experience, the leader in quadrant 1 should function in such a way that he or she trains subordinates and therefore imposes a task-oriented leadership style. As subordinates start being able to accept more responsibility, their leader orientation and style move into quadrant 2, where they must manage both **tasks** and **relationships**. The next quadrant into which subordinates move in the process of task maturity is quadrant 3, where the manager does not help subordinates with the job because they have mastered it and can do it on their own, but rather gives them his or her support. Hence a manager's style of leadership in this quadrant revolves around the exchange of ideas, participation in problem solving and general support. Subordinates learn to manage themselves and move into quadrant 4, where they resolve their own conflict and develop the ability to work together as a group. In this quadrant managers can delegate responsibility because their subordinates are mature enough to accept it. The leadership cycle model presupposes that managerial style must change as a group of subordinates develops and reaches maturity. To be successful, leaders must therefore analyse the situation, determine what degree of training or support is necessary and adapt their style as their subordinates develop.

The Vroom-Yetton-Jago model[13]

Another situational leadership model is the Vroom-Yetton-Jago model, which predicts the degree of group participation in certain situations and then sets standards for the inclusion of subordinates in the decision-making process. This model is therefore an aid for managers to determine how and to what extent subordinates should participate in problem solving. To be able to handle a certain situation, the model isolated five styles of leadership that represent a continuum from authoritarian to fully participative. Depending on the nature of the problem, a specific style may be suitable.

The trait, behaviour and situational approaches or theories of leadership have contributed a great deal to the theoretical body of knowledge of leadership. These days, researchers and managers alike have a better understanding of leadership and how it influences the behaviour and success of organisations. Each of the three approaches, however, has shortcomings. No one group of leadership traits is representative of all leaders, and no single type of behaviour works equally well in all situations with all people. It is precisely because of these shortcomings that research into leadership continues.

12.4.5 Some contemporary perspectives on leadership

Research on leadership behaviour is moving in many directions and new lines of enquiry are opened up in an effort to construct the ultimate leadership model. The following contemporary perspectives are but a few of the numerous enquiries into new leadership models.

Transactional leadership

The traditional management function of **leading** is also known as **transactional leadership**. Transactional leaders do what managers do: they clarify the role of subordinates, initiate structures and provide appropriate rewards. They conform to organisational norms and values. Their style is characterised by objectives, standards, evaluation and correction of performance, policies and procedures. The manager and transactional leader are characterised as directing and controlling in a stable structure and having greater centralised authority. Transactional leadership is characteristic of stable, ongoing situations: exchanges or agreements with followers are developed, pointing out what the followers will receive if they do something right — and wrong. The transactional leadership approach only lasts as long as the needs of both leader and follower are satisfied by the continuing exchange process. It is consequently not a relationship that binds the leader and follower together in a mutual and continuing pursuit of higher purpose. In an environment such as South Africa where change is occurring, a purely transactional style of leadership may be counterproductive.[14]

Charismatic leadership

One area of growing interest in leadership research is the study of individuals who have an exceptional impact on their organisations. These individuals may be called **charismatic** leaders. **Charismatic leaders** have the capacity to motivate people to do more than what is normally expected of them; they motivate subordinates to transcend their expected performance. Charismatic leaders tend to be less predictable than transactional leaders. They create an atmosphere of change and have an emotional impact on subordinates. The phenomenal growth of Microsoft is directly linked to Bill Gates, a typical example of a charismatic leader.

Transformational leadership

Transformational leaders are similar to charismatic leaders, but are distinguished by their special ability to bring about innovation and change. Transformational leaders emerge to take an organisation through major strategic change. They have the ability to make the necessary (successful) changes in the organisation's mission, structure and human resource management. Transformational leadership is most appropriate in dynamic situations such as the current setup in South Africa. The transformation of South African organisations to include all South Africans and to empower them managerially and economically calls for transformational leadership.

Female leadership

As women move into higher positions in organisations, they bring a different leadership style to organisations — a style that is very effective in today's turbulent corporate environment.[15] Although women also possess assertiveness, initiative and aggressiveness, they tend to engage in leadership behaviour that can be called interactive. An **interactive leader** is concerned with consensus building, is open and inclusive, encourages participation by others and is more caring than the leadership style of many males.[16] Interactive leadership is, however, not confined to women. Anyone can develop these qualities, especially because they are consistent with the recent trend towards participation and empowerment.

Dynamic engagement

One new line of enquiry into leadership behaviour is known as **dynamic engagement**.[17] In this case the researchers simply revisited the basics of leadership by trying to single out the five fundamental practices and ten behaviours that leaders use to get 'extraordinary things' done. They asked the leaders to describe themselves when they were at their best, and they asked employees to list the characteristics they admired most in leaders. The first column in table 12.2 shows that these five categories of practices and behaviours are similar to others described in this chapter. The researchers argue that these five categories and ten behaviours can be learnt by most leaders.

Table 12.2
Fundamental practices and behaviours of exceptional leaders

Practices and behaviours of exceptional leaders	Practices and behaviour of President Mandela
Challenging the process ■ Search for opportunities ■ Experiment and take risks	■ He challenged the apartheid system and used every opportunity to change it. His risks included a 27-year prison term.
Inspiring a shared vision ■ Envision the future ■ Enlist others	■ After his release and his inauguration as South Africa's first black president, he inspired every South African with his vision of a democratic South Africa. He enlisted even former opponents as supporters and members of his 'rainbow nation'.
Enabling others to act ■ Foster collaboration ■ Strengthen others	■ President Mandela was instrumental in moving South Africa towards black majority rule, thereby creating an environment of enablement.
Modelling the way ■ Set the example ■ Plan small wins	■ Since his release he has emerged as the world's most significant moral leader since Mahatma Gandhi. Each day he sets the example for reconciliation.
Encouraging the heart ■ Recognise the individual contribution ■ Celebrate accomplishments	■ President Mandela constantly encourages blacks, whites, women and Afrikaners to become part of his vision of one nation, and he gives credit where it is due — even to former opponents.

Source: Adapted from Kanzas, JM & Pasner, BZ, as discussed in Stoner, JAF, Freeman, RE & Gilbert, DR. 1995. *Management*. Englewood Cliffs, NJ: Prentice-Hall, p 488; and Mandela, N. 1994. *Long Walk to Freedom*. Randburg: Macdonald Purnell.

President Nelson Mandela can be described as a leader who practises dynamic engagement and who gets 'extraordinary things' done. Already described by the popular press as one of the 20th century's top ten leaders,[18] it is interesting, as the second column in table 12.2 shows, how the leadership behaviours and practices apply to him.

Charismatic leadership style as well as transformational leadership style would also apply to President Mandela's leadership. The significance of the research summarised in table 12.2, especially the fact that most of it also applies to other leadership styles, is the fact that there is no single 'best' way of leading people to levels higher than their usual performance.

The AMROP study on South African leadership[19]

Research on leadership behaviour is one of the many lines of enquiry into a new management model for South Africa. Of particular importance is a 1996 study by AMROP International on the question of black leadership in South Africa. The survey is a first step in understanding how South African executives from different backgrounds bring different emphasis to their leadership roles. The results of this survey can be summarised as follows.

Creating a vision: looking backwards and forwards

The black executive group has a strong strategic emphasis. Their focus is not so much on short-term hurdles but on longer-term objectives. They are fairly traditional leaders who prefer tried and trusted practices. Their hesitancy to experiment may blind them to opportunities which offer a competitive edge.

They believe that specialist knowledge is an important resource, so they prepare themselves thoroughly, consulting relevant sources of information. This may slow down the decision-making process, taking up time which could be better spent. Greater efficiency needs to be developed.

Developing followership: the value of community

In line with the philosophy of *ubuntu*, black executives maintain a balance between the dignity of position and establishing harmonious interpersonal relationships. Compared with executives from more individualistic cultures, they may seem fairly restrained and hesitant to use their power of persuasion to change others' approaches. This does not mean, however, that they are not in touch with their colleagues, but their relationships have a different basis. A sense of community and respect for others help to create a less adversarial relationship between management and subordinates. Greater emotional investment in the relationship with followers could lead to more inspirational leadership.

Implementing the vision: from control to flexibility

Previous sociopolitical circumstances limited experience in positions of authority and in the implementation of business strategy by this group. Given the watchful eyes of critics, who are constantly alert to confirmation of their prejudices, a careful system approach to implementation is appropriate. At a time when executives have come to rely on intuitive decision making, reliance on procedure and formal communication of directives is quite valuable. But the pressures of time and global competition dictate that greater confidence in exercising and delegating responsibility is essential. Greater experience and success should facilitate a more flexible, hands-on leadership style.

Achieving results: support for success

Fostered by a belief in themselves and a will to win, white South African executives have developed a natural competitiveness. Their black colleagues share their focus on bottom-line achievement, but their striving for individual success is modified by the *ubuntu* philosophy. They are motivated to seek win–win solutions, where success is not achieved at the price of harmonious interpersonal relationships. A greater depth of experience as leaders will boost trust in their own judgment and facilitate greater decisiveness, contributing to greater effectiveness in competition.

Team playing: communalism replaces individualism

A hierarchical, top-down *modus operandi* has been characteristic of South African business. Communication is a powerful value in South African black culture and working for the common good is valued above aggressive competitiveness and individual excellence. This emphasis on teamwork is reflected in black executives' leadership approach: a spirit of cooperation, grassroots support for decisions and encouragement of a free flow of information are its hallmarks. A more Afrocentric view of management brings greater sensitivity to bear on interpersonal relationships, without forfeiting the right to rely on the executive's own judgment in the final analysis. This perspective is very necessary if business is to adjust to a changing South African environment.

Another contemporary perspective on leadership, namely the **attribution theory**, assumes that leaders seek proof or reasons why subordinates act in a certain way, and then modify their behaviour to guide their followers.[20]

The theories of leadership discussed above assume that subordinates' behaviour, job satisfaction and performance can be directly linked to the behaviour of leaders. According to these theories, the subordinates' achievements depend almost completely on the motivation, support and rewards of leaders. The latest research, however, identifies certain internal factors that influence both the job satisfaction and the performance of subordinates without these being derived in any way from their leaders. These factors are known as **substitutes for leadership**,[21] and include, for example, subordinates' ability, experience, need for independence, professionalism and indifference to the organisation's reward system. A rigid reward system, such as that often encountered in bureaucratic systems like universities, robs a leader of his or her **power of reward**, thus reducing and even neutralising the importance of the leadership role. Another example of **substitutes for leadership**, where the leader's role is replaced and neutralised by the traits of followers, is in the casualty department at a hospital. The professionalism and experience of the doctors and hospital staff do not allow them to wait for someone to give orders in an emergency for the simple reason that leadership in this situation becomes superfluous or is largely neutralised by substitute factors.

Against the background of this discussion of the foundations of leadership, there is no doubt that it is a complex concept and that a variety of models have been researched and developed without the **best** characteristics or the **most successful** style of leadership being highlighted. Even though a best theory might never become a reality, each model provides insights into how managers can influence subordinates and obtain their enthusiastic cooperation to attain the organisation's objectives.

12.5 POLITICAL BEHAVIOUR IN ORGANISATIONS AND LEADERSHIP

12.5.1 Introduction

Another general influence on the behaviour of leaders and subordinates in an organisation is the omnipresent phenomenon of politics in organisations. **Political behaviour** in an organisation entails people gaining and exercising power to obtain a specific outcome.[22] This somewhat vague term plays a decisive role in both leaders' and subordinates' behaviour when decisions have to be made and certain people in the organisation have certain preferences about how things should be done. Politics in organisations may involve decisions such as the location of a factory or less important decisions such as what time tea should be served. People participate to advance themselves, protect themselves from others or simply to gain and exercise power. This power can be executed by individuals or groups of individuals.

Politics in organisations

A survey of workers' opinions of how politics works in organisations revealed that 33 % of the respondents held that politics in their organisations influenced salary decisions, while 28 % felt that politics influenced the appointment of new personnel. The respondents also maintained that the phenomenon of organisational politics occurs more at the higher levels of management than at the lower levels.

Source: Griffin, RW. 1993. *Management*, 2 ed. Boston: Houghton Mifflin, p 496.

Politics in organisations is often regarded as dirty play and back stabbing, and even though the concept, like power, is somewhat elusive and does influence behaviour, it is a reality. Management should therefore realise that this does play a role in leadership and that it should be used constructively.

12.5.2 Types of political behaviour in organisations

So far, research has identified four basic forms of political behaviour that occur widely in organisations.[23] The first, **inducement**, occurs when a manager offers or promises something to someone in exchange for that person's support. Thus a manager will 'see' if he or she can perhaps create a post for a subordinate's friend or cousin, if this subordinate is prepared to put in a good word for the manager's section at the evaluation of the management committee.

The second kind of political behaviour is **persuasion**. Persuasion plays on a subordinate's emotions and may even include fear or guilt.

A third kind of political behaviour is the **creation of an obligation**. One manager might, for example, support another in a specific matter, even if opposed to it, being fully aware that the first manager's support will be needed sometime in the future to realise his or her own objectives.

Finally, **coercion** is behaviour that borders on the use of violence to get one's own way. A manager may, for example, threaten to withhold someone's reward or resources in an effort to get his or her own way.

12.5.3 Managing political behaviour in organisations

The question that arises at this point is how management should handle political behaviour in the organisation so that it can be used constructively in the leadership process. Various guidelines, such as the following, have been proposed:[24]

- Managers should be aware of the fact that certain people regard some of their actions as political even if this is not so.
- By granting adequate autonomy and responsibility to subordinates and receiving regular feedback, managers reduce the risk of political behaviour on the part of subordinates.
- Managers should limit the use of power if they wish to reduce the likelihood of being accused of political behaviour.
- Managers should clear the air by handling differences and conflict openly. Frank and open discussion of differences will reduce the likelihood of political behaviour.
- Managers should avoid covert behaviour.
- Management systems that evaluate subordinates realistically, reward systems that are directly linked to performance, and a restriction on competition among

managers in respect of resource allocation can also help to keep political behaviour to a minimum.

Of course, it is far easier to formulate the above guidelines than to apply them in practice. The fact remains that managers should realise that political behaviour occurs in every conceivable kind of organisation, and they should rather try to manage it than pretend that it does not exist. Positive management of political behaviour and conflict in organisations is a decisive factor in successful leadership.

12.6 CONCLUSION

Because of the critical role that managers play in the successful management of organisations, leadership is one of the most important functions of the management process. Leadership, which is defined as influencing and directing individuals' and groups' behaviour to enable them to pursue the objectives of an organisation, is studied from three perspectives, namely the characteristics of leaders, the behaviour of leaders and the situation in which leaders and subordinates function. Although no one group of character traits can be regarded as the 'best' style for a particular situation, the analyses and theories of leadership have provided insights into this complex component of management. Contemporary perspectives of leadership will advance the theoretical body of knowledge of leadership. Political behaviour in organisations is another behavioural factor that can either strengthen or neutralise the influence of leaders, and as such should be managed constructively.

12.7 REFERENCES

1. Genes on the job. *Fortune Magazine*. 13 January 1992, p 66.
2. Reynders, HJJ. 1975. *Die Taak van die Bedryfsleier*. Pretoria: Van Schaik, p 100.
3. Ibid p 78.
4. French, RP & Raven, B. The basis of social power, in Griffin RW. 1993. *Management*. Boston: Houghton Mifflin, pp 77–479.
5. Stoner, JA & Freeman, RE. 1992. *Management*. Englewood Cliffs, NJ: Prentice-Hall, pp 473–474.
6. Griffin op cit p 480.
7. Stoner & Freeman op cit p 475.
8. Griffin op cit pp 481–482.
9. Ibid p 483.
10. Stoner & Freeman op cit p 476.
11. Baird, LS, Post, JE & Makon, JF. 1990. *Management: Functions and Responsibilities*. New York: Harper & Row, pp 302–307.

12. Hersey, P & Blanchard, K. 1988. *Management of Organisation Behaviour: Utilising Human Resources*. Englewood Cliffs, NJ: Prentice-Hall, p 171.
13. For an in-depth discussion of this model see Stoner & Freeman op cit pp 486–489.
14. Grobler, PA. 1996. Leadership challenges facing companies in the new South Africa. Unisa, February. Inaugural lecture.
15. Daft, RL. 1995. *Management*. Fort Worth: The Dryden Press, p 392.
16. Ibid.
17. Based on Kouzes, JM & Posner, BZ. *The Leadership Challenge: How to Get Extraordinary Things Done in Organisations*, as discussed in Stoner et al op cit p 487.
18. *Sunday Times*, 11 February 1996, p 6.
19. AMROP. 1996. The challenge of diversity. Report on the South African executive. Johannesburg.
20. Baird et al op cit pp 310–311.
21. Ibid p 311.
22. Griffin op cit p 496.
23. Beeman, DR & Sharkey, TW. 1987. The use and abuse of corporate power in *Business Horizons*, March–April, pp 26–30.
24. Griffin op cit p 497.

13 Motivation

- What motivation encompasses
- The different motivation theories
- The motivation theories and the motivation process
- Money as a motivator
- How to create jobs that motivate

13.1 INTRODUCTION

Motivation is the number one problem facing managers today.[1] In the past it was believed that if one paid people adequately they would be motivated. However, today it is recognised that South Africans — and workers around the world — do not work for money only. Money is not the only motivator; job satisfaction and empowerment are also important motivators.

Focus

How can South African managers ensure that employees are motivated? The discussion that follows should guide you when confronted with motivational issues. More specifically, our focus in this chapter will be on:
- what motivation encompasses
- the different motivation theories
- combining the motivation theories with the motivation process
- the motivational value of money
- how to create jobs that motivate

Motivation is also the most important hurdle in productivity. The World Competitive Yearbook 1996[2] ranks South Africa 46th on its 'worker motivation' scale. This is lower than many Eastern bloc countries (previously known as communist countries), such as Poland, Hungary, Russia and the Czech Republic.

Diversity in the workplace makes the issue of worker motivation in South Africa even more complex. Motivation theories that apply in North America, Europe and Japan do not necessarily apply to South Africa's diverse workforce.

13.2 WHAT MOTIVATION ENCOMPASSES

There are numerous definitions of motivation. The word 'motivation' is derived from the Latin word *movere*, which means to move. The following is the most common definition of the word: 'A motive is an inner state that energises or moves (hence motivation), and that directs or channels behaviour toward goals.'[3] This inner state of mind that channels a worker's behaviour and energy towards the attainment of goals can be regarded as a process. Figure 13.1 depicts the motivation process in its simplest form.

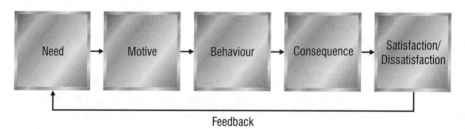

Feedback

Figure 13.1
The motivation process

The motivation process comprises the following interdependent elements:

■ **Need**

A psychological or physiological imbalance may give rise to a need. A physiological need could arise because of lack of food or water. An example of a psychological need is the need to belong or to form friendships.

■ **Motive**

An individual's needs motivate (or drive) him to take action which he believes will satisfy his needs.

■ **Behaviour**

The individual's need will lead to specific behaviour. A hungry person might buy food; a lonely person might join a sports club.

■ **Consequence**

The consequence of the behaviour may be positive or negative. A hungry person who eats something will no longer be hungry; the lonely person could make friends at a sports club.

■ **Satisfaction/dissatisfaction**

The consequence of the behaviour could lead to satisfaction or dissatisfaction. After eating a meal and satisfying his hunger, a person might feel contented. By making friends, the lonely person may satisfy his need to have contact with other people.

■ **Feedback**

Satisfaction is usually short-lived. For this reason the motivation process has a feedback loop.

This process can also be applied in an organisation and in the work situation, because work is one of the ways in which individuals satisfy their needs. Through their work, people can satisfy their need for social interaction, status and power.

Management faces a big challenge when trying to motivate its subordinates. **Needs** and **motives** are extremely complex; we do not always know what our needs are or why we do the things we do. However, managers can observe the **behaviour** of subordinates and infer their needs and motives. Why does a specific mineworker always pitch up late for his shift? Why does his colleague work an additional shift each week? Coming late or working an additional shift is behaviour which can be observed. But what about the needs and motives that cannot be seen?

The focus of this chapter is on the inferences that explain employee motivation. These inferences are experts' explanations of the motivational issues confronting managers. They are not absolute truths; they are theories. These theories are categorised as content theories, process theories and reinforcement theories. The authors of the various theories discussed in this chapter all felt that they had the 'key' to the motivation 'treasure'. However, there is no universal solution to motivational issues, so all three categories of motivation theories are discussed in this chapter.

13.3 THE CLASSIFICATION OF MOTIVATION THEORIES

In this section, we examine the best-known motivation theories. Each theory throws light on motivation and shows how it influences job performance. As mentioned, three categories of theories are distinguished, namely **content** theories, which focus on the 'what' of motivation; **process** theories, which indicate the 'how' of motivation; and **reinforcement** theories, which emphasise ways in which behaviour can be acquired.

Motivation theories in perspective

> The motivation theories which are discussed in this chapter were developed in America. South African managers, however, work with an uniquely diversified workforce and consequently these theories may not always be applicable.
>
> South Africa is a developing country while America is a developed country. Intrinsic motivation of higher-level needs tends to be more relevant to developed countries than to developing countries where lower level-needs dominate.
>
> Even in developed countries the level of needs focus varies. In America people tend to be motivated by needs of self-esteem and self-actualisation (see Maslow's theory). In Greece and Japan security is more important, while in Sweden, Norway and Denmark people are more concerned with social needs.
>
> South African managers have to deal with major cultural differences in their workforce where, for example, the focus on business varies from individualistic approaches to group approaches. Individualistic societies (America, Canada, Great Britain and Australia) tend to have individual-istic approaches to business where self-accomplishment is valued highly. Most South African whites fall in this category. Collective societies (Japan, Mexico, Singapore, Venezuela and Pakistan) have group approaches to business where they tend to value group accomplishment and loyalty. Most black South Africans belong to this group.
>
> Source: Lussier, RN. 1997. *Management: Concepts, Applications, Skill Development* (Instructor's manual). Cincinnati: ITP, p 214.

13.3.1 Content theories

The content theories are associated with the work of researchers such as Maslow, Herzberg and McClelland. The content perspective emphasises the intrinsic factors that influence an individual's behaviour. An effort is made to answer questions such as: 'What needs do people try to satisfy?' and 'What gives rise to individual behaviour?' According to this perspective, people have intrinsic needs that they wish to satisfy or reduce and their behaviour is influenced by them.

The theories of Maslow, Herzberg and McClelland will now be discussed more comprehensively. The objective of the discussion is not to make psychologists out of managers, but to enable managers or potential managers to understand more about the complex nature of worker motivation.

Maslow's hierarchy of needs

One of the most familiar theories of individual motivation was formulated by the famous psychologist Abraham Maslow. Maslow's theory is based on two important assumptions:

1. People always want more, and their needs depend on what they already possess. A need that has already been satisfied is not a motivator — only unsatisfied needs can influence behaviour.

2. People's needs are arranged in order of importance. When one need has been partially satisfied, the next one will come forward to be satisfied. Figure 13.2 illustrates the hierarchical order of human needs according to Maslow's classification.

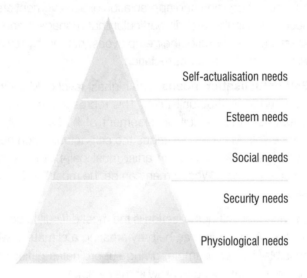

Figure 13.2
Maslow's hierarchy of needs

Let us now briefly examine the five levels in Maslow's hierarchy and their relevance to management.

1. **Physiological needs.** These represent the most basic level in the hierarchy and comprise needs such as food, water and warmth. If these needs are not met, behaviour will be directed towards satisfying them. However, once these needs are satisfied, they no longer influence behaviour. Nowadays most employees belong to trade unions which negotiate for higher wages and fringe benefits and ensure that the basic needs of their members are satisfied. Higher-order needs probably play a greater role in the motivation of the contemporary worker compared to lower-order needs.

2. **Security needs.** Once a person's basic physiological needs have been satisfied, his or her security needs come into play. Security and protection (as opposed to physical and psychological harm), job security, insurance, medical aid schemes and pension schemes satisfy an individual's need for security.

3. **Social needs.** Social needs are man's need for love, friendship, acceptance and understanding by other people and groups. In organisations, people join different groups to satisfy their social needs. By forming work groups and encouraging sufficient interaction among employees, managers can make sure that their subordinates' social needs are met.

4. **Esteem needs.** This level represents people's higher-order needs, that is their need for self-respect and recognition by others. The need for success, self-confidence, recognition and appreciation of achievement are all examples of esteem needs. It is in this area in particular that managers can play a significant role in satisfying the needs of their employees, namely by rewarding high achievement with recognition and appreciation.

5. **Self-actualisation needs.** The highest level of Maslow's hierarchy of needs is the need for self-actualisation. This represents the apex of human needs. Self-actualisation is the full development of humans' potential — to be their true unique self. Maslow[4] describes the self-actualisation needs as follows: 'A musician must make music, an artist must paint, a poet must write, if he is to be ultimately happy. What a man can be, he must be. This need we call self-actualisation.'

The need for self-actualisation is the most difficult to address in an organisational context. A manager can help by creating a climate in which self-actualisation is possible, by, for example, giving subordinates difficult and challenging jobs to master so that they can grow in their work.

The 1990s have seen a sharp upsurge worldwide in re-engineering, mergers, outsourcing and downsizing, affecting company levels that traditionally were havens of job security. In South Africa, organisations previously immune to this type of change have had their foundations shaken by drastic re-engineering programmes, resulting in loss of job security. If they cannot provide job security, what can organisations provide that would make taking up employment attractive? The answer lies in identifying the expectations, needs and desires of employees of the future and matching these with company needs and goals. Young professionals of the 1990s value a balance between job satisfaction and leisure and family activities. They are moving away from 'workaholism' towards 'balance' and 'wellness'. They are interested in quality of life, ethical and environmental issues. They value being able to express themselves and being supported by their managers. They want to be respected for who and what they are.

Source: Brews, N & Martins, N. 1996. The trust gap between employees and employers is widening. *People Dynamics*, vol 14, no 11 (Nov/Dec).

Maslow's hierarchy of needs has great intuitive appeal, which explains its popularity as a way of thinking about the causes of motivation. The hierarchy of needs is generally accepted and applied in practice, mainly for the following reasons:

- The hierarchy is easy to understand and makes sense.
- The theory highlights important categories of needs.
- A distinction is made between higher-order and lower-order needs.
- The importance of personal growth and self-actualisation in the work context is impressed upon managers.[5]

However, from the viewpoint of managerial action, Maslow's approach presents some difficulties for the following reasons:[6]

- During certain periods of their lives, people reorder the levels of the hierarchy. A recent *Wall Street Journal* report cites an example of this among 'survivors' of corporate downsizing. 'These people's esteem, belonging, and even security needs can quickly become unsatisfied, even though they retain their jobs. People can have very meaningful work but as they watch their colleagues being retrenched, their fear is that they may be the next to go, addressing the very basic human security needs.'
- It is very difficult to determine the level of needs at which an individual is currently motivated. Part of the difficulty here is to distinguish between fairly insignificant fluctuations in needs that all people experience from time to time and the more meaningful, less frequent shifts in people's needs.
- It is difficult to measure an individual's needs — a manager must create motivating environments for many different subordinates, each with his or her own needs.
- Individuals differ in the extent to which they feel that a need has been sufficiently satisfied. The extent to which employees are motivated to pursue money, recognition, autonomy, or other need satisfiers differs from one person to the next.

From the above it is evident that there are a number of issues when examining Maslow's theory. Although certain difficulties arise in the practical managerial application of the theory, it still provides an adequate taxonomy of human needs in organisational settings. Its value arises primarily from the description of behaviour, but also because the theory had a major impact on organisational theory and practice.[7]

Herzberg's two-factor motivation theory

Frederick Herzberg conducted a study in the 1950s on motivation among about 200 accountants and engineers employed by organisations near Pittsburgh, Pennsylvania, in the USA.

Herzberg held that factors that gave rise to job dissatisfaction related to job context, and these he called **hygiene factors**. Hygiene factors, as in the medical context, are preventive, that is, their presence will prevent dissatisfaction, but will not lead to satisfaction (see figure 13.3): they will prevent you from 'becoming ill' but will not make you 'healthy'. Hygiene factors cannot motivate. To motivate employees you need to make jobs more interesting and challenging. In other words, job content factors will motivate employees. These factors Herzberg called **motivators**.

Table 13.1 illustrates the difference between motivators and hygiene factors.

Table 13.1
Herzberg's two-factor theory

Hygiene factors	Motivators
▪ Company policy and administration ▪ Supervision ▪ Relationship with supervisor ▪ Working conditions ▪ Salary ▪ Relationship with co-workers ▪ Personal life ▪ Relationship with subordinates ▪ Status ▪ Security	▪ Achievement ▪ Recognition ▪ The work itself ▪ Responsibility ▪ Advancement ▪ Growth
Source: Herzberg, F. 1968. One more time: How do you motivate employees? *Harvard Business Review*, January/February.	

According to Herzberg,[8] the opposite of job satisfaction is not dissatisfaction, as was traditionally believed, but no satisfaction. Removing dissatisfying characteristics from a job does not necessarily make the job satisfying. As illustrated in figure 13.3, Herzberg proposes that his findings indicate a dual continuum: the opposite of 'satisfaction' is 'no satisfaction', and the opposite of 'dissatisfaction' is 'no dissatisfaction'.

When hygiene factors are provided for, people will not be dissatisfied, but neither will they be satisfied. Only motivators such as achievement, recognition, the work itself, responsibility and growth will lead to job satisfaction and motivation.

Herzberg's theory made the following important contribution to the body of knowledge of motivation.[9]

▪ It extended Maslow's ideas and made them more applicable in the workplace.

▪ It focused attention on the importance of job-centred factors in the motivation of employees.

▪ This insight gave rise to increasing interest in job enrichment and the restructuring of work. (Job enrichment is discussed later in this chapter.)

▪ It offers an explanation for the limited influence of more money, fringe benefits and better working conditions on motivation.

■ It points out that if managers concentrate only on hygiene factors, motivation will not occur. Motivators should be built into a position in order to stimulate motivation.

Motivational factors across cultures

A study of work motivation across cultures, namely American, Russian and Chinese, highlighted significant differences in the motivational factors impacting on various cultures. In the Republic of China (Taiwan), two factors, identified as hygiene factors by Herzberg, job security and good wages, are reported as the two top motivators by workers. The American and Russian samples reported two factors, identified by Herzberg as motivators, as their top ratings. (Russian sample: promotion and growth in the organisation and 'feeling in' on things; American sample: appreciation of work done and 'feeling in' on things.)

Source: Silverthorne, CP. 1992. Work motivation in the United States, Russia, and the Republic of China (Taiwan): A comparison. *Journal of Applied Social Psychology,* vol 22, no 17 (September).

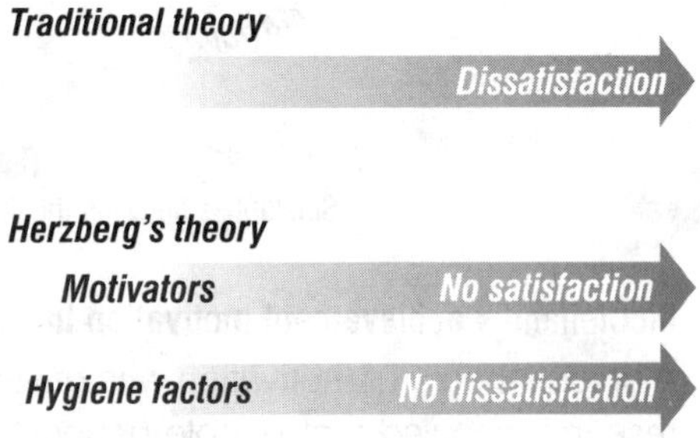

Traditional theory

> Dissatisfaction

Herzberg's theory

Motivators — No satisfaction

Hygiene factors — No dissatisfaction

Figure 13.3
Opposing views of satisfaction and dissatisfaction
Source: Adapted from Donnelly, JH, Gibson, JC & Ivancevich, JM. 1989. *Management: Principles and Functions*, 4 ed. Homewood, Ill: Irwin, p 379.

One major shortcoming in Herzberg's original study is that the sample on which he based his findings was not representative of the general population as it consisted of accountants and engineers. Some of his critics feel that his results would not be applicable to blue-collar workers.

Herzberg's theory has been widely read, regardless of criticisms, and few managers are unfamiliar with his recommendations. The increased popularity of vertically expanding jobs (as discussed later in this chapter) to allow workers greater responsibility in planning and controlling their work, can perhaps be largely attributed to Herzberg's research and recommendations.[10]

A close study of Herzberg's theory shows that what he is in fact saying is that most employees have already satisfied their social and economic needs to such an extent that they are primarily motivated by Maslow's higher-order needs (self-esteem and self-actualisation). However, they must continue to satisfy their lower-order needs in order to maintain their present situation.

Figure 13.4 illustrates the similarities between the two theories.

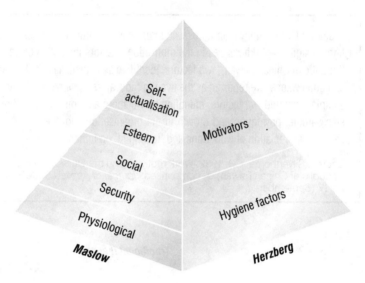

Figure 13.4
Similarities between the theories of Maslow and Herzberg

McClelland's achievement motivation theory

A unique theory of motivation was developed by David McClelland. Although earlier research showed that people generally have a need for achievement, McClelland could prove in his research that some have a greater need than others.

He used the Thematic Apperception Test (TAT) to identify needs. The test comprises a series of ambiguous pictures and the test subjects are asked to write stories about the pictures.

McClelland processed his results and drew the conclusion that different needs predominate in different people. He distinguished three needs:

1. the need for achievement (nAch)
2. the need for affiliation (nAff)
3. the need for power (nPow)

From an organisational perspective, McClelland's theory indicates the following:[11]

1. To function successfully, an organisation should employ mostly employees with a high need for achievement. People with a high nAch enjoy work that offers a

challenge. Such people take the responsibility for solving problems and set fairly difficult goals for themselves. They are usually prepared to take calculated risks and to receive feedback on their performance.

Managers can motivate employees with a high nAch by giving them nonroutine, challenging tasks with clear, attainable goals. Feedback on their performance should be fast and frequent. They should continually be given increased responsibility for doing new things.

2. People with a high need for affiliation are disposed to positive human relations. They need acceptance, support and camaraderie. Such people are often prepared to conform in order to fit in with other people's norms.

People with a high nAff tend to have a low nPow. People with a high nAff usually seek jobs in a service profession such as teaching, human resources management or social work. They tend to avoid management because they enjoy being part of a group rather than being a leader.

Managers can motivate high nAff workers by having them work in teams and giving them lots of praise and recognition. They derive satisfaction from the people they work with rather than from the task itself.

3. Some people have a need to dominate and control: theirs is a need for power. People with a high nPow prefer work where they can direct other people's actions, set goals and make decisions. Such people are well suited to managerial positions.

People with a high nPow tend to have a low need for affiliation. Managers can motivate high nPow employees by allowing them to plan and control their jobs as much as possible. They should be included in the decision-making process, especially when the decision affects them. High nPow people perform best alone rather than in teams. They should be assigned to a complete task rather than just a part of it.

nAch as predictor of success

Need for achievement (nAch) was found to be a significant predictor of success for indigenous entrepreneurs in Transkei. In a research project it was found that entrepreneurs with high and above-average nAch levels tended to engage in more sophisticated business ventures than their counterparts low on nAch. Male entrepreneurs in this study were found to have a higher mean score nAch than their female counterparts. A one-unit enhancement in nAch level of the entrepreneur could induce a more than proportionate rise in the labour growth rate of the small entrepreneurial firm.

Source: Mahadea, D. 1994. Achievement motivation and business success in Transkei. *Development Southern Africa*, vol 11, no 1 (February).

A significant aspect of McClelland's research for managers is that the need for achievement can be acquired.[12] Of importance to South African managers is that McClelland's research showed that people are not static and can improve their own abilities. South Africa's shortage of managers can therefore be alleviated by training managers and potential managers. Workers can also improve their performance if adequately motivated.

13.3.2 Process theories

In contrast to the content theories that endeavour to identify man's needs, the focus in process theories is on **how** motivation actually occurs. The emphasis is on the process of individual goal setting and the evaluation of satisfaction after the goals have been attained.

The best-known process theories are the expectancy theory developed by Victor Vroom,[13] Porter and Lawler's extension of the theory and the equity theory.

The equity theory of motivation[14]

According to the equity theory an individual must be able to perceive a relationship between:

■ the reward he receives, and
■ his performance

The relationship he perceives is based on a comparison of the input–output ratio between himself and someone else whom he regards as his equal. Therefore:

Reward (Individual's own inputs) = Reward (Comparable individual's inputs)

Inputs refer to effort, experience, qualifications, seniority and status. Outputs include praise, recognition, salary, promotion, etc. The 'comparable individual' could be a co-worker in the organisation or a worker in a different organisation doing a similar job. Of importance here is that our definition stresses the word 'perceived' and not actual input or output.

A worker's comparison of his or her own situation with relevant other workers' situations leads to one of three conclusions by the worker: he or she is under-rewarded, overrewarded or equitably rewarded.

If individuals perceive themselves to be underrewarded, they will try to restore the equity by reacting in one of the following ways:

■ reducing their own inputs by means of lower performance
■ increasing reward by asking for a raise
■ distorting the ratios by rationalising
■ trying to get the other individual to change inputs and/or rewards
■ leaving the situation
■ comparing with someone else

However, if individuals see that their reward is greater than their inputs justify, they will also take steps to restore the equity. In such a case they may:

- increase their inputs by higher performance
- reduce their reward by taking a pay cut, for instance
- distort the ratios by rationalising
- try to reduce the other person's inputs or increase his or her reward

Managers should therefore bear in mind that rewards can only motivate if workers perceive them to be fair and equitable.

The practical implications of the equity theory[15] for managers can be summarised as follows: do not underpay and do not overpay. People who are underpaid tend to respond in a counterproductive fashion, such as lowering their performance or stealing from their employers. However, while overpaid employees may improve their performance, the effect will only be temporary. It should also be remembered that, when one employee is overpaid (and perhaps raises his or her performance), others that work with that person will, according to the equity theory, perceive that they are underpaid, and lower their performance, resulting in an overall reduction in productivity.

The application of the equity theory is difficult because feelings of equity and inequity are based on perceptions that people have, which are not easy to control. One approach that managers can follow, is to be open and honest about inputs and outcomes. People tend to overestimate how much their superiors are paid and therefore feel that they are not paid enough. If information about remuneration is shared in a transparent and honest manner, feelings of unfairness may be avoided and the manager's image as a fair person can be enhanced. '

Fair and equitable remuneration

Gain sharing gets back to the simple issue that remuneration has to be fair and equitable at the end of the day ... An unskilled worker does not understand why he should increase his efforts to enhance productivity, when all of the benefits are to go to some remote group of people who are nowhere in sight.

The following question was asked of a shopsteward in a glass manufacturing concern: 'Do you feel that it is wrong to expect employees to work more efficiently and only receive nonmonetary rewards and recognition?'

The answer was:

'Yes, either we should get additional remuneration, or the work to be done must be regulated in a way which is fair and provides regular work for the same number of employees.'

Source: Bussin, M & Thompson, D. 1995. Gaining pace with gainsharing. *People Dynamics*, vol 13, no 6 (June).

The expectancy theory

The fundamental assumptions of the **expectancy theory** are that people will behave according to

1. their perception that their behaviour will lead to a certain outcome, and
2. how much they value the outcome.

André Agassi, before winning the Wimbledon singles title visualised how he would win this title — the ultimate title for any tennis player to win. This motivated him to train for hours each day until each shot was perfected.

The same principles can be applied to the motivation of workers in an organisation. According to the expectancy theory, employees have two key beliefs linking three events. The employee's work **efforts** lead to some level of **performance**. Performance, then, results in one or more **outcomes** for the employee. This is illustrated in figure 13.5.

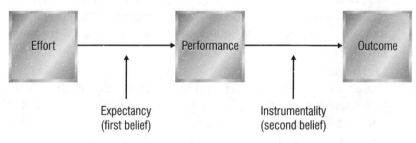

Figure 13.5
Basic concepts of the expectancy theory

The first belief, **expectancy**, refers to the probability that a worker's efforts will enable him or her to attain his or her goals. An expectancy may be high (+1) when a salesperson is sure, for example, to attain his or her goal of increasing the number of units sold per month, provided that he or she works overtime. The expectancy will be low (0) if he or she is convinced that he or she will sell no additional units after hours.

High expectations generally create higher motivation than low expectations. In the above example, the salesperson is likely to work overtime to sell the additional units.

Performance results in some kind of outcome. Increasing his or her sales volume could mean a promotion, bonus, more stress and resentment from other salespeople. If the salesperson does not work after hours, and there is no increase in units sold, the outcome could be friendship with other workers and an average salary.

The second key belief described by the expectancy theory is called **instrumentality**. Instrumentality is the perceived likelihood that performance will be followed by a specific outcome. Instrumentalities can be as high as 1 or as low as 0.

Each outcome has an associated valence. Valence is the value the outcome holds for the employee contemplating it. Valences may be positive, like the promotion mentioned above, or negative, like the stress.

Motivation can be calculated as follows:

Motivation = Expectancy × Sum of (Instrumentalities × Valence)

This calculation is illustrated in figure 13.6.

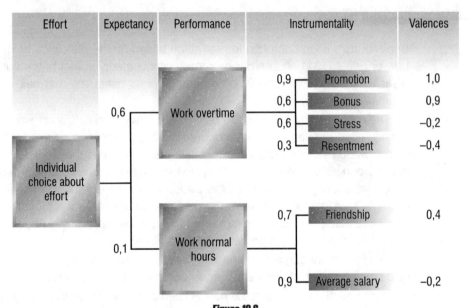

Effort	Expectancy	Performance	Instrumentality		Valences

Figure 13.6
The expectancy theory

The motivation to work overtime can be calculated as follows:

Motivation = Expectancy × Σ (Instrumentalities × Valences)
        = 0,6 × [(0,9 × 1) + (0,6 × 0,9) + (0,6 × –0,2) + (0,3 × –0,4)]
        = 0,6 × [0,9 + 0,54 – 0,12 – 0,12]
        = 0,6 × 1,2
        = 0,72 (or 72 %)

The motivation of the same person to work normal hours should be calculated using the same formula as above. Motivation in this instance is 0,01. This means that there is a 1 % chance that the worker will choose to work normal hours and a 72 % chance that he will work overtime.

People do not actually go through the calculations and choose the option with the highest score. The expectancy theory does, however, specify the important considerations that motivate people's behaviour.

The implication of the expectancy theory for management is that it should create a work environment conducive to hard work, set attainable goals and provide constant training. This should boost the confidence of employees and increase their **expectancies**. Secondly, managers should **identify valent outcomes**. Knowing the content theories should help managers in this regard. **Performance** should be made **instrumental** in positive outcomes. Good performance should be appreciated accordingly.

13.3.3 Reinforcement theories

Behaviourism is an approach to motivation based on the principles of Thorndike's Law of Effect (1911).[16] The basic premise of this theory is that behaviour that has pleasant results will probably be repeated, while behaviour that has unpleasant results will probably not.

The reinforcement theories are based on behaviour modification, which is a systematic effort to shape the behaviour of employees. To encourage specific behaviour, individuals can be rewarded (positively reinforced) as they move closer to the desired behaviour. Another way of reinforcing desired behaviour is through avoidance. Behaviour is reinforced by the avoidance of undesirable consequences. An example here is an individual who sticks to the target date for a project in order to avoid a reminder. He or she is motivated to act in the desired way (the project is on time) in order to avoid the undesirable result (reminder).

Reinforcement can also be negative and here we can distinguish between two kinds of negative reinforcement, namely punishment and extinction.

Punishment, or disciplinary action, is used by managers to discourage (weaken) undesirable behaviour. According to the reinforcement theories, the unpleasant consequences (punishment) of any undesirable behaviour will discourage an individual from repeating the behaviour. However, behaviourists hold that this form of reinforcement is not the most effective. Punishment, it is said, motivates people as soon as it is meted out, but once the negative reinforcement is neutralised, they fall back into their old patterns of undesirable behaviour. The negative side effects of punishment, for example, bitterness and animosity, reinforce the view that it should not be a desirable form of behaviour reinforcement in the workplace.

Extinction can also be used to weaken behaviour, especially behaviour that was previously rewarded. An example here is a subordinate who starts working for a new manager. His previous manager appreciated it if he told tales about his co-workers. The new manager, however, wishes to discourage such behaviour and therefore ignores these tales. If the manager doesn't react to the subordinate's tales, the subordinate's undesirable behaviour will become extinct, and probably not be repeated in the future.[17]

In reinforcement, not only is the **type** of reinforcement used important, but also **when** and **how** frequently it takes place. Various strategies are possible for scheduling reinforcement.

The fixed-interval schedule provides reinforcement at fixed times, regardless of behaviour. A monthly salary cheque does not provide much incentive because the worker becomes used to it.

The variable-interval schedule also uses time as the basis of reinforcement, but the interval differs from one reinforcement to the next. Such scheduling is useful for inspections during which employees are praised or rewarded.

The fixed-ratio schedule provides reinforcement after a fixed number of perform-ances. For example, for every ten new clients that an insurance agent in Johannes-burg recruits, he receives a free air ticket from Johannesburg to Cape Town.

The variable-ratio schedule influences the maintenance of desired behaviour the most by varying the number of behaviours required for each reinforcement. Each performance increases the possibility of a reward — hence employees are encour-aged to increase the frequency of desirable behaviour.

13.4 THE MOTIVATION PROCESS AND MOTIVATION THEORIES

The motivation theories that we have discussed so far could create the impression that there is one best theory for a specific situation. This is, however, not the case. The theories discussed, namely **content**, **process** and **reinforcement theories** are complementary. Each theory is used in a different stage of the motivation pro-cess (see figure 13.7).

In a nutshell

Content motivation theories address the question: '**What** needs do employees have that can be satisfied in their jobs?' Process motivation theories answer the question: '**How** do employees choose behaviour to fulfil their needs?' Reinforcement theories answer the question: 'What can managers do to **shape** employees' **behaviour** in ways that contribute to goal attainment?'

Figure 13.7 depicts the integration of motivation theories into the motivation pro-cess.

13.5 MONEY AS A MOTIVATOR

Virtually all theories of motivation dealt with in this chapter accept that money influ-ences employees' performance to a certain extent.

The monetary reward that employees receive is a package comprising salaries or wages and fringe benefits such as medical schemes, insurance, holiday bonuses, sick leave and housing schemes. In the light of the motivation theories, the following is evident.[18]

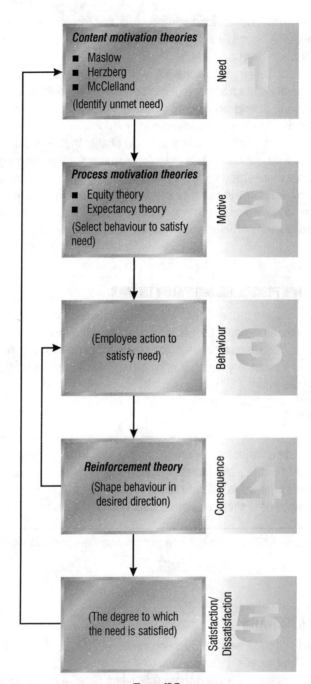

Figure 13.7
The motivation process and motivation theories
Source: Adapted from Lussier, RN. 1997. *Management: Concepts, Applications, Skill Development*. Cincinnati:
ITP, p 379.

According to **Maslow's theory**, lower-order needs can be satisfied by money. **Herzberg's** hygiene factors can be satisfied by money, although, according to his theory, motivators cannot be satisfied by money.

According to the **expectancy theory**, money can satisfy a variety of needs. The theory accepts that if employees perceive that good performance results in generous payment, money can serve as a motivator. The **reinforcement theory** puts forward money as a reward that can be used to reinforce positive job performance.

Therefore, money does play a role in motivation, although researchers agree that a reward system should also satisfy other **requirements**.[19] The idea should be generated among employees that good payment is the result of high performance. Employees should know that other rewards besides money are also linked to high performance. Maslow's lower-order needs and Herzberg's hygiene factors should be satisfied. Employees' rewards should be comparable to rewards given for similar work within the organisation and in other organisations.

Underpayment can have numerous negative effects. If an individual is dissatisfied with the payment received, the result may be poorer performance, strikes, theft and grievances. The dissatisfaction and need for higher pay will also motivate him or her to seek other work. Symptoms of too low payment in the workplace manifest in, among other things, increased absenteeism, high personnel turnover and a poor organisational climate.

Different people have different needs that they satisfy in different ways. As far as possible, the reward system of an organisation should make provision for this. This is especially relevant in South Africa where managers have to motivate a multicultural workforce.

13.6 DESIGNING JOBS THAT MOTIVATE

The last approach to motivation that will be examined in this chapter has to do with designing jobs that can motivate the workers who perform them. The discussion will focus on job enlargement, job enrichment and some aspects of the job characteristics model.

13.6.1 Job enlargement

Job enlargement entails the addition of a variety of tasks to a job to make it 'larger'. Another term used to describe this is horizontal work loading. The concept of job enlargement can be illustrated as follows:

Worker A	Worker B	Worker C	Worker D
Step 1	Step 2	Step 3	Step 4

'Society's collective vision of institutional governance is undergoing a fundamental shift — the replacement of authoritarianism by participation. Such a shift requires profound changes in our assumptions about how successful organisations must work. Technology is changing the nature of work and freeing up time — time that can be devoted to participation. Because technology reduces the number of people required to produce a given good or service, it increases the scope of production for which each worker is responsible. It increases the size of the individual job and associated responsibility. As automation and computers take on the routine or dangerous work, the new worker becomes a manager of exceptions. He or she is expected to access information, understand the context of an issue, and respond rapidly and appropriately to satisfy customers. Technology in the work itself makes each person's impact more significant and his or her commitment and involvement more critical. Most importantly, the characteristics of the new workforce mandate that organisations move to participation.'

Source: McLagan, P & Nel, C. 1996. *People Dynamics,* vol 14, no 5 (June).

According to this example a job comprising four steps will be performed by four workers, each of them specialising in one step. If 60 units of a product are manufactured per day, each worker will have to repeat his step 60 times.

However, by applying job enlargement the task can be redesigned, and will be as follows:

Worker A	Worker B	Worker C	Worker D
Step 1–4	Step 1–4	Step 1–4	Step 1–4

Instead of repeating the same step 60 times, each of the four workers will now produce 15 units of the product on his own. Each employee's work will be more meaningful to him because of this simple redesign.

Despite the above-mentioned advantages of job enlargement, the concept is still criticised. As one worker remarked: 'Before my job was restructured, I had one boring task — now I've got four!' So, although job enlargement increases the variety of tasks, it does not change the challenge that the work offers.

The concept of job enrichment originated as a result of the shortcomings of job enlargement.

13.6.2 Job enrichment

Job enrichment refers to the vertical extension of a job. Vertical work loading occurs when the planning and control of work, previously performed by people in the higher levels of management, are now performed by the person responsible for the actual job. Feedback on his work enables the worker to set new goals aimed at improved performance.

Job enrichment

Implementation of job enrichment programmes in African work settings has to recognise that different people hold various orientations to work. According to Hackman and Oldham (1980), individuals with strong needs for growth respond eagerly and positively to the opportunities provided by enriched work. In contrast, individuals with low needs for growth may not recognise the existence of such opportunities, or may not value them, or may even find them threatening and talk about being 'pushed' or stretched too far by their work.

Source: Blunt, P & Jones, ML. 1992. *Managing Organisations in Africa*. Berlin: Walter de Gruyter.

Herzberg's two-factor theory was discussed earlier on in the chapter. Herzberg[20] identifies job enrichment as an important motivation technique because in job enrichment, greater scope for personal achievement and recognition is built into the job, and this leads to greater job satisfaction.

The elements of job enrichment and their effect on motivation can be illustrated by means of the following example.[21]

The management of an insurance company launched a job enrichment programme for its punch operators because of unmotivated behaviour manifesting in low output, a high incidence of mistakes and absenteeism.

The following changes were introduced:

■ The random distribution of work was replaced by a system in which each operator was made responsible for certain accounts.

■ Certain planning and control functions were added to the punching job.

■ Operators had to liaise directly with clients. If problems arose, the operator and not the supervisor had to sort them out with the client.

■ Operators could plan their own work rosters and daily activities.

■ Each operator was held responsible for his own errors and weekly computer printouts of errors and productivity were sent directly to the operators, instead of the supervisors.

This enrichment effort had impressive effects. Fewer operators were needed, errors and absenteeism declined dramatically and the operators' attitude to their work improved, which meant greater savings for the insurance company.

Job enrichment in its simplest form (figure 13.8) implies the addition of the following to the actual activity:

■ measurable goals
■ decision-making responsibility

■ control and feedback

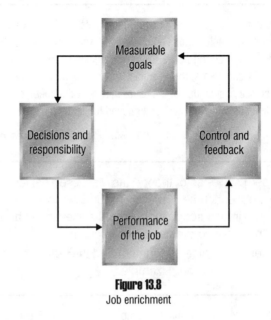

Figure 13.8
Job enrichment

An effective, though simple, way to enrich jobs, is for the manager to delegate more variety and responsibility to employees.

13.6.3 The job characteristics model[22]

The job characteristics model postulates that certain core **job dimensions** create **critical psychological states**, which in turn lead to several beneficial **personal** and **work outcomes**. The model recognises that these relationships are strongest among employees who have a high need for personal growth and development. Individuals not particularly interested in personal growth and development are not expected to experience the psychological reactions to the core job dimensions or the benefits of the predicted personal and work outcomes. Thus the model recognises an important limitation of job enrichment: not all workers can or want to apply job enrichment to their jobs. Furthermore, not all kinds of work or jobs are suitable for job enrichment.

As illustrated by figure 13.9, the five core dimensions indicated in the model are: skill variety, task identity, task significance, autonomy and feedback.

1. **Variety.** The greater the variety of tasks that a worker can use his or her various skills for, the more of a challenge the job will offer.

2. **Task identity.** This is the extent to which a job is performed in its entirety. Tasks are frequently so overspecialised that a worker can only do part of the total task, which leads to low job satisfaction.

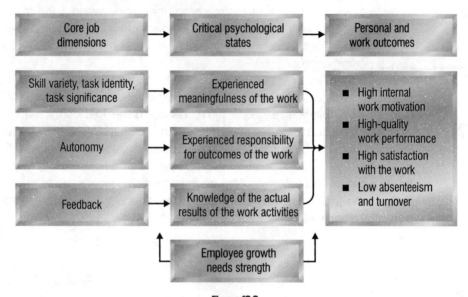

Figure 13.8
The job characteristics model
Source: Greenberg, J & Baron, RA. 1993. *Behavior in Organisations: Understanding and Managing the Human Side of Work*. Boston: Allyn & Bacon, p 139.

3. **Task significance.** This means the extent to which the task influences the lives or work of other people. It is important for people to know that their work is meaningful.
4. **Autonomy.** This refers to the control a worker has over decision making and how the task is performed. This is interrelated with the sense of responsibility that has been cultivated in the person. Management by objectives is a technique used to reinforce this dimension.
5. **Feedback.** This means the extent to which the worker receives direct and clear feedback on the effectiveness of his or her performance. This dimension is also important in terms of correcting deviations and pointing out errors.

The core dimension creates the following three critical psychological states:

1. **Experienced meaningfulness of the work.** The first three factors (variety, task identity and task significance) contribute to a task's experienced meaningfulness. According to the job characteristics model, a task is considered meaningful if it is experienced as important, valuable and worth while.
2. **Experienced responsibility for outcomes of the work.** Autonomous jobs are said to make workers feel personally responsible and accountable for the work

they perform. They are free to decide what to do and how to do it, and so feel more responsible for the results, good or bad.

3. **Knowledge of the actual results of the work activities.** Feedback gives employees knowledge of the results of their work. When a job is designed to provide people with information about the effects of their actions, they can evaluate their performance more accurately, thereby improving the effectiveness of job performance.

From the bases of the proposed relationship between the core dimensions and the resulting psychological reactions, the model postulates that job motivation would be highest when jobs performed score high on the various dimensions. A questionnaire known as the Job Diagnostic Survey (JDS) was developed to measure the degree to which various job characteristics are present in a particular job. The responses to the JDS can be used to predict the degree to which a job motivates the people who perform the job. This can be done by using an index known as the **motivating potential score** (MPS), computed as follows:

$$\text{MPS} = \frac{\text{Skill variety} + \text{Task identity} + \text{Task significance}}{3} \times \text{Autonomy} \times \text{Feedback}$$

The MPS represents an index of a job's potential to motivate workers. The higher the MPS for any given job, the greater the likelihood of beneficial personal and work outcomes, such as high internal work motivation, high-quality work performance, high satisfaction with the work and low absenteeism and turnover of the employee. By knowing a job's MPS a manager can identify jobs that could benefit by being redesigned.

The job characteristics model can guide managers to redesign jobs with the view to enhancing their motivating potential by doing the following:

■ combine jobs, enabling workers to perform the entire job (skill variety, task identity)

■ form natural units that allow workers to be identified with the work they have done (for example, where each punch operator at an insurance company is made responsible for specific accounts instead of a random distribution of work — task identity and task significance)

■ establish client relationships, allowing providers of a service to meet the recipients (skill variety, autonomy, feedback)

■ load vertically, allowing greater responsibility and control over work (autonomy)

■ provide workers with feedback on the results of their work and keep feedback channels open

What workers say about workplace involvement

> In a survey of some South African organisations aimed at establishing an agenda and developing a common vision of democracy at work among South African managers and trade unions, shop stewards expressed the view that they had more say in workplace decisions than before, but that this was limited to how to do their jobs —task-centred involvement — as opposed to power-centred involvement that encompasses strategic and financial involvement.
>
> Source: Mastrantoris, H & Nel, C. 1995. The move towards democracy at work. *People Dynamics*, vol 13, no 8 (March).

13.7   CONCLUSION

In this chapter we studied the theoretical body of knowledge of motivation in detail. We endeavoured throughout to apply the theory in practice because it is essential for contemporary managers to know what motivates their subordinates.

A historical overview of the origin of the various schools of thought was followed by a definition of the best-known content, process and reinforcement theories. In the case of Herzberg and Maslow's theories, we highlighted and discussed the differences and similarities between the two theories.

This was followed by a brief discussion of the role of money as a motivator and the motivation effects of job enlargement and job enrichment. The chapter concluded with a discussion of the job characteristics model.

13.8   REFERENCES

1. Watson, T. 1994. Linking employee motivation and satisfaction to the bottom line. *CMA Magazine*, vol 68, no 3 (April), p 4.
2. *The World Competitiveness Yearbook.* 1996. Lausanne: IMD, p 578.
3. Belelson, B & Steiner, GA. *Human Behavior*. NY: Harcourt, Brace and World, p 242.
4. Maslow, AH. 1943. A theory of human motivation. *Psychological Review*, vol 50, pp 370–396.
5. Donnelly, JH, Gibson, JC & Ivancevich, JM. 1987. *Fundamentals of Management*. Plano, Tx: Business Publications, p 297.
6. Pearce, JA & Robinson, RB. 1989. *Management*. NY: McGraw-Hill, p 450.
7. Barling, J, Fullagar, C & Bluen, S (eds). 1983. *Behaviour in Organisations: South African Perspectives*. Johannesburg: Lexicon Publishers, p 502.

8. Robbins, SP. 1993. *Organisational Behavior: Concepts, Controversies, and Applications*. Englewood Cliffs, NJ: Prentice-Hall, p 210.
9. Donnelly et al op cit p 301.
10. Robbins op cit p 211.
11. Griffin, RW. 1987. *Management,* 2 ed. Boston: Houghton Mifflin, p 393.
12. McClelland, D & Winter, D. 1969. *Motivating Economic Achievement*. NY: Free Press.
13. Vroom, V. 1964. *Work and Motivation*. NY: Wiley.
14. Griffin op cit p 398 and Gannon, MJ. 1977. *Management: An Organisation Perspective*. Boston: Little Brown.
15. Greenberg, J & Baron, RA. 1993. *Behavior in Organisations: Understanding and Managing the Human Side of Work*, 4 ed. Boston: Allyn & Bacon, p 131.
16. Thorndike, EL. 1911. *Animal Intelligence.* NY: McGraw-Hill, p 244.
17. Donnelly et al op cit p 307.
18. Ibid p 317.
19. Lawler, EE. 1981. *Pay and Organisational Development*. Reading: Addison-Wesley, pp 11–25, 61–75, quoted in Griffin op cit p 403.
20. Paul, WJ, Robinson, KB & Herzberg, F. Enrichment pays off. *Harvard Business Review*, March–April, 1969, p 61.
21. Janson, R & Purdy, JR. 1975. A new strategy for job enrichment. *California Management Review* (Summer), pp 55–71, and Hackman, JR & Oldham, G. 1975. Development of the job diagnostic survey. *Journal of Applied Psychology*, April, pp 150–170.
22. The discussion of this theory is based on Greenberg & Baron op cit pp 140–141.

14 Communication and Negotiation

Key issues

- The concept of communication
- The communication process
- Organisational communication
- Barriers to effective communication
- How managers can become better communicators
- How to use communication skills in negotiation

14.1 INTRODUCTION

Communication is an integral part of all management functions. In order to plan, organise, lead or control, managers have to communicate with their subordinates. Decision making necessitates communication, and management-by-objectives relies heavily on the communication skills of managers and subordinates. When delegating or coordinating work, managers have to communicate. Motivating and leading subordinates would be impossible without some form of communication. When controlling activities, managers have to discuss standards, monitor perform-ance and take corrective action.

The links between management and communication are clear when one looks at the roles that managers play (see figure 1.7 on page 14 above). Interpersonal roles involve interacting with employees to motivate them, resolving conflict between dif-ferent departments, and so on. Decisional roles require managers to communicate with each other to establish the most viable alternatives to realise the organisational goals, in negotiating with trade unions, and so on. Informational roles require man-agement to scan the external environment to identify threats and opportunities; they also require management to disseminate the relevant information to the rest of the organisation.

In the light of the above, it can be said that the largest part of each workday is spent on communication. In fact, at all organisational levels, at least 75 % of each workday consists of communication in some form.[1] Communication can therefore be seen as the most important skill that managers should possess.

In South Africa, the skill of communicating is made more complex by the fact that there are eleven official languages. Figure 14.1 illustrates the percentage distribution of the home languages of the South African population.

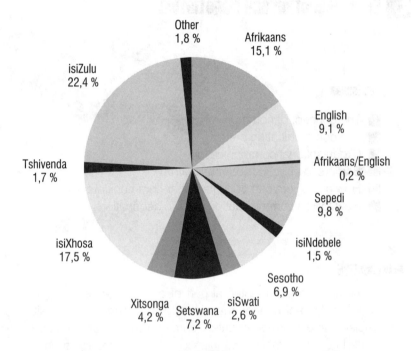

Figure 14.1
Percentage distribution of home language of the South African population
Source: Population Census, 1991. Central Statistical Service, Report no 03-01-06 (1991).

Focus

This chapter looks at communication from a management perspective. Firstly, the term *communication* will be discussed by referring inter alia to the communication process. We also look at interpersonal communication and organisational communication — with the focus on the latter. Communication barriers and strategies to enable managers to become better communicators will also receive attention. Lastly, we shall examine the use of communication skills in negotiation.

14.2   THE COMMUNICATION PROCESS

Communication can be described as the process of transmitting information and meaning. This process is used when there is something that the sender wants the receiver to know, understand or act upon. Implied in this definition is the ability to listen as no meaningful message can be conveyed without a willing listener.[2]

The complex nature of the communication process must be understood if it is to be effective and meaningful. We can best appreciate the communication process if we break it down into various steps, and illustrate them in a diagram as in figure 14.2. Bear in mind, however, that any attempt to illustrate the sequence of communication between two individuals is necessarily an oversimplification. Moreover, the steps in a communication episode are interactive; they do not occur in sequential order.

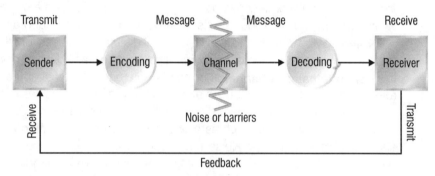

Figure 14.2
Steps in the communication process

Communication takes place between a sender and a receiver. The **sender** initiates the communication. In an organisation, the sender will be a person with information, needs or desires and a reason for communicating them to one or more other people. In the management-by-objectives (MBO) process discussed in chapter 4, the manager can initiate this process by explaining to the subordinate the goals of the entire organisation.

Encoding takes place when the manager translates the information on the organisation's goals into a series of symbols for communication. In this case the symbols used by the manager could be words or pictures. Encoding is necessary because information can be transferred from one person to another only through representations or symbols. Since communication is the object of encoding, the sender attempts to establish mutuality of meaning with the receiver by choosing symbols, usually in the form of words and gestures, that the sender believes to have meaning for the receiver.

The sender has to select a **channel** for transmitting the message. A manager explaining the goals of the organisation to his subordinate can choose one of the

Confusion in communicating

> Lack of mutuality is one of the most common causes of misunderstanding or failure of communication. In Bulgaria and some parts of India and East Africa, for example, 'yes' is indicated with a side-to-side shake of the head; 'no' is indicated with a nod. Visitors who do not share these symbols can quickly experience, or cause, bewilderment when they talk with citizens of these areas. Gestures, too, may be subject to different interpretations. Raising one's eyebrows can have varying meanings, expressing surprise in one context and scepticism in another.
>
> Source: Stoner, JAF, Freeman, RE & Gilbert, DR. 1995. *Management,* 6 ed. Englewood Cliffs, NJ: Prentice-Hall, p 527.

following channels: oral, nonverbal and written. He can choose a one-to-one, face-to-face situation, as individual goals will have to be set for the subordinate.

Noise may be described as any factor that disturbs, confuses, or otherwise interferes with the transmission of the communication message. Noise may arise along the **communication channel** and may be internal or external. If the subordinate referred to in the MBO case above experiences discomfort, such as stress, exhaustion, a dislike for the manager or even hunger, the message may be disturbed or confused. External noise, such as a phone ringing or a noisy air-conditioner, may also disturb the message. Noise may occur at any stage of the communication process, but is particularly troublesome in the encoding or decoding stage. Since noise can interfere with understanding, managers should attempt to restrict it to a level that permits effective communication.

The **receiver** is the person whose senses perceive the sender's message. There may be only one receiver, as in the case of the manager discussing the organisation's goals with a subordinate, or there may be many, such as when a memorandum is addressed to all the members of a department or organisation.

Decoding is the process in which the receiver interprets the message and translates it into meaningful information. It is a two-step process. The receiver must first perceive the message, then interpret it. Decoding is affected by the receiver's past experience, personal assessment of the symbols and gestures used, expectations, and so on. The more the receiver's decoding matches the sender's intended message, the more effective the communication will be.

The receiver has to decide if **feedback** is needed. The subordinate, in discussing with his or her manager the organisation's goal of decreasing the number of rejects in a manufacturing plant, may decide to give feedback to the manager. He or she may tell the manager that his or her individual goal is to decrease the number of rejects that he or she is responsible for to less than 2 %. At this point in time, the role of sender and receiver changes as the subordinate now becomes the sender and the manager the receiver.

14.3 ORGANISATIONAL COMMUNICATION

Managerial communication occurs in three forms, namely intrapersonal, interpersonal and organisational communication. In **intrapersonal communication**, managers receive, process, and transmit information to themselves. In **interpersonal communication**, messages are transmitted directly between two or more people, on a person-to-person basis. In **organisational communication**, information is transferred between organisations or between different units or departments in the same organisation.[3] At Johannesburg International Airport, air-traffic controllers have to communicate with pilots from different airlines to direct the landing and take-off of aeroplanes. They also have to communicate with the Weather Bureau to identify dangerous weather conditions. Different departments at Johannesburg International Airport also have to communicate with each other. The ground personnel at the airport have to communicate with the air-traffic controllers to find out about possible flight delays. They also have to communicate with the information desk to inform them of these delays.

Effective communication can give an organisation a competitive edge. Organisations in which communication systems are effective, are likely to be more successful than those in which they are not. The question now arises: What differentiates an effective communication system from an ineffective one? We will examine this question in the sections that follow.

Internal communication Toyota's biggest challenge

> Brand Pretorius was 1994's Communicator of the Year. During that period, he was managing director of Toyota South Africa. According to Mr Pretorius, communication between Toyota South Africa and its own people is management's biggest challenge. 'We have our own internal marketing department. We constantly strive to emphasise the requirements of a winning company.'
>
> Source: Van der Walt, A, Strydom, JW, Marx, S & Jooste, CJ. 1996. *Marketing Management,* 3 ed. Cape Town: Juta, p 29.

14.3.1 Organisational communication networks

There are two primary organisational communication networks: the formal communication network and the informal communication network. The **formal network** is communication that follows the hierarchical structure of the organisation, or the 'chain of command'. It follows the formal, established, official lines of contact. In other words, it follows the prescribed path of the hierarchical chart and tends to be explicit in terms of 'who should be talking to whom about what'.

The **informal network** involves communication that does not follow the hierarchical path or chain of command. It tells you 'who is **really** talking to whom and about what'. Informal communication refers to links that have grown out of relationships between employees and management and that have little or no correlation with the formal organisation chart. The informal network is very strong in most organisations. It is usually much faster and more accurate than the formal network.

A manager needs to be aware of both networks. Management has more control over the formal network than the informal, while employees have more control over the informal network than management does.

14.3.2 Formal communication

Organisational communication flows in four directions: downwards, upwards, horizontally and laterally. These basic communication flows are shown in figure 14.3.

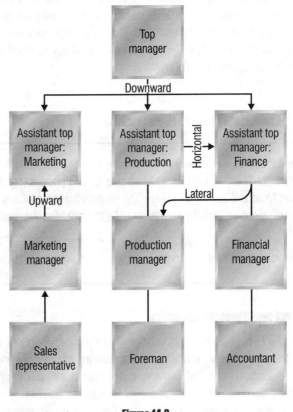

Figure 14.3
Communication flows

Downward communication starts with top management and flows down through the management levels to workers. The major purpose of downward communication is to provide subordinates with information on organisational goals, strategies, policies, and so on. Downward communication is likely to be filtered, modified, or halted at each level as managers decide what should be passed down to employees. Top management at a university may decide to restructure the university and outsource all activities that do not form part of its core business, namely tuition, research and community service. This could mean that cafeteria services at the university will be privatised. This can be communicated to the head of cafeteria services, who will communicate it further downwards to his or her subordinates.

The delegation process (see section 10.4) is a downward communication process. Managers have to communicate with subordinates to explain exactly what is expected of them. This communication process is time consuming and managers are often reluctant to become involved in it. Delegation — and many other processes in the organisation — depends on open communication in order to be effective.

When employees send a message to their superiors they are using **upward communication**. The main function of upward communication is to supply information to the upper levels about what is happening at the lower levels. Managers often learn about customers through subordinates. Subordinates can also communicate with managers through progress reports, suggestions, special requests and so on. Middle management plays an important role in upward communication as those managers usually filter information before it reaches top management. This could lead to vertical information being inaccurate or incomplete if the message is not conveyed clearly. To encourage open communication between subordinate and managers, managers often make use of open-door policies or **management by wandering around** (MBWA). The latter means that managers get out of their offices and talk freely to employees on the shop floor, deal with difficult customers, and so on.

Horizontal communication occurs between people on the same level of the hierarchy and is designed to ensure or improve coordination of the work effort. It is formal communication but does not follow the chain of command. When the head of marketing discusses the appointment of a new salesperson with the head of human resources, horizontal communication takes place. Horizontal communication has the basic task of coordination within departments as well as between different departments. Effective horizontal communication should prevent tunnel vision in the organisation — the idea that a particular department is the only important one in the organisation. Meetings play a decisive role in promoting effective horizontal communication, provided that the right people attend them. When the marketing department meets to discuss the possibility of a new product, managers from the finance, purchasing and operations departments also need to attend to ensure that the manufacture of the new product is feasible.

Lateral communication takes place between people at different levels of the hierarchy and is usually designed to provide information, coordination, or assistance to either or both parties. When the head of human resources explains the new maternity leave policy to a supervisor in a plant, the normal authority path is not followed. However, communication occurs with the knowledge, approval and encouragement of managers who understand that lateral communication may help relieve their communication burden and also reduce inaccuracy by putting relevant people in direct contact with each other.

14.3.3 Informal communication

Communication in an organisation is seen as **informal** when it is not official or sanctioned by management. Commonly called the **grapevine**, information can begin with anyone in the organisation and can flow in any direction.

The grapevine's prime function is to disseminate information to employees (both managerial and nonmanagerial) that is relevant to their needs. The grapevine derives its existence from employees' social and personal interests, rather than from formal organisational requirements.

It should be made clear that rumour and the grapevine are not the same. Rumours — information without a factual base — may just as easily be communicated via formal as informal channels of communication.

Whether they view it as an asset or a liability, managers must understand the grapevine. Since it is always present, speedy, and largely accurate, managers should use it as another means of transmitting information. They should learn who is likely to spread information and 'feed' these individuals selected messages.

14.4 BARRIERS TO EFFECTIVE COMMUNICATION

Whether messages are being transmitted along formal or informal lines, communication barriers can prevent understanding. An examination of all the possible barriers to effective communication is beyond the scope of this chapter. Only those communication barriers common to a typical organisation will be discussed. As shown in figure 14.4, they may be placed in four categories, namely intrapersonal, interpersonal, structural and technological.

14.4.1 Intrapersonal factors

Perception can be defined as the process in which individuals arrange and interpret sensory impressions in order to make sense of their environment (see section 15.3.5). Differing perceptions are one of the most common communication barriers. These differences could be the result of different backgrounds, values, experience,

Intrapersonal factors	Interpersonal factors	Structural factors	Technological factors
■ Perception ■ Individual differences in communication skills	■ Climate ■ Trust ■ Credibility ■ Sender–receiver similarity	■ Status ■ Serial transmission ■ Group size ■ Spatial constraints	■ Language and meaning ■ Nonverbal cues ■ Media effectiveness ■ Information overload

Figure 14.4
Barriers to effective communication
Source: Adapted from Bedeian, AG. 1993. *Management*, 3 ed. Orlando: Dryden, p 527.

and so on. In South Africa managers need to be sensitive to the fact that the same word in different languages may mean different things to different ethnic groups. Not only do we have eleven official languages in South Africa, but these languages also have dialects. To make this situation even more complex, perceptual differences can also arise because of social and gender issues.

People tend to see and hear only what they are emotionally prepared (or want) to see and hear. Furthermore, people seek out favourable messages and ignore unpleasant ones. In other words, they reject or inaccurately perceive information that is inconsistent with their expectations. This phenomenon is known as **selective perception** and it may also be a barrier to effective communication.

People differ in their **ability to develop and apply basic communication skills**. Some people are incapable of expressing themselves orally but are able to write clear and concise messages. Others are effective speakers but poor listeners. In addition, many read slowly and find it difficult to understand what they have read. Such difficulties are potential barriers to effective communication.

14.4.2 Interpersonal factors

The relationship between superior and subordinate is often based on the way each treats the other and how this reciprocal behaviour is interpreted. As superior and subordinate interact, the feelings that arise either limit or encourage the content and frequency of their communications, and the method of their communication. The combination of these elements comprises the **climate** of an interpersonal relationship.[4]

Trust between sender and receiver also plays a major role in the effectiveness of organisational communication. Honesty and openness are prerequisites for effective communication. Distrust between a superior and subordinate can serve only to

The basic communication skills of managers

Theuns Horne, founder member of Hough and Horne Consultants, a communication skills and functional literacy consultancy, recently surveyed the basic communication skills of managers. His study was conducted in order to find out how effective management writings directed at clerical nonmanagerial staff in the banking sector are, what the specific problems are that need to be addressed and how these problems can be rectified. The investigation involved a stratified, random sample of 232 nonmanagerial clerical staff. The findings were that many employees hold educational qualifications at matriculation level or above but the cause for concern is that their writing skills and other verbal and nonverbal communication skills are seriously lacking. The recommendation of the study was that employers should pitch their internal publications for clerical nonmanagerial staff at realistic readability levels of ten to twelve (ie standards eight to ten). The readability levels of printed training materials aimed at clerical nonmanagerial staff should also be scrutinised and, if necessary, revised in order to make them more accessible.

Source: Horne, T. 1993. Written communication: Managers, white collars exposed. *Human Resources Management*, vol 9, no 3, pp 35–36.

Communication in Toyota South Africa

Toyota South Africa is a family-run business. Bert Wessels, chairman of Toyota South Africa, has continued the management style, fostered by the founder of the company, the late Dr Albert Wessels, of adherence to basic values. Emphasis is placed on loyalty, dedication, hard work and commitment. This has led to a high level of involvement, as well as flexibility. This 'Toyota Culture' aspect is seen as important enough to warrant a yearly survey where staff are asked to rate the cultural attributes of the company in order to test whether management's perceptions of the work culture are matched by those of its employees.

Source: Van der Walt, A & Machado, R (eds). 1992. *New Marketing Success Stories*. Johannesburg: International Thomson Publishing (Southern Africa), p 21.

increase defensiveness, and decrease the frequency of open expression and the likelihood of effective communication.[5]

Credibility refers to the perceived characteristics of an information source. Honesty, competence, enthusiasm and objectivity give credibility to a source.[6] When deciding to restructure an organisation, top management should communicate with employees and explain the reasons why they have decided to go this route. Subordinates will regard the reasons as credible only if they perceive top managers as knowledgeable leaders.

The accuracy of communication between two communicators is directly related to how **similar** they perceive themselves to be. Communicators who perceive themselves as being similar are generally more willing to accept each other's viewpoints and to express agreement.[7] Difficulties may arise when subordinates of one religion, ethnic group, gender or even region are supervised by superiors of a different religion, ethnic group and so on.

Major religions encountered in South Africa

> Five of the major religions in the world are encountered in South Africa, namely African traditional religion, Christianity, Hinduism, Islam and Judaism. The workplace needs and realities of these groups are dissimilar. Christmas Day and Good Friday are holy days to Christians. The Diwali and New Year are religious festivals of Hindus. Muslims fast during the month of Ramadan. Jews are not permitted to work on the Sabbath, which begins at sunset on Friday and continues until sunset on Saturday.
>
> Source: Dadoo, Y, Ghyoot, V, Lephoko, D & Lubbe, G. 1997. *Multicultural Sensitivity for Managers*. Pretoria: Tsebanang, pp 33–62.

14.4.3 Structural factors

A person's **status** in an organisation depends largely on the prestige associated with the position he or she occupies. The managing director of JCI Ltd has more status than the financial director. In the Springbok rugby team Francois Pienaar had more status during the World Cup than the rest of the Springbok team. Differences in status are expressed by job titles, imposing offices, and so on.

The influence of status on the direction and frequency of communication has been the subject of many studies. Evidence indicates the following:[8]

- ■ People generally prefer to communicate with individuals of higher status
- ■ People of higher status generally communicate more with one another than they do with people of lower status
- ■ The wider the difference in status is, the greater the likelihood that information will flow from higher to lower status people than the other way around
- ■ In conversations, people with high status generally dominate; and
- ■ People with low status often attempt to gain the favour of those with higher status by displaying respect, offering praise, and agreeing with their views.

Experience shows that the greater the number of management layers a message must pass through, the longer it will take to reach its destination and the less likely it is to be accurate. In effect, layers of management often act as communication filters that distort the transmission of information. The changes that messages undergo as they are successively communicated from layer to layer are known as the **serial transmission** effect.

In organisations which re-engineer (see chapter 2) the elimination of at least one layer of middle management is common. The process of reducing the number of layers in the vertical management hierarchy is called **delayering**. Information technology allows senior management to gain on-line real-time access to information. As a result, middle managers do not act as an information filter and communication should be less distorted.

Information loss

> A study of the transmission of information in 100 business and industrial companies calculated the average loss of information sent from the top of these companies through five layers of management to operatives to be an astonishing 80 %. On the average, only 67 % of a message sent by the board of directors was understood at the vice-presidential level. At the general supervisory level, 56 % was understood; at the plant manager level, 40 % was understood; at the general first-line supervisory level, 30 %; and at the operative level, only 20 %.
>
> Source: Bedeian, AG. 1993. *Management,* 3 ed. Orlando: Dryden Press, p 532.

Interpersonal communication becomes increasingly difficult as the **size of a work group** increases. This occurs in part because the sheer volume of interactions necessary to keep everyone informed tends to make concerted action more difficult.

Spatial constraints refer to physical distances between workers. In general, the shorter the physical distance between two individuals, the more frequently they will interact.

14.4.4 Technological factors

Technological changes have influenced organisational communication in recent years. For example, in making a decision we have moved from a meeting run according to parliamentary procedures to the use of a quantitative tool like simulation (see section 7.7). In exchanging messages over long distances we have moved from messengers to telegraph to telephone to voice mail and electronic mail. Technological changes have an impact on the effectiveness of the **communication media** as well as the **amount** of available **information**. However, it is important to remember that the introduction of new technologies does not replace the use of older ones. The use of electronic mail has not made face-to-face meetings redundant. For this reason, language and meaning and nonverbal cues are also discussed under technological factors.

Language differences are often closely related to differences in individual perceptions. For a message to be properly communicated, the words used must have the same meaning to sender and receiver. A South African organisation doing business with a Japanese counterpart may have difficulty explaining certain words to them. The Japanese, for instance, do not have a word for 'decision making'. They prefer using the word 'choose', which suggests a difficult selection between options in which we can gain some things only by giving up others. Even among South Africans, words are interpreted differently. A South African manufacturer of potato chips used the Swahili word for 'lion' (Simba) as the name for its company. This name was distasteful to some Zulu consumers because of its similarity to the word 'zimba', which means defecation.[9]

Speech is usually accompanied by a variety of meaningful **nonverbal cues**, such as physical posture, head orientation and gestures, facial expressions, and so on. These silent messages assist in the accurate transfer of meaning. Managers in South Africa need to be aware of the differences in nonverbal communication among different groups in South Africa. In African tradition men walk ahead of women to protect them against danger. White South African men, on the other hand, are taught that it is a sign of respect to allow a woman to enter a lift or door first.

The use of an incorrect **communication medium** may also be a barrier to effective communication. Three basic communication media can be used, namely written, oral and multimedia. Written media include electronic mail, faxes, newsletters, and so on. Oral media include face-to-face discussions, telephone conversations, lectures and video conferences. Multimedia transmission refers to written/oral, written/visual and written/oral/visual media.

Managers need to be aware of the comparative effectiveness of the different communication media in different situations. When informing employees about progress in the discussions between management and the labour unions, management must evaluate the effectiveness of the different communication media. Table 14.1 should guide managers in this decision.

Table 14.1
Communication media

Type	Effectiveness
1. Written media	Most effective for transmitting lengthy and detailed material
2. Oral media	Most effective for communications requiring translation and elaboration to be understood by recipients with varying orientations and language skills
3. Multimedia	Most effective in situations such as settling work disputes, communicating major policy changes, and reprimanding work deficiencies
Source: Adapted from Bedeian, AG. 1993. *Management*, 3 ed. Orlando: Dryden Press, p 539.	

Information overload occurs when an individual receives so much information that he or she is overwhelmed by it. To prevent information overload, managers often ask subordinates for an executive summary of a report. Writing this summary is a challenging job as the subordinate needs clear insight into the content of the report in order to identify the key issues.

14.5   HOW MANAGERS CAN BECOME BETTER COMMUNICATORS

Figure 14.2 depicted the different steps in the communication process. During each of these steps the communication barriers discussed in section 14.4 can occur. Managers need to be aware of these barriers to deal with them effectively. Strategies for overcoming various barriers to communication will be discussed in the sections that follow.

14.5.1   The sender encodes the message and selects the channel

When encoding the message, **perception** and **information overload** could be obstacles in the path of effective communication. When messages are transmitted to receivers, senders use their own perception to translate the message so that it makes sense to them. To overcome **perception** barriers, the message that is to be communicated must be analysed in terms of its tone and content. Intonation and facial expression may influence the tone of the message. To formulate the content of the message, the sender has to decide exactly what has to be achieved. The sender can then plan the message to achieve the objective. In formulating the message, choice of words is important. One should avoid using jargon or unfamiliar terminology. The content of the message should arouse curiosity and appreciation.

To overcome **information overload**, the sender should keep the message simple and specific. One should talk within the receiver's framework of experience, keeping the message concise and the objectives clear.

Once the sender has encoded the message, a channel has to be selected. Before sending a message, careful thought should be given to selecting the most effective **channel**. For example, if the top management of an organisation wishes to announce an overall salary increase, electronic mail will be a very effective communication channel, especially if followed by a general meeting at which employees are allowed to clarify uncertainties.

14.5.2   The sender transmits the message

Once the sender has selected a channel, he or she transmits the message through the channel to the receiver. The most significant barrier during this stage in the communication process is **noise**. Noise is anything that interferes with the transmission of the message, including the noise level in the physical setting in which communication is taking place. For example, noisy machinery or equipment may make it difficult to hear. Noise levels should be kept to a minimum.

Timing is another important element in achieving effective communication and it will have a bearing on the communication approach which is adopted. The approach followed during a strike will differ from that just before employees go on holiday.

14.5.3 The receiver decodes the message and decides if feedback is needed

After decoding the message, the receiver decides if feedback, a response or a new message is needed. During this stage in the communication process, trust and credibility, differences in communication skills and emotional factors are common barriers to effective communication.

To overcome **trust** and **credibility** barriers, affection and respect should be offered and earned. Insight into and understanding of the receiver's viewpoint should be shown. An atmosphere of cooperation and harmony should be created. The sender should try to send clear, correct messages, based on facts.

Overcoming **individual differences in communication skills** requires effective feedback. It is essential that communication is always followed up to test whether the message that was sent was properly phrased and whether the intended audience has interpreted it correctly. This can be done by asking questions and motivating the receiver to respond. If a very long message was sent, it should be tested at each important point.

Emotional people find it difficult to communicate effectively. To overcome **emotional barriers**, communicators should remain calm and avoid making others emotional by their behaviour.

14.6 USING COMMUNICATION SKILLS IN THE WORKPLACE

The importance of communication skills in the workplace is nowhere more accentuated than in negotiating to resolve conflict. In the discussion that follows, attention will be paid to a definition of conflict, managing organisational conflict and negotiation.

14.6.1 A definition of conflict

What is conflict? Putnam and Poole developed a definition of conflict that is useful to highlight several critical components of conflict in the organisational arena. They define conflict as 'the interaction of interdependent people who perceive opposition of goals, aims and values, and who see the other party as potentially interfering with the realisation of these goals'.[10] This definition highlights three general characteristics of conflict, namely interdependence, interaction and incompatible goals.

In an organisation, the nature of **goal incompatibility** may vary substantially. Many organisational conflicts stem from contradictory ideas about the distribution of organisational resources. Management and labour negotiate about working conditions and the distribution of wages, or the top management team argues about what capital investments to make in the coming financial year.

Incompatibility is not sufficient condition for organisational conflict. It is only when the behaviours of the organisational members are **interdependent** that conflict arises. For example, one manager may believe in participative decision making, while another may believe in an authoritative management style. This incompatibility may exist harmoniously until their work demands that they become interdependent. If they are asked to work together on a project, conflict could well ensue.

The last critical component in conflict is **interaction**. Conflict involves the **expression** of incompatibility, not the mere existence thereof. This highlights the importance of communication in dealing with conflict. Conflict can be both destructive and productive. It can destroy work relationships or create a needed impetus for organisational change and development. Through communication, organisational members create and work through conflicts in ways that may be either functional or dysfunctional.

As the examples above illustrate, organisational conflict can take place at a variety of levels. At the **interpersonal** level, individual members of the organisation may have incompatible goals, leading to conflict. **Intergroup** conflict considers aggregates of people within an organisation, such as work teams, departments and labour unions, as parties to conflict. **Interorganisational** conflict involves disputes between two or more organisations, such as an organisation and its suppliers or competitors. This level of conflict emphasises the significance of the environment in which the organisation operates.

14.6.2 Managing organisational conflict

We have now developed a conceptualisation of conflict by defining it and noting the levels at which it can materialise. We will now discuss how members of the organisation can attempt to manage conflict.

Avoidance is a technique whereby the conflicting parties withdraw from the conflict. Not surprisingly, this technique is rarely effective. **Problem solving** involves a face-to-face meeting of the conflicting parties for the purpose of identifying the problem and resolving it through open discussion. Another way of managing conflict is to formulate a **shared goal** that cannot be attained without the cooperation of each of the conflicting parties. Where possible, **resources can be expanded** to create a win–win solution to conflict.

Conflict can also be managed by playing down differences between the conflicting parties and emphasising their common interests. The latter is called **smoothing**. When each of the conflicting parties gives up something of value, this is called **compromise**. Management may decide to use **authoritative command** to resolve the conflict and to communicate its desires to the conflicting parties. The **formal organisational structure** can also be changed to resolve conflict. This will result in a change of the communication patterns of the conflicting parties. Examples are job redesign and the creation of coordinating positions. A general strategy for dealing with organisational conflict is **negotiation**. Because of its importance, the next section is devoted to a broader discussion of negotiation.

14.6.3 Negotiation

We are living in an era of negotiation. Negotiation is a fact of life — just as we cannot exist without communicating, so we can barely exist without negotiating.

Negotiation as catalyst for change

A decade ago, South Africa was at war in Angola, world sanctions were in full force, terrorist bombings occurred daily, and a fully fledged state of emergency was in force. Within a few years dramatic changes have taken place: peace in Angola; Namibian independence; the state of emergency lifted; a Government of National Unity planning to solve South Africa's problems. Whereas the price of conflict can only be paid afterwards, the price of peace must be paid beforehand. How did this new way of thinking come about? It has been realised worldwide that great changes can take place through negotiation.

Source: Pienaar, WD & Spoelstra, HIJ 1991. *Negotiation: Theories, Strategies and Skills.* Cape Town: Juta, p 2.

A definition of negotiation

Negotiation can be defined as '**a process of interaction (communication)** between parties, directed at reaching some form of **agreement** that will hold and that is based upon **common interests**, with the purpose of resolving conflict, despite widely **dividing differences**. This is achieved basically through the establishment of **common ground** and the creation of **alternatives**'.[11]

Several points should be clear from the above definition of negotiation. Firstly, negotiation is an exchange of information through **communication**, with the purpose of reaching an agreement between conflicting parties who have certain things in common and disagree on others. This is often the situation between management and labour unions. The survival of the organisation is important to both parties as it secures their jobs. However, management may feel that shareholders are its main responsibility and that wage increases will impact negatively on the organisation's financial results. The labour union, on the other hand, may feel that the welfare of the employees is the first priority — and not the shareholder. As the survival of the organisation depends on the input of both parties, an outcome will have to be negotiated. Secondly, negotiation is regarded as a **process**, not an event. Thirdly, the definition implies that the process should be directed at reaching some form of **agreement**. Fourthly, **common ground** does not refer to what the parties have in common, but what they could become together. Fifthly, the definition refers to the creation of **alternatives**, which implies flexibility in the process. Reference is also made to **dividing differences**, which may be bridged by bringing the parties together physically, especially if both sides are flexible and willing to discuss options. Lastly, the definition refers to **agreements that hold**. This is the real test of whether negotiation has succeeded.[12]

In the section that follows, we look at the negotiation process. It should be clear from the discussion of the different steps and phases in the negotiation process, that communication is an integral part of this process.

The negotiation process

Identifying the potential for negotiation can be viewed as the starting point of the process. The potential for negotiation may be created by a number of factors that operate on an individual or organisation at any given time. Conflict serves as a major stimulus for negotiation. This was the case in Zaïre in 1997 when the conflict between the followers of Mobutu Sese Seko and Admiral Kabila threatened to escalate into a bloody, regionalised war.

Once the potential for negotiation has been identified, a negotiator should be able to anticipate the major events that will occur during negotiation and prepare for them. This preparation phase should include setting objectives, analysing the situation, identifying issues, analysing information on opponents, considering legal and financial implications, deciding on tactics and scheduling feedback.[13] These steps are discussed below.

Step 1: Setting objectives

The preparation phase starts with the formulation of the goals that are to be achieved in the negotiation process. In theory, each negotiator will have objectives that describe the least he or she would accept and objectives that describe the maximum he or she could possibly obtain.

Both Admiral Kabila and Mobuto Sese Seko had aspirations in the Zaïrean conflict to become the single 'strongman', dominating the political, economic and social environment. However, the international environment would not allow this and the parties had to evaluate possible trade-offs.

Step 2: Analyse the situation

This step requires an analysis of one's own and one's opponent's position at the time of entering into negotiations.

Mobuto Sese Seko had to, inter alia, take his ill health into account as well as the disloyalty of his soldiers. Admiral Kabila relied heavily on his military power.

Step 3: Identify issues

Issues are matters of substance that will be discussed with the opponent. Issues may be simple, such as the percentage discount on the price of a new car. However, they may also be more complex, such as reshaping a country's labour laws. Issues may also be subtle, such as the precise wording of a clause in a contract.

A major issue in the Zaïrean negotiations was how to manage a peaceful, effective and sustainable transition from the current circumstances of decaying or collapsed political, economic and social institutions.

Step 4: Analyse information on opponents

It is important to obtain information on opponents, such as their objectives, needs, personalities (if possible), financial position, immediate and pressing problems, value systems, previous negotiating behaviour and personal objectives. However, one should also bear in mind that individuals involved in negotiation change over time. So time and timing are vital in ascertaining the relevance of information.

In preparing for negotiation Admiral Kabila most probably considered his opponent's inflexible will to win, his despotism and incredible wealth.

Step 5: Consider legal and financial implications

It is imperative to consider the legal position of all parties before negotiation. Legal advice may be obtained, depending on the complexity of the issue or contract at stake. Negotiating parties should be fully aware of the stipulations of a contract in terms of the general law of contract. The financial consequences should also be considered before entering the negotiation process.

Both Mobutu Sese Seko and Admiral Kabila had to consider the implications of a negotiated settlement.

The financial implications of incorporating the previously autonomous copper-rich Shaba and diamond-rich Kasai provinces into a unified Zaïre with Kinshasa as its capital had to be considered.

Step 6: Decide on tactics

Parties should prepare themselves for the practical side of the negotiation. Important factors to be considered are the place and time of the meeting, layout of the room, composition of the negotiating team and options that could be posed, to mention but a few.

It was decided that the Zaïrean leaders would meet at a neutral venue where neither party would have a 'home advantage'. The South African ship *Outeniqua* was chosen for this purpose.

Step 7: Schedule feedback

Although feedback cannot be regarded as part of the preparation phase, parties should schedule regular feedback sessions to review their performance and improve their effectiveness in future rounds of negotiation.

Labour relations in South Africa

> 1996 witnessed a number of important legislative developments. The Labour Relations Act became law, accompanied by an amending Act that had been promulgated earlier in the year. Two Green Papers, embodying policy proposals that seek fundamentally to reshape this country's labour laws, were published for comment and debate. A new legislative regime for health and safety in mines was enacted.
>
> Source: Andrew Levy and Associates, Pty Ltd. *Annual Report on Labour Relations in South Africa. 1996–1997*, p 32.

After going through all the above-mentioned steps of the preparation phase, the negotiator will be ready for the actual negotiation. The actual negotiation process will normally go through the emotional, political, problem definition, constructive and socioemotional phases.[14]

Phase 1: Emotional phase

During this phase, the climate for negotiation is established. Negotiating parties make contact by greeting each other. The attitude and manner of greeting could determine the climate for the rest of the negotiations. The climate is largely determined by the socioemotional leader. In trying to resolve the Zaïrean crisis, President Nelson Mandela acted as socioemotional leader.

Phase 2: Political phase

During this phase, a task leader may emerge. He will assist the negotiating parties to agree upon aspects such as the rules, power, authority and agenda of the meeting.

Phase 3: Problem-definition phase

In this phase the group attempts to define the problem, offers trade-offs and implements the agreement.

Phase 4: Constructive phase

During this phase, the group deals with the problem constructively. Experts and task leaders are very active, while the socioemotional leader moves into the background.

Phase 5: Final socioemotional phase

Closure of the meeting takes place. As in the first phase, the socioemotional leader again dominates. The climate for implementing the agreement or re-entering negotiations will be established during this phase.

Negotiation topics between labour and South African management during 1996

> Examples of negotiation topics between labour and South African management during 1996 are the following:
>
> ■ Job-grading system
> ■ Productivity
> ■ Upgrade and extend workers' skills
> ■ Wages
> ■ Paternity leave
> ■ Restructuring of provident funds
> ■ Reduction of the working week
>
> Source: Andrew Levy and Associates, Pty Ltd. *Annual Report on Labour Relations in South Africa. 1996–1997*, pp 44–46.

14.7   CONCLUSION

Communication is an integral part of all management functions. This chapter explained the concept of communication and the communication process. The process starts off with a sender who encodes a message and selects a communication channel. This is followed by the transmission of the message. The receiver then decodes the message and decides if feedback is necessary.

Managerial communication occurs in three forms, namely intrapersonal, interpersonal and organisational communication. The organisational communication network consists of the formal and informal network. Whether messages are sent through formal or informal networks, communication barriers can prevent understanding. These barriers can be placed in four categories, namely intrapersonal, interpersonal, structural and technological.

Managers should constantly strive towards becoming better communicators. They need to be aware of strategies for overcoming communication barriers during each step of the communication process. This chapter dealt with these strategies.

The last part of the chapter was devoted to the use of communication skills in the workplace. Conflict was defined and techniques for managing organisational conflict were discussed. Negotiation was identified as an important technique for managing conflict. We concluded the chapter with a discussion of the negotiation process.

14.8   REFERENCES

1. Maidment, R. 1985. Listening — the overlooked and underdeveloped other half of talking. *Supervisory Management*, August, p 10.
2. Hodgetts, RM & Kuratko, DF. 1991. *Management*, 3 ed. NY: Harcourt Brace Jovanovich, p 370.
3. Ibid p 371.
4. Bedeian, AG. 1993. *Management*, 3 ed. Orlando: Dryden, p 528.
5. Ibid p 528.
6. Ibid p 529.
7. Ibid p 530.
8. Ibid.
9. Dadoo, Y, Ghyoot, V, Lephoko, D & Lubbe, G. 1997. *Multicultural Sensitivity for Managers.* Pretoria: Tsebanang, p 73.
10. Putnam, LL & Poole, MS. 1987. Conflict and negotiation, in Jablin, F, Putnam, L, Roberts, K & Porter, L (eds). *Handbook of Organisational Communication.* Newbury Park, CA: Sage, p 552.
11. Pienaar, WD & Spoelstra, HIJ. 1991. *Negotiation: Theories, Strategies and Skills.* Cape Town: Juta, p 3.
12. Ibid pp 3–5.
13. Ibid pp 26–43.
14. Ibid pp 48–49.

15 The Human Dimension of Management

- The importance of the human dimension of management
- People as a subsystem in the organisation
- The key variables that determine the behaviour of employees

15.1 INTRODUCTION

In our discussion of the various schools of thought on management (see chapter 2) we examined the human relations and behavioural science perspectives. The schools of thought or management theories that developed in the early thirties had their origin in the fact that management found that the principles of the classical theories, namely well-designed tasks and work procedures and systematised production lines, were not the only factors that increase an organisation's productivity (see section 2.4.1). Proponents of this approach maintained that factors that concern the individual in an organisation — psychological, sociological and anthropological factors, including relationships between people — are just as important as physical factors in the successful attainment of the organisation's objectives. It had become apparent that the successful management of an organisation to a large extent revolves around the way **people** in the organisation are managed, and an unprecedented interest in factors such as relationships, leadership, motivation, communication, group formation and teamwork gave rise to an extended body of knowledge on the management of people.

The human aspect of management became so important that industrial psychology and organisational behaviour became fully fledged disciplines in the fifties and sixties to provide answers to questions about the behaviour of people in organisations and what management should do to develop that behaviour to the advantage of the organisation. Interest in the success of Japanese managers in the seventies reinforced the realisation that organisational success depends on **people**. In fact, research into management in the eighties dealt primarily with the excellence of organisations and can be regarded as a revival of the humanist approach. Numerous studies of Japanese management methods concluded that their success could be traced to human factors. The publications of Peters and Waterman showed that human factors were the key to an organisation's excellence, and renewed interest in the role of leadership and corporate culture in the management of people, especially when it comes to implementing strategies.

People are important because they are the only living resource in an organisation and because they are creative — it is people who ensure that the organisational system is designed in such a way that it can adapt to a changing environment. In other words, people determine the potential of the organisation as a system by choosing an appropriate strategy for survival in a turbulent environment, by deploying resources in such a way that the organisation can survive and by ensuring that plans are properly implemented.

Focus

Our focus in this chapter will be on the human dimension of management. More specifically, we will focus on the key determinants of human behaviour. It is not our objective to turn you into a psychologist, sociologist or anthropologist, but the modern manager should understand the basic issues of human behaviour. This should enable the manager to be sensitive to the different values found in the workplace, types of personalities that suit certain jobs, and so on. Understanding the individual is a prerequisite for leading employees (chapter 12), motivating them (chapter 13) and communicating with them (chapter 14).

'I will pay more for the ability to deal with people than any other ability under the sun.'
(John D Rockefeller)

15.1.1 The importance of the human dimension in management

When managers are questioned about their problems at work, one theme crops up time and again — people. Managers often mention how unmotivated some of their subordinates are, the conflict that exists in certain departments or the poor communication abilities of a top manager. Since it is the task of managers to deal with people and have them get on with the job, they must learn more about people in the organisation.

In our introductory discussion on the human dimension of management, we stressed the importance of people in the contemporary organisation. More specifically, people should be considered from the following angles:

■ **People as people**

People spend a large part of their day at work. They work to satisfy their needs. Thus one can say that the work a person does, is a reflection of his needs and objectives. The organisation is one of the instruments an employee can use to realise his objectives. However, if for some reason the organisation blocks the attainment of the needs and objectives of an employee, he may become unmotivated and unproductive.

It is essential, therefore, that managers understand the people working with and under them. A manager is psychologist, sociologist, anthropologist and political scientist, all in one. As a psychologist, the manager must know how different people learn, what motivates them, why their personalities differ, how they perceive things and how they make decisions, to mention but a few aspects. As a sociologist, the manager must know how people function in groups. In his or her capacity as an anthropologist, the manager must know how the values, attitudes and behaviour of various groups differ. Finally, as a political scientist, he or she must have an idea of the role of power in the organisation.

■ **People as resources**

In chapter 1 we defined management as the process in which the organisation's resources are directed towards attaining objectives as productively as possible. People, finance, physical resources and information were highlighted as the organisation's resources. Just as managers must have a knowledge of financial resources (for example, the interest rate on long-term loans at the bank), different types of physical resources (for example, computer equipment, warehouses and office equipment) and the available information resources, they must also have an understanding of human resources. An organisation's human resources are crucial to success for the simple reason that an organisation cannot exist without people. People are the lifeblood of an organisation; this is the resource that gets other resources going.

However, people are the most complex of all resources. They are also the only resource with personal objectives — they strive for higher status, have preferences and dislikes, come from different backgrounds and have different levels and types of experience, and insist on training and development.

■ **People as social systems**

An organisation comes into being when two or more people come together to realise an objective that is too complex for one person alone to attain. An organisation cannot exist without people. If managers wish to understand the organisations in which they work, they must have a knowledge of how people function as individuals, in groups and in teams. Organisations comprise both formal and informal groups. The former develop as a result of organisational structure. Therefore, the employees in, say, the production department, form a group with its own identity which pursues a common objective or objectives, functions inter- dependently and interacts continuously. Informal groups also develop in the organisation on the basis of employees' individual needs — not those of the organisation — which they want to satisfy. Thus one group of employees might play table tennis during its lunch break, while another group might prefer to eat in the cafeteria. It is just as important for a manager to understand the influence of informal groups in the organisation as it is for him to have a knowledge of formal groups.

People as a social system play such a prominent role in the functioning of an organisation that we have devoted an entire chapter (chapter 16) to this sub- system in the organisation.

Work and personality

The work that a person does, reflects his or her personality, needs and objectives. A person who is creative and visionary and a conceptual thinker is likely to be a strategic planner. A typical leadership style of this person would be to lead through own vision and to win cooperation, rather than demand it. This person would prefer a quiet work environmen that allows time for reflection.

Source: McCrae, RR & Costa, PT. 1989. Reinterpreting the Myers-Briggs type indicator from the perspective of the five-factor model of personality. *Journal of Personality,* vol 57, no 1, pp 17–40.

15.2 PEOPLE AS A SUBSYSTEM

People can be regarded as one of the subsystems in the organisation, along with departments, groups, and teams. The individual in the organisation has the same characteristics as any other subsystem. These characteristics, which we mentioned earlier, are the following:

■ A system is complex

People differ in respect of their needs, values, expectations, objectives, and so forth. In addition to being complex, they are also continually changing as they build up experience, are exposed to environmental changes and mature. Thus people cannot be compartmentalised, as is the case with so many other func- tions that managers are concerned with. Each individual is unique, and manage- ment must deal with each one differently.

■ A system can be open or closed

People continually interact with the environment and are influenced by external inputs almost every moment of their existence. An input might be, for example, the fact that the air conditioning in the office is out of order on a hot day, that a colleague has been dismissed or that there is talk of a better-paid job in a neighbouring city.

People, in turn, influence the environment in which they function. The production manager in a fruit juice plant may, for example, invent a new method of canning fruit juice, and this will have a profound effect on the job opportunities of some labourers, among other things.

■ A system strives for equilibrium

People continually strive for equilibrium — either physiologically or psychologically. Thus certain physiological mechanisms create the urge to eat in order for the equilibrium of a hungry person to be restored. A person may experience a psychological imbalance if he has a certain position in the organisation but would actually prefer to be promoted to a higher position. This person will have to mobilise energy to rid himself of this tension.

■ A system can strive towards achieving a multiplicity of objectives

A person, like an organisation, pursues many objectives simultaneously. One of these objectives may be to complete his studies as soon as possible while another may be to spend as much time as he can with his family. These objectives, which are sometimes in conflict, cause tension and imbalance.

It is necessary for managers to be aware of people as open systems to enable them to understand why different people act differently in the organisation, how other systems influence people, and vice versa.

15.3 PEOPLE IN THE ORGANISATION

No two people are the same. The differences between people are easily discernible when it comes to age, sex, marital status or number of dependants, but differences in intellectual capacity, personality, learning experiences, perceptions, values, attitudes, motivation and so forth are far more difficult to ascertain. Managers cannot do their jobs properly if they do not have a sound knowledge of the complex nature of people. Key variables that influence the individual behaviour of employees in an organisation and that managers should know about are depicted in figure 15.1 below.

We shall now discuss each of these key variables in more detail.

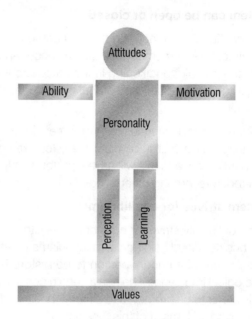

Figure 15.1
Key variables that determine the behaviour of employees

15.3.1 Values and attitudes

A newly appointed managing director of a successful hotel group decides soon after being appointed to close down the casino part of the hotels. The managers of the different casinos cannot fathom this decision because the gambling activities at the hotels generate large profits. What could have driven the managing director to make this decision?

Values play a decisive role in decisions taken in an organisation. Important decisions taken by top management, such as the managing director's decision in the example above, and ostensibly insignificant ones, such as standing back to allow a woman to enter a lift first, are influenced by values. Values are basic beliefs that a certain way of doing things is preferable to another. Thus a moral principle lays the foundation for an individual's values and determines his views on what is right and wrong. **Value systems** refer to the arrangement of values in order of priority for an individual. Every employee in an organisation therefore has his or her own value system. What is important to an individual — values and value systems — influences his or her attitude, level of motivation, perception and individual behaviour, among other things.

An individual's values are fairly stable. This stability can be attributed to the way in which values are acquired. Children are often taught that certain behaviour is always desirable or undesirable. Obedience, for example, is behaviour that is always

Behavioural styles of black South African executives

- **Persuasive** (Getting things done by winning others over to your point of view)

  Black South African executives seek to influence others both through the power of their communications and by example — they gain credibility as much by their actions as by the use of inspiring language.

- **Outgoing** (Emphasising the importance of being extrovert, friendly and informal; being able to establish free and easy interpersonal relationships quickly)

  Black South African executives, on average, tend to be more inner-directed and self-contained than their international counterparts. They feel it's more appropriate to use a formal communication style and to keep people at a distance when involved in a task.

- **Excitement** (Energy, intensity, and a capacity to keep others enthusiastic, motivated and involved)

  When motivating their followers, black South African executives balance a sense of enthusiasm with a concern for realism. They may appeal to followers with a measure of emotion, but will not overdo it, as they regard their followers as having the maturity to be self-motivated to some degree.

- **Restraint** (Keeping a low-key, understated and quiet interpersonal manner; controlling your emotional expressions, and so appearing formal and aloof)

  When they feel it's critical to enhance their own position, black South African executives do express themselves freely. In general, however, they keep a tight rein on their emotional expression within the working environment.

Source: AMROP. 1996. *The South African Executive: The Challenge of Diversity*. Rosebank: AMROP International, p 10.

Cultural literacy

Cultural literacy is the expert knowledge of both surface and core cultural **values**, norms, mores, traditions and operating procedures of a culture. Empirical studies in this field show that expatriates must increase their cultural literacy in order to be successful in their new country.[1]

Globalisation of South African companies is becoming increasingly popular. So, too, is globalisation as a career strategy. Cultural literacy is a prerequisite for success in both cases. Cultural literacy involves more than knowing, for instance, when and how to bow in Japan when greeting a client — it means understanding the deeper core values of the Japanese.

Applying one's own personal values as a guide to understanding foreigners' values can lead to embarrassing and sometimes dangerous incidents in a foreign country.

desirable. In childhood, individuals are not taught to be just a little obedient. This clear black–white distinction between desirable and undesirable behaviour results in the relative stability of values.

When values are questioned, however, they may be changed. Conversely, questioning a person's values may result in those values being reinforced.

Management should realise that employees have different values. A decision that accords with management's values might conflict with the values of certain employees, with the result that those employees might not throw their weight behind the decision.

South African managers need to be very sensitive regarding values based on individualism or values based on collectivism. Generally speaking, black South Africans base their behaviour on collectivistic values, ie the group is more important than the individual. The opposite is true as far as most white South Africans are concerned.

It is interesting to note that, over the past decade, a hostile environment, particularly in the USA and United Kingdom, has made it difficult for trade unions to sustain a significant role and presence. In particular, their collectivist values have been undermined by the rise of individualism.[2]

In addition to knowledge of the values of different employees in the organisation, the attitudes of employees are also a primary cause of individual differences. It is sometimes said that employees have to change their attitudes towards their jobs before they can become productive. If attitude can influence, say, productivity, it stands to reason that managers should have knowledge of the concept of **attitude**.

An attitude can be defined as a permanent, general evaluation of people, objects or events. Managers should be interested in their employees' attitudes because attitudes give warning of potential problems. Attitudes comprise the following three components:

- an affective component
- a behavioural component
- a cognitive component

Suppose you decide to apply for a position at a plant that manufactures chemicals. As a nature lover you are aware of the fact that the organisation dumps its waste in a nearby river, which explains why the fish in the river have been destroyed. At the interview you feel very negative (affective component) about the organisation. This feeling is based on your values and knowledge about the organisation (cognitive component). Because you are desperate for the job, you remain silent about your objections for the duration of the interview, and even nod (behaviour component) when the interviewer mentions the organisation's concern for nature conservation. There is no direct link between your attitude and behaviour, and this is why it is so difficult for managers to predict how an employee is going to act.

People can have thousands of attitudes, but managers are interested in attitudes that are job-related. The three most relevant[3] of these are job satisfaction, job involvement and organisational commitment.

Job satisfaction refers to an individual's general attitude towards his or her job. When managers speak of employee attitudes they more often than not have in mind job satisfaction.

Job involvement measures the degree to which a person identifies psychologically with his or her job. **Organisational commitment**, on the other hand, refers to identifying with one's employing organisation — its goals, culture, and so on.

Although employees continually have new experiences and therefore develop new attitudes, it is extremely difficult to change attitudes. However, management can try to change an employee's negative attitude by changing the following:

- organisational factors
- group factors
- personal factors

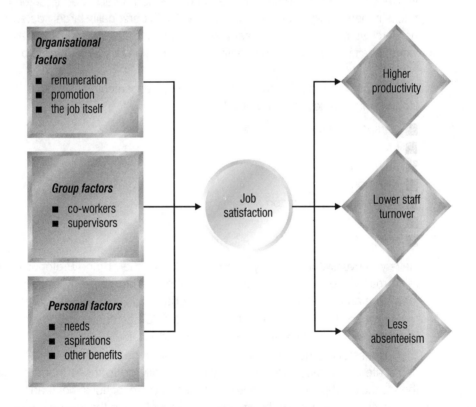

Figure 15.2
Factors that can lead to a change in attitude
Source: Moorhead, G & Griffin, RW. 1989. *Organizational Behavior*, 2 ed. Boston: Houghton Mifflin.

Factors that can lead to a change in attitude are depicted in figure 15.2. The figure shows how important it is for managers to understand how attitudes develop and how they can be changed. Changing an employee's negative attitude towards the organisation can improve job satisfaction, which in turn can generate higher productivity, a lower staff turnover and less absenteeism.

15.3.2 Personality

Why is it necessary for managers to have a knowledge of the different personalities of their subordinates? The answer to this question is already clear when a new employee is appointed. People with certain personality traits are better suited to certain jobs than others. A quiet, reserved person will probably experience more job satisfaction doing something on his or her own than in, say, selling products to customers. Some employees are more conscientious than others and less open to influence and feel that their own hard work will lead to promotion. The fact that some workers are better at some jobs than at others can be ascribed to, inter alia, differences in personality. In a nutshell, an individual's personality largely determines how he perceives, evaluates and reacts to his environment. Individual behaviour in the workplace is a function of the continuous interaction between an employee and the work situation.

The following factors have been found to be particularly valuable in providing insights into employee behaviour:

■ personality type
■ locus of control
■ authoritarianism
■ self-monitoring
■ achievement orientation
■ self-esteem
■ risk profile

Have you ever wondered why people like Sol Kerzner, Brand Pretorius or Mzi Khumalo made it to the top, whereas many other managers seem to stagnate in their jobs? The answer to this question most probably lies in their personality types.

We can distinguish between type A and type B personalities. Some of the behavioural traits of these two types are summarised in table 15.1.

Successful business executives usually have type B personalities. Promotions in corporate and professional organisations 'usually go to those that are wise rather than to those who are merely hasty, to those who are tactful rather than to those who are hostile, and to those who are creative rather than to those who are merely agile in competitive strife'.[4] Great salespeople, on the other hand, are usually type A personalities.

Table 15.1
Traits of personality types A and B

Type A	Type B
■ Unceasing struggle to achieve more in less time	■ Rarely try to complete an increasing number of tasks in a shorter period
■ Competitive	■ Do not exhibit their superiority
■ Impatient	■ Patient
■ Think or do two or more things simultaneously	■ Stay focused
■ Cannot cope with leisure time	■ Can relax without guilt
■ Emphasise quantity of work over quality	■ No need to display achievement
■ Rarely creative	■ Creative
■ Rely on past experiences when making decisions	■ Develop unique solutions to problems

The Myers-Briggs Type Indicator (MBTI) is one of the most widely used tests to determine personality type. Individuals are classified as:

■ extrovert or introvert (E or I)
■ sensing or intuitive (S or N)
■ thinking or feeling (T or F)
■ perceiving or judging (P or J).

The personality type of a person can be ISTJ, ISTP, INFP or any other combination of the letters above. An ENTJ, for instance, will possess the following characteristics:

■ frank, decisive and a leader in activities;
■ develops and implements comprehensive systems to solve organisational problems
■ good at reasoning and talks intelligently
■ good public speaker, and so on.

Managers can use the MBTI to match personalities with jobs.

Locus of control refers to the extent to which a person believes that his or her behaviour directly influences the consequences of his or her actions. Certain individuals believe that they can control whatever they do. Such workers, who have an internal locus of control, believe, for example, that if they work hard they will be promoted. Others again, believe that whatever happens is the result of fate or pure luck. Such people have an external locus of control. It is important for a manager to know that employees with an internal locus of control have better control over their work activities and are more eager to learn about their job than their co-workers with an external locus of control. Internals are also more attuned to success and also try harder to influence fellow employees than do externals.

Internals versus externals

At school there are dramatic differences between internals and externals. The former clearly see the connection between hard work at school and success, while the latter fail to see the link.

Authoritarianism refers to the extent to which an employee believes that there should be power and status differences in an organisation. The more a person stresses these differences, the more authoritarian he is. A manager will therefore give an order to a power-conscious subordinate without expecting much opposition. A manager should also adapt his leadership style in such a way that he gives clear direction to such a subordinate.

Self-monitoring is a relatively new concept and refers to the extent to which an employee is able to mould his behaviour according to that of his co-workers. A person who monitors himself frequently will, for example, check to see how a manager handles a certain situation, say negotiating the purchase of new components for machines, and then act in the same way when in the same situation. A person who seldom monitors himself or herself pays scant attention to how others act in certain situations and follows his or her own ways.

Besides the personality traits discussed above, certain other traits also influence behaviour in the organisation. These include an employee's achievement orientation, self-esteem and willingness to take risks.

15.3.3 The individual's ability

Irrespective of how positive a person's attitude is, it is highly improbable that he or she will be able to write as well as William Shakespeare, play tennis as well as Boris Becker or act as well as Meryl Streep. No two people have exactly the same abilities. However, this does not make one person better than another — it simply shows that people have unique strengths and weaknesses. What is important to a manager is not that people differ, but rather how they differ when it comes to applying their abilities successfully in the organisation.

What exactly does **ability** mean? We can say that it refers to a person's capacity to do the different tasks in a job. So, the ability of a typist is judged on speed and accuracy. The ability of a secretary indicates what her present capacity is to do the different tasks that her job demands of her. In the modern organisation a leader's ability refers mainly to his or her ability to create a vision for the organisation and to share this vision with subordinates.

Managers: born or made?

> Management guru Henry Mintzberg has a definite viewpoint regarding the 'natural endowment' of some employees to become managers — versus others who should not be considered for these positions. He makes the following statements in his book *Mintzberg on Management: Inside our Strange World of Organizations:*
>
> ' ... the (MBA) candidates' leadership and management ability would have to be proven. They would, in other words, be selected not by themselves but by the subordinates who follow them, the peers who respect them, the supervisors who appreciate them. In this way, management training would not be wasted on people who are unlikely to be effective managers — a sizeable number of today's MBA students, I should think.
>
> '... [W]e are seeking to train for administration as well as for business. It could also be argued that we should decouple the two, train people for certain positions in business — namely the more analytical, such as marketing research or accounting — without pretending that we are training them to be managers. But that would require changing a great many established expec-tations, including those of the (MBA) applicants who believe they will attain positions of power quickly because they sat in a classroom for a couple of years ...
>
> 'We have good things to teach to management: let's teach them to people who can use them.'
>
> Source: Mintzberg, H. 1989. *Mintzberg on Management: Inside Our Strange World of Organ-izations.* NY: Free Press, pp 83–84.

Ability comprises two components: intellectual capacity and physical ability. An employee's intellectual capacity refers to his ability to perform actions intelligently. IQ tests are used to determine a person's intellectual capacity. Intellectual capacity includes verbal and nonverbal abilities. Verbal ability refers to, among other things, the ability to think conceptually, while nonverbal ability refers to, inter alia, the way a person perceives and reacts to the world around him or her.

A person's physical ability refers to stamina, coordination, strength, and so forth. This ability plays an important role in more standardised jobs at the lower levels of the organisation. The higher one moves up the hierarchy in the organisation, the more one will have to depend on intellectual capacity.

It is important for the manager to make sure that an employee's ability matches the task that has been assigned to him or her.

15.3.4 Motivation

Because motivation of employees plays such a vital role in an organisation, we have devoted chapter 13 to this concept. In the study of individual behaviour, motivation is probably the concept that receives the most attention. There is no escaping the fact that in any organisation, some employees work harder than others. Why do some workers with fewer capabilities often contribute more to goal attainment than co-workers who have greater abilities? Why do some people work harder than others? These questions and many more are addressed in the chapter on motivation.

15.3.5 Perception

Perception can be defined as the process in which individuals arrange and interpret sensory impressions in order to make sense of their environment.

It is important for a manager to realise that what his subordinates perceive is often different from objective reality. Hence subordinates react not to reality but to what they perceive as reality. Take the example of a rugby match between the Natal Sharks and Gauteng Lions. Two minutes before the final whistle is blown, with the score at a nail-biting 18–18, the referee awards a penalty kick to the Sharks for a dangerous high tackle by the Gauteng Lions' scrum-half. Sharks' supporters are convinced that it was indeed a high tackle and that the referee made a fair decision; Gauteng Lions' supporters feel that it is an unfair, harsh decision. Here the same situation is perceived in two completely different ways by two groups of supporters.

In an organisation, subordinates' perception of a situation plays the same role as in the above example of the rugby match. Even if an organisation has clear objectives that must be attained, employees may perceive these objectives in different ways. These differences in perception depend on who is doing the perceiving, the object being perceived and/or the context in which perception occurs.

A plastic surgeon will notice the wrinkles under a woman's eyes, while a plumber may not even see them. This is an example of perceptual differences that are attributable to the **perceiver**. Employees' interests, expectations and their previous experiences influence what they perceive.

Characteristics of the **object** being perceived can also cause perceptual differences; for instance, exceptionally attractive or unattractive employees stand out among their co-workers. In addition, objects are not perceived in isolation, but are seen against a certain background. The figure-and-ground relationship may also lead to perceptual differences. In figure 15.3 the blue area is first perceived as a vase, that is, the blue area is seen as the subject of the drawing. However, if one sees the blue area as the background, the subject becomes two heads in profile facing each other.

Figure 15.3
Figure-and-ground illustration

The **context** in which an object is perceived also influences one's perception of the object. Factors in the context that may play an important role are the time at which the object is perceived, as well as the working and social environment in which this occurs.

Managers evaluate their subordinates' performance, supervisors check to see that factory workers manufacture a predetermined number of products per hour; and restaurant owners make sure that the waiters and waitresses serve all the tables allocated to them during the lunch period. Judging people, however, is a different kettle of fish. To make this extremely difficult task easier, people often take short cuts. These short cuts can lead to distortion. Because people cannot concentrate on all the stimuli in their environment at one time, they tend to **perceive selectively**. Hence they perceive only bits and pieces. These snippets of information are not chosen uniformly, but selectively, depending on, inter alia, the perceiver's interests, background, experience and attitude. Selective perception therefore helps us to perceive more quickly, but carries the risk that we may make inaccurate assessments of others.

The short cuts that people take are known as **cognitive strategies**. These are short cuts that the brain uses to reduce the mass of information that it is bombarded with so that a person can make more sense of the socialisation process. Two such strategies are heuristics and prejudices. The former entails decision-making principles that an individual uses to draw quick conclusions about other people. Prejudices are the result, mainly, of stereotyping. When we judge employees on the basis of the group to which they belong, we use a short cut known as stereotyping. 'Engineers are poor managers' or 'people who wear bright colours are in a happy mood' are examples of stereotyping.

The **halo effect** means that an individual forms a general impression of another individual based on certain characteristics such as intelligence, appearance or degree of socialisation. At an interview, appearance sometimes overshadows the interviewer's perception of a prospective employee. Thus the interviewer at a firm of architects might decide that an attractive, well-groomed woman will be an accurate tracer without actually studying other qualities she might have.

15.3.6 Learning

The final concept that concerns us in this section is learning. Employees continually learn new things in the workplace. Take a motorcar salesman at Mercedes Benz who must learn all the features of the new Merzedes SLK230 that has just come into the showroom. How can his or her sales manager make sure that the salesperson remembers all these facts in the easiest possible way?

To answer this question, we must first come to grips with the meaning of the concept of **learning**. Any perceptible behaviour change is an indication that learning has taken place. However, what a manager wants to know about learning is whether learning concepts are of any value in explaining and forecasting behaviour. These learning concepts include the concepts of **conditioning** and **shaping**. Knowledge of the two concepts should give a manager more insight into workers' productivity, absenteeism, late arrival for work and quality of work. These concepts also play an important role in changing employees' undesirable behaviour.

Conditioning can be subdivided into classical conditioning, operant conditioning and social learning. Classical conditioning refers to the acquisition of a conditioned response on the basis of an association between a conditioned stimulus and an unconditioned stimulus. At a production plant, for example, management will see to it that all the windows in the plant are washed every time top management from head office visits the plant. If this sequence is performed repeatedly, the employees at the plant will learn to put their best foot forward (conditioned response) when the windows are washed (unconditioned response) — even if they are washed without top management visiting the plant.

However, the acquisition of certain behaviour in organisations will be better understood if one examines operant conditioning. According to this type of conditioning, behaviour is a function of its consequences. People learn to act in such a way that they get what they want, or are able to avoid what they do not want. In this way behaviour is acquired rather than reflexive, as in the case of classical conditioning. If certain behaviour is reinforced by positive consequences, an individual tends to repeat it. Remuneration for certain behaviour is also most effective if it occurs directly after the act and not some time later.

However, individuals also learn by observing and experiencing. This is known as social learning. Workers learn by observing how their colleagues, managers, subordinates, parents, teachers and others act. Perception plays an important role here. People react to their perception of the consequences of a specific action and not to the objective consequences of the act.

Mzi Khumalo: a role model for black South Africans

> Much of what we learn comes from watching role models. One such role model in the new South Africa is Mzi Khumalo, new managing director of JCI Ltd, the seventh largest gold producer in the world and the second largest producer of high-carbon ferrochrome. Khumalo, a dynamic and visionary leader, has personal paper wealth estimated at about R30m.
>
> Source: *Finance Week,* 30 January – 5 February 1997, p 11.

Besides conditioning, as discussed above, learning also occurs through shaping. This refers to a manager's effort to gradually shape an employee's behaviour to the advantage of the organisation. In other words, behaviour is shaped by the reinforcement of each successive step that brings the individual closer to the formulated goal. Reinforcement is discussed in chapter 13.

15.3.7 Individual behaviour

In the preceding sections we discussed a number of concepts that lead to individual behaviour. We referred throughout to the fact that it is vital for managers to have insight into individual behaviour to be able to predict how individuals will react to certain decisions. South African managers, particularly in these times of rapid change, should have knowledge of the influence of their decisions on their subordinates. A manager can predict behaviour only if he is familiar with his employees' values and attitudes, personalities, abilities, motivation, perception and learning.

15.4   CONCLUSION

An organisation without people is unthinkable. Even in plants 'manned' by robots people still play a vital role. As the smallest subsystem in an organisation, individuals have the same characteristics as other systems. People are complex, continually interact with the environment, strive for equilibrium and may have a multiplicity of objectives.

Managers must have knowledge of how people function. This is not an easy task, for no two individuals are the same. However, there are certain key variables that determine the behaviour of employees which managers should be familiar with. These include values and attitudes, personality, ability, motivation, perception and learning. Besides motivation, which is discussed in detail in chapter 13, we focused in this chapter on those variables that determine behaviour.

15.5   REFERENCES

1. Black, JS, Gregersen, HB & Mendenhall, M. 1992. *Global Assignments: Successfully Expatriating and Repatriating International Managers*. San Francisco: Jossey-Bass.
2. Undy, R. 1996. *The Blackwell Encyclopedia of Management*, vol vi, p 573.
3. Brooke, PP, Russel, DW & Price, JL. 1988. Discriminant validation of measures of job satisfaction, job involvement, and organizational commitment. *Journal of Applied Psychology*, May, pp 139–145.
4. Robbins, SP. 1997. *Managing Today*. Upper Saddle River, NJ: Prentice-Hall, pp 358–359.

16 Groups and Teams in the Organisation

Key issues

■ The differences between groups and teams
■ The reasons why people form groups
■ Different types of groups found in an organisation
■ The stages in group development and appropriate leadership styles
■ The emergence of group characteristics
■ Intergroup dynamics
■ Developing groups into teams

16.1 INTRODUCTION

In the preceding chapter we discussed the smallest subsystem in the organisation, namely the individual. We pointed out that an individual functions as an open system and is therefore influenced by external factors, but in turn, he or she also influences the environment. We commented on the complex nature of people and discussed their unique values and attitudes, capabilities and personalities. Although the emphasis in the preceding chapter was on the individual, most employees in the organisation work in groups. Dealing with people — especially when they function in groups — is one of the most challenging tasks facing managers. One of the reasons for this is that the behaviour of a group of people is never equal to the sum of the behaviours of the individuals that make up the group. In a group situation, individuals are often constrained to act in a way that differs from how they would if working alone.

Groups are the backbone of organisations. They are responsible for attaining the goals of different departments and, ultimately, the organisation's goals. Managers are evaluated on the results of their departments as a whole and not the results of individuals. Since managers spend 50–90 % of their time in some form of group activity, the better they understand groups and their performance, the more effective they will be as group members and leaders.[1]

Focus

This chapter deals with groups and teams, and the principles discussed here apply to top management teams, selling teams, rugby teams and others. Because groups can assume so many forms, it is necessary first to discuss the concept of a group and then advance reasons for group formation. Various kinds of groups will be discussed in this chapter as well as stages in group development. As a group goes through different stages, its characteristics start becoming clear — hence the need to study also these characteristics in this chapter. Because there are so many different groups in an organisation, we will also examine interaction between groups, sometimes known as intergroup dynamics. We will also take a look at the bases of interaction between groups.

Teams will also be discussed in this chapter, as well as the similarities and differences between groups and teams, and between group managers and team leaders.

16.2   GROUPS AND TEAMS

The terms *group* and *team* are often used interchangeably, but recent management literature makes a clear distinction between them. A **group** has a clear leader and consists of two or more members who perform independent jobs with individual accountability, evaluation, and rewards. A **team**, on the other hand, has a small number of members with shared leadership and its members perform inter-dependent jobs with individual and group accountability, evaluation and rewards.[2]

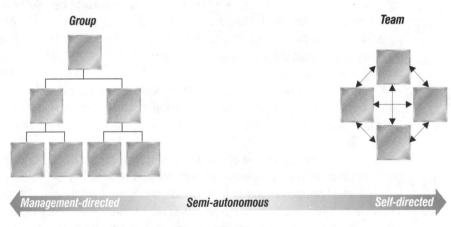

Figure 16.1
Differences between groups and teams

It is not always easy to make a distinction between groups and teams. The best way to explain the difference is to illustrate them on a continuum, as illustrated in figure 16.1.

As illustrated in figure 16.1, groups and teams are on a continuum. Organisations structured along rigid lines of authority where a definite hierarchy exists, consist mainly of groups. The marketing department is a group; so too are the assembly-line workers in a car manufacturing plant with a hierarchical organisational structure. In a group, individuals are usually responsible for making one part of a product and passing it on to the person responsible for the next step in the process.

The lesson of the geese

- When you see geese heading south for the winter flying in a 'V' formation, you might be interested to know what scientists have discovered about why they fly that way. It has been learnt that as each bird flaps its wings, it creates an uplift for the bird immediately following. By flying in a 'V' formation, the flock adds at least 71 % more flying range than if each bird flew on its own.
  Basic truth #1. People who share a common direction and sense of community can get where they are going quicker and easier because they are travelling on the thrust of one another ...

- Whenever a goose falls out of formation, it suddenly feels the drag and resistance of trying to go it alone and quickly gets back into formation to take advantage of the lifting power of the bird immediately in front.
  Basic truth #2. There is strength, power and safety in numbers when travelling in the same direction as others with whom we share a common goal ...

- When the lead goose gets tired, he or she rotates back in the wing and another goose flies point.
  Basic truth #3. It pays to take turns doing hard jobs ...

- The geese honk from behind to encourage those up front to keep up their speed.
  Basic truth # 4. We all need to be remembered with active support and praise ...

- Finally, when a goose gets sick or is wounded and falls out, two geese fall out of formation and follow him or her down to help and protect. They stay with the downed goose until the crisis resolves, and then they launch out on their own or with another formation to catch up with their group.
  Basic truth #5. We must stand by each other in times of need.

Source: Lussier, RN. 1997. *Management: Concepts, Applications, Skill Development.* Cincinnati, OH: South Western, pp 418–419.

Nowadays, many organisations are re-engineering their processes. As a result, teams make the entire product, and not just a part of it. The teams are usually small, consisting of between five and twelve members. Team members share leadership, job responsibility, and so on, and are rewarded for both individual and group performance.

Team playing and the South African executive

A hierarchical, top-down *modus operandi* has been characteristic of South African business. Communalism is a powerful value in South African black culture, and working for the common good is valued above aggressive competitiveness and individual excellence. This emphasis on teamwork is reflected in the black executive's leadership approach; a spirit of cooperation, grass-roots support for decisions, and the encouragement of a free flow of information are its hallmarks. A more Afrocentric view of management brings greater sensitivity to bear on inter-personal relationships, without forfeiting the right to rely on the executive's own judgment in the final analysis. This perspective is very necessary if business is to adjust to a changing South African environment.

Source: AMROP. *The South African Executive: The Challenge of Diversity*. Rosebank: AMROP International, p 18.

By definition, all teams are groups, but not all groups are teams. Therefore, when the term *group* is used in this chapter, it can also refer to a *team.*

16.3 REASONS FOR GROUP FORMATION

If managers wish to know what to expect of the group with which they work, they should know how groups function. They need some idea of why people join groups before they can predict how a specific group is going to function. Bridge players' reasons for joining a group differ from those of squatters holding a protest march through the streets of Cape Town. The reasons for forming a group may range from self-realisation to survival.

In organisations one can distinguish between formal and informal groups. An example of a formal group is the sales team of an organisation selling sprinkler systems in the Free State which has to achieve a specific target. An example of an informal group is a few employees who play darts in the cafeteria during their lunch break.

The reasons why people form formal and informal groups include the satisfaction of their needs, proximity, attraction, goals and economics.

16.3.1 The needs of members of the group

Need satisfaction is often a primary motivating factor in the formation of groups. To understand how people satisfy their needs, read this section in conjunction with chapter 13, which deals with motivation. According to Maslow's hierarchy of need satisfaction, humans start by satisfying their biological needs, and when these have been reasonably satisfied, they move on to satisfying their security needs. Satisfying one's security needs therefore also plays an important role in group formation. Without a group to rely on, employees sometimes feel that they are completely alone when it comes to a management decision that affects them. This 'solitude' may lead to uncertainty. By joining a group in the organisation, employees feel that they have the support of the other members of the group. Interaction and communication between members of a group serve as a buffer between the expectations of management and the sacrifices employees are willing to make for the organisation. New employees, in particular, have to rely on the other members of the group to initiate them into the organisation.

People are social beings and need to interact and communicate with others. This is the second reason why they belong to groups. The group is therefore a social phenomenon.

Trust, a basic element of group formation

One of the worst punishments one can impose on people is to isolate them.

According to Edgar Schein, the unusually low incidence of escape attempts by American prisoners in the North Korean war was because of isolation. The North Koreans made a concerted effort to prevent the formation of groups. Officers were separated from the other ranks. Groups were systematically broken up and prisoners regularly moved to other barracks. This prevented the prisoners from forming groups to devise escape plans. Prisoners were unable to trust each other — an essential element of any escape attempt.

Lastly, people belong to groups for self-realisation. Employees often regard certain groups in an organisation as status groups. Employees might perceive managers who lunch at an exclusive restaurant every day as a status group. Employees with a strong need for self-realisation will strive to belong to such a group.

16.3.2 Proximity and attraction

Interaction between employees leads to group formation. Two important factors in personal interaction are **proximity** and **attraction** The former refers to the physical distance between two employees. Typists will be more inclined to form a group with others working in the same office than with typists in another department. Employees who work in close proximity have plenty of scope to exchange ideas and get to know one another better. Swapping ideas often leads to the formation of a group.

Attraction refers to the extent to which individuals like each other. First impressions are often based on the physical appearance of a person. When we first meet someone, we usually notice their height, mass, clothing, hair and skin colour, and other conspicuous features. People have preconceptions about individuals with specific characteristics and tend to compartmentalise them. A stranger with red hair might immediately be thought to have a fiery temper. Our behaviour tends to be influenced by our preconceptions.

Employees who are attracted to one another are also inclined to form groups. Research has shown that attractiveness 'rubs off'. When an employee befriends an extremely attractive colleague, the less attractive person may subsequently be regarded as more attractive.

16.3.3 Group goals

The goals of a group may also appeal to a person. An employee may, for example, join a group that meets after work to learn more about a computer programme that is to be installed at the office.

It is sometimes difficult to identify the goals of a specific group. If a secretary is transferred from the salary department to the housing department, her new boss may forget to tell her what the goals of the group are. The new employee's perception, attitude, personality and the way she learns will determine how she perceives the goals. By observing the behaviour of her colleagues in the department, she may believe that she knows what goals to pursue. Her perception of the group goals may be correct or completely wrong.

16.3.4 Economics

In many instances, individuals form groups because they believe they will derive greater economic advantage from their work. Individuals working at different points in the assembly plant of an automobile manufacturer in Uitenhage, who are remunerated on a group remuneration basis, will try to function as productively as possible as a group to earn the highest possible wages. By cooperating as a group the individuals obtain the greatest economic benefits.

Individuals also obtain economic benefits by belonging to groups in nontrade-union organisations because they can exert pressure on top management for higher salaries, more leave, a shorter working week, and so on.

16.4　THE VARIOUS TYPES OF GROUPS

Now that we know what a group is and why employees in an organisation form groups, it is necessary to examine the different types of groups found in organisations.

In our discussion of the organisational structures in chapter 9, we studied the allocation of different tasks to specific individuals and groups of individuals. These groups are formed so that the objectives of the organisation can be attained, and they are known as formal groups. Employees are therefore part of the group by virtue of their position in the organisation. Figure 16.2 shows an example of a formal group.

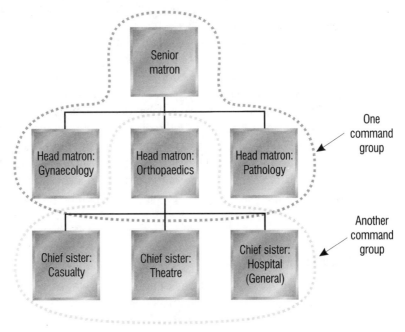

Figure 16.2
Command groups in an organisation

The **command group** — as shown in the above figure — is characterised by a formal organogram and a line of authority. The command group comprises the manager and his subordinates, who report directly to him about their activities in the organisation. In a hospital, for example, the senior matron and her subordinates would be a command group. The existence of a command group is relatively permanent.

A **task group** is another example of a formal group. A task group is created for the purpose of carrying out a specific task or project in the organisation. Once the project has been completed the group disbands. Nurses who occasionally do night shift for extra income form a task group because they have to perform certain tasks on that particular evening, but the group disintegrates when they go home at the end of their shift.

Informal groups develop spontaneously in an organisation, primarily because of the social needs of employees. A **friendship group** is a fairly permanent group and arises from friendships between different people in the organisation. The motivation for their activities is the fact that they enjoy one another's company, often because they share the same interests or hobbies. Interaction between friendship groups usually continues outside the workplace.

Interest groups are less permanent than friendship groups and arise from the common activities or interests of members of the group. Women in management positions may form an interest group for mutual support in an area dominated by men. The advantages of this interest group may extend beyond the social aspects. Information systems can arise which ensure that women are placed in management positions, and management training can be provided for potential female managers. These interest groups can become the means to promote women to management and administrative positions.

The difference between friendship groups and interest groups is often not clear. The relative permanence of interaction between members of the group is usually indicative of the type of group. Although the interests and activities of a friendship group may change over time, the group remains in existence since friendship forms lasting ties among members of the group. An interest group, however, will disintegrate once the interests and activities of its members change.

16.5 STAGES IN GROUP DEVELOPMENT

Groups are not static but pass through four stages. First, members of the group must learn to accept one another. This is followed by communication and decision making, then motivation and productivity, and finally, control and organisation. Managers should understand these four phases and their characteristics, as each phase requires a different leadership style. The stages in group development and appropriate leadership styles will be discussed in the following sections.

16.5.1 Mutual acceptance

In the first stage of group development, prospective members of the group exchange information about themselves. During this stage, the opinions of other members of the group about issues that do not really concern work are tested. Thus one person might ask another what his or her views on the new constitution are, or on working flexitime. Certain issues that apply directly to the group can also be discussed during this stage, for example the group's objectives for a particular project. However, these discussions are not likely to amount to much, because members of the group still do not know how to evaluate other members' opinions. If members of the group already know one another, this stage will be considerably shorter, compared to when the members do not know each other at all.

First-year students at a residential university come from different schools and some may have completed a year of other activities. They are cautious when first communicating with each other or their lecturer because they do not know what the opinions, attitudes and values of the others are — neither do they wish to express their own attitudes and opinions at this stage. Before members of the group trust one another, no meaningful group discussion can take place. However, as they get to know each other, they will be more inclined to test each other's reactions and knowledge. In this way they will learn whom they can trust and whom they should be cautious of. Later when the lecturer asks the group to decide on test dates for that particular subject, and the group's interests become the focus of attention, more interaction among members of the group is elicited.

The most appropriate leadership style during this stage is an autocratic style.[3] The leader needs to spend time with his subordinates to clarify the objectives of the group, decide on plans to attain these objectives, and so on.

16.5.2 Communication and decision making

Once the members of a group accept and trust one another, they will interact more openly. Members of a group tend to tolerate opinions that differ from their own and explore various options to find the best solution for the group as a whole. The students in the above example may therefore decide that it would suit everyone in the group if they were to write their tests on Saturdays so that their tests do not clash with lectures. Before this decision can be taken, however, the group will have to assign roles and tasks to different members of the group. They will elect a class representative and demarcate his specific tasks so that everyone in the group knows with whom they must communicate before making group-related decisions.

The appropriate leadership style in this stage is a consultative leadership style.[4] The leader needs to encourage his people to attain the set goals, but also needs input from them to develop the appropriate group structure and other processes.

16.5.3 Motivation and productivity

In this stage, there is a shift from personal to group interests. Cooperation, rather than competition, is a characteristic of the group. At this stage, members of the group are motivated and perform their tasks creatively. The students in our example above might decide to divide the class into smaller groups so that the various subgroups can summarise different sections of the textbook and swap notes.

Once the group members know what to do and how to do it, the leader should allow them to participate in decision making.[5]

16.5.4 **Control and organisation**

In the fourth stage of group formation the group works together productively to attain the objectives of the group. After consulting members of the group, specific tasks are assigned to different people on the strength of their abilities. Group affiliation is important in this stage, and members endeavour to obey the norms of the group. Group goals are more important than individual goals. Control is exercised over members of the group by, among other things, punishing transgressions of group norms. This punishment may assume different forms, such as ignoring the group member or isolating him or her.

The most appropriate leadership style during this phase is a style of empowerment.[6] Group members should be allowed to make and implement decisions without constantly consulting the leader.

Not all groups complete all the stages explained above — some disband before reaching the final stage, while others omit a stage. So, instead of spending time getting to know and trust one another, members of a group may omit the first stage because their group leader pressurises them into setting a certain target date. If members of the group are forced into the next stage without the previous stage having been completed, they may become extremely frustrated. The group may not develop to its full potential and may become unproductive. Group productivity depends on the successful completion of each stage. A group that completes each of the four stages will be a more mature and purposeful group.

16.6 **CHARACTERISTICS OF A GROUP**

As a group passes through the different stages, certain group characteristics start to emerge. These are depicted in figure 16.3.

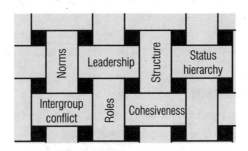

Figure 16.3
Characteristics of a group

To understand group behaviour, it is necessary to discuss the general characteristics of the group as set out above.

In the course of time, a specific **structure**, based on factors such as knowledge, aggression, power and status, develops in the group. The relationship between the positions held by members of the group forms the structure. Members of the group evaluate the position of each person in the group in terms of status and importance, among other things, and on the basis of this, a group hierarchy develops.

In formal groups, **status** is based on position in the formal organisation, while in an informal group it is based on anything that is appropriate, for example, who the captain of a team is, or who the person who can communicate most easily with management. Comembers of the group expect the incumbent of each position to manifest certain behaviour.

The concepts of **status** and **position** are so similar that the two are often used as synonyms. The status that is accorded to a particular position is typically a consequence of the characteristics that distinguish one position from another. In certain cases, a particular status is assigned to a person on the strength of factors such as seniority or age. The oldest worker in a group of bricklayers may be regarded as the best artisan by the group because of his years of experience, and in that particular group will have the most status. This acquired status may have no connection with formal status whatsoever. In this particular example, a young bricklayer could be appointed foreman of the other bricklayers but they will not regard him as their senior.

Each member of the group has an associated **role**, comprising the behaviour expected of the incumbent of the particular position. A superintendent in a hospital is regarded as a manager who must plan and organise activities in the hospital, guide the hospital staff and control the people and activities involved. Hence it is his or her task to see that the entire hospital attains its objectives. The head matron for her part is responsible for the activities of the nursing staff in the hospital's different departments, such as casualties, the maternity section and theatre. The expected behaviour of the nursing staff is not only determined by their peers in the hospital but also by senior nursing staff, other hospital personnel and the superintendent.

Individuals play all sorts of roles because they belong to different groups. Thus supervisors are members of the management team but at the same time members of the group of workers that management must supervise. The behaviour demanded by the different roles is sometimes irreconcilable and the result is that individuals experience role conflict. **Personal role conflict** occurs when the role requirements contradict the basic values, attitudes and needs of individuals in a particular position. The managing director of a hotel group might resign because of top management's decision to open casinos in all its hotels, a decision that goes against his values.

Intrarole conflict occurs when two people have different expectations of a role. It becomes impossible for the person enacting the role to satisfy all the expectations.

Interrole conflict may result when a person has to enact a multiplicity of roles. Sometimes an individual has to play many roles simultaneously, some of which have conflicting expectations. An example here is a hospital superintendent. As a medical doctor, he or she is expected to act according to certain rules. However, he or she is also a manager and must therefore satisfy the requirements of a good manager.

Norms are standards shared by members of a group, and develop from interaction between members. Norms develop in respect of things that the group regard as important. One of the norms in a group might be that members must always strive to improve themselves even if they are doing well in the group. However, norms may also be negative. One of the norms in the sales department of the organisation might be to do as little as possible since other departments are perceived as doing virtually nothing.

Norms may be written, communicated verbally or even be unconsciously shared by members of the group. They are not accepted to the same extent by members of the group. Some norms are accepted in total, while others are accepted only partially. Furthermore, some norms apply to the whole group while others apply only to certain members.

Leadership in the group is one of the critical characteristics of groups. In both formal and informal groups, a leader is someone who motivates his or her subordinates and gives them direction. Since leadership plays such an important role in goal attainment, chapter 12 has been devoted to this topic.

Cohesiveness refers to group solidarity, in other words the way a group stands together as a unit rather than as individuals in a group. Group cohesiveness develops as a result of the attraction that the group has for the individual. The attraction of the group is related to the needs of the individual.

Group cohesiveness, however, does not always have positive results for an organisation. Group thinking may occur in groups with strong cohesiveness, and this may mean that the group's desire for cohesiveness prevents it from considering alternative solutions to problems.

Managers can apply different strategies to encourage or discourage group cohesiveness. To encourage it a manager should:[7]

- make groups as small as possible
- encourage individuals to identify with the objectives of the group
- stimulate competition with other groups
- include people who are similar, although diverse groups usually make better decisions
- ensure that the group is not dominated by one or a few group members
- motivate the group to become successful

To discourage group cohesiveness, managers should not do the above.

Although organisational structures are designed to promote cooperation, most organisations experience internal conflict. Although conflict need not be negative, it can impede goal attainment. Many conflicts are the result of dissension between segments of the organisation — group versus group, department against department, and so forth. The word **conflict** has a negative connotation for many people. Although it can be disruptive, it should not be viewed as detrimental. By managing conflict the strengths and weaknesses of an organisation can be exposed, and something can be done about them. (See chapter 14.)

16.7   INTERGROUP DYNAMICS

The contribution of a group to the objectives of an organisation depends mainly on the group's interaction with other groups and the internal productivity of the group. The interaction may be regular, for example, between waiters and chefs in a restaurant, or irregular, say, between the counter clerks at the post office and the inspectors who inspect the different branches. A manager must understand how different groups interact because sound relations between groups promote the attainment of objectives. We shall now briefly look at a general model of intergroup dynamics to help managers deal with the interaction between different groups in the organisation more effectively. The model is illustrated in figure 16.4.

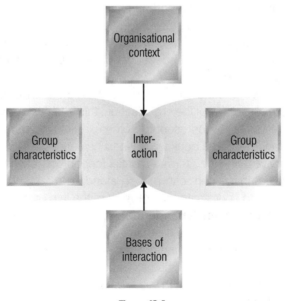

Figure 16.4
A model of intergroup dynamics

Some work can be done only if groups interact. Thus the production department can manufacture products only if the purchasing department purchases the right components at the right time. Group interaction in an organisation occurs within a certain system of organisational rules and procedures, that is, in a specific **organisational context**. Interaction is dependent on the history, traditions and culture of the organisation, and its objectives, remuneration systems and decision-making processes.

Each group is unique. Each group brings its own set of characteristics into the interaction process and this influences the process. Both individual **characteristics**, such as the personality of individuals, and the characteristics of the group, such as group cohesiveness and norms, influence the process of interaction.

The model also focuses on the work relationship between groups, and the reasons for it. Because the reasons for **interaction** are so important, they are regarded as the **bases of interaction**. In the next section we shall examine these bases in greater detail.

16.7.1 Bases of interaction

The factors responsible for groups interacting, also known as the **bases of interaction**, include task interdependence, task uncertainty, time and goal interdependence, resources and localisation.

Task interdependence refers to the extent to which the activities of different groups force them to depend on each other and therefore to act in a more coordinated fashion. Task interdependence is the most powerful basis of interaction between groups in the organisation, and can be subdivided into three kinds of interaction, namely pooled interdependence, sequential interdependence and reciprocal interdependence.

When two or more groups function fairly independently but pool their outputs to attain the objectives of the organisation, this is known as **pooled interdependence**. This relationship is represented in the example in figure 16.5 where it is clear that both branches of the bank will have to be successful if the organisation as a whole is to survive in the long term. Potential for conflict between the two branches is fairly low, and management can rely on standard rules and procedures developed by head office to coordinate the activities of the two branches.

Sequential interdependence requires one group to complete its task before another group can tackle its job. In Volkswagen SA's plant at Uitenhage, the vehicles must first be assembled before they can be spraypainted. So the output of one group here is the input of the next group, but the output of the second group is not part of the input of the first. In this example there is a greater likelihood of conflict than in pooled interdependence.

In **reciprocal interdependence** the outputs of each group constitute the inputs of the other groups in the organisation. This is the most complicated of the three kinds of interdependence and is also the most difficult to manage. The groups are largely dependent on each other, and conflict can easily arise. An example here is the interdependence of the different groups responsible for landing an aircraft. The

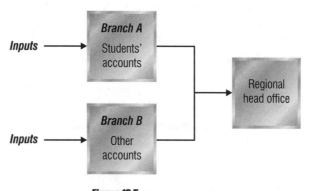

Figure 16.5
Pooled interdependence

control tower at the airport must be in touch with the pilot, the runway personnel must be in touch with the control tower and the maintenance units must be ready to check the aeroplane carefully before it can take off again.

In all organisations there is pooled interdependence among different groups. Sequential interdependence also occurs in complex organisations. The most complex organisations have pooled, sequential and reciprocal interaction between groups. The more complex an organisation is, the greater the likelihood of conflict will be, and the more formidable the task of management to coordinate activities.

We have referred to the changing environment in which organisations in South Africa and throughout the world operate. In these turbulent environments there are many uncertainties that arise because of technological change, economic conditions, legislation, consumer preferences and other factors beyond the control of management. **Task uncertainty** arises precisely because of groups that are unsure of the direction the organisation is taking or because of future events that may affect them and their activities in the organisation.

The importance of objectives in an organisation was discussed in chapter 4. It should have become clear in this chapter that objectives become more specific the lower they are set in the organisational hierarchy. Work groups on the factory floor will have a clear time limit for the completion of different tasks. The fact that broad organisational objectives can be subdivided into specific goals for groups and that these must be realised within a certain period of time leads to interaction between groups to jointly realise the objectives of the organisation. One can therefore say that there is **time and goal interdependence** between groups.

Suppose that two groups of engineers work in a certain organisation. One of the groups is responsible for research into the components used in the products and its results are manifest only in the long term. For this group, the primary consideration is that the best possible material is used in the components, and it therefore takes months to test all the possibilities. The other group of engineers is responsible for manufacturing the product. Its task is to have the product ready for marketing as soon as possible, and these engineers become irritated with the other engineers because they take so long. In this example, the time and goal differences between the two groups influence interaction between them. Management should be sensitive to such differences to ensure productive group interaction.

Organisations have human, financial and physical resources and information at their disposal to actualise their objectives. Each group in the organisation has a claim to the **resources** in order to attain the group objectives. Groups have to interact to ensure that they get their fair share of the resources. The potential for interaction increases if the groups use the same or similar resources or if one of them influences the availability of the resources to the other groups. Take the example of a firm that employs university students during the holidays to relieve the workload of employees. These students are placed in different departments and each of them requires an office to work in. Arguments may arise between the managers of the different departments about the allocation of available office space, computers, and so on, and this may create an unpleasant climate in the organisation.

Interaction as a result of the deployment of resources need not be unpleasant. If the different groups realise that it is a joint effort and not the isolated performance of each group that leads to the attainment of the organisation's objectives, they should be able to make meaningful joint decisions about resource allocation.

Lastly, the greater the **proximity of groups**, the greater the chance of group interaction will be. If members of different groups occupy offices in the same wing, there is a greater change of informal interaction. The pattern of interaction in the organisation can be changed by swapping the offices of different departments.

16.8 DEVELOPING GROUPS INTO TEAMS

Figure 16.1 illustrated a continuum with groups and teams at its two extremes. There is a tendency today towards team development in South African organisations, and organisations worldwide. The following are some of the reasons for this:

- Teams, rather than groups, empower people in the modern organisation.
- Teams are more productive than groups.[8]
- Contemporary management approaches, such as TQM (see chapter 2), rely heavily on teamwork.
- Teams are more flexible and responsive to changes in the business environment.

Turning groups into teams is a process that must be carefully managed. Management cannot place people in teams and expect them to be successful: employees should be trained to function in teams. Managers need to be aware that the management functions, namely planning, organising, leading and controlling, are handled differently in groups and teams.

> The Chrysler Neon, which is now being sold in South Africa, was completely developed by a cross-functional team. (See section 16.8.1.) The new model was delivered in a speedy 42 months and at a fraction of what any other manufacturer's small car has cost. The Neon team knew that if costs weren't rock-bottom, Chrysler would pull the plug.
>
> Source: Woodruff, D. 1993. Chrysler's Neon: Is this the small car Detroit couldn't build? *Business Week*, 3 May, pp 116–126.

To develop groups into teams managers need to be aware of :

■ different types of teams
■ how to create high-performance teams
■ how to transform individuals into team players
■ management functions and teams

The above points are discussed in the following sections.

16.8.1 Types of teams

Teams can be classified on the basis of their **objectives**. The three most common forms of teams found in organisations are problem-solving teams, self-managed work teams and cross-functional teams. These types of teams are illustrated in figure 16.6.

Problem-solving teams are typically composed of employees from the same department who meet for a few hours each week to discuss ways of improving quality, efficiency and the work environment. At City Lodge Hotels, kitchen staff can meet each week to discuss customer complaints, more effective ways of preparing breakfasts, the layout of the breakfast room, and so on. Although this team may suggest improvements, it does not have the authority to implement any of its solutions unilaterally.

Self-managed work teams function autonomously, may make and implement decisions and take full responsibility for outcomes. The management tasks become a team responsibility. These work teams can appoint new employees, authorise equipment purchases, evaluate each other's performance and can even decide who should receive bonuses.

The implementation of self-managed work teams requires the redesign of many aspects of the organisational system. Design changes include flattening the organisation structure, distributing performance-related information to employees, extensive training and development, eliminating status differences, rewarding for performance and skills, and creating conditions for employee empowerment.

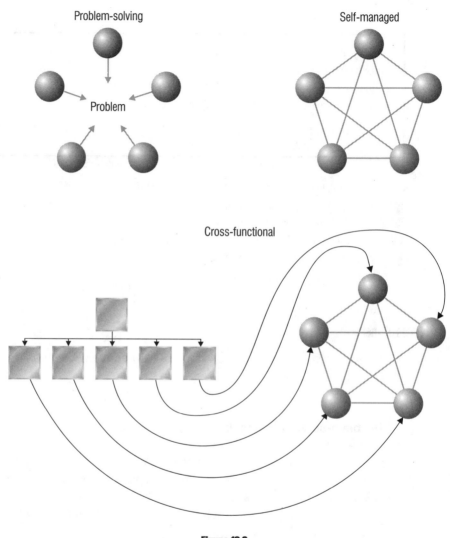

Figure 16.6
Types of teams

Cross-functional teams are made up of employees on the same hierarchical level, such as the marketing manager, financial manager, operations manager, and so on. A cross-functional team usually consists of people in the same organisation but could also include people from other organisations. This type of team is suitable in situations where complex problems have to be solved and the expertise of specialists with diverse backgrounds is needed. The Neon, Chrysler's groundbreaking subcompact, was developed completely by cross-functional teams.

Research on self-managing teams

Research on self-managing teams finds modest evidence of positive impact on attitudinal and organisational performance results. Individuals on these teams tend to report higher levels of job satisfaction. However, counter to conventional wisdom, employees on self-managed work teams seem to have higher absenteeism and turnover rates than do employees working in traditional work structures. The reasons for these findings are, at this point, unclear.

Source: Cordery, JL, Mueller, WS & Smith, LM. 1991. Attitudinal and behavioural effects of autonomous group working: a longitudinal field study. *Academy of Management Journal*, June, pp 464–476.

16.8.2 Creating high-performance teams

To create high-performance teams, managers need to consider several issues.[9]

Firstly, in designing effective teams, managers should restrict the number of people in a team to less than 12. If the team has more than 12 members, the manager should consider breaking the group into subteams.

Secondly, to perform effectively, a team requires different types of skills (see chapter 1), namely technical, interpersonal and conceptual skills. The right mix of these skills is essential: too many people with technical skills, at the expense of those with conceptual skills, will impede the team's creativity. Conversely, too many members with conceptual skills may lead the group to lose sight of current realities.

A third issue is role allocation. The Springbok rugby team will have players with different personalities and preferences. A winning team needs a variety of skills: strong forwards, good ball handlers in the backline, fast wings and a fullback with safe hands. The focus here is on the performance of the team, and not individual performances. This could mean that the best flyhalf is left out of the team because his approach to matches is too individualistic.

In successful work teams people fill the key roles according to their skills and preferences. By matching individual preferences with team role demands (see figure 16.7) managers increase the likelihood that the team members will work well together.

Fourthly, the team should have a meaningful purpose to which all members aspire — a clear vision. This vision should provide direction and guidance under any and all conditions. In developing the Chrysler Neon, all teams and team members were committed to developing a groundbreaking subcompact car at rock-bottom costs.

The purpose of the team is a broader concept than goals. However, a fifth issue that plays a role in creating a high-performance team is that the purpose must be translated into specific, measurable and attainable goals. The designers of the driver's seat for the Neon set specific deadlines for the design of this seat, knowing

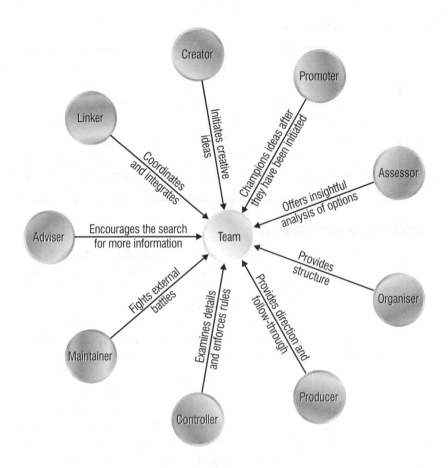

Figure 16.7
Key roles in teams
Source: Based on Margerison, C & McCann, D. 1990. *Team Management: Practical New Approaches*. London:
Mercury Books.

that they played a vital role in completing the car before the International Motor Show
at the end of December 1993. This allowed them to start selling the car in January
1994, at a price of $8 600.

In the sixth place, it should be made clear to team members that each member
will be individually and jointly accountable for realising the team's purpose, goals,
and so on.

Lastly, the appraisal and reward system should be modified to reflect team
performance. Profit sharing, small-group incentives and other system modifications
that will reinforce team effort and commitment should be considered.

> Americans don't grow up learning how to function in teams. In school we never receive a team report card or learn the names of the team of sailors who travelled with Columbus to America.
> Source: Robbins, SP. 1997. *Managing Today.* Upper Saddle River, NJ: Prentice-Hall, p 314.
>
> The same can be said about South Africans, especially white South Africans, who grow up in an individualistic environment where individuals are rewarded for their achievements — often at the expense of other group members who also contributed to goal attainment. Other individual-istic countries include the United States of America, Australia, the United Kingdom and Canada.
>
> Black South Africans, on the other hand, grow up in an environment where the wellbeing of the group is paramount. Venezuela, Colombia, Pakistan and Taiwan are countries where collec-tivism overrides individualism.

16.8.3 Transforming individuals into team members

Transforming individuals into team members is a daunting task in South Africa. The biggest percentage of managers are white males, with predominantly individualistic values, so they are not inherently team players. But what should managers do if they want to introduce teams in the workplace?

Firstly, the selection process should identify those people who possess the inter-personal skills to be effective team players. Secondly, employees should be trained to become team members. Lastly, the reward system should encourage cooperative efforts rather than competitive ones. Recognition should be given to individuals for their effectiveness as team members. This could take the form of pay increases, promotion, and so on.

16.9 TEAMS AND THE MANAGEMENT FUNCTIONS

The management functions are handled differently in groups and teams. Both groups and teams need clear goals, well-developed plans, decision making to per-form at high levels and relevant information. (See part 2.) A major difference between groups and teams is who develops the objectives and plans and who makes the decisions. In a team, the manager should allow the members to become involved in the **planning** function. The manager's role changes to focusing on involving mem-bers and making sure they know the objectives and that they accept them and are committed to achieving them.

As far as **organising** is concerned, both group and team members should have a clear understanding of their level of authority. In groups, authority is held by the manager; in teams, the members have higher levels of authority.

In groups, there is one clear **leader**; in teams leadership is shared. However, in most teams a specific person will be identified as a leader but will share the responsibility with other members. Team leaders empower members to take responsibility for performing the management functions while focusing on developing effective group structures and processes and developing team skills. Team leaders will also be involved in planning and conducting meetings and handling problem members.

Controlling will be the responsibility of team members who will have to identify possible deviations from the planned goals and rectify these deviations.

It should be clear from the above that an organisation should prepare both managers and subordinates if they want to restructure the organisation and turn groups into teams.

16.10 CONCLUSION

One of the most challenging tasks that faces contemporary managers is group and team management in an organisation.

Although groups comprise a number of individuals, the group behaviour of individuals is not equal to the sum of the individual behaviours of the members of the group. The fact that a manager feels he knows his subordinates does not necessarily mean that he can predict how they will act in a group in the organisation.

To know what to expect of a group, it is necessary for management to know how groups function. In the first instance, a manager must know why people belong to groups. Individuals' reasons for belonging to groups include their needs, proximity, attraction and the objectives and economic benefits that the group offers the individual.

Formal and informal groups are found in organisations. Formal groups include the command group and the task groups, while friendship groups and interest group are examples of informal groups that also have a place in organisations.

Groups are not static but develop through four stages. First, there is mutual acceptance between members, followed by communication and decision making. Then comes motivation and productivity, and finally, control and organisation. Each stage requires a unique leadership style.

As groups pass through the four stages, certain characteristics emerge. These include the structure of the group, the status hierarchy, roles in the group, group norms, leadership, group cohesiveness and intergroup conflict.

Groups do not function in isolation, which is why we also studied group interaction in the work situation. To explain this interaction, we put forward and explained a model for intergroup dynamics. We paid special attention to factors that lead to group interaction.

Teams were discussed by looking at the recent popularity of teams. In our discussion we focused on the different types of teams, namely problem-solving, self-managed and cross-functional teams. We stressed that the latter two types could mean that the team members will be held responsible for the entire functioning of the team as they will have authority to make major decisions.

We also looked at the creation of high performance teams and how to transform individuals into team players.

To conclude this chapter, and this part of the book, we looked at how the management functions are handled differently in groups and teams.

16.11 REFERENCES

1. Kolb, J. 1995. Leader behaviours affecting team performance: Similarities and differences between leader/member assessments. *The Journal of Business Communication*, vol 32, no 3 (July), pp 233–249.
2. Lussier, RN. 1997. *Management: Concepts, Applications, Skill Development.* Cincinnati, OH: South Western, p 419.
3. Ibid p 432.
4. Ibid p 433.
5. Ibid.
6. Ibid.
7. Ibid p 429.
8. Peters, T. 1995. When muddling through can be the best strategy. *Washington Business Journal*, 27 January, pp 19–20.
9. Robbins, SP. 1997. *Managing Today*. Upper Saddle River, NJ: Prentice-Hall, pp 311–314.

Part 5

The Control Process

17 Control

- Control as the final component of the management process
- The focal points of control
- The relationship between control and planning and hence the cycle of the management process

---

17.1 INTRODUCTION

Organisations use control procedures to ensure that they are progressing towards their objectives and that their resources are being used productively.

The term 'control' implies that the behaviour of individuals can be influenced in the course of activities and events. In other words, if things are under control, they are proceeding as they should. However, when things get out of control, they become unmanageable and the problems arising from this situation cannot be handled. In management literature, the term 'control' has a specific meaning, namely the process whereby management ensures that the actual activities fit in with the predetermined objectives and planned activities.

Control is the final step in the management process and is an important link in the cycle of the management process. The most brilliant plans can be formulated, the most impressive structures designed and people motivated to attain objectives, but this still does not ensure that the activities will proceed according to plan and that the objectives that management has formulated will in fact be realised. An effective manager is therefore someone who follows up the planned activities, and sees to it that the things that need to be done are in fact carried out and the predetermined objectives attained. It is for this reason that managers at all levels and in all departments should be involved in the process of control. Until the activities of individuals, departments or units are evaluated, that is until actual performance is compared with the standard required, management will not know whether activities are executed according to plan and will be unable to identify weaknesses in the plan or manage-ment effort.

A closer study of the nature of control will highlight the importance of this final component of the management process.

Background

During the 1984/1985 depression, South African managers did not have sufficient financial control over loan capital, and they burnt their fingers when the prime interest rate rose to 25 % per annum. However, in the 1991/1992 depression management was prepared for high interest rates but not for the lengthy duration thereof, and organisations once again ran into difficulties because of poor control.

A South African knitwear manufacturer did not exercise proper control over rising costs caused mainly by wage demands and lost both his foreign and local markets when he was compelled to price himself 'out of the market'.

The B2 bomber of the American air force was supposed to cost $170 million per aircraft, but ultimately worked out at $815 million per bomber! The reason for this was poor control. For example, the air force purchased plastic covers that concealed the screws on the navigators' chairlegs for $118,26 a piece from Boeing, when they could have bought them at $4 a piece from an existing air force supplier.

Source: Robbins, SP. 1991. *Management.* New Jersey: Prentice-Hall, p 565.

17.2   THE NATURE OF CONTROL

The aim of control, one of the four fundamental management functions, is to keep deviations from planned activities and performance levels to a minimum so that the mission and objectives of the organisation can be achieved with as few hitches as possible. Control is therefore the regulatory task of management in that it allows action to tie in with plans, it is an important guide in the execution of plans and it measures the performance of the whole organisation. In a sense control is supervi-sory — it supervises and measures the progress that has been made towards attaining a particular objective. The control task of management determines whether or not there has been a deviation in the plans so that steps can be taken to prevent and rectify errors.

In the control process, management endeavours to make planning and perform-ance coincide — this bridges the gap between formulating objectives and attaining them, and ensures that all activities are performed as they should be. Control is a continuous process and is interwoven with planning, organising and leading. It is probably the most important link in the management cycle. It is the final stage in the process because it evaluates the management effort; the knowledge, experience, information and facts acquired and collected during the control process are the most important inputs in the next round of planning to keep the management process on course. Control also complements planning, because when deviations are encountered, it shows that plans and even objectives need to be revised. Figure 17.1 shows why control is such an important link in the management process. Management formulates plans and uses the control process to monitor the progress of these plans. The control system informs management of the following:

- Activities are proceeding according to plan — that is, the existing plan should be continued.
- Things are not proceeding according to plan — that is, the existing plan should be adjusted.
- The situation has changed — in other words, a new plan must be devised.

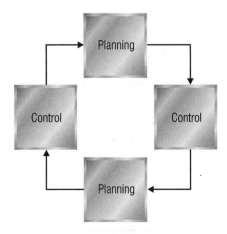

Figure 17.1
The link between planning and control

The management process takes place between planning and control, and successful management is often dependent on sound planning and effective control. The preceding introductory remarks have already partly indicated the importance of control. A few additional remarks are necessary here.

17.2.1 The importance of control

An organisation needs a control process because the best of plans may go wrong. A control process is necessary in an organisation for the following reasons:

- First and foremost, control is exercised to ensure that all activities at all levels of the organisation are in accordance with the organisation's objectives.

- Secondly, control is applied to ensure that the organisation's resources are deployed in such a way that it reaches its objectives. If there is no control, the organisation's resources could be wasted or misapplied.
- Thirdly, control usually results in better quality.
- Control enables management to cope with change and uncertainty. If an organisation is to reach its objectives according to plan, control is necessary. Because of the variables to which an organisation is exposed in the turbulent contemporary business environment, an organisation is seldom able to realise its objectives strictly according to plan. Raw materials may not be delivered on time, labour unrest or defective machinery may delay production, interest rates may influence profitability and competitors may introduce a new product which reduces the organisation's market share. When any of these variables is present, change becomes a reality and the organisation's objectives and plans are invariably affected. As indicated in chapter 3, in the last few years management has been exposed to more change than in the past — hence the need for greater control over the influences of change on the objectives and plans of an organisation.
- The complexity of organisations is another factor. Larger organisations with diverse product lines and decentralised management necessitate comprehensive control systems for the timely evaluation of various product lines and activities of departments. In such complex organisations a small mistake may cost millions of rand. The greater the number of people who join an organisation, the greater the need for coordination, the greater the chance of error and the greater the need for control.

Focus

> Small mistakes do not cause an immediate crisis in the organisation, but over a period of time the incidence of mistakes may accumulate and cause really serious damage. A purchasing manager who neglects to insist on the usual 2,5 % discount given in a particular industry will lose only R2 500 on the organisation's initial order of R100 000. However, once orders amount to R5 million, this 'affordable error' will be in the region of R125 000.

- Competition is a significant factor. In chapter 1 we briefly discussed the disintegration of centrally directed economic systems and showed how a free-market economy can better satisfy the needs of societies. A successful free-market economy, however, also gives rise to more active competition. This in turn necessitates stricter cost and quality control if the organisation is to remain competitive. Globalisation is responsible for fierce competition in international markets.

■ Control facilitates delegation and team work. Managers often fear that subordi-nates will not do the job properly, and they therefore find it difficult to delegate.[1] Hence they tend to avoid delegation and try to do the job themselves. The only way managers can determine whether subordinates are going to perform the tasks delegated to them successfully is by means of a control system. Without a control system it is impossible to determine an employee's progress and ulti-mately the performance of the organisation.

An overview of the control process will help to elucidate the importance of control.

17.3 THE CONTROL PROCESS

We mentioned in the introduction that control is the process in which management ensures that the organisation's objectives are realised or that actual performance ties in with the predetermined standards. More specifically, control is the process in which management ensures that all the organisation's resources are meaningfully deployed so that the mission and objectives of the organisation can be attained. This description implies a process comprising four steps. Figure 17.2 is a schematic representation of the four steps. The process includes setting standards against which actual performance can be measured, measuring actual performance, evalu-ating any deviations that might occur, and taking steps to rectify deviations. Each of these steps will now be discussed briefly.

17.3.1 Step 1: Establishing standards of performance

Establishing standards of performance at strategic points is the first step in manage-ment control. Because of the interrelationship between planning and control, it is said that control starts as early as the planning stage. If one considers that in a certain sense, control means the replanning and reallocation of resources, it is often difficult to distinguish between the two management functions. The control process should actually be a mirror of planning, because plans indicate objectives and set standards or norms that are necessary for control.

A performance standard is a projection of expected or planned performance and, over a period of time, the positive or negative disparity between planned and actual performance is monitored to compare actual performance with the standard possible. In short, setting performance standards is planning which includes the formulation of objectives.

To make the control process possible and meaningful, performance standards should be realistic, attainable and measurable, so that there is no doubt about whether the actual performance meets the standard or not. Although it is difficult to make valid generalisations about suitable standards for different organisations, in any organisation it should be possible to convert a strategy into comprehensive

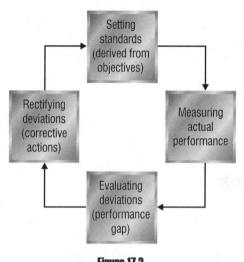

Figure 17.2
The control process

plans and objectives for the future. Suitable performance standards (see section 17.4) can therefore be developed, and they include the following:

- **profit standards**, which indicate how much profit the organisation wishes to make in a specific period
- **market share standards**, which indicate the share of the total market the organisation is aiming at
- **productivity standards**, which are indicated by expressing certain inputs and outputs with a close and significant relationship as a ratio — such a ratio will indicate the relative productivity with which tasks are performed
- **staff development standards**, which indicate personnel training programmes the organisation should provide

Standards are therefore a function of the objectives that are formulated in the planning stage. Performance standards, of which the above are only a few examples, enable management to distinguish between acceptable and unacceptable performance and to keep abreast of the strategy and plans. To be effective, standards should be the responsibility of a particular individual at some strategic point where they can be representative, realised economically and in good time. We shall discuss this at a later stage.

17.3.2 Step 2 : Measuring actual performance

Collecting data and reporting on actual performance — the activities that constitute performance management — are ongoing activities. The complexity of reporting is a function of the type and number of variables (activities) that should be measured and monitored. The assessment of actual performance can also be hampered by what has to be measured.

As with performance standards, the **variables** should be quantifiable to make meaningful comparison possible. A further important requirement for observing performance is that reporting should be absolutely reliable. Unless the data are accurate, control will not be effective. Moreover, observation and measurement should **be in accordance with the control system**, that is, they should occur at the strategic points and according to the standards determined by the control system.

An important aspect of observation, measurement and reporting on the organisation's activities is how much information should be fed back, and to whom. In a fairly small organisation or at the lower levels of management in a relatively large organisation, operations management is usually fully informed and this is not normally a problem. However, as an organisation grows and information on the progress of activities has to be sent to higher levels of management, the issue of control becomes increasingly important. It is here that the principle of **control by exception** comes into play. This means that only important or exceptional differences between actual and planned performance are communicated to top management, and subordinates deal with less significant deviations on their own.

Management information indicates the differences between performance standards and actual performance to enable management to concentrate on the deviations or problem areas. For example, management may be more than satisfied with a report that shows that sales for the year are 10 % higher than the previous year. However, it will feel less complacent if a product that is a market leader shows a decline of 10 %! The minimum of time should elapse between performance and its measurement so that deviations can be identified as soon as possible.

17.3.3 Step 3 : Evaluating deviations

Determining whether performance matches standards entails evaluating differences between actual performance and the predetermined standards.

It is important to know why a standard is merely equalled, and not exceeded, or why the organisation has done considerably better than the standard. The latter could be because of changes in the business environment that could have been even better utilised. The nature and scope of deviations may have various causes. The causes may be fairly obvious or they may be obscure in that they cannot be identified even after further research. It is impossible to make generalisations about the causes of disparities between actual performance and the standard set. It is necessary to make sure that the discrepancies are genuine — that is, the performance standard and the actual performance should be objectively set and observed. If the standard has been set too high, a further study of the differences is unnecessary.

Management must decide whether the differences are significant enough to merit further attention. Upper and lower limits should be set for each deviation, and only those differences that fall outside the limits should be investigated.

All the variables that could possibly be responsible for the deviation should be identified.

The point has now been reached where it is necessary to make decisions about future actions — that is, the final step in control should be taken.

17.3.4 Step 4 : Taking corrective action

Corrective action is action aimed at achieving or bettering the performance standard and ensuring that differences do not recur in the future. If actual performances match the performance standard, no corrective action is necessary, provided that the standards have been set objectively. If actual performance does not match the performance standard, management has three options:

1. Actual performance can be improved to attain the standard.
2. The strategy can be revised to attain the performance standards set.
3. The performance standards can be lowered, or raised, to make them more realistic in the light of prevailing circumstances.

Thus the cycle of the control process has been completed, and corrective action, as explained above, is in a sense the starting point of the next cycle. The concept of control, however, means different things to different people, and often has a negative connotation for those who feel that their freedom and initiative are being curbed. It is important to maintain a healthy balance between measures and people. From a cost point of view one should remember that there are limits to the time and money that can be spent on control — hence the need to examine the focus of control, which is the next topic of discussion.

17.4   THE FOCUS OF CONTROL

In the preceding introductory discussion of control, the importance of control as a fundamental function of management was emphasised. But what should actually be controlled? Which activities in which departments should be controlled? In the preceding section we mentioned that the organisation's activities should be controlled at **strategic points**. What exactly is meant by 'strategic points'? The issues surrounding the design of a control system may be complex and depend on a variety of factors, such as the nature of the organisation and its activities, its size and structure. As a rule, management should identify the organisation's key areas, that is the areas or departments responsible for the effectiveness of the entire organisation. Thus, for example, the production department of a manufacturing organisation is a key area, as is the purchasing department of a chain store. Generally, in a small percentage of the activities, events or individuals in a given process are responsible for a large part of the process. Thus 10 % of a manufacturing organisation's products may be responsible for 60 % of its sales, or 2 % of an organisation's personnel may be responsible for 80 % of grievances. By concentrating on these strategic points, the organisation's main activities are exposed to control.

Management should adopt a more scientific approach to control, which is to consider the organisation's resources. In the introduction we defined management as the process in which the organisation's human, financial, physical and information resources are deployed to attain specific objectives, especially those revolving around profitability. The implication here is that control should focus on the effective management of these resources, as well as the realisation of objectives. Figure 17.3 illustrates the focal points of control.

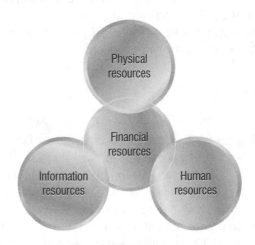

Figure 17.3
The focal points of control
Source: Griffin, RW. 1990. *Management*. Boston: Houghton Mifflin, p 599.

◼ The control of physical resources entails factors such as inventory control, quality control and control of equipment.

◼ Control of human resources involves orderly selection and placement, control over training and personnel development, performance appraisal and remuneration levels.

◼ The control of information sources concerns accurate market forecasting, adequate environmental scanning and economic forecasting.

◼ In figure 17.3 financial resources are situated in the centre of the other resources not only because they are controlled in their own right (for example, cash-flow or debtor control), but also because most control measures or techniques (such as budgets, sales, production costs, market share and various other magnitudes) are quantified in financial terms.

Each of the focal points of control will now be discussed in greater detail.

17.4.1 The control of physical resources

An organisation's physical resources are its tangible assets, such as buildings, office equipment and furniture, vehicles, manufacturing machinery and equipment, trading stock, raw materials, work in process and finished products. Various control systems of an administrative nature can be established to control physical resources, particularly office furniture, equipment and vehicles. Control systems for these resources involve usage procedures, periodic inspections and stock taking, which often fall within the ambit of the internal audit. The control systems for inventories, raw materials and finished products are **inventory control, operational control** and **quality control** Although inventory control falls within the field of purchasing and operations management, it is necessary to make a few remarks about it here. Operational and quality control are mentioned merely to indicate the complexity of **control**

Inventory

'Inventory' refers to the reserves of resources held in readiness to produce products and services as well as the end products that are kept in stock to satisfy consumers' and customers' needs. Inventory normally consists of tangible objects, such as raw materials, components and finished products, but it need not only have to do with manufacturing. For an airline, a seat on an aircraft is inventory, and an unsold seat on a flight is a loss. By the same token, money in a safe in a bank is inventory that can be lent to clients at a certain interest rate, and an empty bed in a hospital ward is 'trading stock'. Organisations keep inventories — and here the word is used in a wide sense — mainly for the following purposes:

- to satisfy the needs of customers and consumers
- in the case of raw materials and components, to keep uncertainties regarding delivery and availability to a minimum so that the manufacturing process is not interrupted
- as a hedge during times of high inflation

A number of reasons why organisations keep inventories can probably be advanced, but the above reasons are sufficient to emphasise one important point, namely the cost of inventories and the need to control that cost. It is estimated that it costs an organisation 20 to 25 cents per rand of inventory per annum to keep inventories. These costs refer mainly to interest, space and risk factors. The most expensive cost is the price of money, or interest, to finance inventories, followed by storage costs, insurance, and so on. Because of the high cost of inventories, it stands to reason that organisations, especially in times when interest rates are high, will try to keep inventory levels as low as possible. Inventory control is introduced to keep inventory, and the costs involved, as low as possible without causing shortages that may delay the manufacturing process or other transactions. The following three control systems are relevant here:

■ The concept of **economic ordering quantity** (EOQ), in use as early as 1915, is based on replenishing inventory levels by ordering the most economic quantity. The disadvantage of this control system is that inventory must be kept, regardless of the needs of the manufacturing department or customer for particular raw materials, components or finished products. This means that items must be kept in stock for indefinite periods in spite of efforts to keep inventory costs as low as possible.

■ The **materials requirements planning** (MRP) system was developed in the sixties to eliminate the shortcomings of the EOQ control system. According to this system, the demand for raw material and components necessary to create a finished product is estimated. With the MRP system, inventories are ordered only when they are needed, and the costs of maintaining inventory levels over extended periods of time are thus eliminated.

■ The **just-in-time** (JIT) system is a refinement of the MRP system and originated in Japan, where it was developed by Toyota in the seventies. The JIT philosophy is the same as MRP in the sense that organisations endeavour to manufacture products without incurring significant inventory costs. In contrast to MRP, where the need for raw materials and components is estimated and they are ordered according to demand, JIT is based on the premise that actual orders for finished products are converted into orders for raw materials and components, which

Toyota and JIT : the origin of the JIT system

The JIT production method, although recent in origin, has become the backbone of Japanese manufacturing. JIT production was developed in the mid-1970s by Toyota Motor Company in response to the energy crisis. Faced with increasing energy and production costs, Toyota had to find a way to make its products more competitive in the international market.

One way to do this was to cut inventory costs. Rather than producing finished goods destined for storage as stock, Toyota decided to produce cars just in time to be sold. It fabricates parts just in time to be assembled into subcomponents and buys materials just in time for fabrication. By using the JIT programme system, Toyota is able to use all materials promptly, incurring no carrying or ordering costs.

Source: Chung, KH. 1987. *Management: Critical Success Factors*. Newton: Allyn & Bacon, p 607.

arrive just in time for the manufacturing process. The success of this complex inventory control system depends largely on reliable deliveries of flawless components, stable relationships with outside suppliers and a reliable labour force.

The preceding discussion of inventory control systems is extremely superficial, the aim being merely to indicate the field of application and the complexity of control systems relating to physical resources.

We next examine an element that is closely intertwined with inventory control, namely operations control.

Operations control

The success of any organisation depends largely on its ability to produce products and services effectively. The focus of operations control is the ability of purchasing and materials management to make available the required quantity and quality of raw materials, components or services at the lowest possible cost. Operations control processes are also designed to determine how effectively the organisation's transformation process works. Well-known techniques that can be applied to operations control include linear programming, PERT and break-even analysis.

Quality control is related to operations management. A few remarks about quality control are necessary at this stage.

Quality control

We mentioned in chapter 2 that quality and productivity have become important issues in management, especially in the USA where business organisations are continually searching for ways to counter the success of the Japanese in American markets. The management approach which emphasises the management of quality is known as 'total quality management' (TQM). Because of its importance, particularly for competition in international markets, it is necessary to say something about quality control.

Japanese products were once regarded as 'cheap goods'. Today the quality of Japanese products is acknowledged globally. Because of the success of Japanese products, especially in the USA, Western managers are realising increasingly that access to international markets depends not only on mass production, but also on quality. Whereas quality control was formerly the responsibility of a single department or section, TQM means that quality is the responsibility of **everyone** in the organisation, from the chairman of the board of directors, down to clerks, purchasing managers, engineers, and selling and manufacturing personnel. Figure 17.4 illustrates the major factors involved in improving quality.

An espousal of product quality at managerial level will ensure that it is included in the mission statement of the organisation, and transmitted to operational levels. The ultimate test of product quality is in the marketplace; that is, whether or not the product satisfies consumers' needs.

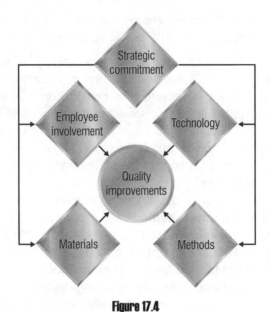

Figure 17.4
Managing quality
Source: Griffin, RW. 1990. *Management*. Boston: Houghton Mifflin, p 651.

A quality control programme

Recent research and articles advocating a systematic quality effort suggest that to be successful, a companywide quality control programme should:

- Reflect total commitment to quality by management.
- Be devoted to prevention rather than appraisal and correction.
- Focus on quality measurement (using feedback).
- Reward quality (employing incentives and penalties).
- Focus on quality training at all levels.
- Stress problem identification and solution (using terms).
- Promote innovation and continuous improvement.
- Promote total participation.
- Stress high performance standards with zero defects.
- Provide calculations and reports of cost savings.

Source: Daft, RL. 1995. *Management*. New York: The Dryden Press, p 521.

Quality control refers to the activities that management performs to ensure a level of quality that will satisfy the consumer on the one hand, and have certain benefits for the organisation on the other. It usually comprises the following steps:

1. The first step in quality control is the definition of **quality objectives** or **standards**. This entails setting standards as prescribed by purchasers, chosen by consumers and necessitated by competition. However, quality means different things to different people. Some might perceive it as value for money, and others simply as the durability of the product. In setting quality standards, management should focus on both qualitative product characteristics, such as reliability, durability, design, style and colour, and quantitative characteristics such as length, height and mass.

2. The second step in quality control is measuring quality. This entails the use of **statistical control methods** to analyse product data with a view to quality; **variation measurement**, that is, measuring variations in materials, processes, equipment and the final product; and the determination of whether or not **specification limits** have been met or exceeded.

3. Thirdly, quality control entails rectifying deviations and solving quality problems in an effort to keep the **cost of quality** as low as possible. This refers to the cost of control as well as the cost of failures, or the cost of poor quality. To be able to decide which products or product processes should be improved, management should conduct quality cost studies. These analyses indicate the cost–quality ratio of the organisation's products and services. Another technique that can be applied to improve quality is **quality circles**. This is a forum of employees who get together to identify aspects of their jobs that impede, prevent or promote quality, and who endeavour, on the strength of their expertise, to find solutions. The influence of quality circles in improving quality is felt not so much in direct savings, but in the positive motivational effect that participative problem solving has on employees.

The preceding discussion of the control of the organisation's physical resources is somewhat cursory and points not only to the complexity of controlling physical resources, but also to the importance of control in the success of the organisation. Aspects of control are expressed mainly in financial magnitudes. Control of the organisation's financial resources is the next topic of discussion.

17.4.2 The control of financial resources

An organisation's financial resources are the second group of resources that management must control. Financial resources and abilities are vital to the success of the organisation and are at the heart of the control process, as indicated in figure 17.3. Not only are financial resources a group of resources in their own right, but the control of financial resources is central to the control of other resources of the organisation. Pure financial control, such as the financial management that ensures that the organisation has sufficient cash flow, does exist, but management must also see to it that cash amounts do not lie in unproductive current accounts. However, financial management has other aspects — too much inventory or unnecessarily high inventory levels lead to excessive costs, and incorrect management information, such as inaccurate sales forecasts, can have a detrimental effect on cash flow. For this reason financial management is pivotal to the control process. We shall now examine two instruments of financial control.

The budget

As part of the planning process management allocates financial resources to different departments of the organisation in order to enable them to attain certain objectives. This allocation of financial resources is done by means of the **budget**. From the point of view of control, management wants to know how the financial resources are applied. The budget is therefore used as an instrument of control.

A budget is a formal plan, expressed in financial terms, that indicates how resources are to be allocated to different activities, departments or subdepartments of an organisation. At the same time it forms the basis for controlling the financial resources, a process known as budgetary control. Budgets are usually expressed in financial magnitudes, but can also be expressed in other units such as sales volumes, units of production or even time. It is precisely because of the quantitative nature of budgets that they provide the foundation for control systems — they provide standards for measuring performance and making comparisons of departments, levels and periods. More specifically, a budget's contributions to financial control are as follows.

- It supports management in coordinating resources, departments and projects.
- It provides guidelines on the application of the organisation's resources.
- It defines or sets standards that are vital to the control process.
- It makes possible the evaluation of resource allocation, departments or units.

Table 17.1
Types of budgets

Type of budget	Focus	Examples
Financial budgets	Focus on cash flow	■ Cash-flow budget ■ Capital budget ■ Balance budget
Operational budgets	Focus on the operational aspects of the organisation	■ Sales budget ■ Income budget ■ Expenditure budget
Nonfinancial budgets	Focus on diverse aspects of the organisation not expressed in financial terms	■ Production budgets in units ■ Sales volumes in units ■ Time projections of projects

Various kinds of budgets, of which a few examples are provided in table 17.1, can be used to make financial control possible across the financial spectrum.

However, budgets are not the only instrument that management uses to apply financial control. To complement the budget, management can use financial analysis, also known as ratio analysis, to apply financial control.

Financial analysis

Managers can learn a great deal about an organisation's affairs by applying financial analyses. Similarly, management can use financial analyses as an instrument of control. In particular, certain financial ratio analyses enable management to control the organisation's financial resources. The same ratio analyses can also provide an indication of the organisation's financial performance. The latter is a reflection of the organisation's total performance in the attainment of its objectives. Table 17.2 indicates the main ratio analyses that can be applied in financial control.

Table 17.2
A few financial ratio analyses

Type of financial analysis and control	Ratio analysis
Velocity of turnover of assets and creditors	Rate of turnover of total assets Rate of turnover of total fixed assets Rate of turnover of current assets Number of days of average inventory Average collection period of debtors Average settlement period of creditors
Analysis of marketing performance	Sales per m^2 of selling space Sales per m^2 of total floor space Sales per member of staff
Analysis of rental paid and marketing costs	Sales per rand of salaries and wages Sales per rand of rent Rent per m^2 of selling space Rent per m^2 of total floor space
Liquidity analysis	Current ratio Acid test ratio
General performance analysis	Value added per m^2 of total floor space Value added per rand of rental paid Value added per rand of fixed capital Value added per rand of working capital Labour efficiency Total efficiency

In addition to the budget and financial ratio analysis that can be used for control purposes, there are the internal financial audit and the formal external audit. These are usually conducted by chartered accountants and auditors.

An aspect that is closely related to financial control and financial management is the third organisational resource, namely information. Without the relevant information or management information, control is impossible.

17.4.3 The control of information resources

All the tasks of management, namely planning, organising, leading and controlling, are dependent on supporting information to function effectively. However, it is the relevant and timely information that is made available **to management** during the management process that is vital in monitoring the progress of goal and objective attainment. Only with accurate and timely information can management implement plans and determine continually whether everything is proceeding according to plan and whether adjustments need to be made. The faster managers receive feedback on what is going smoothly or badly in the course of the management process, the more effectively the organisation's control systems function. In chapter 8 the organisation's management information systems, their influence on management and the control task are discussed in detail.

17.4.4 The control of human resources

Although the control task of management focuses mainly on financial and physical resources, this does not mean that the performance of one of the organisation's main resources, namely people, can be exempt from control. The management of people, that is, the control of human resources, falls within the ambit of human resources management. A few remarks will be sufficient to emphasise the scope of control of human resources throughout the organisation.

The main instrument used to control an organisation's human resources is **performance measurement**. This entails evaluating employees and managers in the performance of the organisation. More specifically, from a control point of view, the performance of individuals and groups is gauged and compared with predetermined standards, as illustrated in figure 17.5. Tasks are subdivided into components and the importance of each subtask is determined so that criteria and measuring instruments can be developed. Performance standards must then be developed, for example 40 production units per hour, an accuracy level of 98 % in tuning machines or a quality level of at least 93 %. Actual performance can be measured against these standards for feedback to and action by management.

Other human resources control instruments include specific ratio analyses that can be applied in respect of **labour turnover, absenteeism** and the **composition** of the **labour force**.

The preceding discussion of the control of an organisation's resources emphasises mainly formal control systems developed by management. As far as informal control systems are concerned, people in the organisation play a decisive role in

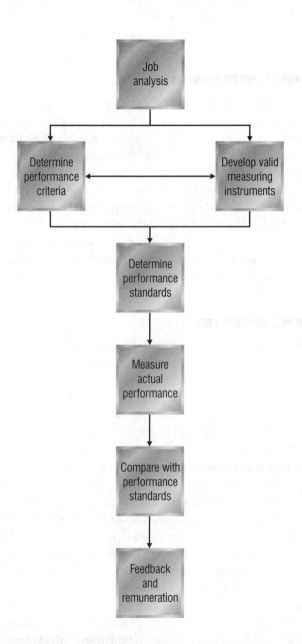

Figure 17.5
The performance measurement process for human resources
Source: Adapted from Griffin, RW. 1990. *Management*. Boston: Houghton Mifflin, p 710.

social control mechanisms. This refers specifically to group behaviour. When a group of people work together on a regular basis, they develop norms that lay down guidelines for the behaviour of the group. These norms, which may include the quality of products, speed of production and reliability, are usually not written down and have nothing to do with the formal organisational structure. Nevertheless, they still have a profound influence on the behaviour of groups when it comes to control or social control. Members of the group subject themselves to the norms of the group because, if they do not, they may be punished by the group — punishment that may range from light-hearted teasing to rejection. Compensation by the group for group cohesiveness and control consists of approval of action, emotional support and the assignment of a leadership role to the leader of the group.

17.4.5 Other dimensions of control

The discussion of the focal points of control emphasised the different resources of the organisation and provided an overview of certain instruments of control. The actual control task, however, is in the hands of management, for the performance of the organisation is ultimately its responsibility. From the point of view of top management, however, it is not good enough to see to the control of individual groups of resources, for the control of the **total organisation** is at stake here — the performance of the organisation as a whole. It often happens in practice that two organisations that apply their resources in different ways are equally successful. One may experience problems with a certain raw material, and the other not; the advertising budget of one may be three times as high as that of the other, and so forth. Thus, in the case of these two organisations, control of the resources of individual groups may yield completely different results, yet both are equally successful. The important point here is that management, especially top management, in addition to controlling individual resources, must also control the whole organisation.

This type of control, known as **strategic control**, is exercised by top management and entails a close study of the organisation's

- effectiveness
- productivity
- management effectiveness.

The chief concern when examining an organisation's total **effectiveness** is determining the extent to which it attains its goals and objectives, as explained in chapter 4. This entails a study of goal attainment and the answer to the question of whether top management is satisfied with the level of goal attainment, especially financial objectives and the way in which the goals and objectives are being realised.

The second overall instrument of control that top management can introduce to evaluate the organisation's performance as a whole, is to study its **productivity**. Productivity can be defined as the relationship between products and services (outputs) and the resources (inputs) used to generate those outputs in an effort to provide an indication of the effectiveness with which the organisation's resources are being deployed.[2] An **improvement or increase in productivity** from one period to the next is represented in an increase in the output/input ratio in the second period, compared to the first.[3] Productivity can be increased in five basic ways:

1. A greater output is made with fewer inputs.
2. A greater output is made with the same inputs.
3. The same output is made with fewer inputs.
4. A smaller output is made with even fewer inputs.
5. A greater output is made with more inputs, but the increase in output is greater than the increase in inputs.

Bear in mind that, according to the productivity concept, an improvement in quality is also regarded as an improvement in productivity, even if a particular output/input ratio remains constant.

The standard of living of communities cannot be permanently improved by means of salary and wage increases, but only by increased productivity.

How do we compare internationally?
– labour productivity in manufacturing in selected countries

Output per worker in 1992 (in 1990 rand prices)	
USA	R181 660
France	R127 170
Japan	R125 600
UK	R94 625
Singapore	R84 340
SA	R34 560
Source: Absa	

It is imperative to improve productivity in South Africa in order to improve the real standard of living of all inhabitants. Management can play a significant role here by increasing the organisation's level of productivity and in this way improving the standard of living of the community. Table 17.3 summarises the role of control in improving productivity in the organisation.

The third dimension of strategic control is measuring management efficiency, which is in fact a management audit of an organisation's main success factors. This approach identifies ten critical success factors such as profitability, the organisational structure, research and development, financial policy, market share, to mention but a few. These factors are measured by an external consultant every year and management receives feedback so that it can take the necessary action.

Table 17.3
A few interfaces between control and improvement in productivity

A: External productivity improvement factors/techniques:

1. The attitude of worker and management to improving productivity.
2. Economic and environmental productivity improvement factors:

- the size of the market
- the stability of the market
- the mobility of factors of production
- the quality and availability of raw materials
- the availability of capital and credit

- the taxation structure
- training facilities available
- research and the exchange of information
- technological innovation and mechanisation
- advantages of location

B: Internal productivity improvement factors/techniques

1. Layout of the factory, machinery and equipment:

- the amount of capital per worker
- material handling

- the maintenance of machinery and equipment
- the layout of the factory

2. Costing and cost-reducing techniques:

- cost control
- budgets and budgetary control
- opportunity cost analysis
- break-even analysis

- control by exception
- organised cost-reducing programmes
- discounted cash-flow calculations

3. The organisation, planning and control of production:

- production, planning and control
- typification, standardisation and specialisation
- work study
- organisational and method study

- inventory control
- value analysis
- other techniques, for example performance research, sampling, simulation, queuing theories, PERT, etc

4. The human resources policy:

- cooperation between management and workers
- selection and placement of workers
- occupational training
- job analysis, personnel evaluation and promotion
- supervision and discipline

- wage incentive and profit-sharing systems
- working conditions and welfare services
- labour methods
- the length of the working day
- the number of shifts

Source: Van Niekerk, WP. 1978. *Produktiwiteit en Werkstudie*. Durban: Butterworth, p 32.

The above overview of a few additional dimensions of control which concern mainly strategic control, emphasises the complexity of the management task. However, the requirements that need to be satisfied in the development of an effective control system are just as important as the various control instruments that can be applied.

17.5   CHARACTERISTICS OF AN EFFECTIVE CONTROL SYSTEM

17.5.1 Integration

A control system tends to become an effective system when it is integrated with planning, and when it is flexible, accurate, objective, timeous and not too complex. **The interface between control and planning** was discussed in the introduction to this chapter. We said that control complements planning because when deviations are encountered, it shows that plans and even objectives need to be revised — control therefore renders the necessary inputs in the planning process. The narrower the interfaces are between planning and control, the better the control system that is introduced will be. This is why it is essential to make provision for control in the planning stage — for example, objectives should be formulated in such a way that they can be converted into standards which can serve as criteria for control. This entails quantifiable objectives. Figure 17.6 is a schematic representation of how planning and control should be integrated.

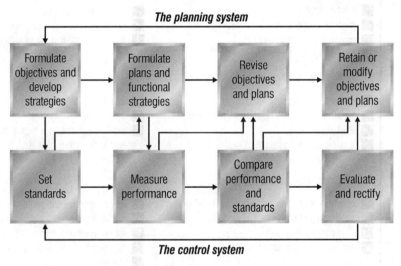

Figure 17.6
Integration of planning and control

17.5.2 Flexibility

The second characteristic of a control system is flexibility. This means that it should be able to accommodate change. Timeous adjustments in objectives or plans should not be regarded as deviations, but as revised objectives or plans, and the control system should be able to adjust to such revisions, within limits, without management having to develop and implement an expensive new control system.

17.5.3 Accuracy

A control system should be designed in such a way that it provides an objective and accurate picture of the situation. Errors or deviations should not be concealed in the data. A total amount expressed in rand certainly does not show a profit, nor does it indicate which products sell better than others. Similarly, production management can conceal indirect costs to make production performance look good. Inaccurate information leads to incorrect modifications of new plans based on unreliable control data.

17.5.4 Timeliness

Timely control data are not obtained by means of hasty, makeshift measurement; control data should be supplied regularly, as needed. A sensible approach is one based on the principle of timeliness.

17.5.5 Unnecessary complexity

Unnecessarily complex control systems are often an obstacle because they can have a negative influence on the sound judgment of competent managers. If managers are hampered by red tape, they may leave the system to keep things going and lose their personal involvement and motivation to see to it that things proceed according to plan. Unnecessary control is equally demotivating for personnel and leads to resistance to control systems.

One should realise that too much information, especially if it is irrelevant, makes great demands on the time and attention of management, which means that the control process becomes too expensive. The unwritten rule of effective control is that control should not become so complex that the implementation of the control system becomes more expensive than the benefits derived from it. At the same time, a system should not be oversimplified to the extent that the essence of control is lost.

17.6 CONCLUSION

Control is one of the four fundamental management functions. It is the final step in the management process and the starting point for planning and strategic development. The control process narrows the gap between planned performance and actual performance by setting performance standards in the right places, against which the performance of management, subordinates and resources can be measured and deviations rectified, if necessary. Control focuses on virtually every activity or group of activities in the organisation, but normally aims at physical, financial, information and human resources. Strategic control focuses on the performance of the total organisation and involves a study of the organisation's total effectiveness,

productivity and management effectiveness. Effective control systems are characterised by the extent to which planning and control are integrated, as well as the
flexibility, accuracy and timeliness of the system.

17.7 REFERENCES

1. Robbins, SP. 1991. *Management*. New Jersey: Prentice-Hall, p 566.
2. Adapted from Cronjé, GJ de J et al. 1997. *Introduction to Business Management*.
   Johannesburg: International Thompson Publishing, p 434.
3. Ibid.

Part 6

· · · · · · · · · · · ·

Contemporary Management Issues

18 The Management of Diversity

Key issues

■ Diversity, culture and management
■ General dimensions of diversity
■ Cultural dimensions of diversity
■ Managing diversity

18.1 INTRODUCTION

18.1.1 Cultural diversity

Throughout history, people have liked, disliked, dominated, ruled and even killed one another solely because of certain characteristics that made one group of people different from another. In many parts of the world people do morally repugnant things to others because they have a different skin colour, have a different faith, speak a strange language, practise uncommon habits or have different values and beliefs which are perceived as weird.

There are many countries in the world today which one could refer to as **radically pluralist**[1] societies. Any such society harbours practically every conceivable kind of human plurality and can therefore be defined as a society with an extremely heterogeneous population in terms of race, ethnicity, culture, language, sexual orientation, religion, conceptions of good or bad, and so on. It is a very complex task to safeguard such a society from the potentially destructive conflicts that arise so easily in radically pluralist societies.[2] South African society can at best be described as a very radically pluralist society which therefore has the potential of destructive conflicts **if a fairness to all its members in terms of the design of its social institutions does not prevail** [3]

18.1.2 Cultural diversity and the business organisation

The significance that cultural differences might have for human relationships becomes clear when one attempts to describe culture. The concept of culture has to do with the fact that human beings are unlike other animals in that they do not merely live in nature but continually change it and form new things out of its resources. Not only the production of food, the manufacture of tools, clothes and arms, the education of children, complex behavioural patterns with respect to sex, parliament and intellectual activities such as science, philosophy and art can be considered to be products of culture, but also the design, construction, implementation and maintenance of societal institutions such as the church, the university and the business organisation.[4]

The political transformation of South Africa to a democracy in 1994 meant new political structures for the country as well as a transformation of our social institutions. Many recognise that nation building will require more than political structures. This is particularly true in the management environment where new structures and approaches are needed to democratise the economy to make possible the economic integration and empowerment of the previously disadvantaged, mostly black, majority of the South African population.

South Africa's radically pluralist society: estimated population of the RSA by population group, 1991 and 1996

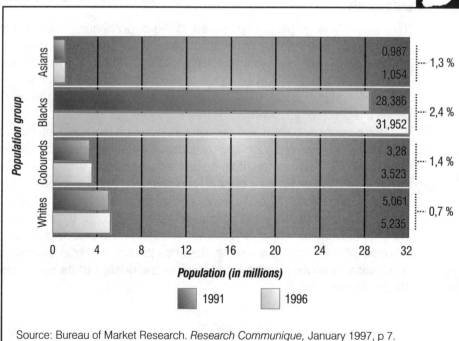

Source: Bureau of Market Research. *Research Communique,* January 1997, p 7.

It is therefore obvious that political transformation does not automatically include social and economic transformation and much needs to be done to make social and economic transformation to a more egalitarian society possible. The wave of transformation sweeping the country also initiated a number of management issues which revolves around the problem of black economic and managerial empowerment. These issues include a wide range of topics such as affirmative action, the economic and managerial empowerment of blacks, the role of women in a white male-dominated business environment, the problems surrounding cultural diversity in the workplace, the demand for the transformation of organisations and the quest for an indigenous African management philosophy.

It is precisely these issues, especially the demand for the transformation of business organisations to reflect the population profile of the country which may become a dangerous variable affecting the maintenance of a workable pluralist society. Can the cultural differences of language, customs, beliefs, values, norms, work ethic and other kinds of pluralism which contribute to the success of many pluralistic societies, be resolved in the South African business environment? Are the characteristics of some cultures necessarily conducive to that which maximises the productivity of business organisations? Because the business organisation is the human race's most important social institution which pushes back poverty and creates wealth, it is imperative that the demand for transformation be dealt with in a scientific way, and not in an emotional and politically driven way.

Focus

If a new approach or orientation to the management of diversity in South Africa can contribute to the more efficient management of its resources as well as to the badly needed improved productivity and international competitiveness, it is only fitting that a South African book on management should explore this issue. The purpose of this chapter is therefore briefly to examine the vast emerging body of knowledge on the management of diversity, the complex interface between culture and management and ways to manage cultural diversity in South African organisations.

18.2   REASONS FOR THE INCREASED FOCUS ON THE MANAGEMENT OF DIVERSITY

18.2.1   What is diversity?

Workplace diversity means the inclusion of people who belong to various cultural groups or people with different human qualities. Figure 18.1 illustrates several important dimensions of diversity. The inner circle represents the primary dimensions of diversity, which include inborn differences or differences that can hardly change and

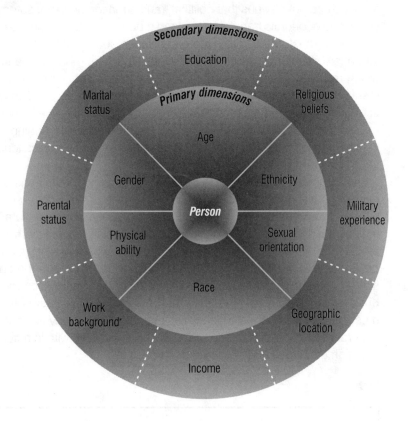

Figure 18.1
Primary and secondary dimensions of diversity
Source: Daft, RL. 1995 *Management*. Orlando: Dryden, p 340.

have ongoing impact throughout one's life.[5] These are age, ethnicity, gender, physical abilities, race and sexual orientation. These dimensions are the core elements through which people shape their view of the world and are closely related to culture.

The secondary dimensions of diversity as illustrated in the outer ring of figure 18.1 can be acquired or changed throughout one's lifetime. These dimensions tend to have less impact than those of the core, but nevertheless have some impact on the way a person sees the world. In South Africa the general dimensions of diversity form part of the debate on transformation, but these dimensions are overshadowed by issues revolving around race, ethnicity and culture. For this reason the general dimensions of diversity will be discussed separately from the cultural dimensions of diversity in order to allow sufficient discussion of the cultural (racial and ethnic) complexities in the South African work environment.

18.2.2 General dimensions of diversity

The worldwide shift in demographics, changing immigration patterns and social change are all factors which affect the work environment. In the USA, for example, the population, and therefore the workforce, is growing more slowly than at any time since the 1930s, the average age of the population is rising, more women are entering the workforce and immigrants will represent the largest share of the increase in the workforce.[6] South Africa is also exposed to similar variables which impact on the productivity of the workforce, transforming it into a diverse workforce which necessitates the management of diversity. A brief overview of the following general dimensions of diversity will help explain the need for the management of diversity:

- gender issues
- age
- marital status
- physical ability

In South Africa it is expected that by 2005 **women** will make up nearly 40 % of the labour force. These changes mean that organisations must deal with issues such as work–family conflicts, child care, dual-career couples and sexual harassment. Seven out of ten women in the labour force have children, which means that organisations should take some responsibility for child care. One issue surrounding gender as a dimension of diversity is the **glass ceiling syndrome** which refers to the difficulty women have of advancing. Only a handful of women reach top management positions in organisations. In the USA it is estimated that men hold 97 % of the top positions.

In the US the supply of **younger** workers is dwindling, with the result that **older** workers represent a significant component of the labour force. This is the same in South Africa in respect of whites, but in the case of young workers the number of entrants is on an all-time high. Both older and younger workers present management with challenges. Older workers are more cautious, less likely to take risks and less open to change. But their experience makes them high performers. Young entrants into the South African labour force will present challenges in the field of communication and management training.

Marital status is a variable which is adding to the complexity of diversity in organisations. The challenge for management is to recognise these differences and use it as a strength. People with disabilities are also subject to stereotyping, prejudices and discrimination. These people prefer managers to focus on **abilities**, rather than on disabilities. Managers should have the knowledge and skills to deal with the above general dimensions of diversity. But managers, especially in South Africa, need to know how to manage **cultural** diversity.

18.2.3 Cultural dimensions of diversity

The cultural dimensions of diversity flow from the racial and ethnic backgrounds of people. Today the cultural dimensions of diversity in South Africa probably over-shadow the general dimensions of diversity. The following are some definitions of the various cultural dimensions of diversity identified in organisations.

1. **Ethnocentrism** is the belief that one's own group, culture or subculture is inherently superior to other cultures and groups. Viewing one's own culture as the best culture is a natural tendency among most people. It is this tendency which makes workplace diversity so difficult to manage, since most theories of management presume that managers and workers share similar values, beliefs, motivations and attitudes about work and life in general. These theories presume there is one set of behaviours that best help an organisation to be productive and successful and therefore should be adopted by all employees. In many countries this is not the case. In South Africa the white male-dominated business organisation is a perfect example of ethnocentrism.

    Two concepts are related to ethnocentrism (racism), namely

    ■ **stereotyping**, which is a perceived or assumed characteristic of a group of people
    ■ **prejudices**, which is a preconceived judgment or opinion about a group of people.

    When these concepts are present in a negative way and are acted upon, it can result in discrimination.

2. A **monoculture** is produced by a standard set of cultural practices. It is a culture that accepts only one way of doing things. The assumption that people who are different are somehow deficient makes it difficult to take advantage of the many values, beliefs and abilities which may enhance the success of the organisation. A monoculture in any organisation creates a dilemma for women, blacks, gays, immigrants and other culturally diverse people who are expected to behave like members of the dominant group. Such diverse employees may feel under pressure to conform or may be the victims of stereotyping.

3. **Pluralism** means that a country or business organisation accommodates several cultures or subcultures. A movement towards pluralism should seek to fully integrate into the organisation the employees who would feel isolated or marginalised.

4. **Ethnorelativism** is the belief that other groups or subcultures are inherently equal. Organisations worldwide are making conscious efforts to shift from a ethnocentric monoculture to one of pluralism and ethnorelativism. Employees in a monoculture, such as is the case in many South African organisations where white males still dominate, may not be aware of the positive values and attributes of other cultures and assume that their own culture is superior. Through effective training employees can be helped to accept different ways of thinking and

behaving. Organisations that overcome the problems of monoculturalism take advantage of the diverse abilities of their human resources.

The reasons for the contemporary emphasis on diversity can now be examined.

18.2.4 Reasons for the focus on diversity

While many of the issues surrounding diversity have been around for some time, many organisations adopt a renewed concern as new trends in the workforce are surfacing. Organisations worldwide are becoming increasingly diverse along many different dimensions, including cultural diversity. Several different factors account for these trends and changes, as illustrated in figure 18.2. A brief overview of each factor will put the renewed focus on diversity in perspective.

Figure 18.2
The changing workplace
Source: Griffin, RW. 1993. *Management*. Boston: Houghton Mifflin, p 577.

The single biggest challenge surrounding the issue of diversity and multicultural management is the **changing composition of the labour force**. Changing demographics in the labour force, together with **legislation** on affirmative action in some countries, are major forces contributing to increased diversity. In South Africa the female component of the workforce rose by 4,3 % a year from 1960 to 1990, compared with 2,2 % for males. It is expected that by 2005, women will make up nearly 40 % of the labour force in South Africa. It is particularly among black women that this trend is occurring.[7] As discussed in chapter 1, the percentage of blacks in top management positions in South Africa is on the increase; a trend which should make a welcome contribution to pluralism in South African organisations.

Another factor contributing to increased diversity in organisations is the **globalisation** of business. More and more organisations are entering the international marketplace, including South African organisations moving into Africa. Many multinational corporations today have more employees outside of their home-base country than within it. Ford, for example today employs less than half its total workforce on USA soil.[8] Some estimate that by the year 2000 half of the world's assets will be controlled by multinational corporations.

The above brief overview of the issues of diversity in international management confirms the importance of examining the influence of culture on management. South African business can now freely do business with the rest of the world, including the rest of Africa. This means that managers must develop new skills and awareness to handle the unique challenges of global diversity: cross-cultural understanding, the ability to build networks and the understanding of geopolitical forces.

Different cultures around the globe treat the same problem differently

Some years ago a study from the MIT Sloan School of Management observed the following

■ When American companies experience economic downturns there is a natural tendency to use employee lay-offs as a principal resolution strategy. Such lay-offs are seen in the USA not only as acceptable, but as a financially responsible mechanism to turn ailing companies around.

■ European companies find that governmental restrictions make it exceedingly difficult and too expensive to lay off employees. (The new South African labour law has the same effect.)

■ When faced with economic hardships, most Japanese companies simply refuse to acknowledge lay-offs as a possible solution.

Source: Steers, RM. 1995. *Impediments to International Management Research.* University of Pretoria Conference on Multicultural Management Proceedings, October, p 1.

As illustrated by figure 18.2, the awareness that cultural diversity **improves the quality of the workforce** is another important reason for the renewed focus on the management of diversity. In fact, most, if not all, South African organisations operating in a period of sweeping transformation should implement strategies to deal with diversity issues.

Table 18.1
South Africa's complex multicultural society

Ethnic group	Numbers (millions)	Percentage (approx)	Percentage of total population	Tribes (numbers)
ASIANS				
1. Indians	1,054	99,0		
2. Other Asians such as Japanese and Chinese	Unknown	1,0		
Total Asian population	1,054	100,0	2,5	
BLACKS				
1. Nguni-speaking people				
— Xhosa	7,668	24,0		
— Zulu	9,585	30,0		290
— Swazi	0,958	3,0		
— Ndebele	0,639	2,0		
2. Sotho-speaking people				
— Tswana	3,514	11,0		
— South Sotho	3,514	11,0		
— North Sotho	3,834	12,0		123
3. Venda -speaking people	0,639	2,0		
4. Tsonga-speaking people	1,597	5,0		30
Total black population	31,952	100,0	76,5	
COLOUREDS	3,500	100,0	8,5	
GRIQUAS	0,040	100,0		
MALAYSIANS	0,160	100,0		
WHITES				
1. Afrikaans	3,100	60,0		
2. English	2,135	40,0		
3. Other (Portuguese, German, Eastern Europeans)	Unknown			
Total white population	5,235	100,0	12,5	
OTHER				
1. Buyse	Unknown			
2. Nunn's	Unknown			
3. Dunn's	Unknown			
TOTAL	**41,941**	**100,0**	**100,0**	

18.2.5 The need for diversity management in South Africa

Supplementary to the reasons for the present worldwide interest in diversity and multicultural management, are the complexities of the South African situation. South Africa has already been described as a radically pluralist society where race and ethnicity are the most visible dimensions of its diversity. Many cultural differences exist between ethnic groups such as Euro-Africans, coloureds, Asian-Africans and blacks. And within each group there are differences. Each of these groups shares a common history, while at the same time maintaining a certain uniqueness.

Imbalances in the South African business world

- Only a few years ago less than 2 % of top and middle management was black, and only a handful of blacks have managed to establish themselves as executives in major corporations. While more than 10 % of the white labour force is in nongovernment managerial positions (all levels of management), the proportion among blacks is only 0,37 %: a ratio of almost 30:1. If middle and top management is singled out and compared, there are 541 top- and middle-level managers per 10 000 members of the white workforce, while the figure among blacks is only two. This is ratio of 270:1. Coloured people at 10 per 10 000, fare marginally better, while Indian people at 95 per 10 000 are still far behind whites.

- Black business faces similar deprivation constraints on black participation in the control of production factors (could not own properly in 'white' areas) and restrictions on the development of black skills (work reservation) have resulted in the concentration of blacks at the bottom of the economic ladder. The availability of capital to blacks is minimal. Only 2 % of all bank credit to individuals and only 3 % of building society loans, go to blacks. Recent estimates indicate that black businesses account for less than 4 % of the number of organisations in the country.

- Investment in the training of blacks for skilled and semiskilled employment is also limited to the total number of artisans and apprentices during the period 1981 to 1989. The proportions for whites were 72,6 % and 68,6 % respectively. For blacks the figures were 5,8 % and 13,8 %.

- Black farmers are confined to 13 % of the land, and using the Gini coefficient as a measure of income distribution, the index makes South Africa's income distribution the worst case among middle-income nations.

Source: Nomvete, BD. 1993. *The Economic Democratisation of South Africa.* Cape Town: The Africa Institute for Policy Analysis and Economic Integration, p 14.

The imbalances between the different ethnic groups in South Africa result in managerial and economic imbalances, and three categories of management problems concerning the South African workplace can be identified and create an urgent need for research and education in this regard.

1. The first issue surrounding the imbalances in South African organisations and which forms an integral part of any policy or strategy on diversity management is the question of **affirmative action**. This is an employment policy which aims to ensure that South African institutions reflect the character of the country as a whole. Many business organisations are developing policies to correct this imbalance.

2. The second management issue with some political undertones is the question of **economic empowerment**. Pressure for the transfer of economic power is evident. The government is being blamed for not doing enough to make black economic empowerment possible. Organisations such as the African Federated Chamber of Commerce (Nafcoc), the Black Management Forum (BMF) and some labour unions propose the 3-4-5-6 policy whereby 30 % of directors, 40 % of senior management, 50 % of middle management and 60 % of the workers of all businesses should be black by the year 2000.[9] Mention is, however, made of who will provide the capital for such a transformation, should it become law. The capital base of black organisations such as New Africa Investments (Nail), Real Africa Investments Limited (Rail) and Thebe Investment Corporation could provide only a fraction of what would be needed for substantial economic empowerment. And the stokvel movement can provide only about R1 billion for this purpose. More and more black consumers are, however, buying insurance policies from not only the black-controlled insurance corporations such as African Life and Metropolitan Life, but also from the mutual insurance giants Sanlam and Old Mutual. Control of these giants could over time change the ownership of the economy overnight.[10] The other question surrounding the transformation of economic power is whether blacks have the entrepreneurial and managerial expertise to make such an urgent transformation feasible.

3. The third management issue which surrounds the debate on managerial and economic transformation in South Africa is the quest for a **new management philosophy**. Activated by the affirmative and empowerment movements and supported by a rich diversity of articles, books and conference papers, this issue is challenging the theoretical foundations of South Africa's Euro-American-Asian management theories, approaches and practices. Based on the premise that the environment of organisations in developing countries is different from that of Western and Asian industrialised countries, management theories and practices developed in the developed-country context may have only limited applicability in the context of a developing country such as South Africa and, for all purposes, a developing continent such as Africa.

The above discussion on the reasons for the present focus on the management of diversity, including a brief overview of the complex South African situation makes drastic measures by South African managers to implement diversity management imperative.

18.2.6 The benefits of diversity management

Organisations in South Africa have generally not been highly successful in managing women and cultural diversity in the workplace. Proof of this is the fact that women and blacks in South Africa are clustered at the lower management levels. This indicates that they are not progressing and that their full potential is not utilised. Managing the issues of diversity and multiculturalism is crucial to organisational success. Table 18.2 lists six arguments which support the belief that managing diversity can improve organisational performance.

Table 18.2
The benefits of managing diversity

Six arguments for managing cultural diversity	
Cost argument	As organisations become more diverse, the cost of a poor job in integrating workers will increase. Those who handle this well, will create cost advantages over those who don't.
Resource-acquisition argument	Companies develop reputations of favourability as prospective employers for women and ethnic minorities. Those with the best reputations for managing diversity will win the competition for the best personnel. As the labour pool shrinks and changes composition, this edge will become increasingly important.
Marketing argument	For multinational organisations, the insight and cultural sensitivity that members with roots in other countries bring to the marketing effort should improve these efforts in important ways. The same rationale applies to marketing to sub-populations within domestic operations.
Creativity argument	Diversity of perspectives and less emphasis on conformity to norms of the past (which characterise the modern approach to management of diversity) should improve the level of creativity.
Problem-solving argument	Heterogeneity in decision-making and problem-solving groups potentially produces better decisions through a wider range of perspectives and more thorough critical analysis of issues.
System flexibility argument	An implication of the multicultural model for managing diversity is that the system will become less determinant, less standardised, and therefore more fluid. The increased fluidity should create greater flexibility to react to environmental changes (that is, reactions should be faster and at less cost).

Source: Stoner, JAF, Freeman, RE & Gilbert, DR. 1995. *Management.* Englewood Cliffs, NJ: Prentice-Hall, p 198.

Organisations who manage diversity and multiculturalism will have a competitive edge in the market, because it means higher morale and better relationships in the workplace. Research has shown that diverse groups tend to be more creative than homogeneous groups. The presence of cultural and gender diversity in a group reduces the risk of 'groupthink' when people contribute freely to a discussion. Moreover, the simple act of learning about other cultural practices enables organisations to expand their thinking about other things as well. South African organisations can certainly expand their thinking on the advantages of diversity management.

The above discussion on the complex dimensions of diversity which include noncultural as well as cultural dimensions explained why organisations worldwide focus on the management of diversity and cultural diversity or multiculturalism. Many South African organisations are grappling with the wave of transformation sweeping the country. They urgently need to implement policies and strategies to deal with the following dimensions of diversity.

- Aspects of diversity which are of a noncultural nature, such as women in the workforce (gender), age, physical ability, sexual orientation and so on.
- Because South Africa is defined as a radically pluralist society in which racial imbalances distorted the racial composition of the economy and the workplace, special attention should be given to policies and strategies which can deal with the cultural dimensions of diversity.

A brief overview of how management should approach the above two categories of diversity will now be given.

18.3   MANAGING DIVERSITY

18.3.1 Introduction

Managing diversity is a management orientation which is not limited to one department or a specific management level of the organisation. It is an overall approach which seeks the commitment of the whole organisation if any success is to be achieved. There is also no one specific policy which necessarily guarantees the required results. And organisations differ in the ways in which they implement a policy of diversity management, as table 18.3 illustrates. This table shows the range of diversity management policies which organisations implement.

The top of the range represents those organisations which are directing very little attention toward managing diversity. These organisations make no effort to promote diversity and do not comply with affirmative action and empowerment standards. The lack of attention to diversity needs within such organisations sends a strong message to their employees that the dynamics of difference are not important. Even more detrimental to the organisation is the outcome of maintaining exclusionary

Table 18.3
The organisational diversity continuum

No diversity efforts:
■ Noncompliance with affirmative action policies
■ Belief in a monoculture organisation
■ No policies on managerial and economic empowerment

Diversity efforts based on:
■ Compliance with affirmative action
■ Inconsistent enforcement of diversity policies
■ Very little is done in the area of managerial and economic empowerment
■ No organisational support with respect to education and diversity training
■ Inconsistent or poor managerial commitment

Broad-based diversity efforts based on:
■ Effective implementation of affirmative action policies
■ Managerial commitment to managerial and economic empowerment — culture of enabling employees
■ Ongoing education and diversity training programmes
■ Managerial commitment tied to organisational rewards
■ Organisational assessment of diversity policies to create an organisational culture which is supportive of diversity.

Source: Adapted from Certo, SC. 1992. *Modern Management*. Boston: Allyn & Bacon, p 586.

practices. Such organisations in South Africa are devastated by mass action, such as that which took place at tertiary education institutions during recent years.

The base of the range reflects organisations who have committed resources, planning and time to shaping and sustaining a diverse organisation. The most effective diversity efforts are developed in conjunction with an organisationwide assessment to determine if diversity goals and objectives have been reached. Assessment interventions are also necessary to create an organisational climate which is supportive of diverse groups.

To reap the benefits of diversity and to create an organisational culture which is inclusive of diverse groups, needs a concerted effort by management.

18.3.2 Strategies for diversity management

Successful diversity management depends on the commitment of the whole organisation. As figure 18.3 illustrates, many spheres of management activities are involved in preparing an organisation to accommodate diversity.

Once a vision for a diverse workplace has been formulated, management can analyse and assess the current **culture** (prevailing value system, cultural inclusion,

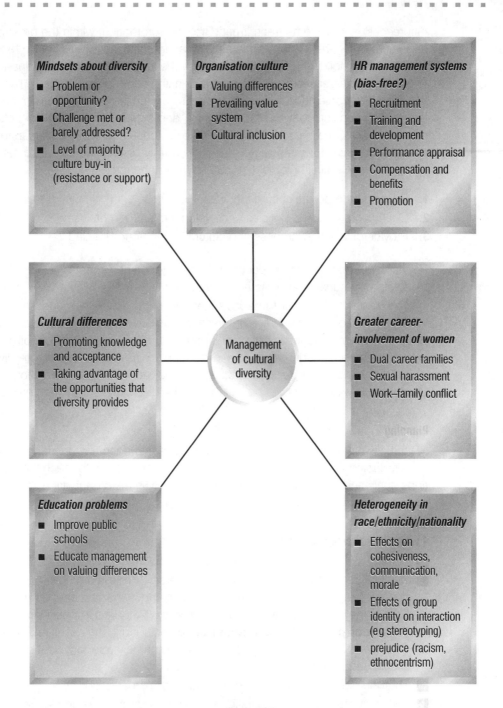

Figure 18.3
The spheres of activities for managing cultural diversity
Source: Stoner JAF, Freeman RE & Gilbert DR. 1995. *Management.* Englewood Cliffs, NJ: Prentice-Hall, p 198.

differences) and systems (recruitment, training, promotion) within the organisation, as indicated by the various spheres of management activity in figure 18.3. This assessment is followed by a willingness (by the leadership cadre of management) to change whatever systems and ways of thinking need to be modified. Throughout this process people need top management's support in dealing with the many challenges and conflicts they will face. Training and support (in the form of delegated power, rewards) are important for the people in pioneering roles. Once management accepts the need for a strategy to develop a truly diverse workplace, three major steps are involved in implementing such a major change:

1. Building a corporate culture that values diversity
2. Changing structures, policies and systems to support diversity
3. Provide diversity awareness and cultural competency training.

For each of these efforts to succeed, top management's support is critical, as well as holding all managerial ranks accountable for increasing diversity.

The implementation of the above steps to bring about the necessary change which will make diversity in the organisation inclusive, is anchored within the four basic management functions of planning, organising, leading and controlling. Planning applies to management's role in developing strategies to promote diversity, while organising, leading and controlling are involved in the implementation phases. The following aspects should be included in the diversity management process.

Planning

Planning is discussed in chapters 4, 5 and 6 as a management function responsible for developing the plans and strategies which are necessary to reach the organisations goals and objectives. In planning for diversity in the organisation, the following aspects should be included.

A vision of a diverse workforce
- What is the organisation's vision of a diverse workforce?
- What is the organisation's definition of diversity? (This is a crucial aspect, especially in South Africa where no-one seems to know what is meant by 'transformation'. In the USA corporations work towards a workforce composition that reflects the **labour pool** and the **customer base**. Included in the definition should also be dimensions other than race and gender, namely age, physical abilities and sexual orientation.)
- The value of women and cultural groups to the organisation.
- The organisation's vision of its identity, as well as that of its employees.
- The opportunities created by diversity.
- Compliance with the law.

Goals and objectives regarding diversity

- Goals and objectives for underrepresented groups over a five-year period.
- Bench-mark goals for each year.
- Composition of gender, religion, age, ethnic groups.
- What should the corporate culture in the organisation be?

Setting recruitment goals for members of underrepresented groups is a key example of planning.

Organising

Organising is discussed in chapter 9 as the division of labour into specific departments and jobs to form a framework for the deployment of organisational resources. Included in organising (organisation design) are mechanisms for coordinating diverse organisational tasks, task forces and teams. To achieve a diverse work environment management will have to work with the human resource department as regards recruitment, appointments, training and maintenance. A **task force** could be established to drive the diversity strategy. The following aspects interfacing with organising should be considered:

Organisation design

- What modifications to the present structure are required to produce the necessary managerial behaviour?
- Will new systems such as mentoring be necessary?
- Is the present structure conducive for the required corporate culture?
- Does the present structure provide for interfaces between the human resource department and other departments? Perhaps in a matrix fashion?

Coordination and interfaces

- Will a task team be the appropriate instrument to coordinate the implementation of a diversity strategy?
- Will the task team have a say in recruitment, training, performance appraisal, rewards and promotion?
- Where will the responsibility for diversity and cultural competency training lie?

Once the organisation begins to appoint diverse groups of employees, they will need to turn their attention to retaining them. This includes education programmes on the value of differences and the advantages of diversity. In the case of working women with families it may also mean utilising the organisation's resources to support their needs in areas like daycare for dependents and flexible work arrangements in keeping with the organisation's policy.

Leading

Leading as a management function was dealt with in chapters 12 and 13. This management function has to do with an effective leadership style, good communication skills, knowledge of how to motivate others and an understanding of organisational culture and group dynamics. Aspects concerning the leading function of management should include the following.

Leadership styles

■ Leaders normally shape organisational values and mindsets about diversity and cultural differences. Do the present leaders (top management cadre) have the necessary competence to shape a culture conducive to diversity?

■ Do the present leaders have the right mindset about diversity? Are they prepared, especially in South Africa, to drop the perception of a middle-aged white male as the ideal employee?

■ Do the leaders need diversity competency training?

■ Do leaders do enough to motivate, encourage and support employees in their efforts to participate constructively in a diverse work environment?

Communication

■ Do the leaders communicate clearly the policies of the organisation regarding diversity?

■ Do the leaders make sure that employees understand what constitutes inappropriate behaviour such as sexual harassment?

Corporate culture

Do leaders 'manage' the corporate culture of their organisations with regard to:

■ values (what values are important)?
■ myths (who are the 'heroes' and who are the 'villains')?
■ norms (how should one behave to get ahead)?
■ differences (can they be accommodated)?

Leaders can also initiate new steps to support the creation of a diverse work environment by moving beyond affirmative action programmes, keeping the doors of the organisation open and opening doors (for diverse appointments) at higher levels in the organisation.

Controlling

Chapter 17 defines the control function as the set of activities which makes something happen as planned. Hence the evaluation activities necessary to ascertain that diversity efforts are part of the controlling role that managers play in shaping a diverse work force. This is a difficult task because many times the most successful diversity approaches simply reveal more problems. In addition, the subtle attitudinal changes in one group's perception of another group are almost impossible to measure. However, the following aspects can be assessed:

■ Is recruitment of underrepresented groups progressing according to the goals and objectives?
■ Are there any incidents of harassment?
■ What happens when illegal behaviour occurs?
■ Is there compliance with the law?

A manager engaged in the controlling function (a member of the task team) with respect to diversity will provide ongoing information of how well the organisation is doing with respect to goals and standards, and he will decide what measures to use for corrective action.

In order for managers to respond to the challenges of working with diverse populations they must recognise the difficulties and needs of employees. People in all groups are struggling to identify how to relate to people who are different from themselves. Most employees want to learn how to handle work relationships without being affected by stereotypes and prejudices. Understanding what people want enables them to relate to one another with acceptance. And understanding the needs of employees helps managers respect and accept others. **Diversity awareness training**, also called diversity competency training, helps people to work and live together and to handle conflicts related to diversity constructively.

18.4   SUMMARY OF THE GENERAL DIMENSIONS OF DIVERSITY

Diversity in organisations means the inclusion of people with different human qualities or people who belong to various cultural groups. The general dimensions which were examined in this chapter includes issues such as women in the workforce, age, people with disabilities and the influence of these dimensions on management. Organisations who manage diversity successfully benefit from such a policy. Many South African organisations are still insensitive to diversity management and should urgently implement policies and strategies to deal with the various dimensions of diversity in its **planning, organising, leadership styles** and its **control** activities.

There are a number of supports available to managers who are facing the challenges of diversity in the workplace. A primary source of support is training programmes to assist managers and employees in working through difficulties they may encounter in coping with diversity. This will be discussed briefly in section 18.6.

18.5   MANAGING CULTURAL DIVERSITY

18.5.1 Introduction

Although most, if not all, texts on the management of diversity in organisations treat the general as well as the cultural or racially/ethnically related dimensions alike, a separate section is reserved to examine the management of cultural diversity or multicultural management. The reason for this is the fact that South Africa is a radically pluralist society in a state of transformation to a full democracy. Because of the political change which took place in South Africa a wave of transformation is sweeping the country. A central (but not necessarily scientific) guideline for the transformation of South African society is that the workforce of public corporations (SABC, Telkom, universities and technikons) should reflect the population profile. Whites view this as a reverse form of job reservation which is to the advantage of blacks only. The wave of transformation also includes South Africa's business organisations. Accustomed to decades of a monocultural approach where things were done the white male's way, South African management now finds itself without answers to the cultural interfaces in the business organisation.

Many whites feel that blacks are unaccustomed to the world of business and management and that they should obtain management skills before they can enter the corporate environment to assume management responsibilities. At the same time blacks view whites as oppressors and stereotyping is rife. In government organisations (parastatals, universities) whites are being weeded out, further adding to a work environment where mistrust, conflict and open hostility prevail. This transformation trend which one finds in South African organisations has two dimensions, namely an **ideological dimension** and a **scientific dimension**.

The **ideological dimension** of transformation is not a new one. Worldwide transformation of institutions, systems and organisations is a continuous process which has to do with change. Transformation is basically a renewal of structures, strategies, organisational cultures, value systems and even power relationships. It therefore includes new thought patterns and paradigm shifts. In a certain sense, transformation represents that which is called a **managed revolution**. Transformation is inspired by many factors such as globalisation, technology, the growth of free markets and political power. In South Africa it is inspired by motives such as the demise of the legacy of apartheid and discrimination, affirmative action and black empowerment, including the aspirations of blacks as the power elite to fully control the country and to Africanise its educational institutions.[11] The question is therefore not who will be affected by transformation in South Africa, but with how much pain, emotion and damage will it be implemented. If it is implemented purely for ideological gain and to please radicals, South Africa's institutions and people can be severely damaged and divided.

The **scientific dimension** of transformation is related to the management of change and in a racial or ethnic context there is much to be said for a paradigm shift in management philosophy. Activated by the wave of transformation and supported by a rich diversity of articles, books and conference papers, this issue is challenging the foundations of South Africa's Euro-American-Asian management theories, approaches and practices. Based on the premise that the environment of organisations in developing countries is different from that of Western or Asian industrialised countries, imported or foreign management theories may have only limited applicability in the context of a developing country such as South Africa. A different approach to management in South Africa may thus represent a scientific dimension to transformation and contribute to more efficient management and higher productivity.

What is needed to eliminate any possible conflict in South African business organisations which may result from ideological transformation, is not only a scientifically based indigenous approach to management, but also knowledge of how to manage people from different cultural backgrounds. It is of paramount importance for South African organisations **to have a common perspective of business** so that the **strengths of diversity** can be used. Managers in South Africa therefore need to

1. understand the way in which culture influences the efficiency of business organisations
2. analyse the critical cultural success factors of the Euro-American-Asian management model
3. analyse and understand the South African and African environment in the context of its cultural variables, and
4. develop conceptual indigenous management models which will deal with the realities of the South African workplace (multicultural management) and engage in continuous multicultural competency training.

Figure 18.4 is an exposition of the above framework for developing a multicultural and indigenous management approach. It is constructed in the same way as **Ouchi's Theory Z** and can be called **Theory A** (for Africa). The basic premise of Ouchi's theory of the early eighties was to draw the best management practices from American (Theory X) and Japanese (Theory Y) organisations and integrate them in one superior approach to deal with the declining productivity levels in the USA. In a similar way South African managers need to draw from the cultural factors which are conducive to efficient management and integrate them in an indigenous approach. Cultural competency training will be necessary to make the implementation of such an approach possible.

Before we discuss the multicultural aspects of management an overview of how culture influences the organisation is necessary. In chapter 11 the influence of cor-

Figure 18.4
Towards an indigenous multicultural management approach for South Africa

porate culture on the organisation was examined. This chapter examines the influence of **external cultural variables** on the organisation.

18.5.2 What is culture?

There are almost as many definitions of the term culture as there are writers on the subject. However, it seems that these definitions — at least to some extent — agree on the variables that make up culture, namely philosophy, beliefs, norms, values, morals, habits, customs, art, literature. Influenced by each other they ultimately influence the behaviour of people and groups.

Culture can be manifested in many ways: dress, language, food, gestures, manners and in various other forms, yet the bulk of cultural components such as beliefs, norms, values, standards, perceptions, attitudes, and priorities are less visible, and hence much harder to deal with successfully. While many people may have problems dealing with foreign customs and language, these are relatively easy components since they are visible and comprehensible. It is much harder to detect and to deal with values, assumptions, and perceptions.

The Indians of South Africa : a cultural profile

Religion	Language
Hindu 63 %	Tamil, Hindi, Telugu, Gujarati
Islam 22 %	Gujarati, Urdu, Hindi
Christians 6 %	
Other 9 %	

Folk tales, proverbs, and idioms are often indicators of a culture's norms and priorities. Culture also has a significant influence on attitudes, priorities, and behaviour. In some Western cultures, including the United States, the culture is youth-oriented. Youth is admired, glorified, and worshipped. In traditional societies old age carries great respect while young people count less. Attitudes toward family members vary in different cultures as well. In traditional societies, the family, including the extended family, is of utmost importance and supersedes everything in society.

Culture has a significant influence on a society's attitude to relations outside the family, money and material assets. In the West wealth is placed in high esteem and at times viewed as a virtue and not just a means.

People's attitudes toward time is also influenced by culture. In industrial societies, time is scarce, carefully measured, and accounted for. Promptness is the norm and tardiness can lead to costly consequences. Arriving half an hour late for a job interview, a final exam, or a court trial can often have disastrous results. In Africa, Latin America and the Middle East, arriving half an hour late is considered early.

From the above exposition of cultural differences between groups of people it is clear that many definitions of the concept are possible. **Culture is basically the way that different groups of people do things differently from other groups, and therefore perceive the world differently.** Because different groups of people (cultures) do things differently, the different cultures of employees of the organisation will influence management differently and will result in different organisational behaviours.

All cultures are, after all, acquired. A baby is not born with a Western culture or a Middle Eastern one. By growing up in a society one absorbs values, norms, beliefs, customs and other cultural traits. Some of them are taught in school; others are conferred by parents and friends. An outsider would, of course, have to invest time and effort to become familiar with the culture.

Culture can be categorised into three levels, as shown by figure 18.5. At the more visible level, culture represents the common behaviour of a specific group of people. In an organisation these aspects of behaviour are taught to new members, rewarding those that fit in and sanctioning those that do not. We say for example, people in one group have for years been 'punctual in submitting reports' or 'very friendly' to students while those in another groups always dress conservatively. Culture at this level is still tough to change, but not nearly as difficult as at the level of basic beliefs and values.

At the deeper invisible level of culture where individuals in a group share beliefs in their minds which they have acquired over a long period of time, values persist over time even when group membership changes. At this level culture is extremely difficult to change since the beliefs and norms of what is good and bad, important and trivial are already in place and other norms are judged by existing ones. These notions about what is important in life can impact greatly on management and the behaviour of the organisation.

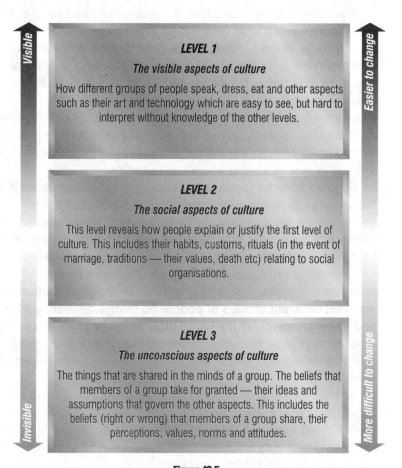

Figure 18.5
The different levels of culture (The iceberg principle)
Source: Based on Schein, EH. 1992. *Organisational Culture and Leadership*. San Francisco: Jossey Bass
Publishers, p 17.

Against the above brief exposition of the nature of culture, we can now examine how it influences the performance of the organisation.

18.5.3 The influence of culture on the behaviour of the organisation

The content of culture (visible as well as invisible aspects) influences the **direction** of **behaviour** and this is precisely the reason why managers are concerned about the beliefs, norms and values of subordinates. The content of culture can therefore be an asset or a liability to an organisation. It is an asset if it eases communication, facilitates organisational decision making and control and facilitates cooperation and productivity. The result is increased productivity since these results are accomplished with fewer resources than would otherwise be possible. Culture becomes a liability when important shared beliefs and values interfere with the needs of the organisation and its customers.

Because of the influence of the cultural content on behaviour, the individual or group

■ may not **want** to behave as called for by the situation
■ may not **understand** how to behave in order to be efficient or
■ may not be **able** to behave appropriately due to a lack of cultural competency, for example communication.

The above situations happen when the cultural content is in conflict with what needs to be done to reach the organisation's objectives. **The more closely actual behaviour matches required behaviour, the more effectively and productively the individual or organisation accomplishes its objectives.** If actual organisational behaviour patterns do not serve the organisation's interests, organisational performance is impaired. Also, if these behaviour patterns are basically inconsistent with the needs, values and skills of the organisation's members, dysfunctional consequences develop, leading to poor performance.

This is the reason why cultural content, and the possible modification thereof, is so important for organisational success. In shaping managerial behaviour the influence of culture can originate anywhere, from an individual to a group, and eventually manifests itself in the corporate culture.

18.5.4 The origin of cultural content

Cultural content, that is the cultural values of an individual or a group, can, as we have pointed out, originate anywhere. In an organisation's external environment, cultural content is produced especially in the **technological, economic, political and social environments**.

The technological, economic and political environments with which organisations interact can be characterised in terms of two critical factors,[12] namely

■ the predictability of future environmental events and
■ the difficulty in obtaining resources from the environment. Variations in the environment on these dimensions have a significant impact on overall organisational behaviour as well as on the behaviour of individuals and groups within the organisation.

The Western industrialised environment represents a high degree of complexity: a large number of organisations are engaged in producing a vast array of products and services. Their characterisation as 'developed' means that the infrastructure is developed, a trained labour supply is developed, the capital markets are developed, and business–government relations are developed to the point of facilitating commerce or at least not hindering it. Thus the difficulty of obtaining resources is comparatively low and predictability is on average relatively high.

The developing country environment, such as those of most African countries, represents complexity of a different kind. Developing countries no longer represent the traditional agrarian society but are on the way to industrialisation and modernisation. Very often, the developing country environment becomes complex because of the nonavailability of resources to meet the high aspirations for development. Complexity is the result not just of what is, but what 'is not'. Organisational means and goals tend to be incongruous and create difficulties for effective management. Furthermore, the developing country environment can be characterised as being on average relatively more unpredictable. The political and legal climates in most developing countries are perceived to be relatively less stable. Very often they also represent certain characteristics of 'loose societies' where 'norms are not well developed', and where lawless, corrupt practices are more the rule than an exception. This type of environment which includes the South African environment also poses problems for obtaining the required economic, technological and skilled human resources.

In a nutshell

> Developed countries have **predictable futures** and resources are developed and available.
> Developing countries have **unpredictable futures** and nonavailability of resources.

In response to difficult and unpredictable economic and political environments in developing countries, organisations are characterised by a **lack of planning for the future, a lack of time management, a lack of entrepreneurship, a lack of risk taking** and a behaviour reflective of a lack of trust in the system.[13]

Thus the challenge facing the manager in a developing country is qualitatively very different from that facing his or her counterpart in the developed world. Hence, managing organisations in a developing country requires some very different approaches and skills in order to be successful. Indigenous management approaches need to address this issue.

Cultural content is also a product of the **sociocultural environment** in which the organisation operates. It is this environment which shapes the beliefs, norms, morals, habits, values and ideas which specific groups of people have in common.

To understand better how culture can impact on management behaviour in a practical sense, we can review how culture affects the interaction of individuals. On the one hand, culture **facilitates** certain behaviours. Members of a cultural group share complementary behavioural programmes which regulate their interaction. Associated with these programmes are values and ideology which provide a guide and a meaning to what they are doing. Implicit in this view is the fact that a culture also **inhibits** other behaviours, behaviours which run counter to the values or practices of the culture. A culture also provides a guide for perception and attribution of others' behaviour. Therefore, within a cultural group, certain behaviours will generate a feeling and response that is **positive** while others will generate a **negative** feeling and response.

Organisations and their employees do not live in a vacuum, and cultural variables are carried into the workplace. Researches in the field of cross-cultural studies of organisations have identified many such values and attitudes. A brief examination of these will help to explain the influence of culture on management.

18.5.5 Cultural dimensions related to work

Many researchers who have studied the influence of culture on management have identified the most important cultural characteristics which relate to the workplace, namely:[14]

1. the way in which members of a cultural group **communicate** with each other
2. characteristics which revolve around **individualism** and **collectivism**
3. attitude to **power**
4. attitude to **achievement**
5. attitude to **conflict**
6. tolerance of **uncertainty**
7. the **dominance** ('masculinity') of certain values

A comparison between Indian and English cultural values and attitudes

Indian people are:	English people are:
more emotional	less emotional
more obedient to seniors	less obedient to seniors
submissive	aggressive
less able to cope with new and uncertain situations	more able to cope with new and uncertain situations
less willing to accept responsibility	more willing to accept responsibility
less disciplined	more disciplined
more modest	more arrogant
less reserved	more reserved
more collectivist	more individualistic
more friendly	less friendly
opposed to change	opposed to change

Source: Tayeb, MH. 1996. *Management of a Multicultural Workforce.* New York: John Wiley & Sons, p 55.

These cultural dimensions manifest themselves in organisations in a number of ways. A brief examination of this is necessary to understand how culture drives behaviour and eventually influences behaviour in the business organisation.

The cultural dimension of communication

It can be argued that cultures can be distinguished from one another by the way in which their members communicate with fellow members and exchange information among themselves. In a **low-context culture**, that is a culture where people are highly individualistic and less influenced by their 'context' (their involvement with their group, such as the African concept of *ubuntu* and the often spiritual influences of their environment), information is explicit and straightforward and vested in words of precise meaning. Low-context cultures include Americans, Germans and other Europeans and Euro-Africans. Afro-Africans, like Arabs and Mediterranean peoples who have extensive information networks among family and friends (*ubuntu*), are examples of **high-context cultures**. This means cultures in which people are deeply involved with each other and where messages appear simple, but are in fact complex. Put differently, in low-context communication the listener knows very little and must be told practically everything and supplied with all the background information, such as when Euro-Africans or whites exchange information. In high-context communication, such as when African cultures communicate, the listener is already 'contexted' and does not need much background information.[15]

In every society both high-context and low-context communication takes place, but at the aggregate level, cultures differ in the degree of 'contexting' considered normal and necessary in every kind of communication, including business communication.

The cultural dimension of individualism versus collectivism

Individualism and collectivism are complicated concepts which can be interpreted in many ways from a cultural point of view. In an **individualist culture** individual members put their own interests above those of the group; their loyalty is first and foremost to themselves. Americans, Britons and Euro-Africans are good examples of members of a individualist culture. In a **collectivist culture**, the group takes precedence over the individual member's interests.

Another way of looking at individualism and collectivism is the extent to which a society values personal autonomy, independence and privacy. In an individualistic culture it is important to individuals to have control over their personal and private lives and to look after themselves and their immediate family. They will not impose on others with their troubles, and do not wish to be bothered by theirs either. In a collectivist culture, people are more dependent on others in their group, both financially and morally. Some researchers believe that avoiders of responsibility too often hide in the collective.[16]

Ubuntu

Ubuntu is a metaphor that describes the significance of group solidarity on survival issues, that is so central to the survival of African communities, which as a result of the poverty and deprivation have to survive through brotherly group care and not individual self-reliance. The key values of *ubuntu* are:

- Group solidarity
- Compassion
- Respect
- Human dignity
- Collective unity

It is our belief that unless the development structures (in organisations), strategies and processes can harness these *ubuntu* values into a dynamic transformative force for reconstruction and development, failure will be almost certain.

Source: Mbigi, L. 1997. *Ubuntu, the African Dream in Management*. Knowledge Resources, pp 2–3.

South African researchers suggest that one of the dimensions of individualism and collectivism revolves around poverty and affluence.[17] According to them the reason why blacks are part of a collectivist culture is because children in townships or rural areas generally grow up under circumstances of profound material deprivation and acute uncertainty. Early in life they learn that no single individual is able to provide for one's needs; that survival as an individual is impossible and that a collection of individuals provide the best chances for survival. In contrast to this, Euro-Africans are individualistically inclined.

The influence of this cultural characteristic is that in a business world or management environment which demands individualism, competitiveness and personal responsibility, the individual who has been socialised into patterns of shared responsibility and noncompetitiveness will be at a distinct disadvantage and will under-achieve relative to his real potential. To remedy this kind of cultural opposites in the organisation, management needs to structure work (see chapter 9, division of work and departmentalisation) and organisations in such a way that teams as well as individuals can achieve.

The cultural dimension of attitude to power

Power is another complex concept which is characteristic of culture. Societies differ from one another in the extent and the ways in which power and authority are distributed among the people. This is reflected in the 'power distance' of the superior–subordinate relationship, such as parent–child, teacher–pupil and manager–

employee. Based on these differences, research in South Africa[18] indicates that whites emphasise **fair** treatment while blacks emphasise **equality**. Both blacks and whites prefer consultation in decision making, but with whites the final decision lies with a single senior while blacks emphasise that the majority viewpoint should be the deciding factor. Organisation design should take cognisance of this fact.

Differences between small and large power distance societies

Small power distance	Large power distance
Inequalities among people should be minimised	Inequalities among people are both expected and desired
There should be, and there is to some extent, interdependence between less and more powerful people	Less powerful people should be dependent on the more powerful; in practice, less powerful people are polarised between dependence and counter-dependence
Parents treat children as equals	Parents teach children obedience
Children treat parents as equals	Children treat parents with respect
Hierarchy in organisations means an inequality in roles, established for convenience	Hierarchy in organisations reflects the existential inequality
Decentralisation is popular	Centralisation is popular
Subordinates expect to be consulted	Subordinates expect to be told what to do
The ideal boss is a resourceful democrat	The ideal boss is a benevolent autocrat or good father

Source: Adapted from Uys, R. 1995. *The New Management Generation: Multicultural Perceptions.* International Conference on Management in Africa, University of Pretoria.

The cultural dimension of attitude to achievement

In all societies the majority of the people want to do well and have certain goals that they strive to achieve. Some researchers, however, argue that people's need for achievement in developed countries tends to be higher compared to developing nations. They also imply that individualistic nations have a higher need for achievement, compared to collectivist ones.[19] From a management point of view the need for high achievement also relates to an ethic of hard work, higher productivity and more competition.

The cultural dimension of attitude to conflict

In every social grouping disagreement and conflicts are bound to occur from time to time, but it seems that cultures develop different ways of handling conflict. In individualistic cultures, conflict is seen as healthy and people are encouraged to bring contentious issues into the open. This trait makes for competition and innovation. In other cultures social harmony takes precedence over an individual's right to express his views, thereby limiting his initiative. .

Tolerance of uncertainty as a cultural dimension

Cultures differ from one another in the extent to which they can tolerate uncertainty or ambiguity. The Germans have very little tolerance for uncertainty compared to the Anglo-Americans and they favour structured organisations with rules and regulations to limit uncertainty.

In South Africa whites perceive themselves as having a strong uncertainty avoidance culture, while perceiving other cultural groups as rating low on the uncertainty avoidance index.[20] Different leadership styles are required for cultural differences revolving around uncertainty avoidance.

The dominance ('masculinity') of certain values as a cultural dimension

In some cultures certain values are viewed as dominant and the extent to which these values dominate others expresses that culture as a 'masculine' culture, such as the acquisition of money and things, not caring for others and so on.

Cultures which associate with masculinity emphasise performance rather than people and reflect assertiveness and competitiveness. South African research[21] indicates that whites rate particularly stronger on masculinity with regard to being aggressive, assertive, competitive and autonomous. With women joining the workplace in greater numbers, a focus on a more feminine leadership style should have added benefits. The question is how to make this happen in a macho male-dominated business environment. Education and cultural sensitivity training seem to be the only solutions.

Many other dimensions of culture, such as that of abstract versus associative thinking, may also be useful in understanding the influence of culture on management. The above dimensions, however, give one a sufficient idea of how it can have an impact on the management process.

18.5.6 Cultural dimensions and the management process

The above brief examination of the various dimensions of culture already shows how cultural values influence management behaviour. The cultural dimensions manifest themselves in organisations in a number of ways. By understanding the impact of culture on the management process, managers should be able to accommodate cultural forces in executing the management process.

Planning

Cultural variables impact directly and indirectly on the planning function of management. Developed societies, for example, tend to have more of a future orientation to events. Future-oriented cultures have relatively less regard for past social customs and traditions and base their decisions on their possible implications for the future. **Planning** for the future is therefore an important aspect of this kind of society and its business organisations. Developing countries tend to be more past-oriented. Past-oriented cultures believe that life should be guided by the customs and traditions of society, regardless of their implications for the future. African cultures tend to fall into this category. Past-oriented cultures do not plan for the future, but live for the moment.[22] In a management context, this results in a short-term orientation to activities and an absence of planning.

Most developed nations also see themselves as being in control of nature and events. In contrast, developing societies see themselves more as being at the mercy of events in the environment. The result of this is that the feeling of being subjugated to nature and spiritual influences would make **planning** and **budgeting** seem pointless, as events could alter their expected outcomes.

Strategic planning it is argued, is a crucial element for the survival and success of a business organisation. Engagement in this activity is hindered in developing countries not only by the present- and past-orientation of such cultures, but also by the relative unpredictability of events in the environment.[23]

Organising

Cultural variables also influence the organisational structure of businesses. Organising, as discussed in chapter 9, comprises structural arrangements and designs for the distribution and coordination of tasks, including the delegation of tasks. With the delegation of tasks goes the delegation of authority and responsibility to do the assigned work effectively. Another concept of organising which goes hand in hand with delegation is decentralisation of decision making. It is the opposite of centralisation, which means that the responsibility and authority for making decisions is maintained at the highest hierarchical levels. Decentralisation means a formal devolution of decision making to lower levels in the hierarchy which, in terms of modern organisational design trends, make such things as downsizing task teams and separate profit centres possible. But cultural variables such as power distance, collectivism and communication may render modern organisational structures in developing countries ineffective. Value conflicts could also come into play in developing countries if it were decided to adopt a matrix structure where the system of multiple bosses is foreign to cultures with a high power distance and low uncertainty avoidance.

Leadership

As discussed in chapter 12, leadership is a complex management function which involves such things as influencing and motivating people, either as individuals or in groups. Leadership also includes conflict management and communication with subordinates. As such it is exposed to cultural influences. Two dimensions which directly affect leadership (and followership) behaviour, are power distance and people orientation. The relatively high power distance and the authoritarian/paternalistic people orientation of developing countries imply a certain type of leadership behaviour and leader–follower relationship. It can be characterised as being more congruent with McGregor'sTheory X leadership model which also presupposes limited and fixed human potential. In contrast, Theory Y leadership, a participative approach which believes that individuals must be given the opportunity to unlock their creative potential, for their own good as well as that of the organisation, will be more favoured in developed countries.

Control

Control is the management function which ensures that actual activities are in accordance with the planned activities. Management takes the responsibility to **account** for the ways in which they execute the plans. Cultural variables also affect the control function of management.

In the case of a cultural dimension such as individualism where the **individual** is emphasised, the accountability of management can be high. In a high-context culture (where people feel that they are subjugated to nature and spiritual influences) measurement systems are usually vague, feelings-based and intuitive. This obviously renders control and accountability ineffective.

18.6 DIVERSITY TRAINING

From the above discussion of the general as well as cultural dimensions of diversity, it becomes obvious that a complex set of management skills as well as management supports are needed to deal successfully with diversity in organisations.

18.6.1 Diversity training

The training of employees is a task which is usually dealt with by human resource management. It is, however, important to mention a few aspects of diversity training to conclude this chapter.

Although the challenges posed by the diversity of the workforce has been the target of researchers and writers on the subject, it has met with mixed reactions from South African practitioners. Some organisations simply ignore it and treat their diverse workforce as if it were homogenous. The results are usually reflected by poor performance of individuals as well as the organisation. **Diversity training** is a learning process implemented to raise managers' awareness and develop competencies concerning the issues and needs involved in managing a diverse workforce.[24]

In order for managers to respond to the challenges of working with diverse populations, they must recognise employee difficulties in coping with diversity. These difficulties include resistance to change, racism, lack of knowledge about other groups, as well as prejudices, biases and stereotypes. Some employees lack the motivation to understand cultural differences, often because of the lack of reward for doing so. Diversity training should therefore focus on:[25]

■ programmes designed to raise participants' consciousness and awareness about differences in values, attitudes, patterns of behaviour and communication that may exist across cultures, and

■ programmes designed to develop new skills and competencies, including communication competency.

Exposure to other people's culture could form a significant step in any cultural awareness training.

18.6.2 Management supports

Another set of supports to complement training in coping with diversity revolves around managerial support from the top, such as:[26]

■ managers who have diversity skills and competence
■ education and training
■ awareness raising
■ peer support in the workplace
■ organisational climate that supports diversity
■ open communication with one's manager about diversity issues
■ recognition for employee development of diversity skills and competencies
■ recognition for employee contributions to enhancing diversity goals
■ organisational rewards for managers' implementation of organisational diversity goals and objectives

Diversity training and managerial support from the top can do much to create cultural synergy and to contribute to higher productivity.

18.7 CONCLUSION

South Africa is a radically pluralist society which includes many dimensions of diversity. Apart from the more general dimensions of diversity such as women in management positions, age and marital status, managers in South Africa have to cope with the cultural dimensions of diversity. These cultural or ethnic influences on the organisation impact on the management process. In developing countries, for instance, planning is nonexistent, organisational structures are rigid, hierarchical and status-oriented, decisions are made on emotional criteria and reward systems seem to be feelings-based.

18.8   REFERENCES

1. Lötter, H. 1993. Pluralism, liberal values and consensus: Like dancing with wolves? *Acta Academia*, vol 25, no 4, pp 13–29.
2. Ibid.
3. Ibid p 14.
4. Ibid p 17.
5. Daft, RL. 1995. *Management.* Orlando, Florida: The Dryden Press, pp 340–350.
6. Certo, SC. 1994. *Modern Management: Diversity, Quality, Ethics and the Global Environment.* Boston: Allyn & Bacon, p 578.
7. Bureau of Market Research, Unisa. 1993. Report no 199.
8. Moorhead, G & Griffin, RW. 1989. *Organisational Behavior.* Boston: Houghton Mifflin, p 671.
9. *Finansies en Tegniek.* 19 May 1995, p 11.
10. Ibid.
11. Esterhuyse, W. *Finansies en Tegniek.* 16 August 1996, p 18.
12. Jaeger, AM & Kanungo, RN. 1990. *Management in Developing Countries.* London: Routledge, pp 11–20.
13. Ibid.
14. Tayeb, MH. 1996. *Management of a Multicultural Workforce.* New York: John Wiley & Sons, p 54.
15. Ibid p 56.
16. Naisbitt, J & Aburdene, P. 1990. *Megatrends 2000.* London: Sidgwick & Jackson. p 338.
17. Uys, R. 1995. *The New Management Generation: Multicultural Perceptions.* International Conference on Management in Africa, University of Pretoria, p 3.
18. Ibid.
19. Tayeb op cit p 59.
20. Uys op cit p 8.
21. Ibid.
22. Jaeger & Kanungo op cit p 135.
23. Ibid p 138.
24. Certo op cit pp 590–592.
25. Tayeb op cit p 185.
26. Certo op cit p 591.

19 International Management

THE NATURE OF INTERNATIONAL BUSINESS

Key issues

■ The nature of international business and the factors that play a role in conducting business internationally
■ The structure of the global economy, that is, the different elements comprising the global economy
■ The main elements of the international business environment and their influence on business organisations
■ The question of how to compete and survive in a global economy (including issues such as organisation size and management functions)

19.1 INTRODUCTION

This chapter explores the global context of management. In the preceding chapters the assumption was made that management (in a given environment) functions within the boundaries of a particular country. We will now extend these boundaries within which management functions, to the international environment. Why is this necessary? Simply pick up any newspaper, magazine, business book or academic text and you will find that the focus is on the global dimensions of business and management. The world's economies are so interdependent that events in far-off locations must be considered by managers no matter where a particular business is located.[1] Business organisations from around the world seem to be entering new markets, preparing to take on new challenges and forming alliances with other firms. This is all done for the same reason — to compete more effectively and more profitably in the global business environment.[2] In order to be successful today, it is imperative that managers understand the global context in which they have to function.

19.2   THE NATURE OF INTERNATIONAL BUSINESS

When you prepared breakfast this morning, you may have used an electric kettle that was manufactured in Holland by Philips or you may have shaved with a razor made in Taiwan. The coffee that you drank was probably made from beans grown in Brazil. You may have driven to work in Korean car (eg Hyundai), or if you made use of public transport (such as a bus) you may have travelled in a vehicle manufactured in Germany. The point is that our daily lives are influenced by businesses from around the world. South Africa is not unique in this respect. The same phenomena can be observed in other countries. We have become part of the global economy where no business organisation can be isolated from the effects of foreign markets and competition.[3] Therefore, in following this trend, we see that more and more businesses see themselves as international or multinational businesses.[4] The question is: To what do these terms refer, and why has this trend developed?

19.2.1 The meaning of international business

We can roughly distinguish four forms of business. Firstly, we can identify a domestic business that seems to obtain all its resources and sell its products and services within the boundaries of a single country. In South Africa, most (but not all) small businesses can be seen as domestic. Examples of such businesses include the local greengrocer, building contractors, spray-painters, plumbers, and so forth. However, it is significant to note that there are almost no large domestic businesses left in the world today. This supports the point made previously about international participation and competitiveness. Most large businesses today can be classified either as an international or a multinational operation. An international business is based mainly in a single country but obtains most of its resources of revenue from abroad. For the purposes of this discussion we can take the CNA group as an example. Almost all its stores are situated in South Africa but many of the books and stationery items it sells are published and manufactured outside the country.

In contrast, a **multinational business** operates in the worldwide marketplace from which it buys raw materials, borrows money and manufactures its products and to which it subsequently sells its products. Toyota is a good example of a multinational company. It has production, distribution and design facilities in various countries and its cars are built with due consideration for local conditions. The Toyota Camry, for example, has been designed in such a way that is allows for the fitting of the so-called 'Africa option'. This means that the vehicle can be modified for the very harsh road conditions found in most African countries. Note that multinational businesses are also referred to as multinational enterprises or MNEs.

The final form of international business is the 'global business'. Such a business operates without the restrictions of national boundaries and is not based in any single home country. Experts seem to agree that no business has truly achieved this level of international involvement.

19.2.2 The reasons for doing business across international boundaries

Having discussed the various forms of business, we must now turn our attention to the reasons why organisations choose to engage in international business. Many benefits are available to companies in the global arena, but the complexity of this business environment also means that international ventures are inherently more risky than purely domestic ones. For managers to justify international activities, the perceived benefits must outweigh the anticipated risks.[5] We can now attempt to identify some of the reasons why firms decide to operate and compete in the international environment. However, before we do so, let us look at the main reason for international trade, known as the **law of comparative advantage**.

The law of comparative advantage is the foundation upon which international trade rests. The law states that production will be located where it is relatively cheapest. A country will specialise in producing and will export those goods that it can produce cheaply relative to the costs of producing the goods in foreign countries and will import those goods that it could produce only at a relatively high cost. Countries specialise in producing various goods and then trade amongst themselves to satisfy local consumption. Initially the applications of the law of comparative advantage rested mainly on the importance of climate and the availability of natural resources as the basis for trade. Portugal would, therefore, be expected to export wine to England, and to pay for the wine, England would export clothing to Portugal. South Africa would again be expected to export gold and minerals and the United States to export wheat.

Modern applications of the law of comparative advantage, however, find the basis for trade in differences in the availability of factors of production such as land, labour and capital.[6] It stands to reason that factors of production that are relatively abundant in one country would tend to be relatively cheap there. Goods that use these abundant factors should then, of course, be relatively cheap in that country. The availability of skilled labour appears to be the most important factor in explaining patterns of trade. The availability of land as well as a country's climate and the availability of natural resources also play a role in determining a country's comparative advantage. In South Africa's case, the availability of natural resources (such as gold, diamonds and other mineral products) has put us into a very strong position as regards international trade relations.

We can now look at the basic **reasons** why a company engages in international business:

■ Access to new markets can play a decisive role in deciding to do business internationally. Should the local market for a certain product become saturated or highly competitive, expansion into international markets in order to find a new and larger market seems to be the answer.

■ Different corporate tax rates and tax systems in different locations provide companies with the opportunity to maximise their after-tax worldwide profits. It is also true that the profit margin on overseas markets itself is very often greater than on local markets. Companies rarely need to incur development costs if the product has already been developed for the local market and the overseas market may give the company access to lower cost structures. It is quite possible that various costs such as labour, materials, transport and financing may be lower outside the home country.

■ Any production process requires a reliable source of the raw material needed for production. Any company that operates in countries outside the home country seems to have a greater capacity than other companies to gain access to a broader range of raw materials.

■ Various incentives can also be made available by the host government. This means that foreign trade and investment are actively encouraged by means of subsidies, tax concessions, interest-free loans, the provision of industrial buildings and training programmes for foreign workers.

■ Economies of scale which are unavailable in a single market may be possible on a global scale. The sheer size of the global market means that, for products or services that can benefit from economies of scale, there is great potential. Motor vehicle manufacturers have found that their markets are essentially global. So, rather than producing locally for the local market, they can achieve substantial cost savings by producing for the worldwide market.

■ Company strengths originating at home can easily be an advantage in the global environment. Things such as a recognised company image, a well-known brand name or a technological breakthrough can all be used as global strengths. The best example in this instance is probably the Coca-Cola company whose trademark is known to virtually everyone on the globe. By capitalising on their brand name, Coca-Cola is today distributed in at least 155 countries around the world.

■ It would seem that international operations create a certain degree of synergy. In other words, having operations in more than one country provides a company with the opportunity to transfer learning from one country to another.

■ The image of being international may increase a company's power and prestige and also improve its domestic sales and relations with various stakeholder groups. The impression is created that because a company is international, its products and services must be world-class. Shareholders may also feel that the value of their shares is enhanced by international recognition.

■ Lastly, there is also the strategy known as 'the best defence is offence'. This means that some companies have found that the best defence of their home market is a strong offence in the foreign competitor's home market. The strategy is to put as much pressure as possible on the competitor in the latter's home market which would result in a pull-back from its foreign activities to protect itself at home.

19.2.3 Trends in international business

In order to understand why different levels of international business have emerged, we must briefly look at what happened in the past. After World War II there was an enormous demand for all types of goods and services which played a vital role in the development of international business. After the war, the United States was by far the dominant economic force in the world. Germany and Japan had been defeated and their economies were almost in tatters. Most of the rest of Europe had been devastated, while many Asian countries had fared no better. The United States government instituted the Marshall Plan, which was meant to help reconstruct the European and Japanese economies. These activities encouraged American firms to be outward-looking and to take a global view of business. They realised that they had enough capital available for proposed international ventures and this led to American firms embracing international business as such.

In the period 1950 to 1960, the multinational corporation was essentially an American phenomenon. American firms simply dominated the international business scene. Countries such as Germany and Japan had been left with no choice but to rebuild from scratch. Even though this may seem to have been a very unfortunate situation, there were definite advantages. These countries were afforded the opportunity to rethink and restructure every aspect of their operations including production, marketing, packaging, distribution, finance and technology.[7] Consequently, even though it took them many years to recover, they eventually did and, as a result, were ready for growth. By the 1970s, American companies had problems of their own. They had grown complacent about their success and, as a result, adopted a more cautious approach to international operations during this period. At the same time Japanese companies were extremely aggressive in international business and were becoming increasing successful in marketing their products worldwide. It seemed clear that American dominance of the global economy was a thing of the past.

The 1970s and 1980s saw a shift in ownership. A number of companies were becoming truly global and their shares were being traded on stock markets right around the globe. Many individuals and organisations were becoming global in that they were investing in many other countries. As a result, ownership of firms could no longer be clearly identified as being Canadian, British, French, American, and so forth. These developments, as well as the emergence of multinationals from Third World countries, global alliances and international debt-financed takeovers, took us into the 1990s. It seems quite clear that firms that are interested in doing business internationally have to be aware of the competitive situations they face in other countries and how companies from distant lands are competing in their home country.

How does a country like South Africa fit into this picture? The years of isolation and sanctions have definitely harmed the South African economy. South Africa has a strongly dualistic economic structure with a more modern formal industrial

economy and a large underdeveloped Third World informal economy, the latter characterised by chronic poverty and unemployment. The modern industrial economy
also suffered increasingly from a lack of international competition, investment and
technological renewal during the years of isolation as indicated in figure 19.1. As a
result, South Africa finds itself largely uncompetitive in many areas. It stands to
reason that South Africa requires international trade and foreign participation in its
economy in order to rejoin the international community.

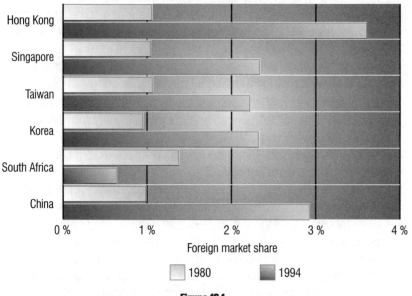

Figure 19.1
Foreign market share — SA pales by comparison
Source: *Finansies en Tegniek*, 23 February 1996, p 20.

Two requirements can be identified as essential in promoting the reinternational-
isation of the South African economy.[8] The first is undoubtedly the encouragement
of an outward-looking mindset amongst important groupings in business. This effectively means that South African business people should prepare themselves to do
business internationally, to focus on overseas opportunities and to make sure that
they always keep abreast of international business developments. The second
requirement is the creation of an investor-friendly climate in the country, and means
unlearning some bad habits. This is an inward focus (the legacy of apartheid) which
leads to a lack of global perspective, and an emerging culture of entitlement. The
latter is not a new problem and has appeared in many countries. It means that many
people feel that the blame for almost all social and economic problems can be laid
at the door of exploitation by some past elite (in South Africa's case the system of
apartheid is being blamed). Consequently, any resources or funds that are pumped

into the country as compensation are demanded as a right. There was and still is a reluctance to face up to the fact that the economic welfare of a country ultimately depends on attributes such as skill, energy, drive, initiative, entrepreneurship, a work ethic and also public morality. Nothing can simply be had for nothing. It is these attitudes and attributes that determine a country's destiny — South Africa is no different.

19.2.4 Ways of doing business internationally

One of the most important decisions that any company has to make, is the appropriate form of entry into a foreign market. Countries can enter a foreign market in any number of ways. We can distinguish between the broad categories, that is, those involving no foreign ownership, joint ventures, strategic alliances, sole ownership or direct foreign investment. Bear in mind that entry decisions are not mutually exclusive — they may involve a variety of forms in combination.

No ownership of foreign assets

Of course, there are many ways in which a company can be involved in foreign markets without ownership or direct investment. We will discuss five possible opportunities of this type.

Exports

This involves selling a product on the international market without manufacturing facilities being established there. This strategy is appropriate if there is capacity at home and the product is able to reach the foreign market timeously and at a competitive price. Exporting is a popular method of entering international markets because it is not a complicated strategy and bears little risk. Exports are relatively easy to undertake and very often this is a company's first step into the international business world. In most instances, exporting does not affect a company's basic mission, objectives or strategies. The company can continue its domestic operations, the only difference being that now some of its output is exported to foreign markets. Should any problems arise in the 'host' country, it is easy to withdraw from the market (that is, the company simply stops exporting).

Any international business strategy does, however, have its drawbacks. In this instance, tariffs or other import costs could constitute difficulties. For example, if tariffs apply to the product in question or if transportation and/or distribution costs are too high, the final price consumers have to pay may be too high to be competitive. Other situations that may affect exports are as follows:

1. If the products are perishable or breakable, it may not be possible to transport them over long distances.

2. If there are nontariff barriers in the foreign market, it may be difficult to gain access to that market.
3. If after-sales service is necessary, a local agent may have to be appointed.
4. Lastly, in a case where the exporter does make use of an agent, his or her enterprise has very little or no control over factors such as price, advertising and distribution.

Licensing

In this instance a company (known as the licensor) grants the rights on some intangible property (be it processes, patents, copyrights or trademarks) to a foreign firm (known as the licensee) for an agreed-upon fee (known as a royalty). This means that the company grants a foreign organisation the right to manufacture its products in the host country or to use nontangible assets such as patents or trademarks. A licensing agreement gives the company access to foreign markets and foreign production without demanding investment in the foreign location. Two definite advantages of licensing are increased profitability and extended profitability. This is especially true in cases where a company is entering less-developed countries where older technology is still being used and even seen as being state of the art.

Licensing does, however, have distinct disadvantages. The first drawback is that should the product or service be successful, the company's revenue is less than it would have been had the company set up operations itself. The company is also dependent on the foreign licensee to ensure proper quality and efficiency standards and to promote the product or service aggressively. If this is not the case, it will reflect badly on the licensor. It is also possible that the licensee may use the knowledge and skill that he or she been given access to and become a competitor of the licensor. The last disadvantage of licensing is its inflexibility. A company can tie up control of its product for a long period of time. If the licensee does not develop the market properly, the licensor may lose some of its potential profits.

Franchising

In this instance the franchiser grants (for a fee) an independent foreign firm the right to use a trademark or any other asset necessary to operate the franchised business. McDonalds and Kentucky Fried Chicken can perhaps be regarded as the best examples of such businesses that have established successful foreign franchises. The advantage for the franchising firm lies in the fact that it can expand rapidly without having to invest any of its own resources. It also need not have any knowledge of local conditions — that is left entirely up to the franchisee. Drawbacks in franchising include the search for appropriate franchisees who have the necessary funds available to set up operations and are capable and competent enough to run this specific business. Such people are not easy to find, especially in foreign locations. The franchiser must also ensure that it keeps control of a needed asset because if it should relinquish control, it will simply create a competitor in the franchisee. The important point here is the following: In order to franchise successfully around the world, a company must have a formula that can be transferred successfully across any national and/or cultural boundary.

Contracts

When a firm enters into a foreign contract, it undertakes to provide general or specialised services in a foreign location for a specified time and for an agreed-upon fee. These services may include management, day-to-day operations and technical expertise. Of course, manufacturing contracts are also a possibility. Contracts are seen as attractive because they allow a company to use their resources effectively. They are mostly short term and the revenues are specified in the contract. Their biggest drawback is also their short-term nature, which means that the company has to spend a lot of time and money negotiating new contracts and drumming up new business.

Turnkey operations

In this type of entry a company will be responsible for the construction of a certain facility, such as a road or water project, for its start-up operations and for the training of local personnel. Once the facility has been completed and is running smoothly, the company transfers (turns over the keys) to the foreign owner(s). This type of project is mostly undertaken in developing countries by companies from developed countries. In some instances they are financed by very large institutions such as the World Bank and they therefore sometimes constitute megaprojects than can only be handled by certain big companies. Projects of this nature include dams, railways, airports, power stations, ports or large industrial plants. These operations (because of their size) can bring a substantial profit for the company concerned. Any cost overruns (for whatever reason) may of course also lead to substantial losses.

Peckish ...

> Mochachos franchises are growing at a dizzying rate from 20 to 60 stores in 15 months. Mochachos Chicken Village rates as the fastest-growing food franchise in the country.
>
> The group will soon launch outlets in Zimbabwe and Botswana, and deals have been signed in Egypt, the United Arab Emirates, Saudi Arabia, Syria, Turkey, Cyprus, and St Petersburg in Russia.
>
> Source: *Sunday Business Times*, 15 September 1996.

Joint ventures/strategic alliances

In the case of a joint venture or strategic alliance two or more firms share in the ownership of a firm on an equity basis. (Note that a joint venture is the traditional term used for such arrangements but today more and more firms choose to call them strategic alliances.)[9] Each party provides a share of the equity or the equivalent thereof in raw materials, cash, physical premises or any other tangible assets. Each investor then has a percentage of ownership relative to the proportion of his or her investment.

Joint ventures or strategic alliances have both advantages and disadvantages. The former include the fact that they allow firms to share the risk and the cost associated with a new venture. They are also an effective way of gaining access to raw materials and technology that previously may have been unobtainable. Major concerns, however, include lower profits, less control and cultural differences. Firstly, profits must be shared between the partners and the profit potential may therefore be lower than if the company were the sole owner of the venture. Secondly, when ownership is shared, decision making must be shared, which implies a loss of control for the company involved. Thirdly, when the two (or more) partners involved are from different countries with different backgrounds, cultures and languages, there are often difficulties in the formulation of joint strategies to manage the organisation. It is vital that partners be chosen with care and that agreement should be reached beforehand on matters such as value systems, mutual respect and conflict resolution.

Direct investment

Direct investment is the decision of the management of a company to manufacture their products abroad without any ties to local companies. It builds or purchases the operating facilities in the foreign country. This approach is deemed to be appropriate where the parent company wishes to retain control of all decisions and policies. The company in question reserves all the profits generated by the 'subsidiary' but also assumes all the risk involved in the latter's operation. A distinct disadvantage of direct investment, however, is that when there are problems in the host country (for example, political upheaval or economic recessions) it is often extremely difficult and expensive to leave the host country.

19.2.5 South Africa and direct foreign investment

Let us now look at South Africa's situation in direct foreign investment. South Africa has just emerged from almost two decades of sanctions, boycotts and especially disinvestment. During the 1980s many multinational companies left South Africa for political reasons (an action known as disinvestment). Today our country has a free democratic society and is once more seen as the 'gateway to Africa'.[10] There has thus been considerable overseas interest in direct investment in South Africa. Most of the new or revived business associations made with South Africa over the last two years have, however, not involved large sums of capital but rather technology, licensing and franchise rights. Those companies that might come in with investment in manufacturing still seem to be holding back.

It is therefore interesting to look at the reasons for this cautious approach (especially by American firms). The first reason is undoubtedly the international competition for capital. Many American companies have invested elsewhere in the world. They will also not simply come back to South Africa because the political climate is right — they need to be lured back with political and social stability, economic growth and the abolition of exchange control. This alone will still not be enough. Problems such as high wages, strikes, low levels of worker education and low productivity need to be addressed. As for American companies, there is also widespread ignorance about South Africa. It is perceived to be the same as the rest of Africa where terrifying violence can flare up at any time.[11]

Despite these very compelling reasons not to invest in South Africa, there may still be those who feel that there are worthwhile opportunities to exploit. British and European companies have, however, seized opportunities wherever they have found them. Since 1991, about 64 British companies have made (direct) investments here. The most notable examples include Cable and Wireless as well as Vodafone which has committed itself to South Africa for the first time. Despite these investments, there is not a great deal of optimism in Britain about the growth of the South African manufacturing sector. Many feel that the lack of skills and the limited size of South Africa's regional market are restraining factors. They also believe that, given the size and the structure of its present economy, South Africa is really only of marginal interest to the rest of the world when it comes to establishing new enterprises.[12] French companies are also belatedly waking up to investment opportunities in South Africa. In February 1996 the food giant Donone bought a R40 million stake in the dairy group Clover SA. Other French companies have also expressed strong interest in investing here. They do, however, believe that the 'window of opportunity' in South Africa will last only a few years.

19.3   THE STRUCTURE OF THE GLOBAL ECONOMY

If managers are to function properly in the global environment, they need to understand the structure of the global economy. Every country (and even regions within a country) is unique, but there are certain basic similarities and differences. We will now describe three different elements of the global economy, that is, mature market economies and systems, developing economies and 'other economies'.[13]

19.3.1 Mature market economies and systems

In a market economy all business is in the hands of private ownership and market factors such as demand and supply determine what business strategies should be. A mature market economy is an economy in which many industries, for example, are dominated by large and successful companies. Mature market economies include the United States of America, Japan, the United Kingdom, France, Germany and Sweden. These countries can be grouped together as they have various things in common. In most of them the free working of the market mechanism determines how resources will be allocated. Private ownership of property is another element that binds them together. Most managers have (or should have) no difficulty operating in this type of economy. The 'rules of the game' (as they pertain to business) apply in most of these countries.

Having discussed mature market economies, we turn to the 'mature' market systems. We will identify three of these market systems. By definition they are a group of countries that engage in high levels of trade with each other. One such mature market system is **North America**. It constitutes one of the largest economic blocs in the world. The United States, Canada and Mexico are major trading partners with each other and together form the North American Free Trade Agreement (NAFTA). NAFTA forms a giant economic bloc in which the United States obviously plays a dominant role. Even before NAFTA was established, the United States already took 78 % and 76 % of the exports of Canada and Mexico (while they took only 20 % and 9 % respectively of United States exports).[14] It is also possible that NAFTA may expand even further and talks on the establishment of a Free Trade Area of the Americas (FTAA) are already well advanced.

The second mature market system that we wish to look at, is **Europe**. Less than ten years ago Europe was still divided into two very distinct economic (and political) areas. The eastern region (also known as the Eastern Bloc) consisted of communist countries such as Poland, Yugoslavia, Czechoslovakia, East Germany, Romania, Bulgaria, Albania and Hungary. These countries were by and large seen as satellites of the former Soviet Union. They relied mainly on government ownership of business and placed great restrictions on all trade. This is in stark contrast to Western European countries (with market economies) who have been trying to further international trade for many years. This has culminated in the formation of the European Community (EC). The ultimate objective of the EC is to eliminate all obstacles to the free flow of imports and exports among member countries. This economic bloc will eventually aim at common customs duties and unified industrial and commercial policies for countries outside the community. The goal is also to have a single currency (to be known as the Euro).[15] However, experts agree that this will only be achieved well into the next century.

The formal members of the EC are Belgium, the United Kingdom, Denmark, France, Germany, Greece, Ireland, Italy, Luxembourg, the Netherlands, Portugal and

Spain. The unification efforts that have been made have not been without contro-
versy and frustration. Members such as Denmark are even threatening to pull out
and go on their own. Recent developments, however, indicate a greater economic
link between the EC and many of the rest of the European countries. For example,
members of the European Free Trade Association (Austria, Finland, Iceland, Norway
and Sweden) or EFTA for short, already conduct more than 60 % of their trade with
the EC, and in 1991 they approved a pact that integrates members more closely into
the EC.

Another complication has also arisen. The collapse of the Soviet Union in 1991
and the profound effect that this has had on many Eastern European countries has
been startling. Communism has failed in most of these countries and they are now
trying to develop market economies. They also want to expand their participation in
international trade. Therefore, countries such as Hungary, Poland, Albania, Bulgaria,
Romania and members of the former Soviet Union have been seeking associate
status with the EC or have negotiated or are trying to negotiate trade agreements
with the EC. The result could be the emergence of a single European market. Should
the Greater European countries (excluding the former Soviet Union) be added to the
EU, it will undoubtedly constitute the largest and most powerful economic market in
the world.[16]

Some interesting facts regarding Europe

> Now it is official: the Greeks smoke the most cigarettes; the French drink the most alcohol; and
> the British have the most efficient car thieves! These are some of the findings of the European
> Commission's statistical service in its first report on the 'human condition'. It also points out
> that French women have the highest life expectancy while Portuguese men have the lowest. The
> Portuguese are also deemed to be Europe's worst drivers. Seventy-eight per cent of the British
> deem work to be the most important aspect of their lives while 99 % of Italians see the work
> ethic as being most important. Britain also has one of the highest crime rates in Europe but its
> murder rate is the lowest. In 1990 there were two murders for every 100 000 members of the
> population. In a relatively peaceful country such as the Netherlands this figure was fifteen!
>
> Source: *Beeld,* 16 September 1995, p 4.

The third mature market system is the **Pacific Rim**. This system refers to countries such as Japan, China, South Korea, Hong Kong, Singapore, Taiwan, Thailand,
Malaysia, Indonesia, the Phillippines and Australia. Japan's international economic
success is of course entirely without precedent. Despite certain setbacks such as
the current slowing down of its economy, Japan is a very formidable international
competitor and remains well poised in all three major economic regions: the Pacific

Rim, Europe and North America. China again can be seen as a strong emerging power in Asia. Its low wage rates make it very attractive to foreign investors. The newly industrialised countries have become a major force in Asia over the last two decades. Known as the **Four Asian Tigers**, South Korea, Hong Kong, Singapore and Taiwan have seen their respective gross national products grow rapidly and they have been particularly effective in developing overseas markets for their goods. Thailand, Malaysia and Indonesia (known as the Baby Tigers) have also made great strides in their economic development and they are now seen as the powerhouses of the future. At present there are also discussions underway to establish a formal Asian economic community much like the EC.

19.3.2 Less-developed economies

In contrast to the highly developed and mature market economies of North America, Europe and Asia, we find the less-developed economies or countries. A less-developed country is characterised by at least two (or more) of the following: low gross domestic product (GDP), slow (or negative) GDP growth per capita, high unemployment, high international debt, a large population, a weak currency, relatively poor consumers and a workforce that is mostly unskilled or semiskilled. The government in most of these countries is, however, actively working to attract investment and stimulate economic growth. India is a good example — many people speak English, the country does indeed have a large number of well-educated people and the nation's economic programme is providing funds for economic development.

Countries in Central and South America seem to have met with some severe economic problems in the 1980s and early 1990s. Argentina, Brazil, Chile and Venezuela have been adversely affected by punishing foreign debt obligations and other countries in the region have suffered from very high levels of inflation. However, even though these Latin American countries are classified as less-developed countries, they seem to be on the rebound again. They have undertaken certain economic reforms including the privatisation of state assets, the signing of free trade pacts with neighbours, the crushing of inflation and the severe curtailment of tariffs. A trading bloc called Mercosur, consisting of Argentina, Brazil, Uruguay and Paraguay, has been formed and has become South America's richest market. Venezuela, Colombia, Peru, Equador and Bolivia have also formed a trading bloc known as the Andes bloc.

When turning to Africa, we see that most African nations are still underdeveloped and that international trade is not a major source of income. Problems such as Aids, overpopulation, poverty, starvation, illiteracy, corruption, war, drought and so on, really give a bleak picture, especially in sub-Saharan Africa. Despite this poor outlook, African countries remain virtually untapped. They do have enormous growth potential that needs to be exploited. As always, South Africa is seen as a special case on the African continent. The years of apartheid and racial segregation, coupled with international isolation, have led to considerable turmoil. The end of the apartheid era has, however, provided South Africa and its region with a major opportunity for higher growth and development. This development is impossible without the involvement of the foreign sector. It would seem that South Africa has a responsibility as the dominant economic force to ensure that the southern African region becomes a zone of prosperity.[17] The success of this region depends largely on how well and on what terms South Africa can reintegrate itself into the global economy.

Managers are therefore presented with a multitude of challenges when they wish to do business with less-developed countries. The lack of wealth on the part of potential consumers and the underdeveloped or weak infrastructure is only part of these challenges. International companies have to set up their own distribution networks, train consumers on how to use their products and provide their workers with the necessary living facilities.[18]

19.3.3 Other economies

Some economic systems simply cannot be classified as either mature markets or less-developed economies. The major area that seems to fall outside of these classifications is the Middle East. This encompasses the Arab nations which rely almost exclusively on oil production. These countries include Iran, Iraq, Kuwait, Saudi Arabia, Libya, Syria and the United Arab Emirates. In the 1970s and early 1980s the oil price reached very high levels and as a result untold wealth was created in many of these countries. They used the funds to develop their own infrastructures and educate their respective populations. A drop in the oil price has forced them to cut back on certain activities, but they are still very wealthy.[19] Since most industrial nations rely, at least to some extent, on imported oil, an understanding of this part of the world is very important to international management. Political instability (as evidenced by the long-standing feud between Iran and Iraq as well as the Persian Gulf War in 1991) and wide-ranging cultural differences have provided managers with extreme challenges. It makes doing business in the Middle East extremely risky and difficult (especially with regards to the social differences).

19.4 ENVIRONMENTAL CHALLENGES OF GLOBAL MANAGEMENT

When operating at international business level, managers have to face the additional challenges that are posed and created by the environment in which they operate. It would seem that the economics, politics and culture of the host country are the decisive factors in this case. Our discussion will therefore centre around the economic environment, the political/legal environment and the cultural environment of international management.

19.4.1 The economic environment

We can identify four aspects of the economic environment that can help managers to anticipate possible economic challenges they are likely to face in a potential host country.

Economic systems

The first factor that a manager must consider is the economic system prevailing in the host country. As indicated previously, most countries today are moving towards so-called market economies. The essence of a market economy (as far as managers are concerned) is the consumer's freedom of choice. Consumers can choose the products they wish to buy and firms can decide what products and services they want to offer. As long as this freedom of choice exists, supply and demand will determine what products and services will be offered and purchased on the market.

Managers must also be aware of the nature of property ownership in the host country. Most countries tend to have a mix of public and private ownership.[20]

Basic economic indicators

When a company is interested in a potential host country, it is worth while to investigate some of its basic economic indicators. This information can be acquired fairly readily from the relevant authorities. In South Africa, for example, the *Quarterly Bulletin* of the South African Reserve Bank and various publications of the Central Statistical Service are important sources of information on, say, total and per capita wealth, import/export statistics, growth figures and total and per capita output of goods and services.

It is fairly simple to acquire the relevant data for developed countries such as Japan, the United States of America and the United Kingdom. In the case of less developed countries (especially certain African and South American countries), managers may experience some difficulties. This is because the information is not as readily available and is sometimes very unreliable as to the accuracy of the statistical measurement.

Natural resources

A crucial aspect of the economic environment in different countries is undoubtedly the availability of natural resources. Even though availability is not a prerequisite for participation in international trade, it still plays a pivotal role in international management. The availability of natural resources differs from one country to the next. A country such as Japan has virtually no natural resources at all. It is therefore forced to import raw materials such as iron ore, oil and other natural resources in order to manufacture for its domestic and overseas markets. One should, however, bear in mind that even though Japan has very limited natural resources, it does have large supplies of capital, entrepreneurship and skilled labour. These factors of production compensate for their shortcoming as regards natural resources. South Africa, in contrast, has large reserves of gold, platinum and a host of other minerals which most countries do not have. However, it does not possess any known reserves of crude oil that can be exploited profitably. South Africa, therefore, exports gold and minerals and imports crude oil.[21] It is clear that oil plays a vital role in the modern global economy with regard to the availability of natural resources. Access to this single natural resource has given the oil-producing countries of the Middle East enormous power in the international economy.

Infrastructure

The importance of infrastructure for companies wishing to conduct business in the international arena cannot be overemphasised. A country's infrastructure comprises its schools, hospitals, power plants, railroads, highways, secondary road system, ports, communication systems, airports, commercial distribution systems, electricity supply networks, and so forth. Again we see that countries like Japan and the United States of America and most of Western Europe have highly developed infrastructures whereas most less-developed countries lack a well-developed infrastructure.[22] Problems with the provision of certain services seem to be a major headache. Power failures as well as communication breakdowns can greatly inconvenience companies that are trying to do business abroad. South Africa can be regarded as a country with a developed (albeit aging) infrastructure, but then only in certain areas. The legacy of apartheid has created a core First World economy with a developed infrastructure, but also a large underdeveloped Third World informal economy where almost no infrastructure exists. These issues need to be addressed urgently in order to attract international investors.

19.4.2 The political/legal environment

Politics plays an important role in the international business environment because it can bring about change. Any sudden change resulting from political developments in a country is known as political risk. In this section we will look at the formal assessment of political risk by international companies. We will also see how governments can protect their countries against the influence of multinational companies by developing national control strategies aimed at increasing their national benefits from foreign investments. The factors we will now discuss represent the main aspects of the international political/legal environment.

Government stability

The stability of the government in any host country is of paramount importance to an international company. This stability can be viewed in two ways, that is, as the ability of a given government to stay in power against other opposing factions in the country **and** as the permanence of government policies towards business. A company that is stable in both these respects will obviously always be preferred, as managers will be able to predict successfully how government decisions will influence their business. Highly unstable governments (in either one of these respects) can, however, effect large-scale change which could affect multinational companies very negatively or even bring their operations to a standstill. The most extreme form of instability would be when a new government takes power. In developed countries such as the United Kingdom, Japan and the United States of America, changes in government usually occur very smoothly and without disruption. In less-developed or Third World countries such as India, Argentina and certainly most of Africa, changes in government could lead to utter chaos. This situation may of course be exacerbated by the policies that could be adopted by the new government. Forced divestment is a very real possibility — this occurs when a government wishes to acquire the assets of a company against the company's will. At worst, the host government can simply confiscate the company's assets (in other words, take them over without any compensation). Alternatively, the host could force the company to sell its assets to local interests — usually the government itself. Forced divestment can take the form of expropriation (usually the takeover of one firm) or nationalisation (usually the takeover of an entire industry). Unstable governments can also cause substantial changes in the tax structure, prices of products, government regulations, employment opportunities and other important elements.

Political risk

Instability implies uncertainty which, in turn, implies risk. We have seen that frequent changes of government as well as an unstable host economy and social upheavals will obviously all increase a company's risk in a particular location. Wars and revolution or incidents of terrorism imply personal and property risks as well as business risks. Even though relatively rare, acts of terrorism can be very worrisome to an international company.[23] This threat can manifest itself in many ways, for example, aircraft hijackings, abductions of business people, terrorist bombings and attacks on employees. Dealing with terrorists does pose problems for international firms. Most are not equipped to deal with terrorist attacks. In the United States and other Western countries companies are also not allowed to make payments of ransom to terrorists. Many companies, however, feel that for ethical reasons, they are obliged to protect their employees and end up making ransom payments. Some multinational enterprises have as a result also developed their own strategies to protect themselves against terrorists for example, by keeping a low profile in a high-risk country through not displaying the company's national flag or logos. An increasing number of enterprises protect their property by introducing strict security measures and teaching their employees what to do in the event of a terrorist attack.

Multinational companies cannot afford to ignore the existence of political risk and so most of them conduct political risk analyses. This means identifying and analysing the sources of risk and the possibility of negative political change that may take place in a (potential) host country. South Africa, for example, is a country where a certain amount of political risk is involved. Even though South Africa has a democratic system of government, there is still a fair degree of political strife and uncertainty coupled with a very high crime rate. International companies wishing to invest in South Africa will have to consider and analyse these political risk factors before deciding whether or not to engage in business here.

Incentives for international trade

The political environment also encompasses incentives to attract foreign business. Governments can offer any number of incentives to encourage foreign investment in their country. These incentives can take a variety of forms, for example:

- reduced interest rates on loans
- subsidies
- tax incentives
- accelerated depreciation for foreign investors

These incentives are usually offered by so-called developed countries. The less-developed countries go even further with the incentive packages they offer. In addition to the lucrative tax breaks that are available, they also try to attract investors with duty-free entry of raw materials and equipment, market protection through limitations on other importers, and the right to take profits out of the country.[24]

Controls on international trade

In certain instances the government of a country may decide that international trade is harming domestic trade. In order to protect domestic business, the government can then decide to implement so-called 'barriers' to international trade. These measures may include the following:

- tariffs
- quotas
- export restraint agreements
- 'buy national' laws
- agreements in which the multinational company agrees to transfer majority ownership to a local investor
- agreements whereby the international company agrees to employ a certain percentage of local labour and management
- subsidies for local enterprises, for example, low interest loans and tax concessions to make local enterprises more competitive

19.4.3 The cultural environment

Effective global management also depends on recognising and accommodating cultural differences found around the world. Culture is a complex environmental influence and can be defined as the sum total of the way of life of a group of people. As a member of a specific community, an individual accepts the culture of that community. This in effect means that he or she acquires the values, symbols, beliefs, knowledge and language of the community/country.

Since there are so many different cultures in the world, an understanding of the impact of culture on behaviour is critical to an international enterprise.[25] It is not easy to identify cultural differences because people study and judge the behaviour of others according to the culture of their own country. In addition, cultural patterns are not static but can change continually. It is very important for international managers to develop a sensitivity to culture — this enables them to be aware of the need to identify cultural variables and adapt their enterprises' activities accordingly. They should be aware of the fact that, firstly, cultures differ and, secondly, that cultures influence behaviour.

Cultural differences develop because different groups of people face diverse environments and cope with them in different ways. Behaviour that is acceptable in one community may not even be tolerated in another. Cultural diversity influences individual perception and therefore individual behaviour. The extent to which Eastern and Western cultures differ from each other can be illustrated by looking at some of the business customs that should be followed when one is in Japan. The box on the next page lists some guidelines that should be followed, and clearly illustrates the gulf between Western and Eastern cultures. We see that a great deal of emphasis is placed on the group rather than personal traits or feelings. If an American businessman, for example, negotiates with his Japanese equal, the latter will spend a great deal of time trying to find out about the American's family and his way of life. In contrast to this, the American will endeavour to close the deal as soon as possible because to him it is the basis of their reciprocal relationship. The Japanese, however, wants to try and build their relationship on mutual trust and respect, which according to his culture, should form the basis of any business relationship. Another example includes the frustration that many American managers have to endure when dealing with the Japanese because they believe that the Japanese continue to raise issues that have already been settled (in other words, issues that have been said 'yes' to). This stems from the fact that the Japanese do not say 'no' in public. Therefore 'yes' does not always means 'yes' in Japan. When a Japanese businessman replies to a question/statement by saying 'yes' (in his own language) he could mean 'yes, I agree' or 'yes, I am listening' or 'yes, I understand'.[26] He thus expresses himself in a very ambiguous manner which is in contrast to the specific language used by most Western businessmen.

Cultural differences based on religion can have a direct impact on business activities. For example, Saudi Arabia nearly restricted a foreign airline from initiating flights when the company authorised 'normal' newspaper advertisements. The advertisements unfortunately featured attractive air hostesses serving champagne to the happy airline passengers. Because alcohol is illegal in Saudi Arabia and unveiled women are not allowed to mix with men, the photo was seen as an attempt to alter or undermine religious customs.[27]

Business customs in Japan

When doing business in Japan, foreign business people should follow certain customs if they wish to be as effective as possible. Experts have put together the following guidelines:

■ Always try to arrange for a formal introduction to any person or company with whom you want to do business. These introductions should come from someone whose position is at least as high as that of the person whom you want to meet or from someone who has done a favour for this person. Let the host pick the subjects to discuss. One topic to be avoided is World War II.

■ If in doubt, bring a translator along with you. For example, the head of Osaka's $7 billion international airport project tells the story of a US construction company president who became indignant when he discovered that the Japanese project head could not speak English. By the same token, you should not bring along your lawyer, because this implies a lack of trust.

■ Try for a thorough personalisation of all business relationships. The Japanese trust those with whom they socialise and come to know more than they do those who simply are looking to do business. Accept after-hours invitations. However, a rollicking night out on the town will not necessarily lead to signing the contract to your advantage the next morning.

■ Do not deliver bad news in front of others, and, if possible, have your second-in-command handle this chore. Never cause Japanese managers to lose face by putting them in a position of having to admit failure or saying they do not know something which they should know professionally.

■ How business is done is often as important as the results. Concern for tradition, for example, is sometimes more important than concern for profit. Do not appeal solely to logic, for in Japan emotional considerations are often more important than facts.

■ The Japanese often express themselves in a vague and ambiguous manner in contrast to the specific language typically used by Americans. A Japanese who is too specific runs the risk of being viewed as rudely displaying superior knowledge. The Japanese avoid independent or individual action and prefer to make decisions on the basis of group discussions and past precedent. The Japanese do not say no in public, which is why foreign business people often take away the wrong impression.

Source: Hodgetts, RM & Luthans, F. 1994. *International Management*. NY: McGraw-Hill, p 62.

Language itself may also have an impact on international management as such. Besides the obvious barriers that are posed to people speaking different languages, subtle differences in meaning can also play a major role.[28] For example, the Ford motor company encountered translation problems with its low-cost truck called the Fierra. When translated into Spanish, the name meant 'ugly old woman'. The same thing happened to Chevrolet when they introduced their Chevrolet Nova. Many Puerto Rican auto dealers showed little enthusiasm for the Nova. The name Nova meant 'star' but, when translated and spoken, it sounded like 'no va' which, in Spanish, means 'It does not go'![29]

19.5 HOW TO COMPETE IN A GLOBAL ECONOMY

To compete in a global economy poses both challenges and opportunities for businesses today. The size of the company is one of the factors that will determine the nature and extent of these challenges. International managers also have to apply the management functions of planning, organising, leading and controlling (as in the case of the management of a local organisation).

19.5.1 Size of the organisation

It would seem that organisations of any size can compete in the global market, although there are some differences in the challenges that face multinational companies, medium firms and small organisations.[30]

Multinational companies (MNCs)

These firms made the decision to compete in the international arena a long time ago. Most MNCs are household names in the global economy. Table 19.1 provides us with a recent list of the world's largest multinationals in different industries.

We know that these firms have a global perspective. As a result they face a number of critical challenges including competitors, customers, suppliers, financial institutions and governments across cultures. They are responsible for transferring capital, technology, human skills and knowledge, technical information and other resources from one market to another. They have a globally integrated strategy and are always seeking new opportunities for expansion, wherever possible. MNCs do allow their local or regional managers to have a differentiated strategy (as long as it remains in line with their global strategy) but they remain accountable to the central authority for their actions. It is vital that managers in MNCs need to understand the issues affecting the global economy and how to react to any changes in global relations. MNCs need to be managed properly because they are major organisations and have a profound effect on millions of people around the globe.

Table 19.1
The world's largest MNCs

Rank and corporation/bank/company	Country	Annual sales/ deposits (in $ million)
Industrial corporations		
1. General Motors	United States	123 780
2. Royal Dutch/Shell Group	Britain/Netherlands	103 835
3. Exxon	United States	103 242
4. Ford	United States	88 963
5. Toyota	Japan	78 061
6. IBM	United States	65 394
7. IRI	Italy	64 096
8. General Electric	United States	60 236
9. British Petroleum	Britain	58 355
10. Daimler Benz	Germany	57 321
11. Mobil	United States	56 910
12. Hitachi	Japan	56 053
13. Matsushita Electric Industrial	Japan	48 595
14. Philip Morris	United States	48 109
15. Fiat	Italy	46 182
16. Volkswagen	Germany	46 042
17. Siemens	Germany	44 859
18. Samsung Group	South Korea	43 702
19. Nissan	Japan	42 903
20. Unilever	Britain/Netherlands	41 262
21. ENI	Italy	41 047
22. EI du Pont de Nemours	United States	38 031
23. Texaco	United States	37 551
24. Chevron	United States	36 795
25. Elf Aquitaine	France	36 316
Commercial banks		
1. Dai-Ichi Kangyo Bank	Japan	435 718
2. The Sumitomo Bank Ltd	Japan	407 105
3. The Fuji Bank	Japan	403 725
4. Mitsubishi Bank and Trust Ltd	Japan	392 208
5. Sanwa Bank Limited	Japan	387 452
20. (!) Citicorp	United States	216 986
Insurance companies		
1. Nippon Life	Japan	157 657
2. Prudential of America	United States	133 157
3. Dai-Ichi Mutual Life	Japan	110 004
4. Metropolitan Life	United States	103 228
5. Sumitomo Life	Japan	94 168
Retailing companies		
1. Sears Roebuck	United States	55 971
2. Wal-Mart	United States	32 601
3. K-Mart	United States	32 080
4. Tengelmann	Germany	23 762
5. American Stores	United States	22 155

Sources: 1. Hodgetts, RM & Luthans, F. 1994. *International Management*. NY: McGraw-Hill, p 33.
2. Griffin, RW. 1993. *Management*, 4 ed. Boston: Houghton Mifflin, p 136.

Medium firms

Most of these businesses prefer to operate in the domestic market rather than enter the international arena. They may still buy and sell products made overseas and compete with businesses from other countries in their own domestic market.[31] Some of these organisations, have, however, ventured into foreign markets as such. For example, African Oxygen Limited or Afrox (based in South Africa) can be regarded as a medium company. It had a turnover of R1,723 billion in 1995. It also exported products to 65 countries during the same period. The volumes of sales overseas were not large but they have managed to establish a viable worldwide market. In Africa itself, Afrox is involved in nine countries (in six of which it can be seen as the dominant force). It is not a multinational company, but Afrox is expanding into foreign markets and plans to increase its export volume by 50 % in 1996.[32] We can deduce that, in contrast to MNCs, medium companies are more selective about which markets they enter, and also tend to rely on fewer international experts to assist them in their foreign dealings.

Small organisations

An increasing number of small organisations have found that they can benefit from the global economy even if they do not participate in foreign operations directly. Some serve as local suppliers to MNCs. A dairy farmer that sells milk to Carnation is actually doing business with Nestlé.[33] Small businesses can also buy or sell their products and services abroad. The local curio industry serves as an example. Various small businesses in South Africa dealing in African curios have managed to establish a successful, albeit small market abroad.

19.5.2 Management functions in a global economy

The management functions of planning, organising, leading and controlling are just as important to international managers as they are to domestic managers. The following sections provide a brief summary of how these functions find application in the international context.

Planning

Planning is important as the primary management function and affects all other management functions. Planning in a global economy affords managers the opportunity to adjust the organisation to the environment instead of just reacting to it.[34] Therefore managers must have a broad understanding of both environmental and competitive issues. They need to understand and be aware of local market conditions as well as technological and institutional factors that will affect their operations. Managers must ensure that the results of an organisation's plans and planning processes provide a unified framework of plans for the accomplishment of the organisation's ultimate goal. Managers also need a great deal of information in order to plan effectively in a global economy. The biggest dilemma they face in planning is that they cannot make the future constant. The planning environment is ever-changing, and the larger the period a forecast (or plan) is developed for, the more vulnerable it is to uncertainty.[35]

Organising

Managers in international business also need to attend to a whole host of organising issues. They must be capable of addressing the basic issues of organisational structure and design, managing change and dealing with human resources.[36] Organising determines the work to be done, classifies and groups the work, assigns the work, delegates the authority to do the work and designs a hierarchy of decision-making relationships.[37] The result of the organising process is an organisation that acts in harmony in the execution of its tasks in order to achieve goals, both effectively and efficiently.

Leading

Leadership styles differ from country to country. It is therefore important for international organisations to employ managers who will be able to identify and understand the needs and expectations of people in the host country. Managers must be aware of how cultural differences will affect individuals, how motivational processes vary across cultures, the role of leadership in different cultures and the nature of interpersonal and group processes in different cultures.[38] Nowadays managers are also faced with another crisis in the work environment. This crisis is a lack of trust. Employees will not follow managers they do not trust. Managers therefore need to develop a style of leadership that negates this lack of trust.

Controlling

International managers should in the final instance, also be concerned with control. The complexity, scale and diversity of multinational activities necessitate this. The controlling function of management is deemed to be critical to the success of an organisation. Basic control issues for the international manager revolve around operations management, productivity, quality, technology and information systems.[39] The control system must also enable the manager to coordinate different units so that they can work towards a common goal. It must also provide the basis for evaluating performance at each level of the enterprise.

19.5.3 South Africa in a global economy

South Africa is in the process of rejoining the international business community after a prolonged absence. We know that participating and competing in a global economy pose enormous challenges. As a country we are faced with various prob-

lems in our participation in international business. The transition to a new dispensation has caused political instability coupled with labour unrest. Low productivity, high
wages, strikes, low levels of skills and other problems have all contributed to South
Africa's dilemma. These are all factors that need to be addressed in order to reinter-
nationalise the South African economy. We have already spoken of other bad habits
that need to be unlearned, namely an inward focus which leads to a lack of global
perspective, and an emerging culture of entitlement. Signs that this is indeed happening are already evident. Rebuilding links and exploring opportunities in the wider
world and increasingly having to deal with foreign interest and competition in their
own country is placing locals under pressure to speed up and get in step with the
global environment.[40] South Africa has been absent from the global community for
a long time and the country is also emerging from this isolation into a world that has
much changed. South Africa's return to the international fold is at a time when accelerated global political and economic change has completely altered the world.
South Africa needs to take note of these issues and incorporate them into plans for
carving out its own niche in the international community. An economic strategy that
will enable South Africa to survive, develop and prosper in the new global environment of today would require at least the following three elements:[41]

1. The first is strengthening the performance and raising the growth potential of the
   South African economy. Eliminating poverty, ensuring economic development
   and upliftment, increasing productivity and other such lofty objectives can only
   be pursued properly from the base of a well-structured, growing economy. In
   order to achieve this South Africa will need to use exports as the 'steam engine'
   of economic growth. South Africa will have to develop its export potential to the
   fullest and also try to improve its productivity so that it can compete in the international market. The bleak picture (as sketched in figure 19.2) will have to be
   eradicated and turned around.

2. The second is to ensure the linking and developing of the economies of the
   southern African region in order to ensure the development of the region as a
   whole. Significant steps towards this goal have already been taken. The Southern
   African Development Community or SADEC (comprising 11 southern African
   states) signed a trade protocol in August 1996 which envisages the elimination
   of import duties over a three-year period. The ultimate goal will be the establishment of a regional free trade area in southern Africa. SADEC has also signed
   protocols that provide for cooperation in the combating of drug trafficking, the
   harmonisation of energy policy and the integration of transport and communication networks. The leading role that South Africa plays in the SADEC is empha-

sised by the fact that President Nelson Mandela was elected chairperson of the organisation by popular acclaim.

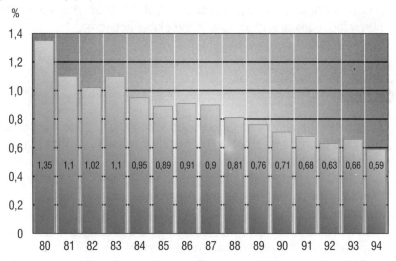

Figure 19.2
SA exports as a percentage of world exports
Source: *Finansies en Tegniek*, 23 February 1996, p 20.

3. The last element is the promotion of an outward orientation of the economies of the region in order to capitalise on the advantages of international trade and to attract inflows of international capital and investment.

South Africa's future economic relations should be built around these strategies. To sum up, its international economic relations should be geared to the following objectives:[42]

■ promoting and deriving maximum benefit from international trade for South Africa and its region
■ attracting production factors and resources to South Africa and its regions
■ promoting greater economic integration of the South African region in order to foster prosperity and development

Recent developments in South Africa do, however, necessitate another look at the South African economy. If this country is to become an 'African Lion' (to be compared with the Asean Tigers), its economy will have to be built on three pillars: social order and stability, steady economic growth and the attainment of national goals. The latter includes, for example, job creation, education and training, housing and proper social services. However, the most important of the three pillars appears to be social order. This refers mainly to the safety and security of people and their possessions. South Africa will have to end the violence and crime permeating the very fabric of its society. It is the only way to restore confidence and ensure domestic and foreign investment. It is the first step towards economic growth and prosperity. Without social order, the other two pillars that have been mentioned can never be built. All three of these pillars are required for South Africa to compete successfully in world markets and as such in the global economy.

18.6 CONCLUSION

Global management has developed into one of the most important features of the world's economy. It is not simply domestic management on a larger scale, but forms an independent field of study. In this chapter we studied the nature of international business by firstly distinguishing between domestic, international, multinational and global enterprises. We saw that managers need not only to understand the process of internationalisation, but also need to be able to manage effectively within their level of international activity. Trends in international business were identified to give you an understanding of how these different levels of business have emerged. The different ways that organisations can enter the international market were also discussed. Three possible options seem to be open, namely where the company involved has no ownership of foreign assets (for example, exports, licensing, franchising, contracts and turnkey operations), where the company is involved in joint ventures/strategic alliances and where the company has a direct investment in the foreign country involved.

In order to compete successfully in the global economy, managers need to understand its structure. We identified three different classifications of the global economy. The first referred to the mature market economies and systems that seems to dominate the global economy of today. North America (in the guise of NAFTA), Europe (as the EU) and the Pacific Rim (a loose affiliation of countries) seem to be the most important economic systems. The second element consists of the less-developed economies in Eastern Europe, South America and Africa. They appear to have great growth potential but are mostly overburdened by economic deficiencies. The last grouping is known as other economies. This refers mainly to the oil-producing states of the Middle East and their unique circumstances.

The environmental challenges that international managers face can be described as complex and daunting. Three elements have to be taken into consideration: the economic, political/legal and cultural environment of the different countries. The different political systems, cultures, languages and many other factors need to be considered before certain decisions can be made.

The basic issues of competing in a global economy may vary depending on whether the company involved is an MNC, a medium firm or a small organisation. Any international organisation must also address the basic managerial functions of planning, organising, leading and controlling.[43] In conclusion, it is essential for all

international managers to adopt a global view of life and the business world if they
wish to achieve success in the international arena.

19.7 REFERENCES

1. Mendenhall, ME, Punnett, BJ & Ricks, DA. 1995. *Global Management*. Cambridge: Blackwell Publishers, p xvii.
2. Griffin, RW. 1993. *Management*, 4 ed. Boston: Houghton Mifflin, p 116.
3. Loc cit.
4. Ibid p 117.
5. Mendenhall et al op cit p 220.
6. Walter, I & Murray, T. 1988. *Handbook of International Business*. NY: Wiley, p 4.
7. Griffin op cit p 118.
8. Mills, D, Begg, A & Van Nieuwkerk, A (eds). 1995. *South Africa in the Global Economy*. Johannesburg: The South African Institute of International Affairs, p 200.
9. Griffin op cit p 120.
10. *Financial Mail Survey*, 30 September 1994, p 29.
11. Ibid p 30.
12. Loc cit.
13. Griffin op cit p 124.
14. Mills et al op cit p 37.
15. Hodgetts, RM & Luthans, F. 1994. *International Management*. NY: McGraw-Hill, p 10.
16. Ibid p 14.
17. Mills et al op cit p 199.
18. Griffin op cit p 127.
19. Loc cit.
20. Ibid p 129.
21. Mohr, PJ, Fourie, LJ & Associates. 1995. *Economics for South African Students*. Pretoria: Van Schaik, p 481.
22. Griffin op cit p 130.
23. Mendenhall et al op cit p 48.
24. Griffin op cit p 131.
25. Hodgetts & Luthans op cit p 59.
26. Griffin op cit p 132.
27. Mendenhall et al op cit p 84.
28. Griffin op cit p 133.
29. Mendenhall et al op cit p 79.
30. Griffin op cit p 133.
31. Ibid p 134.

32. *Finansies en Tegniek,* 10 November 1995, pp 57 and 61.

33. Griffin op cit p 134.

34. Plunkett, WR & Attner, RF. 1992. *Introduction to Management.* Boston: PWS-Kent Publishing Company, p 167.

35. Ibid p 197.

36. Griffin op cit p 137.

37. Plunkett & Attner op cit p 242.

38. Griffin op cit p 138.

39. Loc cit.

40. Mills et al op cit p 200.

41. Ibid p 207.

42. Ibid p 208.

43. Griffin op cit p 138.

20 Ethics and Corporate Social Responsibility

Key issues

- The meaning of ethics
- Ethical decision making
- Managing ethics in the organisation
- The meaning of corporate social responsibility
- Primary and secondary stakeholders in corporate social responsibility
- The social audit

20.1 INTRODUCTION

Ethics and corporate social responsibility are important and much debated contemporary management issues because of the scale and influence of the modern organisation. Organisations and their managers have a real and potential impact on a wide variety of issues extending far beyond their normal business. Read any newspaper or financial magazine in South Africa and at least one article will deal with either ethics or social responsibility in the business context. One of the reasons for the debate is that the actions of organisations impact on the prosperity of entire communities and on the health of the environments in which they operate. Consequently, modern organisations have more power and authority than ever before to pursue their own interests. However, associated with this great power is an increased responsibility towards the stakeholders of the organisation and society at large — and that is what ethics and corporate social responsibility are all about.

Although ethics and social responsibility are not synonymous concepts, they are related because socially responsible decisions often require ethical judgments that fall outside the field of prescribed laws, procedures and previous experience. The manager has the responsibility of judging the fairness and consequences of every demand made on the organisation, and ethics is the foundation on which such decisions are based.

In this chapter the two related concepts of ethics and social responsibility are examined with a view to providing you as students and managers with a framework to help you make ethical decisions about your own actions and about the organisations in which you work.

20.2 ETHICS

Ethics can be defined as the code of moral principles and values that directs the behaviour of an individual or a group in terms of what is right or wrong. Ethics sets standards about what is good or bad in behaviour and in decision making.[1]

The values of individuals are expressed in attitudes, beliefs and judgments about right and wrong. People learn their values from their parents and family, teachers, and the communities they are born into. In chapter 15 personal values were discussed in detail and in chapter 19 we explained how culture influences values, and consequently, how different cultures have different values about what is right or wrong, especially in a business context.

Ethics can be better understood if we compare it with the behaviour of an individual or a group controlled by prescribed laws, on the one hand, and by free choice, on the other.[2] Figure 20.1 illustrates how human behaviour falls into three areas.

| Behaviour directed by prescribed law | Behaviour directed by ethics | Behaviour directed by free choice |

Figure 20.1
Three areas of human behaviour

The first area is that of prescribed **enforceable law** where values and standards are written into a legal system. The behaviour of South African citizens and organisations is governed in many ways by the laws of the country. Individuals and organisations must pay taxes, are forced by law not to take undisclosed sums of money out of the country and are required to buy car licences. At the other end of the scale is the area of **free choice** where no laws direct the behaviour of individuals or organisations and where there is complete freedom of behaviour. An individual's choice to buy a new car or an organisation's decision to give a Christmas party for members of staff are examples of free choice. Between these extremes lies the area of **ethics** In this area no specific laws govern, yet there are certain standards of conduct, based on shared principles and values about moral behaviour that guide the individual or organisation. In the area of free choice the individual and the organisation are accountable only to themselves. By contrast, in the area of prescribed law, accountability is to enforceable laws. In the area of ethical behaviour, accountability is to norms and standards of which the individual or organisation is aware but which are not enforceable.

Ethical questions often appear as 'grey areas' and there are disagreements and dilemmas about proper behaviour. An ethical dilemma arises in a situation where it is difficult to tell right from wrong because all the alternatives have potentially negative consequences.

An ethical dilemma

In October 1988, the French pharmaceutical organisation Roussel-Uclaf faced an extremely difficult ethical dilemma: whether to go ahead with the marketing of RU486, an abortion-inducer, also (incorrectly) known as the 'morning-after' pill. It found itself under pressure from powerful but contradictory forces in the environment, some arguing strongly for keeping the drug off the market, and others insisting that the firm should make it available. The fundamental values involved in the abortion issue made the decision extremely difficult. Many people felt strongly that, although the law might tolerate it, abortion was morally wrong and that to facilitate abortion was therefore unacceptable. Others argued that an organisation had no right to the exercise of legally enforceable rights, and that personal beliefs on abortion were irrelevant. The decision to condemn or accept abortion was made by society, and French society, through its parliament, had already decided that abortion was, if not desirable, at least tolerable and that its exercise was, under certain constraints, legal. The ethical issue was critical to an assessment of the implications of the marketing of the pill for Roussel-Uclaf's image. On the one hand the marketing of such an original and innovative product would give the organisation a lot of prestige. On the other hand, the organisation's slogan of 'at the service of life' would become paradoxical if it sold a product that ended human life at the very outset — although it could also be argued that the World Health Organisation has estimated that out of the 500 000 women per year dying from pregnancy-related complications, 200 000 deaths are due to improperly performed abortions.

The decision announcement was as follows: 'Taking into account the feelings expressed by some French and foreign members of the public ... the Roussel-Uclaf group has decided to suspend distribution of this product as a medical alternative to surgical abortion in France and abroad as of today.'

Source: Ancona, D, Kochan, T, Scully, M, Van Maalen, J & Westney, DE. 1996. *Managing for the Future: Organisational Behavior and Processes.* Cincinnati: South-Western College, pp 24–32.

20.2.1 What is business ethics?

Business ethics is an example of applied ethics where the theory, principles and concepts of ethics are applied to the commercial world of organisational objectives and performance. It is the study of values and conduct in the business environment. Conflict of interest in the business environment gives rise to ethical questions and managers, by definition of the work they do, cannot avoid ethical issues in their day-to-day activities.

Ethical or unethical?

- In your capacity as export manager of an organisation, you have been asked to pay a bribe to an official in a Third World country to speed up the process of acquiring a certain permit. This is accepted procedure in that country, and your organisation will lose business if you do not pay the bribe.
- Your boss says he cannot give you a raise this year becaue of a budget deficit but he will look the other way if you load your expense accounts for a couple of months.
- You are the person repsonsible for completing tenders for the construction organisation for which you work. Other contractors contact you with the suggestion that if you pay each of them a certain amount of money, they will 'fix' their prices so that you can secure the job for your organisation. Your organisation desperately needs the work.

The situations sketched in the above box illustrate typical ethical issues with which managers have to deal. In the following sections we examine **how** managers can make ethically correct decisions.

20.2.2 Levels of ethical decision making

Managers find it easier to decide on what course of action to take if they can identify the level at which ethical dilemmas appear. In business, most issues that managers are confronted with fall into one of five levels, which are not mutually exclusive.[3] These levels are illustrated in figure 20.2.

Ethical questions at the **individual level** arise when people are faced with issues involving individual responsibility, such as being totally honest when completing expense accounts, calling in sick when they are needed at home, accepting a bribe or misusing organisational resources, such as time, telephones and computers, for personal business purposes.

When ethical issues originate at the **organisational level**, the individual dealing with such an issue should consult the organisation's policies, procedures and code of ethics to clarify the organisation's stand on the issue. An example of an issue at this level is when an employee or group of employees is required by the organisation to overlook the unethical behaviour of a colleague whose behaviour benefits the organisation.

Figure 20.2
The levels of ethical decision making

At the **association level**, an accountant, lawyer, medical doctor or management consultant may refer to his professional association's code of ethics for guidelines on conducting ethical business. In South Africa,[4] both the private and the public sectors make extensive use of the services of consultants, some of whom were the victims of the downsizing, re-engineering and affirmative action policies of their previous employers. There is no enforceable code of conduct to regulate the ethical conduct of these consultants to ensure that their clients receive fair treatment and protection of their rights. In recent media coverage on the subject, strong arguments have been made out for creating and enforcing such a code of conduct.

At the **societal level** laws, norms, customs and traditions direct the legal and moral acceptability of behaviour. Many business customs that are commonplace in the Middle East and Asia are not acceptable behaviour in Western countries. At this level a manager may, for example, consult experts on the legal and moral codes of the country he or she is dealing with before reaching a decision on the ethical issue.

Lastly, at the **international level** ethical issues are often muddled by a mix of cultural, political and religious values that influence decisions. An example of an ethical issue at this level would be whether an employee should work for or accept the organisation's policy of doing business with a government that abuses human rights such as making use of child labour.

The ethical levels discussed above can and often do overlap, but it is still useful to identify the level when confronting an issue and to ask whose interests, values, beliefs and economic interests are at stake. Such information can often help to clarify the situation and facilitate better decision making.

20.2.3 **Different approaches to ethical decision making**

Because the ethics of managerial decision making are often complex and managers often disagree on what an ethical decision in a specific situation involves, two factors should be considered, namely (1) the **approach** that the individual manager can use in determining which alternative to choose in a decision-making situation; and (2) **what organisations can do** to ensure that managers follow ethical standards in their decision making.

There are **three fundamental ethical approaches** that managers can use in their decision making on ethical matters when they have to choose between various options and defend difficult decisions. In the following sections, the utilitarian approach, the moral rights approach and the social justice approach are briefly discussed.[5]

When following the **utilitarian approach**, a manager studies the effects of a particular action on the people directly influenced by it and takes a decision that will benefit the most people to the greatest extent. In reaching such a decision, the manager weighs the potentially positive results of the action against the potentially negative results of the action. If the positive results outweigh the negative results, the manager taking the utilitarian approach is likely to follow through with the action in question. Implicit in this approach is that some people (the minority) might be negatively affected by the action. Managers faced with making decisions about pension plans and company-sponsored medical aid schemes are often required to make utilitarian judgments.

Utilitarian ethic in South Africa

> The utilitarian ethic was the basis of the government's decision to provide primary medical services to South Africans living in rural areas and refusing to pay for high-cost, high-risk procedures such as heart and liver transplants. Although a few people needing these procedures will die because the state will not pay, many more people benefit from medical services they would otherwise have had to go without.

According to the **moral rights approach**, the fundamental freedom and rights of individuals cannot be taken away by another individual's decision. Thus an ethically correct decision is one that best protects the rights of those affected by it. Some of these rights and privileges are contained in documents such as the Bill of Rights (part of the South African Constitution) and the United Nations Declaration of Human Rights. A number of the fundamental individual rights protected by the South African Constitution in the Bill of Rights that managers should be aware of, appear in the bobelow.

Rights of South African citizens protected by the South African Constitution in the Bill of Rights

- ■ **Equality.** Everybody is equal before the law and entitled to enjoy rights and freedoms under the law. Individuals cannot be discriminated against on the grounds of race or gender.

- ■ **Human dignity.** Everyone's dignity should be respected.

- ■ **Life.** Individuals have a right to life.

- ■ **Freedom and security of the person.** Individuals may refrain from carrying out any order that violates their freedom of movement or endangers or violates their health and safety.

- ■ **Slavery and forced labour.** *S*lavery and forced labour are not allowed.

- ■ **Privacy.** Individuals may choose to do as they please away from work and have control of information about their private life.

- ■ **Freedom of religion, belief and opinion.** Individuals have the right to practise whatever religion or belief they wish.

- ■ **Freedom of expression.** Individuals may criticise truthfully the ethics or legality of actions of others.

- ■ **Freedom of association.** Individuals have a right to belong to any organisation of their choice and to mix with anybody of their choice.

- ■ **Labour relations.** Workers must be treated fairly by their employers. Workers have the right to strike and join trade unions of their choice. Employers may also form their own organisations in the same way as workers form trade unions. Both workers and employers may participate in these organisations of their choice.

- ■ **Environment.** Individuals have the right to a clean environment.

According to the **social justice approach**, ethical decisions must be based on standards of equity, fairness and impartiality. When managers must decide on how costs and profits generated in organisations should be shared, the basis for ethical decisions should be rules that are fairly and impartially imposed and enforced.

From the above discussion it is clear that ethical issues can be approached from many different perspectives. What then is the best approach to follow? The capitalistic goal of profit maximisation is consistent with the largest benefit for the greatest number of people and therefore the **utilitarian approach** is followed by many business managers. However, the current emphasis in South Africa on individual rights and social justice forces managers to use new approaches. The answer lies in maintaining a fine balance between the various approaches, depending on the situation and the stakeholders involved.

Gain sharing in South Africa

> Although it is common practice in Eastern countries for employers to share their good fortune with their workers, incentive schemes in South Africa were almost unheard of ten years ago. It is only in recent years that the realisation has dawned that both the factors of work ethic and participative management are directly attributable to a more fundamental driving force, namely economic sharing. In 1992 eight companies who had reputedly achieved success in labour productivity were included in a research project. Three out of the eight already practise gain sharing (Con Roux Construction, Golden Lay Farms and Cadac). Gain sharing is a pact entered into between an employer and a group of employees that says: 'Let us take what we achieved last year (or last month) as a fair measure of what we can do and let us try to improve on this. Let us measure our performance from this point onwards. If we can improve productivity, we will share the gains.'
>
> Source: Bussin, M & Thompson, D. 1995. Gaining pace with gainsharing. *People Dynamics,* vol 13, no 6 (June), p 23.

In addition to the formal approaches to business ethics as discussed above, managers can evaluate their decisions according to shortcut 'ethical tests'. These tests are based on common sense and the inherent morality of human beings. They are easy exercises to test the ethical quality of decisions. For example, the manager can ask himself the following questions:[6] Is it the truth? Is it fair to all concerned? Will it build goodwill and better friendship? Will it be beneficial to all concerned? The decision is probably ethically correct if the answer to all four questions is 'yes'.

Another informal approach to ethically sound decision making is to follow a few simple guidelines[7] such as **the golden rule** that says, 'Do unto others as you would have them do unto you'. This includes not knowingly harming others. The **intuition ethic** claims that people have a moral sense about what is right or wrong and that we should follow our 'gut feeling' about what is right. The **means-ends ethic** warns that we may choose unscrupulous but efficient means to reach an end if the ends are really worth while and significant. One should make sure that the ends are not the means. The **test of common sense** asks: 'Does the action I am getting ready to take make any sense?' The message here is to think before acting.

20.2.4 Steps in the ethical decision-making process [8]

In the preceding sections we learnt how a manager faced with an ethical decision must investigate all the variables pertaining to the specific issue and then take a decision based on the appropriate approach or combination of approaches. The actual steps that are followed in this process of decision making do not differ much from the decision-making process discussed in chapter 7, but the emphasis is on ethical considerations, as depicted in figure 20.3.

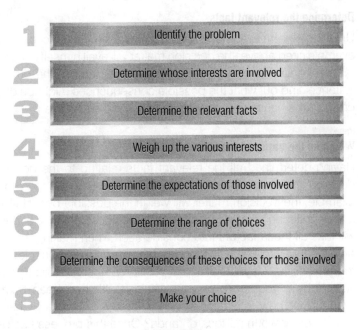

Figure 20.3
Steps in the ethical decision-making process

Identify the problem

The ethical problem should be specifically defined. Here it is important not to confuse the ethical problem with the associated symptoms or problems. For example, suppose the organisation you work for is compromising on the quality controls of a drug sold to pregnant women to meet an urgent and large order. Your ethical problem here is whether you have the right to endanger the life of foetuses and pregnant women. The quality control of the drug is not the real ethical problem.

Determine whose interests are involved

A decision with ethical consequences can affect many stakeholders such as customers, suppliers, employees, shareholders, the government, environmental lobby groups and many others. Before any ethical choice can be made, it is essential to determine whose interests are involved and how the various stakeholders would react and be influenced by the various scenarios created by different choices. Say, for instance, in the example cited above, that many deformed children are born as a result of the poor quality of the drug taken by their mothers while they were pregnant. Stakeholders here would be customers (mothers and babies), the organisation, employees and shareholders who will be affected by costly court cases, and also the government, which will act against a drug company that compromises on the quality of drugs taken by pregnant women.

Determine the relevant facts

Unless all the relevant facts are examined, no ethical choice can be made. In the example cited above, the decision maker will avail himself or herself of all the relevant facts relating to the compromised quality control of the drug. He or she will, for instance, find out what the possible consequences might be of a batch of defective drugs to the health of pregnant women and their babies.

Weigh up the various interests

Having determined all the relevant facts relating to the decision to be taken, the decision maker must now judge whose interests are the most important. In our example, the decision maker will weigh the possible benefits to the organisation of a large order against the possible negative consequences of defective products and will take all these factors into consideration when making the final ethical decision. An ethical way to weigh the various interests is to reverse roles with the other parties to the conflict. Put yourself in the position of the other party. How would you feel if your baby's, your own, or your wife's health had been harmed by a defective product? Or, how would you as chief executive officer feel if the organisation were to lose an order worth millions of rands? Once this process has been completed, the decision maker should be in a position to make a judgment about whose interests are the most important.

Determine the expectations of those involved

In complicated ethical decisions, many stakeholders have expectations which are based on actual and tacit agreements. The end user has a legitimate expectation to receive a safe drug while the client has a legitimate expectation to have his order delivered on time. The expectations of all the stakeholders should be taken into consideration when a decision is reached.

Determine the range of choices

A range of choices is available in any given decision-making situation. The decision maker must first determine what can be done, before deciding on what to do. In the case of our example, he or she could decide to cancel the order, or to remain silent and go ahead with the processing of the order, or to discuss the problem with his or her superiors. Another alternative is to speak to the press if forced into a decision that he or she is not comfortable with.

Determine the consequences of these choices for all those involved

This is not an easy exercise, because it is difficult to predict the consequences of the various alternatives with any certainty. However, this is an important step in the ethical decision-making process. In our example the decision maker may judge that by keeping silent, a number of deformed babies could be born. On the other hand, he or she might lose his or her job if the order is cancelled.

Make your choice

The decision maker should now be in a position to make a reasoned judgment, taking into account the facts, the stakeholders, the consequences of each possible option and the weighed reasonable expectations of all involved. The decision ultimately taken may of course still be the wrong one, but at the very least a rational process has been followed and the decision taken represents the best judgment of the decision maker.

Having discussed both the formal and informal approaches to ethical decision making as well as the steps that managers can follow to solve ethical problems, what can **organisations** do to ensure that managers follow ethical standards in their decision making?

20.2.5 Managing ethics in the organisation

In section 20.2.3 two important aspects were identified that are particularly relevant to the complex issue of ethics in organisations. The first was the **approaches** that individual managers can use in their decision making. The second was the question of **what organisations can do** to ensure that managers follow ethical standards in their decision making.

The first and most important requirement to foster a culture of good ethics in an organisation is **leadership by example**. In a report on ethics policy and practice issued by 250 large American companies including Boeing, Xerox and Johnson & Johnson,[9] the crucial role of top management was emphasised as one of the most important aspects of ethics in organisations. According to the report, the chief executive officer and senior managers need to be openly and strongly committed to ethical conduct and should provide constant leadership in reinforcing ethical values in the organisation. This commitment should be communicated as often as possible in speeches, directives and organisational publications. Most importantly, their actions should set the example for ethical standards in their organisations.

Another way of managing ethics in the organisation is by means of a **code of ethics**.[10] Many organisations that attempt to set an internal standard of behaviour in ethical matters, develop a corporate code of ethics. An organisation's code of ethics sets out the guidelines for ethical behaviour within the organisation. A code usually comprises a written statement of a company's values, beliefs and norms of ethical behaviour and is usually developed by top management. Ideally, a code of ethics should provide employees with direction in dealing with ethical dilemmas, clarify the organisation's position in specific areas of ethical uncertainty, and in general achieve and maintain organisational behaviour which the organisation views as ethical and desirable. The written code of conduct is followed by an implementation strategy where values and beliefs are translated into specific ethical standards of behaviour and communicated to employees.

An organisation can create various **ethical structures**[11] to implement ethical behaviour. An **ethics committee**, usually consisting of senior executives, can be established to judge the doubtful ethical behaviour of employees and to discipline where necessary. An organisation can also appoint an **ethical ombudsman** who is an official with the responsibility of receiving and investigating ethical complaints and to alert top management to potential ethical issues that might create problems. **Ethical training programmes** at all levels of the organisation can also help to entrench ethical behaviour in organisations.

Whistle blowing in an organisation occurs when the dishonest or unethical behaviour of an employee or the organisation is reported by another employee to the management of the organisation or to outsiders such as newspapers or the police. Whistle blowing can only be effective if whistle blowers are protected by the organisation. If they are not protected, they will be harassed and the individual or organisation may continue with unethical or illegal activities.

20.2.6 A last word on ethics

Although various approaches, guidelines and strategies for ethical decision making in organisations have been discussed in this chapter so far, it is important to realise that each ethical issue is different and that there is no general rule which is applicable to all ethical problems. Also, the decision maker is personally responsible for his or her decisions. If decisions have negative consequences, individual managers and the organisation must take full responsibility for such decisions, regardless of what the organisation's rules or code of ethics prescribe. Also, business problems are often complex. Gross violations such as fraud and theft can easily be judged and dealt with, but subtle issues, such as discrimination or misleading consumers, are far more complicated and require a great deal of discretion on the part of the managers dealing with them.

20.2.7 Ethics and social responsibility

The relationship between a manager's ethical standards and the organisation's social responsibility can be explained as follows.[12] Ethics is the **individual manager's** guide for assessing the 'rightness' of potential actions by the organisation. Individual managers' ethical standards are the 'filters' that screen the organisation's actions according to what is right and what is wrong. Ultimately, managers should weigh each demand made on the organisations they work for according to their own ethical standards, as well as the organisation's code of ethics which forms the foundation for their decision making on the complex issues of social responsibility.

20.3 CORPORATE SOCIAL RESPONSIBILITY

In chapters 1 and 3 we discussed the organisation as an open system and described how it interacts with the environment in which it operates. Because the organisation is an open system, managers cannot make decisions based solely on economic considerations. The organisation is interrelated with the whole social system in which it functions and to make socially responsible decisions, managers should consider all possible stakeholders. **Corporate social responsibility**[13] implies that a manager, in the process of serving his own business interests, is obliged to take actions that also protect and enhance society's interests. The overall effect is to improve the quality of life in the broadest possible way, regardless of how quality of life is defined by society. The manager becomes concerned with the social and economic outputs and with the total effect of the organisation's actions on society.

20.3.1 Levels of social responsibility

Capitalism is based on the ideas of Adam Smith[14] who believed that in the long term, public interests are best served by individuals and organisations pursuing their own self-interest and that government interference should be kept to a minimum. The economist, Milton Friedman, elaborates on the ideas of Smith and says that when an organisation makes a profit it is being socially responsible. Friedman believes that diverting organisations from the pursuit of profit makes the economy of a country less efficient. According to him, private organisations should not be forced to accept the responsibilities belonging to government. Friedman's view represents the one extreme of the debate on social responsibility. At the other extreme there are those who argue that social responsibility policies should be part of company mission statements. Most managers' views fall between the two extremes. Figure 20.4 illustrates the **levels of social responsibility**[15] in which organisations engage.

Social obligation

Because society allows organisations to exist, organisations owe it to society to make profits. According to the social obligation view, the generation of profits within the legal framework of the society in which the organisation operates, represents socially responsible behaviour by the organisation. Thus the socially responsible behaviour of the organisation consists only of its economic and legal responsibilities. **Economic responsibilities** include the maximisation of profits, the provision of goods and services to society at a reasonable cost and the creation of jobs where applicable. **Legal responsibilities** refer to the organisation's obligation to comply with the general civil and criminal law that applies to the public and also to laws that regulate business activities. In South Africa in recent years, consumer and environmental movements have made much progress in convincing the government to

Figure 20.4
Levels of social responsibility

introduce laws that govern business in the areas of protecting the environment and consumer safety. Furthermore, labour practices are fully governed by new progressive labour laws in South Africa.

Social reaction

The social reaction view holds that organisations owe society more than the mere provision of goods and services. Organisations should at least be accountable for the ecological, environmental and social costs resulting from their actions. Ideally, organisations should also respond to society's problems, even those for which they are not directly responsible. Thus socially responsible behaviour as defined at this level includes voluntary actions by the organisation such as supporting worthy causes that will help solve some of society's problems.

Social responsiveness

Social responsiveness refers to the socially responsible actions of organisations that exceed social obligation and social reaction. Organisations engaging in socially responsive behaviour actively seek to prevent and find solutions to the social problems of society. Socially responsive behaviour includes civil responsibilities such as supporting or opposing public issues and responding to the present and future needs of society by trying to fulfil needs. It also implies communicating and liaising with the government and other organisations about existing and anticipated socially desirable legislation and community programmes. The box below contains examples of how South African organisations engage in socially responsive behaviour.

Socially responsive actions by South African organisations

> Murray and Roberts places five per cent of its ordinary dividend into its foundation for social investment. The Colgate-Palmolive South Africa Foundation finances multicultural youth programmes. Pick 'n Pay has made its mark as South Africa's 'green company', particularly supporting environmental initiatives. Eskom's social investment concentrates on electrification. Gencor has explored ways to recycle former mining properties for community investment purposes, including schools and training centres. Liberty Life has given high priority to early-childhood care. In conjunction with the Reconstruction and Development Programme (RDP), many companies are linking their social investment to explicit projects in skills training and job creation. Shell and BMW adapted their strategies to address RDP goals.
>
> Source: Alperson, M. 1995. *Foundations of a New Democracy: Corporate Social Investment in South Africa.* Johannesburg: Ravan, p 14.

20.3.2 To whom is business responsible?

Socially responsible activities by organisations can be classified in terms of the stakeholders affected by the actions of the organisation. A stakeholder is 'any individual or group who can affect or is affected by the actions, decisions, policies, practices, or goals of the organisation'.[16] The stakeholders in organisations can be classified in terms of **primary or secondary stakeholders**.[17] Primary stakeholders are those identified in the microenvironment and market environment discussed in chapter 3, while secondary stakeholders are found in the macroenvironment of the organisation.

Primary stakeholders

The primary stakeholders who are affected by the social involvement of enterprises include the **owners** who are interested in the pursuit of profits, the achievement of objectives, the effectiveness and efficiency of the organisation, productivity, the promotion of the organisation's image and public relations, the quality of service rendered, environmental management and environmental control. **Stockholders and the board of directors** look at the promotion of the company image, earnings on shares and profit-sharing. **Employees** are concerned with training and development opportunities, their conditions of service, working conditions, remuneration, security, self-actualisation and job satisfaction, the protection of minority groups and the safety and health of the working environment. **Suppliers** are important stakeholders because they supply raw materials, loans and credit to the organisation and are affected by decisions made by the organisation and the socially responsible behaviour of organisations. **Customers** are concerned with the provision of safe products of good quality. Service of a high standard, product improvement, consumer protection and marketing actions are areas of concern to customers.

Secondary stakeholders

Secondary stakeholders include the local community and the country as a whole. **Local communities** demand social responsibility from enterprises in areas such as environmentalism, community development, ecological control, low-cost housing, support of health and medical services, training and development of the local population, donations to churches and religious institutions, sponsorships for schools and sporting bodies, preservation of historical buildings and the creation and promotion of an economic infrastructure. **The country as a whole** benefits from the support of countrywide projects and campaigns. Nature conservation, support of educational programmes, upliftment of the poor and illiterate, financial support of education and training, the promotion of the arts and sciences, welfare and international relations are the areas of social responsibility in this category. Since the early 1970s,[18] South African organisations have become increasingly active in the area of social investment in the country. The political reforms initiated in the early 1990s accelerated the social change process in the country and social investment began to gain momentum.

South African organisations' involvement in the social change process

In 1990 the Liberty Life Foundation pledged R100 million over five years for investment in education. A year later 15 organisations, including Anglo American, Gencor, JCI, Shell, Southern Life and Standard Bank, joined forces with a spectrum of political parties, trade unions and black advocacy groups and pledged R500 million to launch the Joint Education Trust. These initiatives illustrate the process through which organisations in South Africa began to take a more active role in the social change process. Since 1990 corporate social investment began to gain momentum and this can be attributed to the following factors: (1) organisations decentralised some of their corporate social investment programmes to regional operations where management and employees understood local community needs; (2) they published more information about their spending and began networking with each other to share resources on individual programmes or to link up in particular regions; (3) foreign organisations began exploring how they could contribute to redevelopment in South Africa; and (4) local corporate social investment programmes linked up increasingly with the Reconstruction and Development Programme (RDP). Today many social upliftment and social investment programmes are financed and managed by corporate South Africa.

Source: Alperson, M. 1995. *Foundations of a New Democracy: Corporate Social Investment in South Africa.* Johannesburg: Ravan, pp 6–11.

The example above shows how the social and economic effects of organisations' decisions can positively affect the interests and wellbeing of many people. However, the interaction between the organisation and its shareholders can also have serious repercussions for the organisation when things go wrong. The *Exxon Valdez*[19] incident discussed below illustrates the problems and issues a large organisation faces in a crisis and illustrates the responsibility and accountability of organisations towards their many stakeholders.

The effects of the Exxon Valdez disaster on Exxon

In 1989 the *Exxon Valdez* ripped open its bottom on Bligh Reef off the Alaskan coast and dumped 11 million gallons of crude oil. It was America's worst oil spill ever and the disaster sparked an outburst of reactions, from congressional hearings, state and federal legislative proposals for new preventative measures to many environmental studies and innumerable lawsuits. Apart from polluting the water and shorelines the spill also damaged one of the world's major fisheries and killed more than 36 000 migratory birds, including at least 100 bald eagles. A grand jury indicted Exxon in February 1990 by which time they also faced fines totalling over 6 million dollars if convicted on the felony counts. More than 150 lawsuits and 30 000 damage claims were reportedly filed against Exxon, most of which had not been settled by July 1991. While the charge against the captain of the *Valdez* of having a blood-alcohol content of above 0.04 % was dropped, he was nevertheless convicted of negligently discharging oil and ordered to pay 50 000 dollars restitution to the state of Alaska. He was also ordered to serve 1 000 hours cleaning up the beaches. Exxon executives and stockholders have been besieged with court cases, as well as by environmental groups, the media and public groups over the crisis, and have paid 300 million dollars in damages to 10 000 commercial fishermen, business owners, and native Alaskan villages.

Source: Weiss, J. 1994. *Business Ethics: A Managerial, Stakeholder Approach*. Belmont: Wadsworth Publishing Company, p 28.

20.3.3 The social audit

Many South African organisations are involved in socially responsible actions and to evaluate whether they are meeting their social objectives they need to measure the effectiveness of their actions. For this reason, many large organisations include a social audit in their annual reports. A social audit[20] is a measure of an organisation's social behaviour in the form of an inventory that identifies and describes specific information on the current and anticipated socially responsible plans and results of an organisation. The objective of a social audit is to measure an organisation's overall contribution to its social goals by comparing the social costs and social benefits of its programmes. Elements that are measured include the social and ethical impact of the organisation on communities, customers, employees and society in general. The basic steps in a social audit are monitoring, measuring and evaluating the performance of a company in its conduct of socially responsible activities.

In South Africa,[21] where the socially responsible programmes of organisations are increasingly linked to the social development goals of the government as originally set out in the Reconstruction and Development Programme (RDP), there seems to be a need for organisations to be measured in terms of their support of these goals. An organisation's commitment to factors such as transparency, good governance, progress in affirmative action, consultative labour forums and the management of diversity tends to go unnoticed unless it is measured. Currently no such enforceable audits have to be completed by South African organisations, but specific initiatives, such as the King Committee's report on corporate governance, encourage organisations listed on the Johannesburg Stock Exchange to comply with a recommended code of conduct. This nonenforceable code suggests that organisations disclose separately earnings of executive and nonexecutive directors, implement worker participation and affirmative action programmes and establish separate audit and remuneration committees. The King Committee's report relies on peer pressure and public exposure to ensure compliance. Table 20.1 contains examples of indicators that can be assessed by means of a social audit.

Table 20.1
Examples of indicators assessed by a social audit

Indicator	Description
General satisfaction	Staff perspectives on what factors contribute most to job satisfaction and company performance, company culture, staff turnover, absenteeism, illness, stress levels, staff development, return on investment by shareholders (dividends)
Material rewards	Wages, salaries, hourly rates, total wages bill, percentage of industry/area averages, salary differentials
Participation	Formal levels of representation for decision making, quality of representation, spheres of staff control, quality of participative structures
Affirmative action	Number of selected groupings at different levels, degree of career mobility, recruitment figures, equal employment opportunities, training days and representation, literacy levels, suppliers and distributors
Community investment	RDP impact, housing, social investment as a percentage of labour, education support in communities, staff modes to travel to work, contribution to public debate and influencing peer companies
Environment	Recycled paper, health and safety, staff understanding of environmental impact, product development
Customer/public perspectives	Measure influence and recognition, fair trading policies, pricing, advertising and marketing

Source: Adapted from Rosmarin, K. 1995. Counting social profit and loss. *People Dynamics*, vol 13, no 6 (June), p 21.

20.4 CONCLUSION

In this chapter the important concepts of ethics and social responsibility were examined. Although ethics is not synonymous with social responsibility, the two concepts are related in the sense that socially responsive decisions require value judgments that fall within the field of ethics. Various important aspects of ethically and socially responsible decision making were discussed in an attempt to continually highlight the situation in South Africa. Ethics and social responsibility are the topics of many media reports and debate in South Africa and for the contemporary manager to perform effectively, a thorough knowledge of these concepts is necessary.

20.5 REFERENCES

1. Daft, RL. 1988. *Management,* 2 ed. Orlando: Dryden, pp 92–94.
2. Ibid.
3. Weiss, JW. 1994. *Business Ethics: A Managerial, Stakeholder Approach.* Belmont: Wadsworth, p 10.
4. Van Rooyen, M. 1995. Codes to distinguish consultants from con artists. *People Dynamics,* vol 14, no 5 (June), pp 26–31.
5. Pearce, JA & Robinson, RB. 1989. *Management.* NY: McGraw-Hill, pp 153–154.
6. Lussier, RN. 1997. *Management: Concepts, Applications and Skill Development.* Cincinnati: South-Western, p 56.
7. Weiss op cit p 80.
8. Based on Voice, P. 1994. Social Responsibility and business ethics. *African Management Programme.* Unisa: Centre for Business Management, pp 181–202.
9. Daft op cit p 108.
10. Ivancevich, JM, Donnelly, JH & Gibson, JL. 1989. *Management: Principles and Functions,* 4 ed. Homewood: Irwin, p 657.
11. Daft op cit p 109.
12. Ivancevich et al op cit p 660.
13. Shaw, WH & Barry, V. 1992. *Moral Issues in Business,* 5 ed. Belmont: Wadsworth, p 212.
14. Lussier op cit p 59.
15. Ivancevich et al op cit pp 638–643.
16. Freeman, RE. 1984. *Strategic Management: A Stakeholder Approach.* In Weiss op cit p 32.
17. Donnelly, JH, Gibson, JL & Ivancevich, JM. 1992. *Fundamentals of Management.* Boston: Irwin.
18. Alperson, M. 1995. *Foundations for a New Democracy: Corporate Social Investment in South Africa.* Johannesburg: Ravan, pp 4–11.
19. Weiss op cit p 28.

20. Pearce & Robinson op cit p 148.
21. Rosmarin, K. 1995. Counting social profit and loss. *People Dynamics,* vol 13, no 6 (June), pp 18–21.

Index

Note:

Page numbers referring to the text are in ordinary type: 123
Page numbers referring to figures are in bold blue type: **123**
Page numbers referring to tables are in bold black type: **123**